VISIONS
OF
INFAMY

VISIONS

OF

INFAMY

*The Untold Story of How Journalist
Hector C. Bywater Devised the
Plans that Led to Pearl Harbor*

WILLIAM H. HONAN

ST. MARTIN'S PRESS
NEW YORK

Portions of chapter 1 appeared in *Naval History*, summer 1990. A portion of chapter 18 appeared in *The New York Times Magazine*, April 4, 1982. Portions of chapters 1, 5, 11, and 22 appeared in a different form in *American Heritage*, December 1970. A condensation appeared in *MHQ* in 1991. An earlier version of this entire book was published in September 1990 under the title *Bywater: The Man Who Invented the Pacific War* in Great Britain by Macdonald & Company (Publishers) Ltd. To these publishers and periodicals, the author extends his thanks.

Design by Robert Bull Design.

Original maps by Arnold Bombay. Map on page 147 from *The Valor of Ignorance* by Homer Lea.

Library of Congress Cataloging-in-Publication Data

Honan, William H. (William Holmes)
    Visions of infamy : Hector C. Bywater / William H. Honan.—1st ed.
       p.   cm.
    Includes bibliographical references.
    ISBN 0-312-05454-8
    1. World War, 1939–1945—Campaigns—Pacific Area—Forecasting.   2. Bywater, Hector C. (Hector Charles), 1884–1940.   3. Journalists—Great Britain—Biography.
4. Journalists—United States—Biography.   I. Title.
D767.9.H66 1991   940.54'26—dc20   90-23703

First Edition: August 1991
10 9 8 7 6 5 4 3 2 1

For Nancy, Bradley, Daniel, and Edith

All that I have said and done
Now that I am old and ill
Turns into a question till
I lie awake night after night,
And never get the answers right.
Did that play of mine send out
Certain men the English shot?

—W. B. Yeats

CONTENTS

MAPS

PREFACE

HECTOR C. BYWATER—a convivial, pub-crawling English and American journalist, author, spy, and raconteur who knew more about the navies of the world in the 1920s and 1930s than a room full of admirals—had an obsession. Although most of his contemporaries looked upon it as idle speculation, Bywater devoted himself to figuring out the shape of a possible future war between Japan and the United States.

By 1925, sixteen years before Japanese forces struck at Pearl Harbor, he published a plan that accurately predicted the entire course of the Pacific war. The fulfillment of his prophesy was no accident. What Bywater wrote powerfully influenced Admiral Isoroku Yamamoto, the architect of the Pearl Harbor attack and many of Japan's subsequent moves in the war, and a host of future leaders of the United States Navy.

Bywater imagined that Japan would make a surprise attack against American naval forces in the Pacific and launch simultaneous invasions of Guam and the Philippines. By taking such bold steps, he calculated, Japan could build a nearly invulnerable empire in the Western Pacific.

He also surmised that, given time, the United States would counterattack. The immense ocean distances separating the adversaries after the fall of Guam and the Philippines would be unprecedented. But ultimately, Bywater believed, the United States would be able to reach Japan by pursuing a novel campaign of amphibious island-hopping across the Central Pacific. The result would be "ruinous" for the aggressor. With that outcome in mind, Bywater published his ideas in the hope of deterring Japan from attempting any such adventure.

His two books—*Sea Power in the Pacific* and *The Great Pacific War*—and numerous articles on Pacific strategy—many written in his capacity as European naval correspondent for the *New York Herald*, the Baltimore *Sun*, and later, *The New York Times*—attracted only momentary notice from the public and were soon forgotten. But for professional navy men on both sides of the Pacific, Bywater's work became required reading. Indeed, Bywater was soon recognized as the successor to Admiral Alfred T. Mahan as the world's leading authority on naval theory and practice.

Until now, historians have believed that Yamamoto's war plan was conceived independently, or at least that its origins "remain obscure," as the American military writer Ronald H. Spector recently observed in his authoritative *Eagle Against the Sun*. But today, half a century after Yamamoto unleashed Japanese forces in the Pacific, it can be shown that while serving as naval attaché in Washington in the late 1920s he reported to Tokyo about Bywater's war plan and then lectured on the subject, adopting Bywater's ideas as his own. Years later—long after it had become encoded in his mind—Yamamoto followed Bywater's plan so assiduously in both overall strategy and specific tactics at Pearl Harbor, Guam, the Philippines, and even the battle of Midway that it is no exaggeration to call Hector Bywater the man who "invented" the Pacific war.

One may ask why, if Yamamoto was so deeply influenced by Bywater's analysis, he was not deterred from attacking Pearl Harbor by Bywater's unwavering conviction that Japan would lose a war against the United States. The answer is paradoxical. Yamamoto wholly accepted Bywater's belief that Japan could hold out against the United States for only about a year and a half, and for that reason vigorously opposed the resort to war. Once he became convinced that war was inevitable, however, Yamamoto came to believe that carrying out Bywater's strategy would place Japan in the strongest possible position to press for favorable terms in a negotiated settlement.

Bywater's influence on the American Navy was also profound—so much so that many high-level officers considered him "a prophet." He was the first analyst to publicly spell out the revolutionary concept of island-hopping across the Marshall and Caroline chains that became a fundamental of American strategy during the war. A year and a half after Bywater published this plan, the U.S. Navy drastically revised its top-secret "War Plan Orange"—the official contingency plan for war against Japan—discarding the idea of a reckless transpacific lunge that Bywater had shown to be doomed to failure and adopting in its place his careful, step-by-step advance.

It should not be surprising to discover that naval leaders like Yamamoto and his various American counterparts were deeply affected by a foreign strategist. Such cross-cultural influence occurs virtually all the time in naval and military science. The Prussian author Karl von Clausewitz was read just as avidly by American, British, and French generals who took part in the First World War as by his fellow Germans. Kaiser Wilhelm II, the emperor of Germany, returned the compliment by reading and at one time attempting to memorize long passages from Mahan. And Heinz Guderian, the German general who developed Nazi Germany's Panzer Corps, acknowledged after the war that he had drawn his ideas on the use of fast-moving armored divisions from the writings of the British Army officer John F. C. Fuller, the French leader Charles de Gaulle, and the British military writer Basil Liddell Hart—the latter a friend and colleague of Bywater on the London *Daily Telegraph*.

Does it matter *where* such ideas originate? Frequently not; however, without Bywater the Japanese probably would have launched a very different offensive in 1941, and that might well have set the stage of history quite differently.

The purpose of this book is to tell the story of Hector Bywater, which, until now, has remained unknown. In fact, apart from an article by the author that appeared some years ago in *American Heritage*, Bywater's name is virtually absent from the literature of World War II. The reasons for that omission will be examined in the Epilogue.

Meanwhile, the following pages seek to bring to life a singular individual through whom we may witness the pageant of naval history from the first testing of high-speed armored warships at the Battle of the Yalu River in 1894 to the Second World War. Bywater's story includes his early fascination with the Japanese Navy, his daredevil adventures as a British Secret Service agent, his early recognition that the Pacific would become the scene of a titanic struggle, his long-running debate on the physical possibility of a Pacific war with none other than Franklin D. Roosevelt, his solving a key tactical problem with model ships on a pond just outside of London, and then—most remarkably— the way in which both the Imperial Japanese Navy and the United States Navy absorbed his ideas and put them to the test of war.

Yamamoto is a recurring figure in Bywater's life. Both born in the year 1884, the two men were often influenced by the same world events at the same time in their lives. At least once, Bywater and Yamamoto met face to face and whiled away an evening discussing the prospects for peace and war over a bottle of Scotch. But the two came into repeated conflict as international tension increased in the late 1930s. In fact, it has been suggested by one of Bywater's former colleagues that once Yamamoto commenced actual preparations for a surprise attack based on Bywater's strategic ideas, he came to look upon Bywater like the protagonist in Alfred Hitchcock's *The Man Who Knew Too Much* and decided to have him eliminated.

Whatever the truth about his sudden death, Bywater's life also was filled with mystery and paradox. A large and imposing individual, there was much of the actor about him. He could hold a packed pub room in rapt attention when he told anecdotes, recited poetry, sang, or recounted how he had mischievously pulled Mussolini's leg when *Il Duce* invited him to inspect the Italian Navy. But there was also a compulsively hidden side to Bywater. For nearly a decade he lived a double life as an agent for British Secret Service and later Naval Intelligence, deceiving not only the Germans from whom he extracted a bounty of naval secrets but his friends and neighbors in Britain and the United States.

Nevertheless, he was nothing if not quintessentially British. Coolly precise, wry-witted, and steel-nerved, Bywater used to say he was drawn to the navy by the accidents of having been born on Trafalgar Day and by his surname. Long before his twenty-first birthday, which fell on the centennial of Nelson's victory at Trafalgar, his command of naval science and history was expert. He seemed to speak and write on the subject effortlessly and unerringly, as if he had absorbed several centuries of his nation's collective memory of seagoing as naturally as breathing.

Although renowned for his penetrating intellect, unaffected by the illusions that blinded so many in his generation, Bywater's private life was storm-tossed. He resigned in a fit of temper from the two daily newspapers he worked for the longest, fought with and divorced two wives, excoriated the frequently bumbling British Admiralty, and once indignantly rejected the offer of one of his country's highest decorations —the Order of the British Empire.

In the last analysis, however, one marvels at his daring, dazzling mastery of all things naval, and remarkable but as-yet unacknowledged influence on the history of our time.

—W. H. H.
Masons Island, Connecticut

1

TORPEDO ATTACK

NIGHT HAD FALLEN. The sea off the north coast of China lay flat and gleaming like an enormous field of coal. A foaming path, glinting with phosphorescence, was slowly ploughed across this dark waste by a column of eleven torpedo boats bearing the insignia of Imperial Japan. Tense young officers commanding the diminutive steamers were gripped with the knowledge that their mission was historic. But others in the crew gazed dreamily overhead. It was the kind of deeply peaceful night that tempts sailors at sea to think of their loved ones far away.

The date was February 8, 1904. Czarist Russia and Imperial Japan, long in contention for mastery of East Asia, were finally on the brink of war. Ambassadors had been recalled from Moscow and Tokyo. The world waited with a thrill of horror for the news that a state of war existed—but, as yet, there was no declaration.

Russia's powerful Asiatic Fleet was based at Port Arthur, a sheltered bay on the coast of northern China. Hoping to throw the Russians off balance, the Japanese naval commander—feisty, British-trained Heihachiro Togo—requested permission to make a surprise attack even before war had been declared. Tokyo approved. Immediately, Togo dispatched eleven torpedo boats to sneak up to the Russian anchorage under cover of darkness and fire their weapons.

As the Japanese column approached Port Arthur, two Russian patrol craft suddenly blundered in the darkness directly through their line, causing two of the attacking boats to collide in an effort to escape being seen. It was too late. The Russian patrol wheeled about and sped back to their anchorage. For the Japanese, however, being discovered like this turned out to be a stroke of good fortune. They followed the Russian boats through treacherous waters and were led directly to their targets. Even so, the outcome was not assured. The Russian patrol boats might be able to alert their comrades and have them lay down an impenetrable blast from their small-caliber, quickfiring guns. Furthermore, the "automobile," or self-propelled, torpedo, at this stage in its development, was erratic and unseaworthy, often proving as great a danger to the ship that launched it as to its intended victim.

As a light snow began to fall, the Japanese suddenly found themselves at the center of a vast city on the sea, surrounded by fantastic, shadowy shapes surmounted with rows of twinkling lights and, higher still, funnels as tall as factory chimneys. Quickly, the Japanese captains selected their targets and reduced speed lest the enemy be alerted by a sparkling bow wave or a telltale tongue of flame licking from the tops of their funnels.

HECTOR BYWATER HAD a grandstand seat from which to observe the spectacular outbreak of the Russo-Japanese War—a conflict that influenced his thinking more acutely than any other in his lifetime. Now twenty years of age, he had just been engaged as a reporter by the *New York Herald*, and it appears he wrote his very first article as a working journalist about the Port Arthur raid.

A tall, slim young man with a notably high-domed forehead, an olive, almost Mediterranean complexion, and penetrating, steel-gray eyes, Bywater—the second son of middle-class parents—had been attracted to naval affairs while still a boy by the accident of having been born on October 21, Trafalgar Day. That was the day when Admiral Horatio Nelson's victory over the combined French and Spanish fleets in 1805 was celebrated throughout the British Empire. The Royal Dockyards were thrown open to the public, and the majestic, sea-scarred fighting ships of the world's greatest navy were displayed for admiration and wonder. Bywater's visits to the Royal Dockyards were his "nearest conception of heaven," he later wrote. On those occasions, he astonished the official guides—metropolitan policemen as a rule—by "shyly but firmly correcting the misinformation they dispensed to visitors," as he put it. It was a simple matter to catch their mistakes, he explained, because, even as a boy, he "knew almost by heart the ship tables and data published in *Brassey's Naval Annual*, *Jane's Fighting Ships*, and other textbooks."

His fascination with the Japanese Navy took hold when he was only ten and wrote an essay about the Battle of the Yalu River—the decisive sea battle of the Sino-Japanese War. It became his first article accepted for publication. Years later, Bywater recalled that this precocious effort "only escaped getting into print by an editor's chance discovery of the author's tender age."

It is not difficult to imagine what attracted him to the subject. The Battle of the Yalu had been a remarkable upset victory for Japan. Any naval expert would have said that when a squadron of unarmored British-built Japanese cruisers encountered a superior force of Chinese ironclads of German construction that September morning in 1894, the huge 12-inch Krupp guns of the Chinese battleships—which heaved a shell nearly ten times the weight of those thrown by the 6-inch quickfirers on the Japanese cruisers—should have speedily settled the issue. Yet, by late afternoon the Chinese fleet had suffered the loss of five ships sunk or driven ashore, while on the Japanese side, only the flagship *Matsushima* had been seriously damaged.

The battle was important for technical reasons, too. As Bywater later wrote, it was "the first occasion on which high-speed warships, quickfiring ordnance, and smokeless powder had been tested in actual warfare," and the remarkable conclusion was that the generally regarded *weaker* force had won. Before the Chinese had been able to bring their heavy-caliber weapons into action, the more nimble Japanese gunners "overwhelmed the Chinese with a tornado of shell from their quickfiring guns." It seemed that one need not penetrate the armor of the enemy in order to prevail in naval combat. Light cruisers could defeat even heavily armored men-of-war by showering them with high-explosive shell, blasting away funnels, masts, ladders, unprotected bridges and observation posts, and all other superstructure, and killing or wounding any exposed crew members. A warship subjected to such a bath of fire might not sink but would lose its fighting power and become easy prey for an adversary's torpedo or ram.

For his fourteenth birthday, Bywater would long remember, he was given a copy of H. W. Wilson's *Ironclads in Action*. Although compelling to read, this was no juvenile book of wonder, but the most penetrating study of naval warfare of its time. Ranging from a detailed description of the battle between *Monitor* and *Merrimac* in March 1862 to the British bombardment of Alexandria twenty years later, Wilson made revelations such as that *Merrimac* might have destroyed *Monitor* had she been provisioned with solid shot instead of shell and grapeshot for attacking wooden ships. Wilson explained how Farragut ("the ablest admiral since Nelson") had overcome the natural advantage of forts over fleets in his successful attack on New Orleans in the American Civil War. And, discussing the Battle of Lissa, in which four British frigates defeated a much larger Franco-Venetian squadron in 1811, he showed how Italy "chose the royal road to defeat" by building a great fleet of ironclads without training officers and men to handle them expertly.

The statistics in Brassey's *Naval Annual* and Jane's *All the World's Fighting Ships* were devoured by Bywater much the way other boys gobbled up rugby or baseball facts and figures. With all the data packed into these encyclopedias before him, he could match the British battleship *Royal Sovereign* in hypothetical combat against *Gheorghy Pobyedonosets*, a Russian battleship of comparable size and modernity. He could see that *Royal Sovereign*, because of her superior speed and the greater range of her main battery, should be able to keep at a distance from *Pobyedonosets* where her 13.5-inch rifles would be lethal while she remained beyond the reach of the shorter and smaller-caliber guns of her adversary. If, however, the visibility were limited and the warships had to close to within, say, 2,000 yards in order to see what they were shooting at, *Sovereign*'s advantage would be nullified, and *Pobyedonosets*' main battery of six major-caliber guns might overwhelm *Sovereign*, which carried only four heavy weapons.

About the only fictional writing Bywater enjoyed in his youth was the work of the man he regarded as the master—Rudyard Kipling. In midlife, he wrote to the Nobel laureate and declared that by the age of twelve he had read every book Kipling had written. Even so, it was not Kipling's fiction or poetry that Bywater singled out for praise. His favorite, he wrote, was *A Fleet in Being*, a slim volume of eighty-four pages published in 1898 in which Kipling recounted his cruise with the Royal Navy aboard a scout cruiser taking part in maneuvers along the Irish coast. *A Fleet in Being* contained some fine, close-up reporting and a few memorable flourishes, such as when Kipling described a battleship "cleared for action, naked and grim, like a man swimming with a knife between his teeth."

Born in the Tottenham section of London on the seventy-ninth anniversary of Trafalgar, Hector Charles Bywater was the youngest of four children of Peter Daniel Bywater, a hugely built Welshman whose outsized physique, bushy beard, and mischievous eyes gave a hint of the pirate captain. The elder Bywater wandered the world for much of his life, counting among his occupations traveling salesman, engraver, Pony Express rider (which led to his friendship with William "Buffalo Bill" Cody), Secret Service agent in the Union Army of the United States, and teacher of Greek and translator of ancient languages—whence the naming of his sons Ulysses and Hector. Even with four young children, he crossed and recrossed the ocean and, at one point, took his family to live in Cambridge, Massachusetts, for four years—where Hector would urge the family to visit the Charlestown Navy Yard to see "Old Ironsides" and the other warships in port.

The Bywater family returned to England and, shortly after Hector's thirteenth birthday, put to sea again. These were the years Bywater later referred to as his *Wanderjahre*, and they included sojourns in the United States, Canada, West Africa, and a long stay in Germany. Soon after the turn of the century, the family scattered. Hector wound up in New York. His fluency in German, which would equip him for becoming one of Britain's most successful Secret Service agents, was fine-tuned—oddly enough—on the streets of New York. From age seventeen to age twenty, he worked as a streetcar conductor and later clerk for the Union Railway Company in Brooklyn, a firm whose work force was composed almost exclusively of recent German immigrants.

Living in Brooklyn, Bywater spent much of his free time at the bustling Brooklyn Navy Yard, which had built warships for the United States government in both the Civil War and the Spanish-American War, and sporadically in between. Since visitors were welcome, he could poke around in the engine houses where mechanics fashioned the huge, steam-powered machinery that could push a ship around the world; stroll along "Cob Dock," made of cobblestones brought to the yard as ballast in sailing ships; explore the "pyrotechnic laboratories" where ordnance was manufactured; and crawl through the cigar-shaped "Intelligent Whale"—one of the first submarines ever built, which became an exhibit at the yard after being condemned by the U.S. Navy in 1872.

A particular attraction was the battleship *Connecticut*, whose prodigious keel was laid down on March 10, 1903. Up to that time, the biggest warship constructed at the yard had been the 6,700-ton *Maine*, which blew up and sank under suspicious circumstances in Havana harbor, thus helping to incite the Spanish-American War. *Connecticut* was to have a displacement about two-and-a-half times that of *Maine*. A special launching way, long remembered as "The *Connecticut* Way," had to be constructed to support this 456-foot-long monster. Bywater was especially interested by the low profile of the battleship. From her plans, freely published in the press, he could see that her main battery of four 12-inch guns would be only 18 feet above the waterline, as compared to a height of 22 to 25 feet in most foreign battleships. This low-slung silhouette would make *Connecticut* harder for an enemy to see and hit, but in heavy seas the gun turrets might become flooded and unable to fight. Furthermore, the gunports—holes in turrets through which guns projected—were so large that enemy shells could readily plunge through them. Excessively large gunports were a common defect in American battleships, and Bywater had doubtless heard the scuttlebutt that when *Kearsarge* visited Germany in 1903, her crew covered the gunports with canvas painted to look like steel to hide their vulnerability.

Bywater used such giblets of information to write a tryout article or two for the *New York Herald*, the daily newspaper where, in January 1904, he landed his first job as a reporter at the age of nineteen. It was no accident that of all the dozen newspapers in New York City, he was drawn to the *Herald*. This was the paper that lavished more space than any other on naval and maritime news. If the navy decided that the barnacles on the hull of *Hercules* were to be scraped off at the League Island Navy Yard, this fact was duly published in the *Herald*. On one not atypical day, four of the *Herald*'s six editorials dealt with maritime subjects. No wonder the *Marine Journal*, a shipping publication, praised the *Herald* for having done more for the maritime industry "than all the other daily publications in the United States combined."

The man responsible for this journalistic obsession was James Gordon Bennett, the flamboyant and tyrannical publisher. A lean aristocrat with an imperious gaze and tigerish temper, Bennett was given to indulging his passions and perversities. One of the latter was that when in command of his steam-schooner *Namouna* (which *Herald* staffers nicknamed "Pneumonia"), Bennett would not change course to allow another vessel the right of way. Once when cruising the Aegean, he came on collision course with an American warship on maneuvers. At what seemed like the last possible moment, one of Bennett's top editors, who happened to be a guest on the bridge, impulsively grabbed the wheel and swung *Namouna* to port to avoid what seemed like certain disaster. The "Commodore"—as Bennett liked to be called—was so outraged that he forced the man ashore on a tiny, uninhabited island, and only after his other guests persuaded him that he might be committing murder did he send a boat back to rescue him.

Bennett's infatuation with the sea, as well as his shrewd eye for talent, led him to recognize Bywater's ability almost immediately. It was his practice to have a specially marked copy of the newspaper sent to him every morning. At the top of each article, the reporter's name would be written in red pencil and the editor's name in blue. A land-lubberly error in a nautical story would unloose a fiery reproach. "Doesn't that damned fool O'Rourke know enough never to call a funnel a 'stack'?" Bennett would thunder. By the same token, a reporter who handled nautical news with finesse was heaped with praise. "First-class job by Bywater!" Bennett would exclaim, and so delighted was he with Bywater's writing that in less than a year he rewarded his young recruit with the title of European naval correspondent—a position Bywater would hold, off and on, for the next seventeen years.

Shortly after he started work for the *Herald*, the office was thrown into an uproar. Dispatches came clacking into the telegraph room reporting that in the night Japanese torpedo boats had made a surprise attack against the Russian fleet at Port Arthur. Bywater had learned enough Morse code so that as news stories came in by wire he could read the "ticker tape" over the telegrapher's shoulder and shout bulletins to the rest of the staff. Bent over the "inker," which printed the ticker tape, he called out that the 6,600-ton cruiser *Pallada* had been torpedoed. Next, he cried, a torpedo had sunk the great battleship *Retvizan*, built only two years before for the czar's navy at Cramp's Shipyard in Philadelphia. Finally, called Bywater, the mighty *Czarevich*, a Russian battleship of French construction, had been sunk. Russian gunners on the great ships had fired furiously but blindly, and consequently the Japanese torpedo boats—Bywater knew the names by heart—*Shirakumo, Akatsuki, Asahiwo, Kasumi*, and the others had escaped unscathed.

Bennett and his editors planned lavish coverage. Under an eight-column banner headline reading SEVEN OF RUSSIA'S BIG SHIPS ARE DISABLED BY JAPAN, they clustered on the first news page a group of photographs of the principal combatants. Several ferocious-looking Russian battleships were shown pumping up clouds of soot and steam beside pictures of the diminutive Japanese torpedo craft. There were also news stories and reactions from around the world. The main analysis of the action was written by Commander J. D. Jarrold Kelley, a former naval officer handpicked for the job by Bennett. But there was more to be written, and either Bennett or Kelley assigned Bywater to research and write what seems to be his first article published in the *Herald*.

Alongside Kelley's analysis the next day, there appeared a survey of the warships of the Russian and Japanese navies. Most of the article consisted of a list of the names, tonnage, and last-known station of some 250 Russian and Japanese warships. What made it distinctive is that the list was preceded by several introductory paragraphs that sparkle with canny observations—such as that the passage of warships through the Indian Ocean is appreciably slowed because vessels in those waters "quickly get a foul bottom." The wording would be echoed years later in one of Bywater's books. Moreover, the exuberance and polish of these paragraphs make it clear that whoever wrote them was reveling in his element.

2

"WAR WHEN JAPAN IS READY"

BENNETT'S COVERAGE OF the outbreak of the Russo-Japanese War was an extraordinary feat. Not only had he set up the first international wireless-and-cable relay to get immediate news from a distant battlefront, but he had had the prescience to post a reporter at Port Arthur and another at Chemulpo, Korea, to cover the outbreak of war when it happened. Due to one delay or another, the communiqués from these well-placed reporters were a long time in coming, but when they arrived in New York they made the *Herald* the only newspaper in the world to publish eyewitness accounts of the two spectacular naval engagements that began the conflict. Bywater's exposure to these dramatic reports prompted him to ponder the strategic lessons of the war, and eventually to recognize that in many respects this war resembled nothing quite so much as a possible future war between Japan and the United States.

One of Bennett's reporters, Francis McCullagh, was aboard the British steamer *Columbia* at Port Arthur on the night of February 8, 1904. His ship stood in the outer roadstead almost within hailing distance of some seventeen Russian warships anchored there. Soothed by the sound of Russian sailors chanting evening prayers in the chill night air, McCullagh wrote that he "felt as safe lying on the edge of that mighty fleet as I would have in the heart of London." He declared he was convinced of "the impossibility of the Japanese ever attacking Port Arthur."

After composing a few hundred words in that vein, he turned in for the night. Abruptly and rudely McCullagh was awakened by "three muffled explosions followed almost immediately by the discharge of ships' guns." He told how he got dressed, went up on deck and watched the vigorous play of searchlights and gunfire for a while, but soon retired again, feeling certain "it's only practice." Even the next morning when he saw the battleships *Retvizan* and *Czarevich* aground in the harbor entrance, McCullagh assumed they must have collided in the night during an exercise. Later in the day, however, when a squadron of Japanese cruisers steamed into view and began shelling the harbor at long range, showering *Columbia* with steel fragments, McCullagh realized he was in the midst of an undeclared war. He finished his dispatch, put it with cash in a cigar box, and tossed it to a sampan. The cigar box was handed over to a steamer bound for Cheefoo up the coast, from where the story went by wireless and Atlantic Cable to the home office of the *Herald*. No reader consumed it more eagerly than Bywater.

Meanwhile, Willmott Lewis, a young Englishman on the staff of the *Herald*, who wore Panama hats at a tilt, wrote an "exclusive" on the action off Chemulpo. Bennett featured it not only for its stirring drama, but because Americans found that they had unexpected stakes in the outcome.

Chemulpo was the name of a port on the west coast of Korea known today as Inchon and now famous as the site of Douglas MacArthur's amphibious assault in the Korean War. The Japanese were first to recognize the port's strategic possibilities. A few hours before the torpedo boats struck at Port Arthur, a Japanese cruiser squadron under Rear Admiral Sotokichi Uriu convoyed troop transports to Chemulpo, where 3,000 infantrymen landed and moved inland to capture Seoul. Also in the harbor was the fast, new Russian cruiser *Variag*, and the aged gunboat *Korietz*, but they had made no effort to interfere with the landings.

Early the next morning, after the Japanese troops were all safely ashore, Uriu withdrew his cruisers to the mouth of the harbor. From there he sent a message to the commander of *Variag* declaring that a state of war existed and that unless the Russian warships surrendered or left the harbor, it would be his unpleasant duty to attack them at anchor.

Willmott Lewis was the only reporter in the city who got wind of Uriu's ultimatum. He hired a launch and struck out into the harbor, notebook in hand. The Russian warships were then stripping for action, Lewis reported. Captain Rudnev, the commander of *Variag*, had elected to run the gauntlet of Japanese cruisers in the hope of reaching the safety of Port Arthur. Everything on his decks not essential to survival was thrown overboard; a wooden mast that could not be taken down was chopped down. "The situation of the Russian vessels could scarcely be worse," wrote Lewis. "The crew could only hope to die bravely." As the two Russian warships made their way to open water, the band on *Variag* playing "God Preserve the Czar," they received "vociferous cheers" from the crews of four neutral warships in the harbor.

In a very real way, as Lewis made clear to his readers, *Variag* was a surrogate American warship. Like the battleship *Retvizan*, torpedoed a few hours earlier at Port Arthur, "the Russian American-built cruiser," as the *Herald* described her, had been constructed by the William Cramp and Sons yard in Philadelphia, one of the leading U.S. shipyards. Both *Retvizan* and *Variag* embodied the last word in modern naval engineering, and their delivery to the Russian government had marked the entry of the United States into the lucrative international warship market.

But American sympathy was drawn, also, to *Variag*'s adversary— the clean-cut, forty-six-year-old Uriu, who had received his naval training at Annapolis under a program to admit foreign cadets. During a year of preparatory school at Middletown, Connecticut, Uriu had become an ardent Christian. At the Naval Academy, he was elected president of the Annapolis YMCA. He became an expert boxer, and once —back home in Japan, so the story went—when challenged about his religious conversion he silenced his questioner with a knockout punch to the chin. With such stories in the American press, Uriu had a following.

Variag came zigzagging out of the mouth of the harbor at her remarkable top speed of 23.5 knots, but as soon as she cleared the entrance, the Russian captain found himself surrounded by a semicircle of eight enemy warships. The Japanese cruiser *Asama* was the first to come within

range of *Variag*, and, at 6,800 yards, according to Lewis, opened up
with an 8-inch broadside. *Variag* was struck twice amidships at the
waterline, disabling two boilers and slowing her speed. Furthermore,
the ship began to list so heavily to port that the guns in her port battery,
even when elevated, pointed into the sea. Another shot found the bridge
and twisted it out of recognition. Captain Rudnev was wounded in the
face, his drummer boy and bugler standing to either side were killed
instantly. Still another shell struck a magazine, which set the ship afire.

Several Japanese cruisers, including Uriu's flagship, *Naniwa*, now
came within range. Japanese gunners ignored *Korietz*, but the sea around
Variag was lashed to foam by near misses and the deck of the Russian
cruiser was bloody. Ten of the ship's twelve gun-captains were quickly
killed. One shell passed between the arm and the body of a gunner who
had his hand on his hip, then struck the forecastle and killed every other
man on it. After fourteen minutes of this fierce bombardment, 109
Russian sailors lay dead or dying on deck. Listing and ablaze, *Variag*
limped back to Chemulpo, followed by the unscathed *Korietz*. *Asama*
pursued them for a while, hoping for a chance to ram, but both Russian
warships escaped that humiliation only to be scuttled by their crews at
anchorage.

Bywater read of these momentous events with fascination. From
Brassey's *Annual* and Jane's just-published encyclopedias of the Russian
and Japanese navies, he knew all specifications of *Variag* and the Japanese cruisers ganged up against her, and details about the torpedo boats
and their Russian victims. He could play the battles, shot by shot, over
and over again in his mind. He was also beginning to do something he
could not yet articulate. The budding strategist was beginning to think
in geopolitical terms. He was almost ready to grasp the central strategic
lesson to be learned from this clash of arms—that the outcome would
be determined not by the potential resources of the adversaries (which
would make Russia the obvious victor), but by the *actual* resources that
each side could deploy in the war zone. Russia, after all, possessed a
navy much more powerful than Japan, but most of her warships were
thousands of miles away in the Baltic. Likewise, Russia's industrial capacity was many times that of Japan's, but it was an open question as
to whether or not she could make that superiority felt at the battlefront.

Meanwhile, being at the *Herald* allowed Bywater to read each article
that arrived by cable, whether published or not. Hanging around the

office after hours, he befriended the night editor, John T. Burke, and was able to converse by wire with reporters covering the action. As for his own contributions, Bywater wrote articles for the *Herald* on a variety of aspects of the war.

An illustrated Sunday feature headlined SURGERY FOR THE STEEL SKINS OF BATTLESHIPS, which appeared a month after the outbreak of war, is obviously Bywater's handiwork. His theme is that the material consequences of the Japanese surprise attack were less devastating than originally feared because warships that have been torpedoed and sunk in shallow water may be quickly repaired and raised by divers using underwater welding equipment—a new technique. "It is evident," Bywater observes, shaking a finger at czarist Russia, "that *Retvizan* and *Pallada* and the other battleships and cruisers did not carry trained submarine craftsmen, and this is but one evidence of the unpreparedness of Russia for war—at any rate, naval war." He then explains how divers for the British Navy were trained at a diving tank at Portsmouth, England. It was unusual, of course, for a New York reporter to illustrate a common practice by citing a British training program rather than one nearer home, and thus the article brings to mind that English boy whose "nearest conception of heaven" had been the Royal Dockyards.

Even more detailed—and telltale—knowledge of the British naval scene is displayed when he tosses in the fact that "the great firm of Siebe, Gorman and Co., of the Westminster Bridge road, London, sent out upward of 250 complete diving dresses to Nagasaki for the use of the Japanese Navy." Bywater adds: "This firm is the contractor for diving dresses to the British Navy, and has furnished tutors and teachers for the recently established naval diving schools in Japanese arsenals."

He also includes a grimly amusing anecdote of the kind for which he would become renowned. This, too, is set at Portsmouth. "A graduate seaman diver," Bywater relates, "was sent below to scrape the bottom of the battleship *Goliath*, and was down so long that a peremptory signal was given at last to him from above to come up. No notice was taken of this, and presently, to the amazement and alarm of his masters, his tools began to float upward one by one and appeared on the surface. Feeling certain now that a tragedy had happened, a second seaman diver was dressed and sent below, only to find that the supposed dead man was fast asleep sitting on a steel rail right underneath the keel of the immense battleship."

Another *Herald* story bears other marks of Bywater's writing. The assignment had been a routine one of the kind given to a new reporter—to tell how subzero weather affected maritime activities at the port of New York. Bywater sets the scene by describing the Holland-America liner *Statendam* as "a huge ice palace of grotesque design." Coming to its pier, the ship was coated with at least six inches of ice from stem to stern, and the crew had to chop their way out of the cabin with axes. He then interviews the captain—evidently in German—to get an exact description of the course taken, gales and blizzards encountered, and other exact details guaranteed to delight Bennett. Bywater is vivid, precise, technically astute, and able to confidently underplay the sensational, as when he describes how another great ship swinging into its slip crushed a small steam launch.

Despite the opportunities in New York, Bywater departed for England after being a reporter for a little more than a year. A passport application indicates that he left on February 12, 1905—just after the first anniversary of the Japanese attack at Port Arthur. Yet he hardly severed connections with Bennett and (according to a subsequent job application) left for Britain as the *Herald*'s European naval correspondent—a part-time job but a prestigious connection.

Imbued with the reportorial feats of McCullagh, Lewis, and others, Bywater yearned to witness a great naval action, and thought he had a better chance of finding one from a base in London. Furthermore, his twenty-first birthday would fall on the centennial of Nelson's victory at Trafalgar. The occasion would be gloried in throughout the British Empire, but nowhere more splendidly than in London. Bywater must have felt an irresistible tug to be there.

He could not have foreseen that the Trafalgar centennial would serve to focus his attention once again on the Imperial Japanese Navy. As the Russo-Japanese War progressed, Japan scored a tremendous naval victory, annihilating an entire Russian fleet at the Battle of Tsushima on May 27 and 28, 1905—and this triumph seemed to many in England reminiscent of Nelson's feat at Trafalgar. In the century between the two battles, no naval commander—not Sampson at Santiago nor Dewey at Manila Bay—had come as close as did the diminutive Togo to matching Nelson's victory. Once details of the Tsushima action became known, the British public was reminded that Togo had received seven years of his naval training in England, and that his flagship *Mikasa* (among other

Japanese warships in the engagement) was of British construction. At the opening of the battle, Togo's message to the fleet had been a reverential translation of Nelson's last order: "England expects that every man will do his duty." At Tsushima, Togo signaled—not from the signal yardarm of *Mikasa* but from the masthead, where all could see the colors—"The fate of the Empire depends upon your actions. You are expected to do your utmost."

Bywater read about Tsushima shortly after he reached London. By then, the Russo-Japanese War had lasted fifteen months. For that time, Togo had managed to keep the Russian Asiatic Fleet bottled up in Port Arthur, smashing at it when the Russian ships, like the ill-starred *Variag*, once tried to put to sea. As a result, the Russian Baltic Fleet under the command of Zinovi Rojestvensky had been dispatched on an epic, 18,000-mile journey to relieve the fleet at Port Arthur. Togo was waiting for it in the Straits of Tsushima. When the rivals met, Rojestvensky's ships were low in the water, laden with coal for a long voyage; Togo's faster warships carried a minimum supply of coal and thus even increased the disparity in the speed of the two fleets. (It would occur to Bywater—and to many Japanese as well—that Japan would have a similar advantage if a hostile American fleet should hazard the long trek across the Pacific to Japan.)

At first, Togo surprised Rojestvensky with a daring turn that briefly exposed his ships to heavy fire, but that put the fleets roughly in two parallel lines. In short order, the faster Japanese column forged ahead and swung in front of the Russian line. That classic maneuver is described as "crossing the T," which means presenting heavily armed broadsides of one's own ships to relatively lightly armed bows or sterns of the enemy, and so outgunning him. In fact, Togo's maneuver was more exquisite and devastating. When the Japanese column surged in front of the Russian column, Togo was not only facing his broadsides against Russian bows but, by outdistancing Rojestvensky's rear, was placing all his own warships simultaneously in action against just a portion of Rojestvensky's.

The result for the Japanese was even better than mathematical probabilities might suggest. Although Russian armored ships outnumbered the Japanese by fourteen to twelve, every major Russian vessel was sunk or captured, and, on the Japanese side, not a ship was lost or crippled. The Russians lost 4,830 men, Japan only 117. Rojestvensky himself was

CROSSING THE *T* AT TSUSHIMA

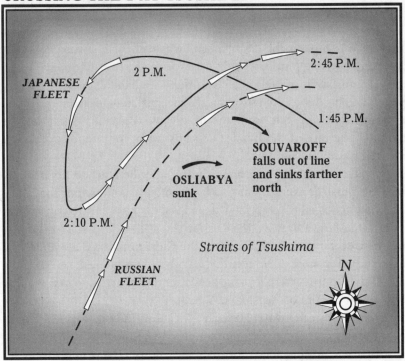

Togo's maneuver was more exquisite and devastating than merely facing his broadsides to Russian bows.

transferred successively from three sinking ships, finally to wake up in a Japanese hospital with a fractured skull. "Rarely, if ever, in the annals of war," wrote Bywater in later years, "has the Goddess of Victory showered her favors with so lavish a hand."

Four-and-a-half months after the battle, when late reports of it still provoked amazement, Britain celebrated the Trafalgar centennial. The *New York Herald*'s report with a London dateline was clearly the work of its new twenty-one-year-old European naval correspondent. Nelson's column at Trafalgar Square, wrote Bywater, was decorated with flowers "sent from all parts of the Empire which had been pouring in for the last week." Memorial services for Nelson were held in churches, and actors and statesmen gave public readings of Kipling's "Recessional." Nelson's ship *Victory*, preserved at the Portsmouth naval base, was "brilliantly illuminated," and British warships throughout the world were instructed to "parade their crews."

The *Herald* story was too brief to cover events at Royal Albert Hall, jammed to capacity with more than 8,000 people. But even a raging fever could not have kept Bywater away. The crowning moment of the entire centennial celebration, according to the London *Times*, occurred during a brief speech at the Albert Hall by Captain Kaburaki, the Japanese naval attaché in London. There was "great applause" when Kaburaki arose to accept on behalf of Togo a bust of Nelson and a wedge-shaped piece of timber from *Victory*. Then Kaburaki spoke with great solemnity: "The spirit of the Navy of Great Britain is also in the Navy of Japan," he said. This was greeted by "a perfect roar of cheers." Kaburaki alluded to Togo's Nelson-like signal at Tsushima and grandly swept his hand, pointing to signal flags draped around the gallery that spelled out Nelson's message to the fleet. The crowd exploded in cheering. Kaburaki then read a cable just received from Tokyo: "Heartfelt thanks to accept centenary present on this memorable day. Togo." Thunderous applause made the old hall tremble.

Bywater was also interested in the implications of Tsushima for naval practice in the future. At first, he became convinced that the Japanese had prevailed not only because Togo exploited tactical advantages but because of the effectiveness of Japanese 6-inch quickfiring guns—just as at the Yalu eight years before. Rapid fire seemed the key.

He knew, of course, the arguments of big-gun enthusiasts who insisted Rojestvensky's Baltic Fleet had been "literally pounded out of existence by a succession of smashing blows from the Japanese 12-inch guns," as Bywater expressed it in an article written soon after Tsushima. But he could not resist the conclusion that the Japanese had won by firing a "constant stream of high-explosive shell" that transformed the Russian ironclads into "spouting volcanoes of fire, metal splinters, and noxious gases." Even if these missiles failed to penetrate, "their bursting gradually loosened rivets and wrenched plates, thereby doing incalculably greater damage than the clean penetration of a 12-inch armor-piercing projectile." What the Yalu had suggested now seemed conclusively proved, as far as Bywater was concerned. Heavy guns, it appeared, which were aimed and fired with tortoiselike deliberation, had been outstripped by rabbitlike quickfirers.

Over the next few years Bywater changed his mind. He probably caught wind of the reports of British naval attachés present at Tsushima. Royal Navy observers had been allowed aboard Japanese warships when they went into action. One of these officers, William Pakenham, stated a key tactical lesson in a report to the British Admiralty. "When 12-inch guns are firing," Pakenham wrote, "shots from 10-inch guns pass unnoticed, while, for all the respect they instill, 8-inch or 6-inch guns might just as well be pea-shooters." These words were cited as "momentous" in the report of the Admiralty's Committee on Designs in 1905, which had been charged with creating a new line of British fighting ships. It had become clear to both Japanese and British naval authorities that 12-inch guns, when fired in salvos according to methods worked out by the gunnery expert Percy Scott, could be handled with remarkable accuracy, and, in addition, threw the greatest weight of metal with the highest speed. These were considerations certain to affect the outcome in any ship-versus-ship combat. Consequently, before the end of 1905, Japan laid down *Aki* and *Satsuma*, the first battleships designed to take advantage of the lessons of Tsushima. Britain followed by laying the keel of *Dreadnought*, which gave its name to the new class of all-big-gun battleships. The so-called dreadnoughts would dominate battleship design for a generation, until the threat of air power impressed gunnery specialists, who then began to slather battleships with high-angle anti-aircraft weapons.

By at least 1912, Bywater got the message. "Tsushima," he wrote, "had taught that not the quickfirer but the big gun was the decisive factor in naval combat."

IF THE *HERALD'S* preeminence in naval coverage attracted Bywater to the newspaper, one of James Gordon Bennett's fixations very likely influenced him after he came to work there. Bennett held the opinion that sooner or later Japan would attack the United States. Since that view was unusual for its time, and since Bywater eventually came to share it (although for quite different reasons), it seems likely that Bywater's thinking about possible Japanese aggression in the future owes a debt to his long-time employer.

"Mr. Bennett for many years has been convinced," wrote a former *Herald* editor, "that war between Japan and the United States will come when Japan is ready to strike the blow." It was not Japan's surprise attack at Port Arthur that persuaded the Commodore of this inevitability; he had formed his opinion much earlier, probably during the summer of 1897 when Japan acted provocatively toward the United States in response to the introduction of a resolution in the U.S. Congress proposing the annexation of Hawaii. Japan protested through her ambassador that Hawaii's independence was "essential to the good understanding of the Powers that have interests in the Pacific," and she dispatched her cruiser *Naniwa* to Hawaii to drive home the point.

Japan quickly backed down. Her ambassador insisted that his protest had been merely an "inquiry," and *Naniwa* departed after a brief stay. Nevertheless, Americans were alarmed and Hawaii-annexationists in Congress gained considerable support. The U.S. Pacific Fleet was strengthened as an era of good feeling toward Japan came to an end. Bennett was one of those swept up in this earliest outbreak of "yellow-peril" fever. A few months later, amid clamor for a declaration of war against Spain, he opposed American intervention in the Caribbean for fear that Japan would seize the occasion to attack the fleet in San Francisco Bay.

So certain was Bennett that Japan would make war against the United States, he equipped *Herald* foreign correspondents with special code books with which to elude Japanese censors in reporting what one of his editors described as "information concerning any conflict between American and Japanese forces." With the outbreak of the Russo-Japanese War in 1904, although most Americans sided with Japan, Bennett argued in an editorial that if the *Herald*'s "sympathies are with the white race rather than the yellow race, why that is, after all, its indisputable right." He never wavered in his conviction that sooner or later Japan would strike America. As late as 1914, Bennett maintained a dozen reporters in China and Japan—an extraordinary number for a Western newspaper even at a time when foreign correspondents came cheap—to await the collision.

Bennett's belief in the inevitability of war between Japan and the United States marks him as the earliest prophet of a Pacific war. Heretofore, historians have accorded that distinction to Homer Lea, a bizarre militarist who wrote of a likely war ahead in 1909. But Bennett, long since converted, welcomed Lea to the fold like a fresh recruit to a venerable cause. He hailed Lea's book, *The Valor of Ignorance*, in the *Herald* with a five-column headline—UNITED STATES CALLED A CRUMBLING GIANT—and trumpeted the author with feature stories and provocative editorials.

Bywater, of course, read Bennett's diatribes against Japan. And he recognized them as jingoistic fulminations riddled with strategic and tactical absurdities—hostile Japanese warships could no more enter San Francisco Bay than could the American fleet go on a shooting spree in

Tokyo Bay. Powerful shore-based batteries would tear such intruders to pieces. In contrast, Bywater would write of a possible war in the Pacific with technical mastery and true prophetic insight. Still, his employer's Japanophobia did alert Bywater to a possibility that dominated his thinking for much of the rest of his life.

CHAPTER

3

"OUR SPLENDID SPY IN GERMANY"

IT WAS 1909. Somewhere in Germany. The German kaiser, Wilhelm II, had long since read and methodically annotated his copy of Alfred Thayer Mahan's book *The Influence of Sea Power upon History*, and had been convinced that naval power was the foundation of world power. A German naval buildup was well underway, although wrapped in secrecy. Some of those entrusted to guard it became aware of a tall, young Englishman with a swarthy complexion who had taken a disconcerting interest in German naval activity.

The young man had been picnicking at naval anchorages, sightseeing at the Kiel Canal, and asking questions of naval arms manufacturers. The most disturbing thing about him was that he spoke German with such idiomatic polish that he could pass for a native. Counterespionage agents had interrogated his landlady and surreptitiously searched his apartment—to no avail. Nevertheless, a senior naval intelligence officer believed he was on the trail of a genuine spy who would, sooner or later, make a fatal slip.

Catching a British spy and holding an espionage trial keenly interested the German Admiralty. Such trials offered opportunities to convince the budget-conscious Reichstag of the navy's importance—why else would Great Britain want to spy on it? After a widely publicized trial at which two British officers confessed before a Leipzig court that they had been collecting information for a "naval Baedecker" compiled by the British Admiralty, Alfred von Tirpitz, the chief of the kaiser's navy, remarked that "every spy caught is worth a new cruiser."

In a short while, German diligence was rewarded. The suspect was observed visiting a naval base on the North Sea. He was followed as he took a train to an inland city and was observed posting a letter in a mailbox. The naval intelligence officer watched as a policeman, accompanied by a plainclothesman, touched the suspect on the arm.

"Would you mind coming with us to show your papers?"

The tall Englishman assented with a casual air and was ushered into a cab. At the Town Hall, he was met by the local chief of police and a man he recognized as a senior naval intelligence officer.

"Did you post some letters just now?" he was asked.

The suspect admitted mailing a letter. He described the envelope, named its addressee, and outlined the contents—it was written to a friend in Leeds and contained only idle gossip. A policeman brought in a sealed sack from the mailbox. Envelopes were spread out on a table. The chief of police went through them until he came to the one the suspect had described.

"You permit me?" he asked, picking up a letter opener. The suspect nodded, hardly daring to believe his captors were falling for one of the oldest tricks in the spying trade—that of mailing an innocent letter to a friend when posting a coded intelligence report, so that if one is caught one can point to the innocent letter. The contents were exactly as the suspect had described. The Germans scrutinized the letter with a magnifying glass and tested it for invisible inks. It was checked against a code book brought from Berlin; nothing useful was discovered.

At midnight the suspect was released with the explanation that the police were on the track of a criminal who closely resembled him in appearance. The interview ended with both parties lying politely—the Germans about a fictitious thief they were pursuing, the suspect about his acceptance of their story. The young man then returned to his room, where he calmed himself with a double brandy and soda.

Bywater had become a British Secret Service agent. Apart from the few tips his father may have passed along from his experience as an agent for the Union during the American Civil War, Bywater developed his technique intuitively. He seemed to have a natural feel for clandestine work and soon became one of the best spies the Royal Navy ever had. By 1911, when he had served as an agent for two years, Sir John Fisher was exuberantly describing him in letters to Winston Churchill, the first lord of the admiralty, as his "splendid spy in Germany."

Those in the know heaped praise on articles Bywater sent back to British naval and military journals. The *United Service Magazine*, a periodical devoted to naval and military affairs, stated in 1910 that the British public owed a large debt "to Mr. Bywater, whose monthly articles on the German Navy afford more information on this very difficult subject than do the writings of all the rest of the naval correspondents put together." Tributes to Bywater were also paid by the Germans, sometimes unwittingly. On one occasion, von Tirpitz appeared before the Reichstag to respond to Bywater's needling the German Navy for its "abnormal excess of officials" in dockyards. He did not refute Bywater's charge but lamely tried to justify the fact that there was one overseer for every seven hands in German dockyards whereas the ratio was one to thirty in British yards.

Leaving aside all ethical questions, the nine years from 1909 until the Armistice that Bywater spent as an undercover agent were excellent preparation for his career as a journalist. He was well aware of this connection and once wrote that an intelligence agent is like a newspaper reporter "in that he is generally trying to procure information which the other side is unwilling to divulge. In both cases the work involves not merely the collection of basic facts, but also their analysis and logical amplification by methods of deduction." In time, Bywater would become a past master of procuring information the other side was unwilling to divulge, bringing to light the secret growth of the German, Italian, and Japanese navies. His years as a naval spy also made him a student of naval science and practice, giving Bywater the foundation for writing a seminal book on Pacific strategy.

The invitation to move to Germany came from his older brother Ulysses, or Uly, who had settled in Europe after the Bywaters went their separate ways at the turn of the century. Uly had become deputy consul general for the United States in Dresden. Two years older than Hector, he was said to be "a charming young man; slightly immature and lacking in force." But Uly had no trouble in making life in Dresden sound attractive. The philosopher Herder had called the city Germany's Florence, and indeed it was a capital of culture, beautiful and baroque. The composers Schumann and von Weber had lived there, and so had Schiller when he finished *Don Carlos* and Wagner when he came to supervise the premiere of *Rienzi*. When Uly arrived in Dresden, the old opera house was still a glory, and the remarkable Zwinger Museum with its charming pavilions housed a splendid collection of old-master paintings as well as world-renowned scientific exhibits. Both Bywater brothers were fine amateur musicians; they doted on German opera and had a sophisticated taste in the arts. They were also remarkable linguists. Hector's German was flawless—and now he had begun to speak French. Uly was proficient even in Swiss dialects. A language barrier hardly existed for either brother.

In his letters to New York, Uly mentioned other attractions of Dresden—festive restaurants, cafés, beer gardens, and pretty English girls who strolled along the Elbe's grassy banks on warm Sunday afternoons. Dresden had an English-speaking colony of several thousand residents, and more during the opera season. English people had found Dresden "a clean, cheerful city . . . a place in which men are gregarious, busy, full of merriment," as Anthony Trollope wrote.

But more than Dresden's social and cultural life beckoned to Bywater. In 1907, the chief fascination of naval observers in both the United States and Great Britain was the German Navy. A European naval arms race had been underway for several years, and now the emergence of the all-big-gun dreadnought had come as a stroke of luck to Germany. By outmoding all previous battleships, it wiped out Britain's naval superiority and held out the possibility that any nation able to afford a new fleet of dreadnoughts might eclipse British sea power. Kaiser Wilhelm took up that challenge, and the German Navy was growing at an enormous rate. Such activity naturally aroused curiosity in Britain and America, where experts wondered about the design and fire power of the kaiser's new warships.

There had been rumors of extraordinary accuracy in German naval rifles tested at target practice in the Baltic, but reliable information was scarce. The Germans were also believed to be experimenting with a new type of diesel engine to revolutionize submarine propulsion, and there were intriguing bits and pieces of information suggesting feverish activity at coastal fortifications. All this made Germany a magnet for a student of naval affairs in 1907, and so Uly's invitation to Hector had proved irresistible.

Uly had a secret to tell when Hector arrived. Once—five years earlier—in order to get a job in the U.S. Consular Service, he had passed himself off as an American citizen, born in Boston. It had seemed a harmless deception; passports were then almost unknown and nationality was not a matter of serious concern. But now with the international situation heating up, things were getting a bit sticky, Uly said. His job with the American Consulate in Dresden was the third he had held based on the fiction of his American citizenship, and if the truth came out, he would lose his job and be disgraced. Hector would simply have to go along with the ruse, reassuring everyone that both Bywater brothers were American citizens. Hector agreed, taking a step that would lead to deeper deception once he became a British agent.

For the time being, it was easy for the brothers to pose as Yankees. They could speak of their schooling in Cambridge, Massachusetts, of visiting "Old Ironsides" at the Charlestown Navy Yard, and they could even drop remarks about their "Uncle Maurice," who was, in truth, an Episcopal minister living in Seattle who had earned the distinction of delivering the benediction when Knute Nelson was sworn in as governor of Minnesota.

Hector soon found a job as copy editor on the *Daily Record*, an English-language weekly serving the English and American community in Dresden. It summarized world news on its front page and covered Dresden and Germany at large on inside pages. Hector, meanwhile, kept his post as European naval correspondent for the *New York Herald* and began writing on naval affairs for specialized publications in England —notably the *Navy League Journal*, a pulpit for the Navy League of Great Britain; and the *Naval & Military Record and Royal Dockyards Gazette*, a weekly with close ties to the British armed services. These markets for his writing gave him the reason and the funds to travel widely and visit German naval bases on the North Sea coast. He did so well in ferreting out information on fortifications, warship construction, and gunnery practice that in April 1908 he began writing regular columns for both the *Navy League Journal* and the *Naval & Military Record and Royal Dockyards Gazette*.

Bywater commenced this work as a genuine admirer of Germany. He had made a number of German friends in New York and on previous visits to Germany, and his reading of Carlyle's *Frederick the Great* had given him a sincere appreciation of the qualities that had raised Prussia to major-power standing in Europe. Gradually, however, he became disturbed to see that von Tirpitz's propaganda system, used to stimulate public interest in the navy, consistently portrayed Britain as an implacable foe determined to frustrate Germany's hopes of commercial and colonial expansion. In time, it appeared to him that the whole of the German naval effort was directed against Britain.

According to a friend, Bywater was now "an affable and entertaining companion . . . possessed of robust common sense and a suave, tactful manner." Such charm, combined with his language ability, gave him access to German and foreign society in Dresden. He benefited, too, from a rich baritone and his knowledge of lieder, which ranged from art songs by Schubert and Schumann to pop favorites like "Gaudeamus" and "Was Martin Luther Spricht." In time, he developed an affection for German war songs. Bywater regarded them as among the best ever written and learned to sing them like a native—a useful talent.

Once, at a beerfest, he broke into the mystical, staccato strains of "Song of the Sword," the anthem written by the poet Körner a few hours before he fell in battle at Leipzig. So impressed was a group of German officers that it was not long before one of them felt comfortable enough to reveal details of the top-secret 16.5-inch "Big Bertha" howitzer developed specifically to attack Belgian forts. The details, naturally, speedily appeared in one of Bywater's communiqués.

Love struck the Bywater brothers almost simultaneously. Uly married Marguerite d'Arx, a Swiss who had come to Dresden for the high life, and Hector married Emma Robinson, a beautiful young woman from Yorkshire who had been touring the Continent with her aunts. Even as he started a family, however, Hector was entering the world of the undercover agent. Although he would eventually write two books and a score of articles about the Secret Service and British Naval Intelligence, which he served successively, he took pains to conceal his personal involvement. Because one of his revealing letters has come to light in a Texas archive and because in later years he told his son which of the "capers" recounted in his books and articles in the third person were in fact experiences of his own, it is possible to piece together his career as a secret agent.

Shortly after he began to write regular columns from Dresden about the German Navy, Bywater received a visit from an Englishman who told him that if he ever took a holiday in England it would be to his advantage to call a certain friend of his. Intrigued, Bywater pursued the suggestion on his next visit to London. Telephoning the number he had been given, he was directed to 2 Whitehall Court, a palatial structure that looked like a French chateau in the heart of the government section of London. The building housed the Authors' Club, the Golfers' Club, and the Junior Army and Navy Club. Bywater was told to take the elevator to the top floor, just above the Authors' Club. He followed the instructions apprehensively because he still had no idea of what he was getting into. At the top landing, his identification was checked by two men who appeared to be carrying concealed revolvers. When satisfied, they instructed him to climb a flight of stairs and enter a suite of rooms in what was evidently the attic.

In one of his books, Bywater described the scene:

> The apartment, large and airy, is furnished as an office. Its most conspicuous feature is a huge steel safe, painted green. The walls are adorned with large maps and charts and one picture, the latter depicting the execution of a group of French villagers by a Prussian firing squad in the war of 1870. There are three tables, at the largest of which sits an elderly man, grey-haired, clean shaven, wearing a monocle. His figure inclines to stoutness, but the weather-tanned face, with its keen grey eyes, stamps him as an out-of-door man. He is, in fact, a post-captain on the retired list of the Royal Navy.

This gentleman was to play a large role in Bywater's life over the next six years, although throughout most of that time he would be known to him only as "C." He was Sir Mansfield Cumming, the head of the newly formed Foreign Section of British Secret Service—officially known as M.I.i(c)—a power in the world at that time. Unlike today's Secret Service chiefs who inspire novels and movies, C was completely unknown during his lifetime. Many high-ranking government officials, including some who communicated with him regularly, did not known his identity.

Bywater recalled that C began the interview by explaining in an avuncular manner that he was the head of an agency within the Foreign Office whose specialty was gathering information from around the world that might have a bearing on the security of the British Empire. Quite obviously, he said, the growth of the German Navy was a matter of serious concern, but dependable information about it was exceedingly hard to come by.

He went on like this:

> We are almost entirely dependent on the naval attaché's reports and such news as Tirpitz chooses to give the German press, which is precious little. Then we get reports from an agent in Brussels, and occasionally from two very dubious agencies in the same city which make a business of prying into the military secrets of all the big powers and selling information to the highest bidder. The stuff I have from this source struck me as being highly suspicious and probably worthless. The fact is we have no means at present of obtaining trustworthy news from Germany. If the Germans really wanted to spring a big naval surprise on us, apparently they could do so without our having the slightest warning.

C said he knew all about Bywater's background and was confident that he would be able to perform an invaluable job for his country. So as not to arouse suspicion, he should continue to work for the *Daily Record* in Dresden and to contribute articles to the service publications for which he was currently writing, but he should start sending reports back to C immediately. The first of these should cover the fortifications on Borkum, a small island off the Friesland coast that was one of the key strategic positions in the North Sea. Where were the bomb-proof shelters located, and how many were there? How many 28-centimeter howitzers in fixed positions, and how many mobile 4.1-centimeter high-velocity guns in among the sand dunes? Where were the main and emergency wireless stations located? Where were the secret telegraph and telephone cables leading from the garrison headquarters to the mainland? A map would be helpful.

"You must exercise extreme caution," C warned, "and understand that if you should be caught violating the German law against espionage you would be disavowed by the British Foreign Office and would have to fend for yourself. His Majesty's Government cannot be implicated under any circumstances."

Bywater responded that the British government ran no risk of exposure from him since both he and his brother had represented themselves as Americans. C was enchanted with this piece of news. He urged Bywater to have Ulysses take advantage of his official position in Dresden to certify him as an American citizen—a simple procedure used before passports became common to facilitate the identification and movement of foreign travelers in Europe. C may also have had in the back of his mind that if war came between Britain and Germany, with the United States remaining neutral, establishing Bywater as an American might permit him to remain inside Germany to continue his work for the British Secret Service—a ploy that C did indeed pursue in 1913. (Meanwhile, Uly did precisely as C requested as soon as Hector returned to Germany, certifying the registration of American citizenship of one Hector Charles Bywater along with ten other individuals then living in Dresden.)

Intrigued by the prospect of such risky work as C outlined, Bywater was aware that his wife back in Dresden was now pregnant. Getting up his courage, he explained to C that he was honored by the invitation but, also mindful of his approaching fatherhood, he would be glad to know how much he would be paid.

C said he was surprised to hear any mention of monetary compensation since it was a patriotic honor to serve one's country in time of need. Bywater persisted, firmly yet politely, and as he spoke, C recalled the reports by Bywater he had been reading in the *Navy League Journal* and the *Naval & Military Record*, which packed more fresh and vital information into a column of newsprint than he could get from all the naval attachés and agents in Europe. Consequently, C relented. In short order, the two men shook hands and the newest recruit to the British Secret Service was strolling confidently along the Victoria Embankment, having been promised the pay and allowances of a lieutenant commander in the Royal Navy.

CHAPTER
4

CRUEL YEARS

"SECRET SERVICE ACTIVITIES," Hector Bywater once wrote, "must often come into provocative contact with the strongest emotions of the human soul. Love, hate, fear, revenge, greed: each and all of these passions play their part in such work."

That statement was made after nearly a decade of undercover operations, which followed his recruitment in London by C, and one can only guess at the hours of toil and sacrifice, the months and years of living with fear, the constant degradation of preying upon human weakness, and the rare, exhilarating moments of triumph that are compressed into those words. Still, it is possible to gain more than a glimpse of Bywater's life as an agent by "decoding" certain passages in his published writing. For example, in a chapter of *Strange Intelligence*, the book that he and his friend H. C. Ferraby wrote in 1931, there is an account of a six-month-long adventure by an unnamed British agent in Germany and

Austria prior to the First World War. Bywater told his son that this particular chapter was based on his own experience.

He had been assigned to gather information about German warships at the Schichau yard at Danzig (Gdansk), German submarines being fitted out at the navy yard north of Danzig, and the seaplane trials at the Putzig Naval Air Station. He accomplished all this and a great deal more.

"It was cold as only Danzig can be," he began, reporting an episode that displays his instinctive grasp of the art of espionage. "I put up at the 'Reichshof,' and spent the first day in paying one or two genuine business calls, being careful to let the desk people know where I was going. On the second day," he continued, "the usual batch of mail arrived for me. This further established my respectability with the hotel people and, of course, with the police, who in every German seaport were known, at that time, to take special interest in English visitors." (Bywater never revealed to his readers that he had pretended to be an American.)

He then explained that before every trip he would arrange to have business letters forwarded to the hotels at which he was planning to stay. If the letters were casually inspected, or even steamed open, their effect would be to dispel any suspicions that might have been aroused. "It was a simple precaution," he wrote, "but I always found it effective."

Although the Germans were "ravaged by spy fever," it proved easy for Bywater to enter the Schichau yard and wander around inside for three hours. Workmen were supposed to show identity cards, but since there were 3,000 of them the formality was largely ignored. All one needed to pass was the look and dress of a shipyard worker, the ability to speak idiomatic German, and, of course, nerve.

"I went in with Jacobs, a Pole, whom I knew to be trustworthy," Bywater wrote.

He was an electrical fitter, and was then working on board a cargo steamer which had been built by the firm. I was able to make a close inspection of the [battleship] *Konig Albert*. She had her guns in position, but was less advanced than we had believed. The battle cruiser [*Ersatz Kaiserin Augusta*] was in the main building-slip, having been laid down the previous autumn. She had been reported to us as being almost a replica of the *Derfflinger*—of which we had pretty full details—and her appearance, although the hull had not been entirely plated up, confirmed this.

Access to the navy yard north of Danzig proved more difficult. It was isolated on the west bank of the Vistula River. A ferry ran between the yard and a landing on the opposite shore, but this approach seemed unsafe. Bywater got a general view of the yard by taking the steamer that ran between Danzig and Neufahrwasser, but the submarines, which were his objective, were invisible inside sheds.

"Eventually I did get in," he wrote—without revealing how, "and had a good look at four submarines on the stocks and two that were in the fitting-out basin; but it was exceedingly risky, and I cut the visit as short as possible." He stayed long enough, however, to master a problem that had plagued British efforts to monitor the growth of the German submarine flotilla. Previously, British agents had been confused as to the actual number of submarines completed because boats built at Danzig were sometimes sent to the Krupp-Germania yard at Kiel for machinery overhaul and boats built at the Germania yard were sent to Danzig to receive certain items of equipment. By figuring out these routines, Bywater developed a system that made it possible to accurately count the number of submarines in service and under construction on a monthly basis.

His next stop was Zoppot, a beach resort farther north, from which he could observe exercises at the nearby Putzig Naval Air Station. He saw six seaplanes in action and made notes on the hangars, repair shops, and oil tanks. "By this time," he recalled, "I had been long enough in the district, and judged it adviseable to cancel an intended visit to Elbring, where the Schichau firm had another big yard which specialized in destroyer construction."

He returned to Berlin and spent a couple of days preparing his reports and encoding them before departing for Munich to meet a Czech informant who was employed at the Skoda plant in Pilsen, which made all the heavy guns and armor for the Austrian Navy. Valuable information was received and dispatched to London before he moved on to Düsseldorf to visit, without any difficulty, the Ehrhardt gun shop, which was building 3.4-inch and 4.1-inch guns for new cruisers and an experimental light gun for submarines.

Essen was a disappointment. An informant who had promised to accompany Bywater on a visit to the Krupp works where the German Navy's huge, new 12-inch guns were being machined never showed up. "I thought it best to leave Essen at once," he wrote, "as his absence was suspicious. I never heard from this man again, but as there were no unpleasant developments, it was probably a case of 'cold feet.' However, I avoided Essen for several months after that."

Since the weather by this time had become warmer, Bywater proceeded north to Kiel. He visited the Howaldt and Krupp-Germania yards, and got a look at the new submarines at the latter but regarded the government yard as too closely guarded to be entered. There was, however, fair compensation. "I found a delightful spot a few miles northwest of the entrance to Kiel harbor where the U-boats came out to do diving practice," he wrote. "Several days were profitably spent here. I discovered, among other things, that the German boats were sluggish in diving compared with ours, and took nearly a minute longer to submerge. The boats appeared to be handled with extreme caution, probably due to the scare which had been caused by the sinking of *U-3*."

The tour had its lighter moments. After meticulously inspecting the battleship *Markgraf* at the Weser yard in Bremen and then pushing on to Hamburg to scrutinize her sister ship *Grosser Kurfurst* at the Vulcan yard and the battle cruiser *Derfflinger* at the Blohm and Voss yard, Bywater took an excursion steamer bound for Cuxhaven. Passing the Blohm and Voss yard, he pointed to the *Derfflinger*, the first such ship to be fitted with 12-inch guns, and innocently asked a guide if it was a torpedo boat.

"The guide nearly had apoplexy," Bywater reported gleefully. " '*Ein Torpedo-boot! Herr Gott!* Why, that's a battle cruiser, the largest in the world!'

"He was so appalled at my ignorance that from then on he insisted on giving me details on every ship we saw. Unfortunately, they were all wrong. But I did not enlighten him."

Bywater kept busy throughout the cruise making notes on the local mine-sweeping flotillas. At Cuxhaven, he saw that the new battle cruiser *Von der Tann* happened to be in port, and "though the risk was considerable," he determined to visit her. He struck up an acquaintance with a man in the shipping business who said he had some friends aboard *Von der Tann*. Then, "by very tactful maneuvering," Bywater wangled an invitation to accompany this gentleman when he went aboard to see his friends.

"We went across [the harbor] in a launch," he reported, "but on arriving at the ship's ladder I remarked to my companion that, being a foreigner, I might not be welcome on board. He then spoke to the officer of the watch, who was one of his friends, explained who I was (or, more strictly speaking, who he thought I was), and I was promptly invited to come up." Bywater spent two hours on the ship, noting such details as the cramped crew accommodations, which indicated that *Von der Tann* was not intended to keep the sea for long periods of time, and the effective isolation of the 6-inch guns, which meant that they could be knocked out only by a direct hit. Back in his hotel room, he wrote an elaborate report. "This was the first German battle cruiser," he declared triumphantly, "to be personally inspected by a British Secret Service man."

Bywater pressed on to Vienna where the head of the Austrian Navy League granted him an interview, blissfully unaware of the true identity of the man to whom he was talking. He then dropped by Trieste for a look at battleships under construction at the Stabilimento Tecnico, moved on to Pola, the chief naval harbor, where he gathered "a mass of information" from a local shipwright about the four Austrian dreadnoughts of the *Viribus Unitis* class, and then made his way down the Dalmatian coast to Cattaro, where he collected information about the German U-boat headquarters in the Mediterranean.

Thus far Bywater's tour had seemed remarkably safe, but there was a nasty surprise waiting for him when he checked in at the guest house in Berlin that he frequented. A man named Schneider, who had previously provided him with useful information, showed up in "a state of extreme nervous tension." The police, Schneider said, were on his trail. He believed he had been shadowed for several days, his mail was being opened, and he expected to be arrested at any moment. He had not been able to sleep and now had decided to go to the police and confess. By implicating Bywater, Schneider said, he hoped to get off lightly. He had simply come to warn Bywater of what he intended to do.

Bywater recalled:

> I argued with him for a long time, assuring him that his fears were baseless, and pointing out that even confession would not save him from a stiff term of imprisonment. But it was all in vain. . . . It was clearly a case for drastic methods. Schneider made for the door, but I reached it first, locked it, and put the key in my pocket. He struggled with me and I had to hit him—hard. . . . He collapsed in a chair. I gave him a drink and then produced a revolver, just for moral effect. Then I talked to him.

Bywater's talk, mixed with threats and "play with the revolver," went on through the night. By morning, Schneider was in "a more pitiable state of terror than before" and swore he would not go to the police and would do whatever was demanded. Bywater then compelled him to write and sign "a full confession of the work he had done for me—giving dates and all details." He put the letter into an envelope and addressed it to the chief of police in Berlin. "Now, Schneider," he said, "if in the future I have any reason to doubt you, this envelope goes in the post at once. You must see that there is no escape if you give me away."

Revolver in hand inside his coat pocket, Bywater marched Schneider down to the street, summoned a taxi, and dropped him off at his home. As Schneider was getting out of the cab, Bywater told the driver to take him to the Friedrichstrasse station, then looped around to the Anhalter station and subsequently changed trains several times to be sure he was not being followed as he made his way home. "It was always a risky business dealing with such people," he commented grimly, "for a man who will sell his own country will, as a rule, think nothing of selling those for whom he works. . . . In dealing with one of his kidney you cannot afford to observe Queensbury rules."

BY SEPTEMBER 1910, the appeal of a spy's life had paled, and Bywater was anxious to return to England to establish himself as a journalist. Bidding farewell to Ulysses, he, his wife, and their infant son born that year moved to a small apartment at 39 Blandford Square in the northwest section of London. Bywater donned the striped trousers, long-tailed morning coat, silk top hat, gloves, and spats worn by Fleet Street reporters of the day as he sought employment.

He found that his old friend John Burke, who had been night editor of the *Herald* when he was working in New York, had become chief of the *Herald*'s London bureau. And since James Gordon Bennett, the autocratic publisher of the *Herald*, remained an admirer of Bywater's writing, it was easy for him to land a job working for Burke in the London bureau, pulling down $125 a month. Among other assignments, he covered the visit to England of Togo, the Japanese hero of Tsushima, in July 1911. At the admiral's press conference, Bywater—probably prompted by Bennett—asked Togo about the possibility of war between

Japan and the United States. Togo dismissed the idea as "mere moonshine."

Apart from seeking a job on a London daily newspaper, Bywater's chief preoccupation was to find a publisher for a book-length manuscript he had written about the menace of the German Navy. A number of his letters have survived in the papers of J. L. Garvin, the tall, gangling, and eternally spouting editor of the London *Observer*, known affectionately on Fleet Street as "The Garve."

"During my present brief stay in England," Bywater wrote to Garvin on November 11, 1910, "I have taken the opportunity to prepare for publication in serial form a mass of information which I have accumulated in the course of my long residence in Germany relative to the naval issue. These articles are of a thoroughly comprehensive nature, and contain a good deal of information never before published, and I venture to think they may be worthy of your consideration." Under his signature, Bywater wrote, "Berlin correspondent of the Navy League, etc."

As a strong advocate of the British Navy and a close friend of Sir John Fisher, The Garve was a regular reader of the Navy League's journal, and he doubtless recognized Bywater's name. He asked to see him immediately. From Bywater's next letter to Garvin, dated November 24, it appears that the older man took an immediate liking to him. He offered to read Bywater's manuscript and recommended that he send it to the London *Daily Mail*. Garvin also offered to write a letter of introduction for him to the editor of the *Mail*.

The following month, by which time Bywater had moved his family to Grove Park, a suburb of London, he wrote to Garvin again. Since their last correspondence, he declared, he had briefly visited Germany. Doubtless, it was on a clandestine errand for C, for although holding down a job at the *Herald*'s London bureau and now also serving as a research assistant for Archibald Hurd, the diminutive, peppery naval correspondent of the London *Daily Telegraph*, Bywater continued to work for the Secret Service. "I am hoping that you have found time to read my stuff," he continued, adding: "By the way, have you ever thought of having 'Naval Notes' in the *Observer*? If this idea appeals to you at all, I could guarantee to supply you with earlier and more interesting information—particularly as regards German and Austrian progress—than appears in any of your competitors. As for remuneration, that would be a secondary matter."

Two weeks later, the impatient young author still had not heard from Garvin. He wrote to him again: "Could you find it convenient to let me have the ms. of my book back? . . . As time is passing and the book, or much of it, deals with transient things, I must try to do something with it immediately, unless it is to adorn the w.p.b. [waste paper basket]."

There is a gap in the surviving correspondence between the two men, but from Bywater's final letter to Garvin, dated March 4, 1911, it is clear that he finally read Bywater's manuscript and reacted with enthusiasm. Even with Garvin's endorsement, however, Bywater was unable to place it with a publisher. "After this experience," he concluded glumly, "I would consign the book to the fire if it were not for your strong recommendation. It seems to me that the naval situation bids fair to become acute within the ne[xt] few months, and that the moment is not inauspicious for the appearance of articles on the lines of my own. . . . I should be very grateful if you could let me have another suggestion."

With the prophetic declaration that "the naval situation bids fair to become acute," the Bywater-Garvin correspondence breaks off, although a friendship had developed between the two men that would eventually lead to The Garve's appointing Bywater naval correspondent of the *Observer* in 1923. In 1911, however, the difficulty Bywater was experiencing in finding a publisher for his work about the rise of the German Navy lay not in his writing ability nor in any journalistic shortcoming but in the fact that the leaders of Fleet Street—like so many British intellectuals of the day—were deaf to warnings about Germany's preparations for war. Under such circumstances, the best Bywater could do with his manuscript was turn it over to Archibald Hurd, for whom he was now working, for whatever use he could make of it.

With the outbreak of the First World War in 1914, the idea of a handbook on the German Navy suddenly became a commercial proposition, and the *Daily Telegraph* agreed to act as publisher if Hurd would write such a book. Thus, Bywater's "mass of information . . . accumulated in the course of my long residence in Germany" finally broke into print, although not in the form Bywater originally conceived and not under his own name. The 168-page volume was entitled *The Fleets at War*, and Hurd listed himself as the sole author. A brief two-paragraph preface included the statement: "Grateful acknowledgment is made to Mr. H. C. Bywater for valuable assistance in preparing this volume." Hurd had not simply stolen Bywater's work. He himself was well in-formed about the German Navy, having published a book on the subject only the year before. Furthermore, instead of limiting this new book to the German Navy, Hurd made it a comparison between the British and German navies. The material on the British Navy was evidently all his own. Still, since *The Fleets at War* is densely packed with firsthand observations about German warships, dockyards, and personnel, it ap-pears that Hurd adopted large segments of Bywater's manuscript whole-sale.

Years later, when Bywater was preparing his entry for British *Who's Who*, he counted among his books *The Fleets at War* followed by the phrase "with Sir Archibald Hurd"—an attribution never acknowledged by Hurd, who consistently named himself the only author. A few months after *The Fleets at War* was published, Bywater and Hurd collaborated on another *Daily Telegraph* war book, this one being a summary of the first hundred days of naval combat, entitled *From Heligoland to Keeling Island*. At last, Bywater's name advanced to the title page, yet he never mentioned this book in any of his lists of publishing credits. Evidently, he regarded their second collaboration as hack work. *The Fleets at War*, however, was precious to him; after all, he had repeatedly put his life on the line gathering the material that went into it.

SURVEYING THE DARKENING world in the spring of 1913 from his garret at Whitehall Court, C, the sharp-chinned chief of the British Secret Service, recognized that war with Germany was not far off. Since Bywater had been his most effective spy in Germany, he began to con-sider possible ways of returning him there and keeping him inside Ger-many after the expected hostilities broke out. He remembered that Bywater had been certified as an American citizen while living in Dres-den, and soon C learned of an opening—a clerk's job—on the staff of the American embassy in Vienna. Since Bywater was then almost twenty-nine years of age with nine years of experience as a professional jour-nalist, he was obviously overqualified for such a position, yet it seemed to C a satisfactory cover under which Bywater might continue his ob-servations of the German Navy. Consequently, C urged him to apply for the job. No doubt under instructions from C, Bywater lied on several counts in his letter of application dated May 20, 1913, addressed to the chief of the Bureau of Appointments of the U.S. State Department. After expressing his interest in the position of embassy clerk, Bywater stated: "I am thirty-one years old, having been born in Boston, Massachusetts, on October 21, 1882." Actually, he was twenty-eight years old, born in London on October 21, 1884.

When he received an application in response, Bywater filled it out, repeating his false claims. In seeking references, he obtained a letter from his uncle, Maurice J. Bywater, who was then rector of St. John's Episcopal Church in Seattle. It was not necessary to have his uncle join in the deception; his Seattle residence added credibility to Bywater's claim to American citizenship. "He is not only a linguist," Reverend Bywater wrote of his nephew, "but a scholar of the languages of Europe."

There is no indication in the file on Bywater in the National Archives in Washington that American authorities ever suspected they were being duped. Nevertheless, the job went to someone else—a man named Schlesinger, who was possibly an American agent. But Bywater and C did not give up. Nine months later, Bywater received word from Uly that his former boss in Dresden had been moved to Munich and was looking for a deputy. Would Hector be interested? On March 14, 1914—just four months before the outbreak of the First World War—Bywater addressed a letter to the director of the U.S. Consular Service, applying for the job. "Several times in the last few years," wrote Bywater, "I have made endeavors to enter the [U.S. Consular] Service. Last spring, when the appointment clerk to the Vienna Embassy fell vacant, I applied for it, and the application forms, duly filled out, together with various credentials sent in at the time, will doubtless be on file. . . . I may add that I am a native-born citizen."

Once again, someone else got the job. But it was not for lack of effort—nor from an excess of scruple—that Bywater remained in London as war clouds gathered over Europe. Fate would grant him other opportunities to exercise his exceptional skill and daring—as well as his ability to pass himself off as a German.

"MY GOD, IT'S happened!" Bywater exclaimed to his son in August 1914 when from a train window he spotted a newspaper headline announcing WAR DECLARED! Unlike millions of his countrymen, he would never don a uniform; Bywater was far too valuable as a spy. By early

1915, he was transferred from C's Secret Service to Naval Intelligence. Now that war had broken out, his undercover work was, if anything, even more dangerous than before. Soon after his transfer, a fellow agent named Johnson who lived nearby in Bromley was killed in the line of duty, and Bywater's son remembered him being "very cut up about it for a long period of time."

On at least one occasion, he was sent to the United States. For several weeks in the fall of 1915, Bywater wore dark glasses and publicly complained of having trouble with his eyes. The object, he later explained to his son, had been to create a pretext for visiting New York—he would have to go there, he told friends and neighbors, to be treated by an American ophthalmologist.

The real reason for his trip was that German agents in New York had been planting delayed-action incendiary bombs in the coal bunkers of British ships just before they set out across the Atlantic. Forty-one vessels were fire-bombed in this manner, and many went to the bottom. Bywater's job was to infiltrate the German-American community in Hoboken, New Jersey, a suburb of New York City, which was suspected of harboring the bomb-makers.

It was a sensitive assignment. The United States was still neutral, and it would not do for a British agent to be exposed operating in New York with the apparent complicity of the United States. Once again, Bywater posed as an American. And, using his language skills, he quickly penetrated the ship-bombing ring and alerted the bomb squad of the New York City Police Department. It turned out that the bomb factory had been on board the German liner *Friedrich der Grosse*, which was interned at Hoboken. A number of German operatives, led by an advertising man named Wolf von Igel, were arrested, tried, and imprisoned for the duration of the war.

Back in London early the next year, bearing an American Flyer model train as a gift for his son, Bywater was kept busy translating German publications and captured documents, and frequently disappeared for a week or more on a clandestine mission. By the war's end, he was bone-weary, so run-down in fact that he asked the British government for a year's leave with pay. Unlike almost all other veterans, he pointed out, he was leaving the service of his country with no record that could be made public, no rank or honors, no pension, not even a uniform. Some sharp words were exchanged between Bywater and the Admiralty after his request was turned down. Finally, the government offered him an Order of the British Empire (OBE)—a paper honor Bywater indignantly rejected.

Long after the war, he summed up his feelings in *Strange Intelligence*:

> Needless to say, [an agent's life] entailed constant and serious personal risk. In the pursuit of his avocation the secret agent hazarded his liberty, and not seldom his life. Day and night he lived under a nerve strain which never relaxed. . . . The work itself was thankless, perilous and distinctly unremunerative, and those who engaged in it too often found themselves caught in a web of intrigue and misunderstanding which has outlasted the war, and from which some may never hope to escape. It is safe to say that none of the survivors would ever dream of taking up Intelligence work again, under any circumstances whatsoever.

These had been cruel years for Bywater. No matter how prophetic his book was, the publishing world had spurned it. And when he finally saw it in print, the credit went to another man. Furthermore, after having been lured with an appeal to patriotism into the shadowy world of espionage, and having made great sacrifices, he felt unfairly recompensed. By the time of the Armistice, he was thirty-four years old and the father of two children. A son, Hector junior (called Robin), had been born in Dresden in 1910, and a daughter, Sylvia, had come along in 1914. Yet Bywater had no job and no visible means of supporting his family.

Throughout these years, however, Bywater had tested and perfected the reportorial skills with which he would penetrate the secrecy cloaking the postwar growth of the German, Italian, and Japanese navies. And he had accomplished something even more important. He had learned —more viscerally than he could have discovered at any college or university—that the job of the naval journalist is not a game for the easygoing or faint of heart. Every wile, every strategem, every scrap of knowledge about his subject and about human nature, had a place in the handbook of the correspondent who would delve into vital secrets of national power. "Nearly every valuable item of news," he wrote of his work before and during the war, "had to be excavated by personal effort and at personal risk." That was a lesson worth the considerable price Bywater had paid to learn it.

CHAPTER

5

THE FLEET STREET PRESS GANG

B Y THE SPRING of 1920—when Bywater's imagination was captured by the naval rivalry developing in the Pacific—he had become a leading member of the "Fleet Street Press Gang." This was the circle of naval experts in London who used to gather informally after work at a Fleet Street pub, such as The Old Bell or The White Swan (known to regulars as "Ding Dong" and "The Mucky Duck"), and pass an evening over a few pints of bitter, swapping stories, rumors, and theories about the navies of the world. Most of the Press Gang worked for one of the newspapers on or near Fleet Street, although they had lightheartedly adopted the name of their drinking society not from the printing presses on Fleet Street but from the notorious press gangs of the eighteenth century that seized men for service in the Royal Navy.

Bywater had earned the esteem of his colleagues by having published a number of impressive articles on naval subjects in such major London newspapers as the *Daily Graphic* and the *Pall Mall Gazette*, technical journals like the *Engineer, Scientific American*, and *United Service Magazine*, and the two "bibles" of naval writers—the Navy League's weekly, now called the *Navy*, and the service-oriented weekly with a highfalutin name, the *Naval & Military Record and Royal Dockyards Gazette*. Ever since 1908, Bywater had been writing regularly for the latter two publications, and he was now billed in both as "our former Berlin correspondent." Being an expert on Germany and the German Navy accorded him the special status enjoyed by an experienced Kremlinologist today.

Furthermore, he was good company in a pub. An engaging conversationalist and raconteur, Bywater was quick-witted enough to be quoted in newspaper columns. When an American journalist happened to ask him what he thought of Congressman Fred Britten's proposal that English and American diplomats should meet in Canada to resolve their differences about naval disarmament, he quipped: "I'm very much afraid that this fellow aspires to be the Britten that rules the waves." The remark wound up in W. A. S. Douglas's popular column in the Baltimore *Sun*.

When the occasion permitted, Bywater could quote poetry or sing songs and ditties for an entire evening without repeating himself. And he could convulse his audience with stories, like the one about a magician and a parrot. The magician earned his passage on a transatlantic liner by performing tricks. He kept the parrot on a perch beside him strictly for ornamental effect, but gradually the parrot learned the tricks and would give them away to the audience behind the magician's back. Suddenly, during a performance, the ship struck an iceberg and quickly sank. The magician was clinging to some floating wreckage when the parrot swooped out of the sky and landed on his shoulder, saying: "That's a damn good trick! Where'd you hide the ship?"

But jocular though Bywater could be, the British naval tradition was something he took with the utmost seriousness. Britannia, not Congressman Britten, still ruled the waves, and those on familiar terms with His Majesty's ships and the men who commanded them stood close to the seat of imperial power—and close, as well, to the soul of their seafaring nation. A remark by Lord Bolingbroke, the eighteenth-century British statesman, was one Bywater particularly liked to quote. "Like other amphibious animals," the orator had proclaimed, "we [Englishmen] must come occasionally on shore, but the water is more properly our element." He meant not only that Great Britain depended for her national existence on trade and commerce from across the sea, but that she depended upon a strong navy to protect that traffic. The members of the Fleet Street Press Gang saw themselves as the high priests who led the empire in its devotion to that belief.

The sea obsessed these men. In 1918, when writing a memorial tribute to Earl Brassey, the founder of Brassey's *Naval Annual* who was idolized by the Fleet Street Press Gang, Bywater made a point of the omnipresence of the sea throughout Brassey's exemplary life. He noted that no small portion of Brassey's six-volume work, *The British Navy*, had been written, as Brassey himself expressed it, "under conditions far from favorable, in a scanty cabin, six feet square, rocked on the uneasy billows of the open ocean." Later, when Brassey decided to run for Parliament, Bywater recalled, he deliberately selected a seaport constituency and then made a point of doing all of his campaigning within sight of the sea. "There was certainly nothing of the fine-weather yachtsman about him," Bywater concluded. "He loved the sea in all its moods."

"The three most beautiful things in the world," the members of the Press Gang used to say, "are a fighting ship, a nubile woman and a fast racehorse—in that order." They thought of a low-slung, new battleship, bristling with the most powerful ordnance known to man, cleaving the sea at 26 knots, as one of the highest expressions of human achievement. Kipling had captured their infatuation in *A Fleet in Being*, a slim volume that Bywater told the poet laureate was the book most often cited for admiration when navy correspondents gathered to discuss their craft. "A modern man-of-war photographed in severe profile is not engaging," Kipling had written after attending maneuvers of the Royal Navy's Channel Squadron,

but you should see her with the life hot in her, head-on across a heavy swell. The ram-bow draws upward and outward in a stately sweep. There is no ruck of figure-head, bow timbers or bowsprit-fittings to distract the eye from its outline or the beautiful curves that mark its melting into the full bosom of the ship. It hangs dripping an instant, then, quietly and cleanly as a tempered knife, slices into the hollow of the swell, down and down till the surprised sea spits off in foam about the hawse-holes. As the ship rolls in her descent you can watch curve after curve revealed, humoring and coaxing the water. When she recovers her step, the long sucking hollow of her own wave discloses just enough of her shape to make you wish to see more. In harbor, the still waterline, hard as the collar of a tailor-made jacket, hides that vision; but when she dances the Big Sea Dance, she is as different from her Portsmouth shilling photograph as is a matron in a mackintosh from the same lady at a ball. Swaying a little in her gait, drunk with sheer delight of movement, perfectly apt for the work in hand, and in every line of her rejoicing that she is doing it, she shows, to these eyes at least, a miracle of grace and beauty.

Almost to a man, the Press Gang supported retention of a big fleet in the period between the two world wars. It was not simply that they saw the navy as the backbone of national defense; even after the horror of Jutland, all of these men professed admiration for what Bywater once described as "the grim splendor of naval combat."

Not surprisingly, most of the members of the Press Gang listed as their favorite recreation "seagoing" or "going to sea as often as possible." The navy indulged them just enough to keep them tantalized, generally offering the members of the Press Gang two- or three-week cruises during the annual naval maneuvers at the end of the summer. But apart from an occasional joy ride, and partying during Navy Week in August and on Trafalgar Day in October, the high and mighty British Admiralty saw little reason to cater to the press. Most of the naval heroes of the First World War, such as Admiral David Beatty, took particular pride in the "silent-service" tradition of the Royal Navy and openly despised the publicity-seeking Royal Air Force. Sir Dudley Pound, who served as first sea lord from 1939 to 1943, simply never granted a reporter an interview. Fisher and later Winston Churchill, of course, were just the reverse, courting the press in every way possible. But since the Beattys and Pounds were many and the Fishers and Churchills few, the members of the Press Gang did not have easy access to the object of their fascination.

Between the two world wars, the Admiralty held no regular press conferences and had no press-information officers to provide assistance. The only tools the accredited naval correspondent might have in those days were an Admiralty pass, his personal friendships among naval officers, and his wits. If, for example, he wished to check on a rumor about an impending reduction in the size of the fleet, a report of an accident, an important promotion, or the results of the sea trials of a new ship, he would walk a few blocks over to the massive, white-stone Admiralty Arch on Trafalgar Square where navy headquarters had been located since 1911. After presenting his pass to the doorkeeper at the back entrance, the reporter would ask to see one or another officer whom he thought might confirm or deny what he had heard, or at least be willing to swap information. The doorkeeper would place a call for him and he might or might not be received. If exceptionally lucky, someone within might slip the reporter a mimeographed copy of one of the famous "prayers"—a memorandum from the first lord (civilian head) of the Admiralty that customarily began "Pray explain the lack of . . ." or "Pray dispatch the *Hood* . . ." Such a find would almost invariably result in a news story. The industrious naval correspondent would also scavenge such publications as the semiofficial *Naval & Military Record and Royal Dockyards Gazette*, as well as the AFOs (Admiralty Fleet Orders), which reported the movement and disposition of warships. And then, of course, he would visit the Royal Dockyards.

"Once a week we would make the rounds of the dockyards—Portsmouth, Devonport, and Chatham—to see what was going on," recalled Raymond Blackman, a former editor of *Jane's Fighting Ships* and the longest surviving member of the old Press Gang, who died in May 1989. "We would know what ships to expect because we would have been reading the AFOs, but we would want to have a look for ourselves. If a ship interested one of us for some reason, that man would go up and make his number [identify himself in naval parlance] and probably be invited to go below. If the captain knew him, or of him, which was usually the case, he'd have him in his cabin and serve pink gin." Blackman added: "I felt as if I hadn't visited a ship until I'd had six pink gins." Pink gin, almost a Royal Navy staple, was made by the steward. He would pour a couple of drops of angostura bitters in a gin glass, swirl it around, and throw the bitters in the sink, then add gin and water. What was left of the angostura bitters faintly colored the gin pink.

Even if not chatting with a captain or an admiral, drink flowed freely for naval correspondents when they visited the dockyards. Unlike the American Navy, which has been dry ever since the abolition of the wine mess in 1914, the Royal Navy has for centuries regarded alcohol as a part of its daily life. It is now legendary that the officers of the British battleship *Royal Oak*, sunk at Scapa Flow in 1939, first realized that they had been torpedoed when the gin glasses shook or shattered in their hands. Traditionally, at the cocktail hour, Royal Navy warships fly the long green and white "gin pennant" (the old Number Nine, or Starboard, pennant, nowadays occasionally emblazoned with the figure of a gin glass). The flying of the gin pennant is the traditional means of signaling to other ships in the harbor that one is "pushing the boat out" in the wardroom bar. Any officer, or visiting correspondent, may then consider himself invited aboard, and of course he reports to the bar or wherever liquor is being served.

"There was a time when a few seconds' exposure [of the gin pennant] above the signal locker would have boats heading down like a swarm of bees," recalled Sir Terence Lewin, the first sea lord and subsequently chief of the Defense Staff, in a letter about the custom of the gin pennant to the London *Daily Telegraph* in 1978.

Between freely flowing spirits in Fleet Street pubs, on the one hand, and aboard Royal Navy warships, on the other, it is hardly surprising that alcoholism became the chief occupational disease for the members of the Fleet Street Press Gang. Bywater was only one of many affected by it. Although never seen "worse for wear"—the expression for drunkenness in London pubs—Bywater's personal physician stated that by the end of his life Bywater had become an alcoholic.

Sometimes the encounters between the Fleet Street Press Gang and the bottle were amusing. Bywater, for example, used to relish telling the story about what navy gin did to Thomas (Tommy) Woodroofe at the Naval Review at Spithead following the coronation of King George VI. It seems that Woodroofe, a retired navy officer who reported on naval affairs for the BBC, had a great thirst for pink gin. At Spithead, Woodroofe boarded a ship from which he would be reporting "live" for the BBC, and was invited to the captain's cabin. There he imbibed even a bit more pink gin than customary for himself. And then, taking note of the fact that the fleet was strung with colorful electric lights, Woodroofe weaved his way to the ship's wireless room where he was handed a microphone and given the signal to commence his broadcast. Swaying back and forth, Woodroofe was able to say only: "The fleet's all lit up!" before sinking with a blissful expression into the arms of a startled radio operator. "If the fleet was lit up," Bywater would remark dryly, "so indeed was Tommy Woodroofe."

But drunkenness took its toll. Bywater's best friend, H. C. Ferraby, naval correspondent of the London *Daily Express*, "drank his lunch" every day at the old Press Club, just off Fleet Street, and returned to his office to sleep it off. On New Year's Eve, 1942, Ferraby went to the Press Club as usual and made his way to the bar, which was at the top of a flight of stairs. At some point during the evening, Ferraby bid all "Go' bless," wobbled over to the door, tumbled down the stairs, and broke his neck.

THE MAN WHO set the pace for the Fleet Street Press Gang, and exerted a powerful influence on Bywater, was Frederick T. Jane. A boundlessly energetic naval artist, novelist, and encyclopedist, Jane founded the illustrated naval annual *Jane's Fighting Ships*, which today has become a major publishing industry. The youngest son of the vicar of Uppottery, in Devon, Jane had been fascinated by warships ever since, as a young boy, he and his brothers built model ships and fought mock naval actions on the village pond at Uppottery. He never lost his love of models and games, and just before the First World War he published a book about the Naval War Game, which he had invented some years before. His purpose was "to afford a means of working out any strategical problems or . . . particular tactical theories under conditions as nearly as possible resembling real war in miniature." Jane's *Kriegspiel* was played by British naval officers at the War College at Dartmouth, and may have influenced Bywater—also an avid warship model-builder and war-gamer—in doping out an imaginary naval engagement in the Pacific, which would later inspire Isoroku Yamamoto.

Another of Jane's fascinations was a questionnaire he drew up for the purpose of testing one's ability to identify warships. Typical questions and answers might be these:

Q: What postwar cruisers carry as many as four funnels?
A: Only the American *Omaha* class and Japanese *Jintsu* class.

Q: What new cruiser has a short, heavy quadripod mast surrounded by towering bridgework?
A: The Italian *Bande Nere*.

Jane made a practice of carrying his questionnaires around with him to spring one on an unsuspecting naval eminence who might cross his path. It was considered remarkable for anyone to give correct answers to 5 percent of the test questions, although Jane himself, whenever subjected to similar examination, was rarely at a loss for a prompt, accurate answer. Bywater once wrote of him: "Jane could, and repeatedly did, astound the most experienced naval officers by his uncanny familiarity with the minutest detail of every vessel of war that floated during his lifetime. Upon being shown at sea a squadron of ships of uniform design, he could instantly name each unit, though even to the trained eye they seemed alike as peas."

Jane's questionnaires made for good sport in a Fleet Street pub, but there was also a serious purpose behind them. Quick and accurate ship identification could be a matter of life or death in wartime. One even had to be on the lookout for disguises. During the early days of the First World War, the German raider *Emden* scored a coup when her crew rigged up a dummy fourth funnel to prevent the ship from being recognized. She slipped unchallenged into the harbor at Penang and surprised and sank the Russian cruiser *Jemtchug* and the French destroyer *Mousquet.*

After Jane's death in 1916, the dean of the Fleet Street Press Gang became Archibald Hurd, the diminutive, dapper, and frequently pugnacious naval correspondent of the *Daily Telegraph.* As we have seen, Hurd had made good use of Bywater as a research assistant and ghost writer before and during the war, and would eventually—after a bitter struggle—be succeeded by Bywater at the *Telegraph.*

By the end of the First World War, Hurd's preeminence among naval writers derived partly from his long experience in the field, partly because the *Daily Telegraph* gave its naval correspondent a byline and more space than any of its competitors, and partly because he was uncommonly successful at ingratiating himself with the brass hats. Aside from his friendship with Sir John Fisher, Hurd became a particular favorite of admirals Sir Reginald Baker, Sir Edmund Fremantle, and Sir John Jellicoe, the commander of the British fleet at Jutland. In fact, Hurd became so thick with the Admiralty that he once resigned from the Navy League in protest against the league's indulging in some polite questioning of the sea lords. On another occasion, the editor of the *Telegraph* had to caution Hurd against becoming too much of an Admiralty spokesman. Hurd stoutly defended his journalistic integrity, but the fact is, he had progressively bartered away his independence in exchange for privileged access to power—a common but always fatal failing among journalists. It was largely because of his too-cozy friendships in the navy that Arthur Watson, the editor of the *Telegraph*, insisted on Hurd's resignation in 1927 and hired in his place Hector Bywater—a man whose independence of the Admiralty, as we shall see, was beyond question.

Bywater had two especially close friends in the Press Gang, both born in the same year as himself—1884. The first was H. C. Ferraby, a slightly built, thin-faced Irishman, known on Fleet Street as "Ferrets." Bywater befriended him during the war when Ferraby was an official naval war correspondent. Ferrets got his start writing about the sea as a teenage apprentice working for the *Army and Navy Gazette*. For the next thirty years, with time out for the war, Ferrets served as naval correspondent of the London *Daily Express*, a newspaper given to sensationalism and not taken seriously in Admiralty circles. Only close to the end of his life were Ferraby's talent and authority recognized when he was appointed naval correspondent of the Manchester *Guardian* and the British Broadcasting Corporation. Throughout his life, he remained a loyal friend of Bywater, generously lending a hand with the manuscripts and galley proofs of each of his books. Ferraby was the author of a few books on naval subjects himself, including the collaboration with Bywater entitled *Strange Intelligence: Memoirs of Naval Secret Service.*

Bywater's other close friend in the Press Gang was Francis E. McMurtrie, known on Fleet Street as "Mac" or "Ferenz." One of the legendary characters in the Press Gang, Mac was a tall, sinewy, and prematurely stooped, almost hunchbacked Scotsman who invariably wore pince-nez glasses. A former colleague described him as "the perfect picture of a secretary bird." Poor eyesight had prevented Mac from entering the navy. The best alternative he could find was a job as a clerk for a sea-salvage firm called The Ocean Tug and Salvage Company. During the First World War, he worked for the Admiralty as a civilian, then returned to The Ocean Tug and Salvage Company and gradually inveigled his way into journalism. For years, McMurtrie bounced around Fleet Street, briefly holding jobs as naval correspondent for the *Daily News, News-Chronicle, Daily Telegraph*, and *Sunday Express*. His amazing mastery of his subject always impressed prospective employers, but he was such a slow and graceless writer that the jobs rarely lasted. Mac was, however, single-minded in his devotion to naval knowledge, and became famous for his "card-index" memory. Prominent authors, politicians, admirals, and even the sea lords themselves were known to turn to him for help in tracking down an obscure bit of naval information or lore of the sea. After Admiralty briefings got started just before the outbreak of the Second World War, whenever the officer in charge began to fumble over a fact he might look up and call out: "Is that right, Mac? How many tons is she?" Hovering somewhere at the back of the room, McMurtrie would mutter the correct answer.

In his prime, Mac may well have had a greater command of naval facts and figures than Fred Jane. As one of his former colleagues recalls: "If you asked him how many *Formidable*s there had been, he unhesitatingly replied: 'Five,' and would give the dates of each. If you asked him who commanded the *Terrapin* in 1897, Mac would report the captain's name and reel off the details of his service record."

McMurtrie was intensely shy, but also craftily effective in harvesting information. When a great warship came into port, for example, the crew was naturally anxious to greet their wives and loved ones rather than recount their experiences to a reporter. But McMurtrie would often manage to get aboard before any of the wives, and would immediately start asking questions. His persistence could be irritating, however, and on one occasion after he boarded a warship he was invited to give the junior officers a lecture on an obscure aspect of naval history. The young officers were too junior in rank to protest, and Mac too full of himself to realize he was being made a fool of.

By 1923, McMurtrie landed the one job for which he was exquisitely suited. Maurice Prendergast, who had been the editor of *Jane's Fighting Ships* since Jane's death in 1916, had been born deaf and now began to lose his eyesight. Consequently, McMurtrie and Oscar Parkes, a practicing physician and gifted naval artist, succeeded Prendergast as co-editors of the annual. McMurtrie edited the text and Parkes the pictures. But the two men—each of whom considered himself the first apostle of Fred Jane—often quarreled about warship identifications. Parkes, who used to entertain the Press Gang at the piano singing songs for which he had composed his own high-spirited and gently mocking lyrics, once poked fun at McMurtrie's obsession with naval trivia in a song that included the lines:

> He'll tell you the name of the bos'n's mate
> In the Channel Fleet of sixty-eight.

So intense did the squabbles between McMurtrie and Parkes become that they occasionally broke into print. Once, for example, the *Daily Telegraph* published a photograph of four Spanish warships at sea. Parkes wrote to the *Telegraph* to point out a mistaken identification in the photograph caption. The next day, McMurtrie wrote to the *Telegraph* to correct Parkes. "I am in agreement with Dr. Parkes," Mac began,

that three of the Spanish Nationalist warships which recently appeared on your Picture page are minelayers. I believe them to be the *Jupiter, Neptuno*, and *Marte* (ex-*Saturno*), since the *Volcano* is reported to have proceeded to Cadiz to repair damages. But I cannot agree with your correspondent that the fourth ship illustrated is either the *Huesca* or *Teruel*, ex-Italian destroyers. In my opinion she is the *Calvo Sotelo*, which was built for Mexico as the "transport-gunboat" *Zacatecas*, but was taken over by the Nationalists at Cadiz.

Fred Jane would have been proud of such disciples.

SEIZE THE DANUBE POSITION

ONE DAY IN the spring of 1920, Bywater's eye was caught by a minor news item on the next-to-last page of the *Naval & Military Record and Royal Dockyards Gazette*. This tabloid, with its colorful masthead adorned by crossed sabers, spears, flags, and bunting, was read like a house organ by members of the Fleet Street Press Gang. Affectionately, they referred to it as the Dockyard Liar.

The small-type headline that attracted Bywater's attention read: UNITED STATES AND THE PACIFIC. The item consisted mainly of a long quotation from an American service journal, the *Army and Navy Register*, that stated that "the activities and ambitions" of Japan have created "a dire and ominous situation" in the Pacific. As a result, the item continued, the American secretary of the navy, Josephus Daniels, had announced that the newly formed U.S. Pacific Fleet would remain in that ocean indefinitely, and he said he wanted to build a $75-million naval base at San Francisco to provide facilities for it. Bywater had been following the growth of the Japanese Navy with keen interest, and now he was intrigued to see that naval competition between Japan and the United States was being taken seriously by sober-minded analysts in America.

After turning the matter over in his mind for several days, Bywater, who was still writing a weekly column for the Dockyard Liar, decided to devote his next piece to "Sea Power in the Pacific," as the headline phrased it. This was his first published essay on naval strategy in the Pacific—the joining together of a man with the subject that would dominate his thinking throughout his adult life. "Sea Power in the Pacific" would soon become the title of his third book, which laid the foundation for his magnum opus, *The Great Pacific War*, a few years later.

"Many people in this country have no doubt been surprised to learn, that . . . there exists in the Pacific Ocean a 'dire and ominous situation' for which 'the activities and ambitions of Japan' are held responsible," Bywater wrote, referring to the news item that had first caught his attention. In view of the great difference in the industrial power of Japan and the United States, he continued, it is "scarcely credible" that Japan would risk a war with America. Nevertheless, "since the contingency is one accepted as possible by American service papers of standing, it may be of interest to examine the composition and strength of the two fleets which would be involved in a struggle for the mastery of the Pacific."

He then sized up both the American and Japanese navies. He began with the observation that the United States had opened "a new epoch" in naval history in August 1919 when she moved a powerful fleet of oil-burning superdreadnoughts (led by the first electrically propelled flagship, *New Mexico*) through the recently opened Panama Canal into the Pacific Ocean. An equally mighty U.S. fleet remained in the Atlantic, and, as a result of the canal, the Atlantic and Pacific fleets could be united within two weeks—long before any enemy would be able to concentrate a major force to attack either coast of the country. The result, declared Bywater, had been the creation of a "gigantic force." Its only lack, in Bywater's estimation, was a shortage of fast cruisers for scouting and raiding the commercial shipping of a potential enemy.

In contrast, he continued, the Japanese Navy was at present "rather weak," although its announced "eight-eight" program, which called for the construction of eight new battleships and eight new battle cruisers, would greatly bolster its effectiveness. In addition, Japan's large force of fast cruisers would constitute "a serious menace to American shipping" in the event of a conflict.

But the decisive factor in any future showdown between the two powers, Bywater went on to say, would be geography. The positions of Japan and the United States, and the immense size of the Pacific Ocean, would outweigh any foreseeable disparity in the strength of the battle fleets that they might bring to bear. To begin with, Japan's relative isolation was a profound advantage. Furthermore, wrote Bywater, the U.S. fleet would be severely handicapped in a future Pacific war because of "a lack of adequate base facilities" for a large force in Asian waters, and by the difficulty of "transporting material to the war zone across seven thousand miles of ocean." This was not to say that Japan could defeat the United States in an all-out war; indeed, if the conflict were "prolonged" and the United States had time "to mobilize its almost unlimited resources," the ultimate victor "would hardly be in serious doubt." On the other hand, he continued, if Japan did not recklessly attempt to grab Hawaii or land troops in California (as sensationalists like Homer Lea had forecast), but limited her objective to seizing the Philippines and Guam—possessions in the Western Pacific America had taken from Spain in 1898 at the conclusion of the Spanish-American War—"the problems of strategy which American commanders would have to deal with . . . . might well prove insoluble."

Bywater's conclusion was a sharp departure from the complacent conventional wisdom of the day, which held that the United States Navy could "whip the Japanese Navy with one hand tied," in the words of a widely quoted American admiral. Bywater saw that the United States had overextended herself in the Pacific. Her recently acquired territories west of Hawaii were so far from the nearest American naval station that they could not be defended against a locally based aggressor.

Over the next few months, Bywater returned again and again to the situation in the Pacific in his columns for the Dockyard Liar. On June 9, for instance, he found the American and Japanese battleship-building programs "strikingly similar." The recently launched 35,000-ton American superdreadnought, *Maryland*, and the latest Japanese man-of-war, *Mutsu*, could almost have been sister ships, although the *Maryland* appeared to have slightly better armor protection and the *Mutsu* had a 2.5-knot edge in speed. Also, the 45,000-ton *South Dakota*–class battleships then under construction in the United States and the fully comparable *Akagi*-class monsters on the ways of Japanese shipyards suggested that the technical experts in these "leading Naval Powers" had not lost their faith in the primacy of the big ship with big guns.

Three weeks later, in an article headlined PACIFIC ARMAMENTS, Bywater observed—not without a trace of nationalistic envy—that Japan and the United States were now "setting the naval fashions." The "remarkable resemblance between American and Japanese naval designs" made it clear that a naval arms race was in progress. Quite obviously, the two powers were reacting to each other. No sooner had Washington announced that the Navy Department was contemplating the arming of all future battleships with colossal 18-inch guns than a statement was issued from the Naval Ministry in Tokyo to the effect that the projected battle cruiser *Hatsuse* had been designated for 18-inch guns. And both Japan and the United States were known to be building copies of the long-range German *U-142*–class submarines. The capabilities of these extraordinary vessels, which carried unusually heavy armament and had a range of approximately 20,000 miles, suggested that they were being constructed for offensive commerce-raiding operations rather than defensive missions against attacking enemy warships. "Each [power] is trying to outdo the other in the production of fighting ships," Bywater wrote, "and while Japan cannot hope to compete successfully against her wealthier rival as regards numbers, she seems determined not to be left behind in respect of individual power."

Bywater was hardly the first Western thinker to focus on the strategic importance of the Pacific Ocean. William H. Seward, the American secretary of state who negotiated the purchase of Alaska from Russia in 1867, predicted that the Pacific would become "the chief theater of events in the world's great hereafter." In the 1890s, such spokesmen as Alfred Thayer Mahan, the American naval officer and preeminent authority on naval strategy, as well as James Gordon Bennett of the *New York Herald*, pressed for recognition of the importance of the Pacific. Mahan, well versed in classical history, had likened America's decision on whether or not to annex Hawaii to the "momentous" decision of the Roman senate to occupy Messina and thus for the first time expand the Roman Empire beyond the Italian peninsula.

Nor was Bywater alone in imagining that Imperial Japan might enjoy an advantage over the United States in a future Pacific war. Homer Lea's *The Valor of Ignorance* had gone so far as to forecast Japan's domination of the Pacific and capture of California, Oregon, Washington, and Alaska. Lea's book was followed by a score of imitations by American and Japanese authors. In 1911, even Mahan, while dismissing Homer Lea's nightmare vision as "improbable," observed that it was not inconceivable that the new Japanese Navy might one day defeat the American Navy in pitched battle in the Pacific. And thus, from about 1909 onward there had been whispers and gossip in ships' smoking rooms and in imperial hotel bars throughout the Far East that Japan was poised to strike at America and that she had cunningly contrived a way to gain the upper hand.

What was new and different about what Hector Bywater was writing in 1920 was, first of all, his clear-sighted recognition of exactly how far Japan could and could not go in a war against the United States. Japan, he understood, could snatch American territories in the Western Pacific and thereby build a nearly unassailable ring of insular territories around herself, yet she did not have it within her power to seize Hawaii let alone seriously menace the continental United States. In the second place, Bywater foresaw that such an aggressive move by Japan might well be in the cards, so to speak. He perceived that "a new epoch" in naval history had begun. Bywater was the first journalist of his generation to grasp the fact that the central arena in the struggle for naval supremacy had shifted from the North Sea and the Mediterranean, where Great Britain and Germany had vied with each other since the turn of the century, to the Pacific Ocean. The Pacific, as Bywater saw it, was no longer an exotic backwater, nor even merely the scene of a possible future war, but the fateful setting in which the victorious allies of the First World War would test each other to determine who would be the mistress of the seas in the twentieth century.

"When the German High Seas Fleet surrendered for internment on the 21st of November 1918," Bywater would shortly write,

> a brief but pregnant chapter in the history of sea power was brought to a close. The next chapter may be said to have opened in August 1919, with the passage of the newly created United States Pacific Fleet through the Panama Canal en route to its base in San Francisco Bay. By the disappearance of the German Navy the strategical situation throughout the globe was profoundly modified. . . . [There had been] a gravitation of naval power from West to East, from the Atlantic to the Pacific.

Maurice Prendergast, a fellow member of the Fleet Street Press Gang, was among those who acknowledged Bywater's prescience. "Few at that moment perceived how tremendous was the transformation," wrote Prendergast in the *Navy*, looking back on what Bywater had written in 1920 and 1921.

> Naval policies still appeared to revolve, but in a dull and un-natural manner, round that vacuum where once the German Fleet had existed. As time went on, we began to perceive, how . . . the naval cosmos had instantly dissolved and regrouped itself around a new, central sun—the Rising Sun of Japan. The magnetic pole of maritime affairs had not vanished with German sea power; it had only altered its position and required rediscovery. . . . Mr. Bywater clearly expounded the elements of the new naval situation.

In the summer of 1920, realizing that he had found a subject of great timeliness and importance, Bywater started to work on a book he would title *Sea Power in the Pacific: A Study of the American-Japanese Naval Problem*. This was the book in which he would first spell out a collection of revolutionary ideas for the employment of naval power in the Pacific, later to be amplified in his novel *The Great Pacific War*, which would have such weighty consequences in the years to come.

By this time, Bywater had moved his family of four into a comfortable, semidetached brick house at 23 Whitmore Road in Beckenham, a middle-class suburb ten miles south of the center of London. Both of his children were now of school age, and on weekends the Bywaters found time to bicycle and picnic in the countryside. If he was good company in a pub, Bywater was also a caring father. He was forever encouraging his son to build model ships, and when "Robin," as the boy was called, seemed unresponsive, Father swallowed his pride and brought home model airplanes, one of which—powered by a pneumatic cartridge—was a real success. He adored his little Sylvia and loved to toss her into the air until she squealed with delight. Even though they were very young, Bywater used to recite for his children long passages from Goethe and Schiller in German, and would entertain them by singing everything from lieder to the rollicking drinking songs he had picked up while living in Dresden. He also used to delight them with his ready stock of doggerel, including one nonsense rhyme he evidently learned in the United States:

Said the Reverend Henry Ward Beecher
To a hen: "You're a beautiful creature."
The hen upon that
Laid an egg in his hat
And thus did the Henry Ward Beecher.

Bywater established a workplace for himself in the attic. At one end, there was a brick fireplace with a grate for burning large chunks of anthracite. Smut, his black cat, invariably curled up nearby. In fact, it was usually at the insistent strutting and meowing of Smut that Bywater would put down his morning newspapers and make his way upstairs to work. He sat at a rolltop desk in front of his old-fashioned Oliver typewriter—a large, cumbersome machine in which the capital shift key raised half of the machine rather than depressed the bank of keys. Bywater would type occasionally, but his first drafts were characteristically written in longhand in blue-lined notebooks with black speckled covers.

In writing *Sea Power in the Pacific*, he had no desire to stir up enmity between Japan and the United States; a war between the two powers would be "a terrible and protracted struggle," he wrote in the book's preface. His object was "to bring to light certain facts concerning the strategical situation of the rival Powers the full significance of which does not appear to be realized either in Japan or the United States." Accordingly, he stated, "such modest influence" as his book might exert would be "in the direction of peace rather than of war."

After setting forth his ideas about the "new era of naval power" and the "gravitation from West to East" in the first chapter of *Sea Power in the Pacific*, Bywater proceeded to compare and contrast the American and Japanese navies, expanding upon what he had written for the Dockyard Liar. Making use of his large library and calling upon his encyclopedic naval knowledge, he could not only survey both navies and point out their strengths and weaknesses, but could bring up esoteric bits of information, such as the fact that the American dynamite cruiser *Vesuvius* of 1886 carried pneumatic guns considered so lethal that they would "abolish warfare at sea by making it too destructive." He also recalled the embarrassment over the battleships *Indiana, Massachusetts,* and *Oregon* of 1890 whose unbalanced turrets "caused the ships to heel over when these weapons were trained on the beam."

Turning to the Japanese Navy, Bywater raised a few eyebrows among his readers by observing that the all-big-gun battleships *Aki* and *Satsuma* had anticipated by "many months" Lord Fisher's more-famous *Dreadnought*, which gave its name to a new generation of battleships in 1909. In addition, he provided full details on the new battleship *Nagato* and revealed theretofore secret information about Japan's four projected 45,000-ton battleships, the last two of which did not yet even have names but were known only as "C" and "D." Furthermore, Bywater reported, "the modern Japanese submarine is probably the most strongly built vessel of its type in the world" owing to the enormous depths and erratic currents of the Japanese coastal waters in which they had been designed to operate.

Unlike so many of his contemporaries, he gave no credence whatsoever to the disparaging stereotypes and caricatures of the Japanese prevalent in England and the United States. Bywater praised the typical Japanese sailor for his "courage and contempt for death," which had been heroically demonstrated in Japan's wars against China and Russia, yet he did not succumb to the temptation to portray such men as fanatics. "Great discretion" and "prudence," Bywater wrote, are as much a part of the Japanese national character as heroic courage. He cited Admiral Togo's practice of refusing to expose his ships to unnecessary damage once an objective had been achieved.

Even more important than ships and men, continued Bywater, elaborating on a theme sounded in his first essay on the Pacific in the Dockyard Liar, were geographical considerations. Lord Salisbury's advice to the British people to "study big maps" was "equally applicable to the American people of the present generation," he wrote. And a study of the map of the Pacific revealed the crucial importance of a remote speck of an island called Guam. Distances are so enormous in the Pacific, and so unyieldingly difficult to move a navy across, that the position of Guam—a stepping-stone between Hawaii and the Philippines—was "unique, commanding, and of supreme importance, the veritable key to the Pacific." In fact, Bywater added, "We may, indeed, go further, and say that the issue of an Americo-Japanese war would primarily be decided by the fate of Guam." His point was that while Hawaii was too far distant from the Philippines to protect them, Guam, only 1,500 miles to the east, was ideally situated to serve as an advance American naval base for the defense of the Philippines. Consequently, if Guam were developed as a first-class naval station, "no Power would venture to molest the Philippines"; whereas, if the United States left Guam in its undeveloped state with primitive anchorage facilities that could not begin to service a battle fleet, the Philippines would remain in peril. Furthermore, Bywater went on to say, the need to fortify Guam was more urgent than ever since the League of Nations' mandating to Japan of the former German Caroline, Marshall, and Mariana islands had surrounded Guam with "a cordon of potential Japanese strongholds and naval bases." This analysis, focused on the crucial importance of Guam, would soon win the enthusiastic endorsement of the leaders of the American Navy, and would become the subject of heated debate at the upcoming Washington Conference on the Limitation of Naval Armaments.

The most remarkable part of *Sea Power in the Pacific* was a penultimate chapter entitled "Possible Features of a War in the Pacific." The challenge of writing such an essay as this, of course, was to try to figure out what course Japan might take in a war against the United States, and Bywater conceived of a bold and highly unorthodox plan. To begin with, he imagined that Japan would start hostilities by aiming a blow at the only major force in the Pacific preventing her expansion —the American fleet. The best way to eliminate this force would be to launch a surprise attack. "It is reasonable to infer from their conduct on previous occasions," he wrote, "that the Japanese would act with swiftness and energy once a rupture had become inevitable. In 1894 a Japanese naval squadron began hostilities against China a week in advance of the formal declaration of war; and the famous torpedo attack on Port Arthur in February 1904 took place only a few hours after the Japanese Government had signified its resolve to terminate negotiations with Russia."

Now, however, Bywater guessed that Japan might attack with not just a handful of torpedo boats but a major force whose object would be that of annihilating the U.S. fleet rather than merely chipping away at it. With the American fleet *hors de combat*, Japan could seize Guam and the Philippines in almost leisurely fashion. Bywater wrote:

> In view of the overwhelming strategic importance of Guam, this island would doubtless be the first Japanese objective. The reduction

of its feeble defenses would be a simple matter. . . . If the expeditionary force reached Guam at dawn, the Japanese might count on having firmly established themselves on the island by nightfall. A simultaneous attack on the Philippines and Guam, would place no abnormal strain on Japanese naval, military, and shipping resources. In the case of the Philippines expedition, the landing itself would doubtless be made at one or more points where there were no seaward defenses. The complete subjugation of the islands would not be attempted at once; it would suffice if the principal harbors were seized, garrisoned, and hastily fortified, an operation for which two weeks would be a liberal time allowance. The conclusion is that within a fortnight after the beginning of hostilities, the United States would find herself bereft of her insular possessions in the Western Pacific, and consequently without a single base for naval operations in those waters. Those who demur to what may seem a somewhat startling statement are invited to examine the premises on which it rests, and to judge for themselves whether any other inference can be drawn therefrom.

Bywater acknowledged that this scenario would be impossible if the United States developed Guam and established a major naval presence there. But barring such admittedly costly preventive measures, Japan could quickly take possession of a far-flung East Asian empire reaching from the Kurile Islands in the north, down through Korea, Manchuria, Formosa, and the Philippines in the south, and extending westward through the Caroline, Marshall, and Gilbert islands. Having thus expanded her borders, declared Bywater, paraphrasing what he had written in the Dockyard Liar, "the problem confronting the United States would become well-nigh insolvable."

Here was a war plan that was daring indeed—not only because it depended upon surprise and exact timing, which are always difficult to achieve in a tactical situation, but because the seizure of territories 1,800 and 1,400 miles south of the Japanese home islands seemed to flout the nearly sacred principle of naval strategy known as concentration.

The principle of concentration had been forcefully expounded by Mahan in his lectures to students at the Naval War College in Newport, Rhode Island, which were published in 1911 and widely quoted by naval authorities throughout the world. Mahan explained the principle by recalling a land battle. It was the Danube campaign of 1796 in which the Archduke Charles, the Austrian general, had triumphed over two of

Napoleon's ablest commanders, Jean Baptiste Jourdan and Jean Victor Moreau.

The Archduke Charles, Mahan related, had made a study of the military history of Bavaria—an area that had been fiercely contested over the previous three centuries. He concluded that the force that controlled the Danube River between Ulm and Ratisbon (now Regensburg) invariably dominated the entire region. There were two fundamental reasons why. First, the stretch of the Danube between Ulm and Ratisbon was centrally located, being about midway between the bases in the east and west from which the opposing armies usually marched. Second, the Danube was a formidable obstacle. The riverbanks were steep and the bridges all well fortified. The result was that the force that occupied "the Danube position," as Mahan phrased it, could use this great natural obstacle to divide and conquer an opponent. The force astride the Danube, since it controlled the bridges, could quickly concentrate on either side of the river whereas the attacking army was always at the disadvantage of being on one side of the river and cut off from the other, or else on both sides of the river and unable to unite when the need arose.

With this in mind, the Archduke Charles stationed his troops along the Danube between Ulm and Ratisbon. And sure enough, the advancing French armies, which together greatly outnumbered the forces of the archduke, separated when they came to the river, one to the north and the other to the south. As soon as this division took place, the Archduke Charles gathered his forces on the north side of the Danube and hurled his full strength against Jourdan's army, battering it back across the Main and to the Rhine. "It matters not if Moreau gets to Vienna, provided I meantime crush Jourdan," the archduke had said. Once Jourdan was indeed crushed, the archduke turned and flung his entire strength at Moreau, mauling him severely as he retreated through the Black Forest and back across the Rhine. "Had the archduke divided his force, half against Jourdan and half against Moreau," Mahan commented, "it would have mattered greatly had Moreau reached Vienna. . . . Jourdan would have been on hand to join his colleague. As it was, when Moreau was nearest Vienna, Jourdan was back at the Rhine in rapid retreat; and there was nothing left for Moreau but to retire precipitously, or else be cut off by an enemy superior to himself."

Although division of the enemy and concentration of one's own

THE DANUBE POSITION

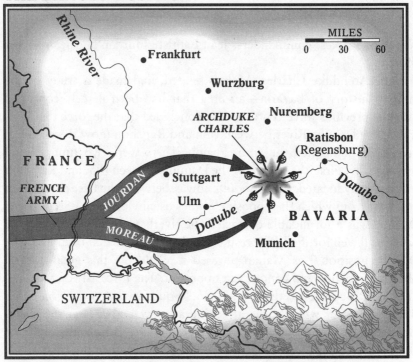

Mahan drew on a famous land battle to illustrate the importance of naval concentration.

forces is "the prime object . . . the A.B.C. of military efficiency in war," Mahan went on to say, this disposition is far more critical and urgent for navies than land armies. Since armies are relatively slow moving, he explained, a commander may keep his forces dispersed and rely on the fact that it will take considerable time for his opponent to mobilize and concentrate his troops. On the sea, however, where large forces move with much greater speed, a fleet must remain concentrated and ready for action at all times. Throughout history, Mahan insisted, it had been disastrous whenever France divided her navy between the Atlantic and the Mediterranean, when the British fleet was split between the Mediterranean and the Channel, when Russia kept half her forces in the Pacific and half in the Baltic, and it would be equally calamitous for the United States, prior to the opening of the Panama Canal, to divide her navy between the Atlantic and the Pacific. "Should then war arise with a European state, or with Japan," he declared, "it would be open to either enemy to take the Danube position between our two divisions, as Togo did between the [Russian] Port Arthur and Baltic Squadrons."

Furthermore, said Mahan, in a warning to all who might be tempted to disperse naval forces:

> It is necessary . . . to guard against a mistake so common that it seems almost a permanent bias of the human mind in naval matters. It is one that has come home to myself gradually and forcibly throughout my reading. . . . I knew long ago, and quoted in these lectures, Jomini's assertion that it is possible to hold too many strategic points; but it is only by subsequent reading that I have come to appreciate how common is the opinion that the holding of additional ports adds to naval strength. Naval strength involves, unquestionably, the possession of strategic points, but its greatest constituent is a mobile navy. If having many ports tempts you to scatter your force among them, they are worse than useless.

The resounding message for Japan—and, as we shall see, Mahan was interpreted precisely this way by Japanese naval strategists—was that the Imperial Navy would invite disaster if it dispersed its forces throughout a Pacific island empire or gave in to the temptation to seize "too many strategic points" in the Pacific, which might oblige her to divide her fleet.

The Japanese were not alone in this interpretation of Mahan. As late as 1935, while a member of the American military mission to the Philippines, Dwight D. Eisenhower declared that the Japanese were unlikely to invade the Philippines because they, like everyone else, could see that any such move would "introduce an element of extraordinary weakness in the Japanese empire" by dividing it "militarily into two parts." Douglas MacArthur, who headed the military mission, concurred and continued to press this case in the fall of 1941.

What Bywater had grasped back in 1920 was that by lunging to the south and seizing the weakly defended Philippines and Guam, Japan would be closing a gap in her defensive perimeter. Leaving these territories well garrisoned, she could then retire her fleet and concentrate it in a veritable Danube position in the Bonin (Ogasawara) Islands only 600 miles southeast of Tokyo. Far from being scattered then, the Imperial Navy would command a central rallying point, or naval redoubt, from which to pounce upon enemy forces and destroy them.

No published naval analyst had seen the Pacific with such clarity.

* * *

BY THE FALL of 1921, Bywater had completed a few chapters and an outline of *Sea Power in the Pacific*. He submitted this material to Otto Kyllmann, the tall Englishman of German extraction who served as chairman of Constable & Company, a highly regarded medium-sized London book publisher. Kyllmann, who like many Britishers-by-adoption was a zealous patriot, was an ideal prospect for Bywater's book. Although widely known as an editor whose stable of writers included George Bernard Shaw, Havelock Ellis, Walter de la Mare, Katherine Mansfield, and George Santayana, Kyllmann's deepest interest was not fiction, poetry, or philosophy but foreign affairs. After hours, he used to lumber upstairs to the attic over the office of Constable & Company at 10–12 Orange Street, just off Leicester Square, to the space rented to the intellectual monthly *Nineteenth Century and After*, which devoted its pages to scholarly essays about Britain and the world. Kyllmann would pore over manuscripts, correspond with authors, and otherwise assist the editors in producing the bulky magazine that frequently ran to some 200 pages per issue.

Kyllmann was intrigued by Bywater's prospectus and summoned the young writer to his office for a talk. Kyllmann was then "a formally but untidily-dressed elderly man" who frequently "shuffled about the office with shoelaces untied," according to a young publisher who bought an interest in Constable & Company at about this time. "He wore old-fashioned eyeglasses attached to a black ribbon. . . . His conversation was disconcertingly punctuated by sudden snorts and grunts." Occasionally, Kyllmann would take a pinch of snuff, "indulging thereafter in a Homeric bout of sneezing. Some of the snuff fell on the grey woolen cardigan which, incongruously, he wore with a short black coat, striped trousers and a blue and white spotted bow tie."

Somehow, the chemistry was right; Kyllmann would eventually serve as editor for all of Bywater's future books. He encouraged Bywater to complete *Sea Power in the Pacific* and promised favorable terms. The contract was signed on November 3, 1920, and Bywater delivered the manuscript a few months later.

A series of fourteen letters that Bywater wrote to Kyllmann during 1921 survive in the files of Constable & Company, and they present an engaging picture of a young author torn between politeness and a fierce desire to protect what he considered his masterpiece and call the world's attention to it. "I venture to think that early publication would have an advantageous effect on the sale of the book," wrote Bywater, observing that "the American-Japanese question is coming in for a good deal of attention at present." He received his galley proofs on March 1, corrected them, and sped them back to Kyllmann in less than five days. Page proofs were returned in a single day. "Would it be convenient if I called next Wednesday between 10:30 and 11:00 A.M. . . . regarding the appearance of the book in America?" he wrote on March 6. Kyllmann couldn't be bothered and turned him over to an underling. A week later, Bywater was still fretfully hopeful that "everything necessary has been done to safeguard [the] copyright . . . since, from what I hear, it seems not improbable that the book may enjoy a fairly large sale in the United States, and I am naturally anxious to know whether my interests will be protected." The following day Bywater was still wondering if a publication date had been set. The date, according to a handwritten note by Kyllmann on this letter, was May 12. A week later, the anxious author was urging that a second copy of his book be sent to Frank C. Bowen, a fellow member of the Fleet Street Press Gang who had promised to review it, since the first copy had been lost evidently due to "a postman's blunder." Bywater also proposed that copies of his book should be offered for sale to "leading Americans resident in London" and to "members of the Japan Society," and that advertisements should stress the fact that the book contained "exclusive information" on "the political and strategic significance of the ex-German South Sea Islands [the Caroline, Marshall, and Mariana islands] and the only account which has appeared up to now of the Japanese submarine flotilla."

Bywater's final letter in this series was a shout of triumph. He reported to Kyllmann that the editor of the *Atlantic Monthly* had just sent him an advance copy of a "rave" review of his book by Admiral William S. Sims, then president of the United States Naval War College, which would appear in the November issue of the prestigious American magazine. It was a stroke of luck for Bywater that the *Atlantic Monthly* had invited Sims to review his book, since Bywater had referred to Sims in *Sea Power in the Pacific* as "one of the most highly esteemed officers in the service." Sims could not have helped being pleased by that, but even more importantly, as we shall see, Sims had been immersed in the study of Pacific strategy for a number of years and had reached some of the same conclusions as Bywater. Bywater's letter to Kyllmann enclosed a copy of the review in which Sims praised *Sea Power in the Pacific* for covering "all phases of a highly technical study in a way which the lay reader should find easily understandable, and most interesting, and which the student of war will recognize as authoritative in its assemblage of facts." Sims concluded: "The reading public is fortunate in having presented to it at this time a treatise so thoroughly excellent, by a writer both authoritative and impartial."

"You may possibly deem it worthwhile," a joyous Bywater wrote to Kyllmann, "to reproduce some of his favorable comments in a future advertisement of the book."

AN EXHILARATING
POSSIBILITY

$\mathcal{S}$CARCELY TWO MONTHS went by after the publication of *Sea Power in the Pacific* in Britain and the United States when the Office of the Imperial Navy General Staff in Tokyo had Bywater's book translated, mimeographed, and distributed to top naval officers as "material for strategic studies." It was an immediate sensation. Bywater's name soon became a household word in the upper echelons of the Japanese Navy.

It was not the first time a foreign naval writer had excited interest in Japan. At the turn of the century, Mahan's major work, *The Influence of Sea Power upon History*, and the Russian Admiral Stephan Makarov's *Consideration of Questions of Naval Tactics* had been translated into Japanese and read avidly by the naval officer corps. A decade later, Homer Lea's *The Valor of Ignorance* had been translated into Japanese under the title *The War Between Japan and America*, and it sold what was then considered a remarkable 40,000 copies. But the demand for the books of Mahan and Makarov was never as great as that for *Sea Power in the Pacific*, and Homer Lea's lurid vision of Japanese troops storming over the continental United States was not taken seriously by any but the most fanciful of Japanese officers.

So "heavy" were requests from Imperial Navy men for copies of Bywater's book that by June 1922 the Office of the Navy General Staff granted permission to *Suiko sha*, the highly influential professional association of officers of the Japanese Navy, to publish *Taiheiyo kaiken ron*, as *Sea Power in the Pacific* was translated. The book was distributed to a wide circle of naval officers, although not to the general public. Copies were marked "Not for Sale." In fact, *Sea Power in the Pacific* was never made available to the Japanese public. In a short while, however, *Taiheiyo kaiken ron* became required reading at both the Imperial Naval Academy and the Naval War College.

There are a number of reasons why Bywater's book aroused such interest in Japan. To begin with, the publication was well timed; *Sea Power in the Pacific* appeared at the height of the postwar Japanese-American naval arms race, which had stirred deep emotions in Japan as in the other major maritime powers. Furthermore, Bywater's book was one of the first major assessments of the growing naval power of Japan written by a foreign specialist, and a British specialist at that. "Mr. Hector C. Bywater is a noted British naval expert," wrote one prominent Japanese military analyst in 1921, admiringly introducing Bywater to his readers. "Before the war, he was in Berlin as a correspondent for a British publication, and was well acquainted with the naval power of Germany. He has recently cast his eye in the direction of Asia. . . . The views he expresses on a possible Japanese-American naval war should be regarded as those of an authority on naval matters."

But the main reason why Bywater's book excited the Japanese Navy is that it spelled out a thrilling plan of conquest for Japan. *Sea Power in the Pacific* asserted that by making a series of swift, bold strokes to the south, Japan could create a vast Pacific empire. Never mind that Bywater had written that the United States could win in the long run by applying her crushing political and economic power, inspiring rebellion in China, Korea, and Formosa, and bringing Japan to her knees by means of a strangulating blockade. "No facile successes achieved in the beginning [by Japan] could avert the most ruinous consequences to the Island Empire," Bywater had warned. But elsewhere in the book, notably the chapter entitled "Possible Features of a War in the Pacific," he had declared that by seizing and quickly fortifying the inadequately defended American insular territories in the Western Pacific, Japan could forge for herself a nearly impregnable empire, the defeat of which would pose a "well-nigh insolvable" strategic problem for the United States. Firebrands in the Imperial Navy fastened their attention on that and ridiculed Bywater's caveats as a typical Western attempt to belittle Japan and undermine her self-confidence.

To appreciate the excitement with which Bywater's ideas were received in Japan, it is necessary to understand how different they were from the purely defensive war plan Japanese officers had been living with for the previous decade and a half. After the Russo-Japanese War, which ended in 1905, a Japanese contingency plan for a possible war against the United States was drafted and finally adopted in 1907. Although subject to annual review after 1913, it remained substantially unchanged. The authors of the plan were two young officers on the faculty of the Naval War College at Tokyo—Tetsutaro Sato, who was known as "the Japanese Mahan," having written the Naval Academy's textbook on Mahan; and Saneyuki Akiyama, a brilliant but eccentric young officer who had served as an official observer with the American fleet when it annihilated Cervera's squadron in the Spanish-American War in 1898. During the Russo-Japanese War, Akiyama was Togo's chief strategist, and it was he who planned the trap for Rojestvensky that became the Battle of Tsushima.

The Sato-Akiyama strategy for war against the United States had been approved at the conclusion of a full-scale defense review in 1907, attended by members of the army, the navy, and the government's political leadership. Because the army carried more weight than the navy, and was still preoccupied with the danger of Russia, the greatest attention was devoted to plans to defeat a Russian attack launched from northern Manchuria. Lesser consideration was given to such possible future adversaries as the United States, Germany, and France.

The Sato-Akiyama contingency plan was essentially a naval ambush based on the presumption that the United States would attack. Japanese light forces were to harry the enemy as he approached Japan, but the main battle fleet would simply lie in wait. The Americans would have clear sailing as far west as Hawaii, but after they struck out into the Western Pacific they would be set upon by wolf packs of Japanese submarines and destroyers that would tear down their strength, reducing the attacking fleet by approximately 30 percent. The notion of weakening the enemy prior to a decisive Tsushima-like battle was a favorite of Akiyama's. When planning Togo's tactics as the Japanese fleet awaited the arrival of Rojestvensky near the Strait of Tsushima in 1905, Akiyama conceived a seven-stage battle that would commence with rapierlike daylight thrusts by elements of the main fleet, and nighttime destroyer and torpedo-boat attacks to cut down the enemy's size and confuse his commanders on the eve of a major engagement. Togo was ready to put the plan into action, but his scouts were not able to locate Rojestvensky's fleet the day before the all-out battle.

After the American fleet entered Japan's home waters, according to Sato and Akiyama, the Japanese main fleet would intercept and destroy it—probably in the vicinity of the Bonin (Ogasawara) Islands 600 miles southeast of Tokyo. Any survivors attempting to struggle back to Hawaii would be relentlessly pursued night and day. The Japanese fleet was sure to be victorious in this fight-to-the-finish for several reasons: the American sailors, like the Russians before them, would arrive at the scene of the battle physically and psychologically exhausted; the American ships would not be in fighting trim but would be heavily laden with fuel for the long voyage home; and finally, the Japanese spirit of *issho kemmei* (total commitment) would be invincible.

At all costs, as Sato and Akiyama saw it, Japan must avoid a protracted war in which the relatively limited Japanese industrial capacity would be matched against vastly superior American resources. For Japan to win, the war would have to be largely a struggle between navies—a limited war like the Russo-Japanese War, not a total war such as the American Civil War, which involved nearly all the resources and territories of the combatants. Consequently, the decisive fleet engagement had to take place as soon as possible. At one stage in the updating of the Sato-Akiyama plan, when it was feared that the American fleet might not venture across the Pacific, provocation was added to speed up the American response. Immediately after a declaration of war, the Japanese main fleet was to assault the Philippines. The object was not to secure an advance base of operations as in Bywater's scheme; the Japanese strategists regarded such a base as worse than useless since it might necessitate the division of the fleet—a prospect that was anathema to followers of Mahan. The Philippines were to be attacked, according to

Sato and Akiyama, specifically to outrage the American people so as to ensure that the main fleet of the U.S. Navy would be hastily dispatched to seek revenge.

Another key element in the Sato-Akiyama strategy, which would soon assume the proportions of an obsession in the Imperial Navy, was that Japan must have a navy at least 70 percent the size of the American fleet. Such a navy would be "sufficient to defend but insufficient to attack," as the saying went. Its size was based on the aforementioned premise that it would be possible to whittle down the American fleet by 30 percent as it crossed the Western Pacific. After that, if the Japanese fleet had started at 70 percent the size of the American fleet, the two forces would be roughly equal by the time of the decisive engagement, and then the *issho kemmei* of Japanese sailors would provide the winning edge.

Clearly, in Sato and Akiyama's thinking, a future war against the United States would be a repetition of the Russo-Japanese War. The American Pacific Fleet was seen as a stand-in for Rojestvensky's Baltic Fleet, which had come churning halfway around the world to attack the fresh, battle-ready Japanese in their home waters. The result, the Japanese strategists confidently predicted, would be another Tsushima.

Over the years, the soundness of the Sato-Akiyama scenario had been tested in tabletop war games, fleet exercises, and strategic studies based on what were conceived to be the lessons of the First World War. Invariably, the plan was upheld. In addition, intelligence reports received by the Imperial Navy General Staff strengthened the belief that the U.S. Navy could be led into the sort of trap envisioned by Sato and Akiyama. In 1916 or 1917, the Japanese Navy learned that the American plan "Orange"—the code name for the official American contingency plan for a possible war against Japan—was built around the concept of dispatching the U.S. fleet to the Western Pacific. And in October 1920, the Navy General Staff received a copy of the secret plan drafted by a team of American strategists spelling out how the U.S. Navy expected to respond to a Japanese attack by waging a transpacific war.

By 1921, the basic assumptions of Sato and Akiyama had been reinforced by a great many other Japanese strategic thinkers, including those who disagreed on the details or even questioned whether or not Japan could actually win a war against the United States yet had no better strategy to recommend. For example, in 1914, Hironori Mizuno, the superintendent of Naval Archives for the Navy Ministry who had written the classic Japanese study of the Battle of Tsushima, published a fictional sequel to his book about Tsushima entitled *The Next Decisive Battle*. One of the rare Japanese naval officers on active duty to comment in print about the possibility of a Japanese-American war, Mizuno pictured in this work an enormous Japanese expeditionary force seizing both the Philippines and Guam only to become stranded in the Philippines after the Japanese Navy is defeated in an epic naval battle.

Mizuno's aim was to call attention to the relative weakness of the Imperial Navy at the outset of the First World War and thus to campaign for a bigger naval budget. But *The Next Decisive Battle* also had the effect of underscoring the already widespread belief that the Japanese Army and Navy existed for the purpose of defending the homeland and protecting vital Japanese interests on the Asian mainland—in Formosa, Korea, and China—rather than for risky adventures in the South Seas.

Another influential writer who sought to discourage Japanese interest in the Pacific islands was Kojiro Sato (no relation to the naval strategist Tetsutaro Sato), a retired lieutenant general who in 1921 published an analysis of the military and naval problems posed for Japan by the United States. Later the same year, Sato published a novel telling the story of a Japanese-American war. In both books, his purpose was to combat the defeatism of Mizuno, and he argued that if it came to a showdown in the Pacific, the Imperial Navy could sweep the U.S. Navy from the seas. Guam, the Philippines, and even Hawaii were of little consequence, in Sato's view. If it should happen that the Japanese fleet greatly outstripped the American Navy at the outset of hostilities, he wrote, Japan might gobble up the South Sea islands with impunity, but the empire should "make no great sacrifice" for them. Even if the Americans were to develop modern naval bases in these islands, they would not be of much use, he believed. Guam, according to Sato, was so flat that enemy warships in the harbor could be seen at all times and would make perfect targets for Japanese gunners, whose ships would not even have to enter the harbor in the manner of Admiral Dewey at Manila Bay in order to pour a lethal fire on the hapless Americans. And the Philippines, although affording more suitable naval bases, Sato declared, could be readily cut off from all lines of supply by the Japanese fleet.

Consequently, as Sato saw it, the best possible course in a war against the United States would be to ignore all outlying naval bases and concentrate on following Togo's strategy of ambush that had led to the great victory at Tsushima.

> If the American expeditionary forces are to be met with the present naval strength of Japan, there will be no alternative but to employ a strategy similar to that adopted when the Russian Baltic Fleet was awaited during the Russo-Japanese war. . . . Our best strategy will be to employ the method suggested by Sun Tzu "to wait at rest for the exhausted." The Japanese will wait at rest for the exhausted American fleet to come. . . . A fleet of warships, like a bullet, will become weaker the farther it is removed from the point of departure. If the American fleet should come near the gate of Japan, it will be like a bullet which goes in a tottering manner, so that it will be so weak that it can be sunk with a single blow.

Despite the fact that the Sato-Akiyama plan dominated Japanese thinking about a possible future naval war, the notion of invading the Philippines was certainly not unheard of by the time Bywater's *Sea Power in the Pacific* made the rounds of the Imperial Navy. Many Japanese officers had come across the idea in Homer Lea's *The War Between Japan and America*, or in novels by Japanese imitators of Lea, such as Yasushi Shirokita or Ryusen Oto, who published war fantasies in which Japan snatched the Philippines and Hawaii on her way to conquering vast areas of the continental United States. But these novels were the work of amateurs ignorant of the limitations of naval power and thus were not taken seriously by service professionals.

Also, a number of Japanese writers, beginning with Toru Hattori, who visited the South Sea islands in 1877, had considered the Philippines ripe for colonization and commercial exploitation. Yet virtually no influential Japanese thinker grasped the strategic importance of the Philippines—not even after the United States annexed the islands at the conclusion of the Spanish-American War in 1898, nor after the Japanese annexation of Korea in 1910.

In 1908, Tetsutaro Sato had advocated in his treatise *On the History of Imperial Defense* the importance of "avoiding the continent and advancing on the sea." Yet, as the scholars Mark Peattie and David Evans have pointed out, "he spoke in only the most generalized terms, referring only to the prospects for Japanese trade and immigration in that part of the world." During the First World War, junior Japanese officers had talked informally about invading the Philippines. In fact, in

1919 the possibility was raised at a joint army-navy meeting, yet no specific plans were drawn or authorized, and no construction programs developed to build the troop transports and landing craft that would be required by any such venture. Some officers in the Navy Ministry spoke of the possibility of acquiring bases in Borneo, and Navy Minister Tomosaburo Kato recognized a need for patroling the South China Sea, but he and his staff planners refused to commit the navy to defend the former German Pacific islands when given to Japan by the League of Nations. The drumbeat for the southern advance and formation of the Greater East Asia Co-Prosperity Sphere, popularized by such writers as Murofushi Takanobu in the mid-1930s, would not be heard for many years to come.

In such an atmosphere, Bywater's *Sea Power in the Pacific* was heady stuff indeed.

8

"SPECIAL LINE ON JAPANESE INFORMATION"

IN THE LATE summer of 1921, a pair of American newspapermen staged a raid on the British literary and journalistic establishment. If their methods were a little crude by proper British standards, at least their aim was lofty. Paul Patterson, the tall, dynamic publisher of the Baltimore *Sun*, and John Heslup Adams, his slightly built, bespectacled managing editor, who was cruelly hobbled with arthritis, had decided that their newspaper would be second to none in its coverage of the coming naval disarmament conference.

The major maritime powers of the world—all reeling from the effects of a deep postwar recession—had gladly accepted an invitation from President Warren Harding to participate in "a conference on limitation of armament . . . to be held at Washington." Leading statesmen from Britain, Japan, Italy, and of course the United States would attend the historic gathering. Consequently, Patterson and Adams had sailed for London to recruit a glittering array of commentators who would write special articles for the *Sun* during the conference. One of their prizes was Hector Bywater.

The Baltimore *Sun*'s engagement of Bywater to analyze developments from a naval expert's point of view was to have important consequences. Apart from giving Bywater a pulpit from which to address a broad international audience, it would forcefully bring his writing on Pacific strategy to the attention of such men as Franklin D. Roosevelt and the leaders of the American and Japanese navies.

In seeking out the most challenging writers, Patterson and Adams were not merely aiming to increase circulation for their newspaper. Unlike Pulitzer, Hearst, and James Gordon Bennett before them, they were old-fashioned idealists whose aim was to work for lasting peace; if the Baltimore *Sun* should benefit from their efforts, then so much the better. Patterson had written to one of his contacts in England just before sailing:

> This is not a business matter in the ordinary sense, but an effort on the part of the *Sun* to leave nothing undone to advance the purposes of the Disarmament Conference, in which it is profoundly interested. . . . The *Sun*'s motive in this arises from its ardent desire to see a reduction in armaments. While it recognizes the difficulties in the way, the *Sun* feels that the financial situation the world over, makes the prospect of something worthwhile being done at the conference greater today than is likely to be the case for many years in the future. . . . Consequently, it proposes to spare no effort to make both its news reports and its comments upon the subjects arising during the conference as full and authoritative as possible, to the end that public sentiment, insofar as it may influence the delegates to the conference, shall be both wisely guided and crystallized.

Patterson, one of the rare newspaper editors to make a successful leap from the newsroom to the business office, had brought about a radical change in the appearance of the *Sun*. He removed classified advertising from the front page and went on to revamp makeup and typography throughout the newspaper. By 1921, the *Sun* was recognized as one of the smartest and most innovative newspapers in the country, and it had established a significant readership in the nation's capital only thirty miles away.

J. H. Adams, Patterson's painfully shy, teetotaling companion on the journey to England, whose arthritis would soon confine him to a wheelchair, was widely respected as the conscience of the *Sun*. His famous assistant, H. L. Mencken, once declared that Adams was the only journalist he ever knew "who never made a visible compromise with his convictions." Furthermore, wrote Mencken, Adams "simply could not tolerate loose thinking, snap judgments, defective information." Getting to the bottom of matters was a cause Adams served "with romantic devotion."

The Baltimoreans met with a series of disappointments soon after establishing themselves at the fashionable Savoy Hotel in London early in September. George Bernard Shaw, it seemed, did not deign to reply to their invitation to discuss the possibility of his writing for the *Sun*. John Maynard Keynes, the Cambridge economist, gave them "a cold turn down," according to Patterson's diary. The first group of British journalists they met also displayed an astonishing lack of interest in the coming conference. "The newspaper editors can't quite understand why we came over here," Patterson confided in his diary. He declared that the only man they had met who had been thinking about disarmament was Henry Noel Brailsford, the Socialist editorial writer of the Manchester *Guardian*. The Americans lost no time in signing up Brailsford for a series of articles.

One of the editors of the *Morning Post* amused the two Americans by explaining that "the English couldn't be expected to be interested in disarmament just now as Charlie Chaplin was due to arrive in England," and then he added quite earnestly that Britain "deserved" a few laughs since the country had been "fed up with serious matters for seven years." But jovial flippancy aside, the horrors and grief of the war years had created a genuine yearning for disarmament in Britain as elsewhere throughout the world, and it was only a matter of time before Patterson and Adams were able to tap that sentiment. After several days of searching, they scored a coup by signing up H. G. Wells to travel to the United States to cover the conference for the *Sun* as one member of a syndicate of American and British newspapers. Next, Patterson and Adams convinced C. P. Scott, the well-known editor of the Manchester *Guardian*, to exchange editorials with the *Sun* in an arrangement that was to last out the decade, and they hired as a columnist Henry W. Nevinson, one of the most experienced British war correspondents. To balance the liberal Brailsford, they engaged J. St. Loe Strachey, editor of the conservative London *Spectator*, along with H. W. Massingham of the *Nation*. Prominent French, Italian, and Chinese correspondents were also lined up. (To express the Japanese point of view, the *Sun* had already hired Hitoshi Suzuki, a Japanese correspondent based in Nagoya, and K. K. Kawakami, the well-known Washington correspondent for several major Japanese daily newspapers.)

Bywater's name was high on the Americans' list of people to see. *Sea Power in the Pacific*, they knew, had sold extremely well, having already gone through three printings in the United States. Moreover, the book had been highly praised by the critics. The *Sun* itself had hailed Bywater's book by stating: "Seldom does one find these matters more succinctly and yet so intelligently set forth." The *Sun*'s reviewer had also commended Bywater for the clarity and liveliness of his writing, remarking—with what must have been music to the ears of such no-nonsense journalists as Patterson and Adams—"any fears of tiresome profundity will be quickly dispelled."

Furthermore, professional opinion on *Sea Power in the Pacific*, the Baltimoreans were aware, was also strongly favorable. In addition to being praised by William S. Sims in the *Atlantic Monthly*, a recent issue of *Proceedings* of the U.S. Naval Institute, which Patterson may have been given by his father-in-law—an admiral who fought with Dewey at Manila Bay—devoted a review of unprecedented length (nineteen pages) to *Sea Power in the Pacific*. Calling the book "the most important recent estimate of the situation in . . . the Pacific," the *Proceedings* essay described Bywater as "a very prominent writer on naval affairs and international subjects" whose regular contributions to such periodicals as the *Naval & Military Record and Royal Dockyards Gazette* were "noted for their detailed accuracy." After an exhaustive summary of the book, the reviewer observed: "Probably no time could be more opportune for its arrival than that immediately preceding the disarmament conference, which has every likelihood of becoming a world event of the first importance."

Thus, Bywater seemed an ideal guest writer for the *Sun*, both for the vigor and clarity of his writing and for the timeliness of his special knowledge. Adams invited him to the Savoy on the afternoon of September 8; he arrived punctually. Patterson's telegraphic diary explains what happened:

> H. C. Bywater called at Hotel in response to our letter, had brief but interesting talk with him—looks like our best bet from Naval Expert Standpoint; Brailsford thinks well of him; writes now for *North American Review* and *Atlantic Monthly*; did stories on Japan for *New York Herald*; keen and businesslike; owing to short time for talk arranged he will come up to London to see us Tuesday (our idea is to get series preliminary articles and others as needed during conference).

Three days after having met Bywater, Patterson ruminated in his diary: "I think Bywater is our best selection provided his terms are not too high. He claims to have special line on Japanese information." Patterson then outlined the coverage of the conference he was planning, which would place Bywater as his number-two man, second only to H. G. Wells.

Bywater, also, must have done some heavy thinking after this encounter. Accepting any offer that Patterson and Adams might make would mean breaking with the *New York Herald*, which had given him his first newspaper job in 1904 and published his work, off and on, over the past seventeen years. Bywater had served as a correspondent for the *Herald* in New York, London, Dresden, and Berlin and then, once again, London. Over all those years, whenever he had been in need of a few pounds sterling to help make ends meet, there had always been the *Herald* to turn to. He could dash off a column or two, and the pay was unusually good for grub-street work. Leaving the *Herald* would be an emotional wrench.

And yet, the fact was that James Gordon Bennett, the *Herald*'s publisher who had been Bywater's patron, had been dead for three years. Furthermore, by 1921 it was evident that the *Herald* was on its last legs. From the high point of its circulation of 500,000 after the Spanish-American War, *Herald* readers had dwindled to a mere 55,000. The paper was now owned by Frank Munsey, the sharp Yankee trader from Maine who bought and sold newspapers like horses, and who, it was generally known, had been despised by Bennett. As to what sort of treatment a writer might expect from Munsey, Paul Patterson had left his employ in disgust in 1911 and had perhaps told Bywater a thing or two about him.

For the present, Bywater continued to be given generous space allotments by the *Herald*, and a fairly free hand to write all he wished about the Japanese Navy, or whatever piqued his interest. Still, there was little of the old newspaper remaining to inspire his loyalty, and indeed scant hope that it would even survive. The Baltimore *Sun*, in contrast, held out the prospect of good pay from a robustly healthy newspaper that could place Bywater's articles and essays on the breakfast tables of the power elite in Washington.

On September 13, the Americans met with Bywater again at the Savoy and this time they struck a deal. "1 P.M.—Luncheon with Bywater and conclusion of arrangement with him," Patterson wrote in his diary. "We are to get 1,000 words cable a week and two Sunday articles each month of 3,000 words each over three-month period—arrangement to be continued if conference lasts longer."

The next day the American pilgrims departed from England on the steamship *Olympic*, jubilant over their success. In less than two weeks, they had signed up a remarkable array of talent. Even John Maynard Keynes, although not able to cover the conference for the *Sun* because of a previously planned trip to India, had abandoned his haughty manner when he realized he might have offended the Baltimoreans and invited them to tea at the Oxford and Cambridge Club. Likewise, George Bernard Shaw finally got around to replying to their letter and received Patterson and Adams at his home at 10 Adelphi Terrace, apologetically explaining that he had made a prior commitment to write about the conference for William Randolph Hearst. "Some of my friends have told me I ought to have nothing to do with Hearst," Shaw said to Patterson and Adams, alluding to the fact that Hearst was antidisarmament, anti-Japanese, and even anti-British. "I tell them that the fact that he seems eager to print my compositions proves him a connoisseur and a gentleman."

No reporter has ever covered a high-level international conference quite the way Hector Bywater handled the Washington Conference for the Baltimore *Sun*. He never came within 3,000 miles of where the delegates were meeting, but he found out more about what was actually taking place there than most of the delegates and all of those who sat in the press gallery—a group of some 400 writers from around the globe led by the editors of *The New York Times* and the London *Times* and including such celebrated figures as Wells and William Jennings Bryan, the one-time U.S. secretary of state and three-time presidential candidate. The first of Bywater's remarkable articles for the *Sun* appeared on November 11, 1921, heralded by a boxed announcement at the top of the front page of the newspaper:

H. C. Bywater
has been a close student of international naval affairs for the past
18 years and is recognized as the authority on naval matters.
The first of his preliminary articles on naval disarmament
appears in the editorial page of
THE SUN
Today

Inside, an editorial saluted Bywater's arrival, remarking that his book *Sea Power in the Pacific* was "generally spoken of as a standard work on the political as well as the strategic problems of the Pacific Ocean," and that Bywater, aside from his other accomplishments, "has specialized in Japanese political affairs."

Even this generous introduction could not have prepared readers for the prophetic nature of Bywater's opening essay. In this 2,000-word debut, Bywater anticipated the proposal with which Charles Evans Hughes, the American secretary of state, would electrify the world at the opening of the conference the next day. The Hughes proposal, although derived from a resolution put forward in the U.S. Senate some months earlier by William Borah of Idaho, was one of the best-kept diplomatic secrets. No foreign government had been notified in advance. Not even H. G. Wells, who had a reputation for prophecy, had been able to divine what the Americans had up their sleeves.

The only genuine method of reducing naval arms, wrote Bywater the day before the conference began, would entail "the ruthless scrapping" of battleships—the ultimate weapon of the 1920s. Such scrapping could be carried out by Great Britain, the United States, and Japan in the ratio of ten-to-ten-to-five, respectively, "without prejudice to the relative standing of the three powers," he declared. If, however, naval reduction were construed to mean only the decommissioning of warships (which could later be recommissioned), then "the reduction would be more apparent than real." No proposal for actual scrapping would win immediate support, Bywater continued. Indeed, the Japanese would resist it "with passionate indignation" since Japan "has condemned itself to virtual penury in order to build battleships." Nevertheless, he concluded, "unless this were done no real reduction of naval armaments could be achieved."

And that, as it turned out, was just about what Secretary Hughes said the next morning in the large, white-paneled Daughters of the American Revolution Hall at Seventeenth and B streets as he addressed the delegates of nine nations. The three major naval powers—Great Britain, the United States, and Japan—declared Hughes, should scrap a total of sixty-six battleships, thus fixing their total capital-ship tonnage by a five-to-five-to-three ratio (roughly 500,000 tons each for the United States and Britain; 300,000 tons for Japan). As Hughes named the great vessels that he proposed to cut up for junk, a list that included several veterans of Jutland, David Beatty, the British hero of Jutland who was present, "staggered, leaned forward in his chair, his eyes widening and then narrowing," according to one reporter. Other admirals were seen to grow red-faced. When Hughes enumerated the Japanese battleships he would have scrapped, including the soon-to-be-launched 34,000-ton *Mutsu*, which had been built with donations from schoolchildren and laborers, the Japanese delegates were observed to "stir in their seats" yet their faces remained "immovable." Hughes offered two other propositions as well—that there be a ten-year moratorium on capital-ship construction, and that afterward a 35,000-ton, 16-inch-gun limit be observed.

Less than a week after the conference began, Bywater contributed an article to the *Sun* that demonstrated the potency of the "special line on Japanese information" he had told Patterson and Adams he possessed. He accurately predicted: "Japan will . . . request from America a definite pledge not to proceed with fortifications and harbor developments in the Philippines, Guam, and Hawaii, and to dismantle existing island forts in the Western Pacific." It was a remarkable stroke of reporting. Bywater had managed to reveal Japan's secret compromise proposal one day before Imperial Navy Minister Tomasaburo Kato presented it to Hughes and British Prime Minister Arthur Balfour in a private meeting at the U.S. Department of State. At this first of a series of confidential meetings, Kato made Japan's acceptance of the naval ratio contingent on the nonfortification of the American islands closest to Japan—those that the United States acquired in 1898 after the war with Spain and whose defenses a penurious U.S. Congress had not been willing to finance. Four days later, Bywater published an even more precise report on Kato's still-secret proposal. "Judging from information I have just received from Tokyo," he stated, "the Japanese will endeavor to make any reduction of their own armaments conditional on a pledge from America that she will not fortify the Philippines or Guam." Bywater added caustically: "America should be on her guard against any such insidious proposals." He pressed the point: America's strategic position in the Western Pacific is "bad enough as it stands today," but it would become "infinitely worse" if she were persuaded "to forgo her clear right and title to make Guam and the Philippines secure against summary capture." This, after all, had been the central thesis of *Sea Power in the Pacific*; namely, that the key to the Pacific from America's point of view was the development of Guam as a first-class naval station.

There was yet another card being played at the secret negotiations conducted by Hughes, Balfour, and Kato, and Bywater turned up that one as well. He wrote that it was "incredible" that the Japanese would ever agree to scrap the battleship *Mutsu*, which they had made such sacrifices to build. "Japan definitely plans to keep the ship [*Mutsu*]," Bywater stated flatly on December 3. He added a suggestion—"America could end the deadlock on the tonnage ratio question by conceding *Mutsu* to Japan." He was prophetic once again, for that is precisely the bargain Hughes and Balfour were in the process of striking with Kato. Tomosaburo Kato finally agreed to accept an inferior naval ratio in exchange for America's pledge not to develop a naval base west of Hawaii and a reprieve for the *Mutsu*.

As the conference went on, Bywater supplied yet more revelations from Japan. At one point he reported that the Japanese were engaged in secretly building a new class of submarine so large it could be described as a "submarine cruiser." Undersea vessels in this 2,000-ton class were on the stocks at Kure, Kobe, and Sasebo, he reported. What was significant about such warships was their extraordinary range; they were capable of crossing the Pacific, attacking American shipping, and bombarding Portland, Seattle, San Francisco, and Los Angeles before heading home. Despite "the intense secrecy in which the Japanese naval authorities have always shrouded this [submarine] branch of their service," Bywater added in an article he published in the *Atlantic Monthly* at this time, "a careful analysis of information that has reached this writer from a well-informed quarter shows Japan to have ordered from 90 to 100 submarines of all types since the year 1903."

Like most reporters who delve into forbidden areas, Bywater rarely revealed his sources. Nevertheless, a number of them are relatively easy to bring to light. He naturally made use of a number of native Japanese informants. In the preface to *Sea Power in the Pacific*, for example, he thanked Seizo Kobayashi, the London naval attaché, and his assistant, K. Kurokawa, "for kindly supplying me with valuable notes on the administration, organization, and personnel of the Imperial Japanese Navy." Kobayashi, in particular, greatly impressed Bywater. Years later, when Kobayashi, by then a vice admiral, shared the command of one of Japan's largest peacetime naval maneuvers, Bywater referred to him in an article as "one of the most brilliant commanders in the Japanese Navy." Kobayashi, who went on to become the Japanese governor-general of Formosa and had a reputation for being pro-British, was doubtless of assistance to Bywater after his departure from London.

Another important source of information for Bywater was the Japanese press. Although he never learned to read or speak Japanese, he was a regular reader of the English-language *Japan Advertiser* and *Japan Weekly Chronicle*, both of which published extensive translations and summaries of news and editorial opinion in the Japanese press. Making use of such sources, in one article for the Baltimore *Sun*, for example, Bywater was able to characterize and quote from such Japanese newspapers as the Tokyo *Asahi*, the Osaka *Asahi, Yorodzu, Yamato, Yomiuri, Miyako*, and *Jiji*.

Bywater's principal source of secret information from inside Japan between about 1920 and 1934—his "special line on Japanese information," as he put it to Patterson and Adams—appears to have been Malcolm D. Kennedy. A graduate of Sandhurst, the British military academy, Kennedy was invalided out of the service in 1917 and from then until 1934 lived in Tokyo, serving as a correspondent for the Reuters news agency for the last nine of those years. Because the Reuters job was only part-time, Kennedy was encouraged to accept free-lance assignments from editors, scholars, or writers such as Bywater. When Kennedy was asked to confirm his relationship with Bywater in 1982, he was eighty-eight years of age and mentally failing; he immediately recalled Bywater's name and that he had had some connection with him, but little else. There is, however, corroborating evidence in Kennedy's six books about Japan. For example, *Some Aspects of Japan and Her Defense Forces*, which Kennedy published in 1928, contains all the information about the Japanese submarine force that Bywater revealed in earlier news articles and is authoritative on numerous other naval subjects as well. Moreover, a journalistic squabble between Kennedy and A. Morgan Young, the editor of the *Japan Weekly Chronicle*, which broke into print in the pages of that journal in 1925, suggests that Kennedy was Bywater's source of information for a controversial series of articles about the planned expansion of the Japanese Navy that Bywater wrote for the London *Daily News* and the Baltimore *Sun* at that time. Finally, Kennedy's books are sprinkled with complimentary (and in one instance gently chiding) references to Bywater.

The fact that Bywater had the services of a man like Kennedy, who spoke and read Japanese fluently and had been professionally trained in military science, goes a long way toward explaining the extraordinary series of reportorial coups from Japan that Bywater scored throughout the 1920s and 1930s. Kennedy, to be sure, does not deserve all the credit; Bywater's expertise in naval matters was unmatched, and Bywater knew—from his days as a secret agent in Germany—the right questions to ask and how to piece together the answers from incomplete information. Still, one cannot understand Bywater's achievements without first recognizing Kennedy's contribution.

Brilliant as was Bywater's reporting and commentary on the Washington Conference, it included one important lapse. Even the hard-nosed Secret Service agent in Bywater could not completely resist the worldwide jubilation that greeted the December 10 announcement that the United States, Great Britain, Japan, and France were about to sign a treaty agreeing to respect each other's Pacific dominions and to submit any disputes that might arise there to international mediation. Bywater proclaimed the four-power treaty America's "greatest diplomatic triumph of her history," and then surprisingly repudiated the case he had been arguing so vehemently for more than a year concerning the vital necessity of the United States' developing Guam as a naval base. Japan and the United States, he wrote in the *Sun* the day after the new treaty was announced, had been on a collision course. It was "certain" that sooner or later America would develop naval stations in the Western Pacific, yet Japan "was determined to make the fortification of Manila or Guam a *causus belli*," thus creating a "hair-trigger" situation in which war between the two countries was "only a question of time." The four-power treaty, however, had made the possibility of war in the Pacific so "remote" that "questions of naval strategy have ceased to be of prime importance for the time being," and it was now "very unlikely" that the United States would, or should, develop Guam, Manila, or Midway as naval bases. In his next dispatch, Bywater was joyously proclaiming: "We stand at the threshold of a new epoch of prosperity for shipping and the commercial world in general."

If euphoria over the signing of the Washington Treaty was to last more than a decade for most of his contemporaries, it clung to Bywater for precisely eleven days. On December 15, the Washington conferees announced a second treaty—the so-called five-power agreement between the United States, Great Britain, Japan, France, and Italy, in which the 5–5–3–1.75 naval ratio was adopted. Japan, in exchange for her acceptance of the medium-level tonnage (a capital-ship fleet of 315,000 tons as compared with 525,000 tons each for Britain and the United States and 175,000 tons each for France and Italy), was given an assurance by the United States that she would not create naval bases in the Western Pacific. In addition, Japan was permitted to retain her cherished *Mutsu*.

The nonfortification proviso was precisely what Bywater had condoned, even applauded, less than two weeks earlier, but now, the reality of the United States tying her hands brought him to his senses. In a major essay for the *Sun* written on December 22, Bywater praised "the splendid work performed at Washington" in gaining acceptance of the five-to-five-to-three naval ratio, but pointed out that the decision about Pacific naval bases was "overwhelmingly to the advantage of Japan." He warned: "It is an open question whether America has not committed a grave mistake in agreeing not to develop naval stations in the Western Pacific." The United States may regret, Bywater wrote, that she has made Japan "strategically supreme in that quarter of the globe." It was a warning that he was to sound with ever greater urgency throughout the coming years.

The Baltimore *Sun*'s intensive and intellectually broad coverage of the Washington Conference earned recognition for the newspaper both at home and overseas. No small share of the credit, Paul Patterson and J. H. Adams well knew, belonged to Hector Bywater, whose reportorial newsbreaks and penetrating, often prophetic analysis had gained a wide following. Adams generously pointed this out in a letter to Bywater as the conference was winding down. "I want to tell you that it is not only my opinion, but that of everyone in the office," Adams wrote to Bywater on January 3, "that your articles have had very much to do with the success of the *Sun*'s handling of the conference, which is generally conceded here even by our enemies."

A few weeks later, Adams wrote to Bywater again, this time asking him to continue to write regularly for the *Sun* after the expiration of their original agreement on February 15. Bywater was to be the *Sun*'s European naval correspondent. The pay was good—fifty pounds a month—and Bywater's contributions would be given a prominent position opposite the editorial page, unless, of course, they appeared on the front page. It was an ideal arrangement from the writer's point of view, and it proved to be a long-lasting one. "Did you read Bywater in the *Sun*?" sailors and statesmen would ask each other throughout the 1920s.

CHAPTER

9

BYWATER VS. ROOSEVELT

SOON AFTER COVERING the Washington Conference, By-water was drawn into a debate with a former assistant secretary of the United States Navy named Franklin D. Roosevelt. The issue between them was whether or not a Japanese-American war was a physical possibility, given the vastness of the ocean that separated the two powers. The debate was conducted on occasion by proxy and sometimes by direct exchange in the pages of newspapers—including the Baltimore Sun—magazines, and books.

To get in the last word, Bywater wrote his fourth book, called The Great Pacific War. It was an imaginary yet meticulously realistic account of a future war between Japan and the United States, written as if by a historian piecing the story together after the war had taken place. Bywater's first objective in this book was simply to show that the two foremost Pacific powers could indeed enter into a decisive struggle. He also sought to demonstrate the best possible strategy for each country, and then show that the United States inevitably would be the victor. It is surely ironic that the writing of *The Great Pacific War* was prompted by the man who would later be at the helm of the United States government when Japan put Bywater's ideas to the test.

The Bywater-Roosevelt debate took place after the two men had shifted from their original stance, like a couple of wrestlers circling each other before coming to grips. In the end, both Bywater and Roosevelt wound up taking a position on the possibility of war in the Pacific diametrically opposed to the one he started with.

Before the Washington Conference, Bywater had written that distances across the Pacific were so enormous that neither Japan nor the United States could significantly harm each other. The vastness of that ocean was not often given due appreciation. For example, compare the Atlantic with the Pacific. While New York is 3,500 miles from Liverpool, England, the distance between San Francisco and Yokohama by way of Honolulu is 6,300 miles—almost twice as far. The steamship route from the Panama Canal to Yokohama with a stop at Honolulu is close to 10,000 miles.

One of the ironies of the advent of steam power, Bywater liked to point out, was that modern technology had precipitously *decreased* the range of warships. In the days of sail, a fleet of fighting ships provisioned with dry stores could keep the sea for months at a time and bring its guns to bear on virtually any maritime or coastal target around the globe. Not so in the modern age. In the 1920s, many capital ships could cruise nonstop for 10,000 miles, but there was no such thing as "cruising" in wartime. Proceeding in a straight line at an economical speed would make a ship in a war zone a sitting duck for submarines. Modern warships in hostile waters had to necessarily move at a fast clip, frequently on a zigzag course, and carry extra fuel in case they ran into bad weather or other unforeseen obstacles.

Had Commodore George Dewey's squadron been based at San Francisco in 1898, it would have been madness for him to sail for Manila Bay to attack the Spanish fleet. Dewey's ships could not carry enough fuel to get home in case they were forced to retire. Luckily for the United States, Dewey had concentrated his ships at the British colony of Hong Kong, and by an even more remarkable stroke of good fortune, much-needed supplies reached him there the day before the governor of the colony insisted that he remove his ships from British territorial waters because Spain and the United States were at war and Britain wished to remain neutral. Japan, also, closed its ports to him. Furthermore, even coming from the China coast, if Dewey had not succeeded in destroying Admiral Montojo's fleet when he entered Manila Bay, and if American troops had not captured Manila two months later, Dewey might have become stranded in the South Pacific or had his squadron interned at a neutral port.

A possible means of increasing the range of warships was to direct them to rendezvous with colliers to replenish their bunkers on the high seas. But even when such linkups were scheduled to take place in placid harbors in time of peace, this practice was fraught with danger. In 1908, America's "Great White Fleet" on a world cruise came perilously close to running out of fuel in the middle of the Pacific when colliers failed to arrive at three successive points of rendezvous. Only by inducing commercial dealers to break their contracts with other buyers in order to sell coal to him was the American commander, Charles S. Sperry, able to nurse his fleet along to Manila and then Yokohama without embarrassment, but in time of war such mishaps could spell disaster.

Keenly aware of all this, Bywater assumed that Japan and the United States were simply too far apart to be able to engage in a fight to the finish. "Humanly speaking," he had written in the Baltimore *Sun*, "Japan is invulnerable to attack." He used the same locution in *Sea Power in the Pacific* to describe the immunity of the United States. "Every intelligent American knows," he wrote, "that his home coasts are, humanly speaking, secure against invasion from the Far East."

Of course, the same could not be said of the American outposts in the Western Pacific. Guam and the Philippines were so remote even from Hawaii that they could not be defended against a nearby aggressor. The only way the United States could protect these newly acquired territories, Bywater wrote, would be to develop Guam as a first-class naval base. But now that the United States had renounced that prerogative in the Washington Treaty, Japan was left "strategically supreme in that quarter of the globe." Presumably, Japan could snatch these distant American possessions whenever it suited her, and leave the United States with the virtually insoluble problem of how to get them back.

As time went on, however, Bywater began to feel a good deal less sanguine about the stalemate in the Pacific. He suspected that the latest technological developments in warfare might be changing the old calculations. For example, might not the long-range submarines such as Germany built during the last year of the First World War, and such as both Japan and the United States were known to have under construction, bring the two powers within reach of one another? "The big submersible cruiser will have a longer reach than any other species of war-vessel," Bywater wrote in an article for the *Atlantic Monthly* in February 1922. "It would, for example, be perfectly feasible for a boat of this type to leave its base in Japan, cross the Pacific Ocean, and remain off the American coast for a month or more, doing all the damage that it could—sinking ships, laying mines off harbor mouths, and even bombarding coastal towns within range of its guns."

Furthermore, if the Washington Treaty had ruled out the possibility of stationing a fleet in the Philippines or at Guam, might not a powerful force of submarines and aircraft based at Manila be just as effective in defending American territories in the Western Pacific? This, too, he contemplated in the *Atlantic Monthly* article, speculating on the strategic effect of basing "a large flotilla of submarines" and "a hundred aeroplanes, each armed with one or more bombs of the heaviest description, held in readiness at Cavite and other strategical points in the [Philippine] island group."

Bywater was troubled by other imponderables as well. Now that the Washington Treaty had been signed, and warships were being scrapped and plans for new bases shelved, would these new realities stimulate efforts that were inconceivable previously? With battleships restricted in number and tonnage, would the cruiser take on a new importance? Finally, now that the development of advance naval bases had been prohibited by treaty, would other means of moving a fleet across vast ocean spaces be devised? These were formidable questions. Bywater wrestled with them in a series of thoughtful articles after John Heslup Adams named him European naval correspondent for the *Sun*.

By February 1923, he finally abandoned the idea that Japan and the United States were unable to make war in the Pacific. In the advent of hostilities, he wrote, once again for the *Atlantic Monthly*, the Japanese superiority in fast, new cruisers and submarines could wreak havoc with American shipping. Such action would never force the United States into submission, he cautioned, but it would be "a serious matter." Thus, Bywater concluded, "The widely held idea that a war in the Pacific must speedily end in deadlock, in which neither opponent could inflict any appreciable damage on the other, is seen to be fallacious." A war between Japan and the United States, he was saying, was in fact a deadly possibility.

Over the succeeding months, Bywater became increasingly convinced that the Washington Treaty had not prevented war, but, in fact, had done the very opposite—baited a trap for Japan that, sooner or later, she would be drawn into. He made this observation in an essay for the *Navy*. "As things are at present," he wrote, "there is no physical impediment to the extension of Japanese sovereignty over the richest territories of the Pacific such as the Philippines, the Dutch East Indies, even Australiasia. Japan may be innocent of imperialistic ambition, but the temptation to exploit the unique strategic position in which she has been placed by the Washington Treaty may sooner or later prove irresistible."

Just as Bywater was coming to see the Washington Treaty as a snare and a delusion, Franklin Roosevelt—ever a creature of political instinct—was absorbing the popular optimism generated by the signing of the Washington Treaty and profoundly changing his way of thinking.

After having demonstrated political flair during the six years he served as assistant secretary of the navy, Roosevelt had been tapped in 1920 to run for vice president on the Democratic ticket with James M. Cox, the genial but colorless governor of Ohio. Cox and Roosevelt were soundly defeated by Warren Harding and Calvin Coolidge, and although Cox returned to Ohio and disappeared from national political life, Roosevelt was clearly a rising star. In August 1921, however, after falling into the icy waters of the Bay of Fundy from the yacht tender of his friend Van Lear Black, chairman of the board of the Baltimore *Sun*, Roosevelt contracted infantile paralysis.

At first, his recuperation was dishearteningly slow. But as Roosevelt began to regain strength, he took an interest in the progress of the Washington Conference. Among the books he purchased and read at this time were Bywater's *Sea Power in the Pacific* and Walter Pitkin's *Must We Fight Japan?*—both of which argued that as things then stood in the Pacific, Japan could gobble up the Philippines and Guam with impunity. Such action by Japan, they believed, would lead to deadlock. Roosevelt carried this one step further and leapt to the conclusion that since neither power could strike a deathblow to the other, neither would be tempted to start a war.

Moreover, Roosevelt sensed that the signing of the Washington

Treaty had significantly altered the climate of public opinion in the United States and throughout the world. The desire for peace and disarmament, he believed, had come to dominate public thinking. Roosevelt expressed this conviction in a letter to a friend in 1923: "President Harding's Washington Conference of 1921 has, without question, removed the greater part of the indefinable something which has bred suspicion and competition first in the defense departments, then in Congress, and finally among a large body of people who followed the doings of government." And thus, moved both by personal conviction and political expedience, Roosevelt adopted what was essentially a pacifist foreign policy.

It was a remarkable turnabout for a thoroughgoing navy man. Even as a boy, Roosevelt had been fascinated by stories about the involvement of his forebears in sea battles of the Civil War. He himself had come within a week of entering the U.S. Naval Academy at Annapolis, and withdrew only because his parents insisted that he prepare himself at Groton and Harvard to take over his father's business interests. After that, his love of the sea was restricted to his favorite recreation—sailing off the coasts of Maine and New Brunswick—until 1913 when President Wilson's newly appointed secretary of the navy, Josephus Daniels, invited Roosevelt to serve as assistant secretary of the navy. "All my life I have loved ships and been a student of the Navy," Roosevelt told Daniels, "and the assistant secretaryship is the one place, above all others, I would love to hold."

During his years as assistant secretary of the navy, Roosevelt allied himself with the big-navy enthusiasts on the General Board, an advisory group of senior officers headed by Admiral Dewey. Repeatedly, he supported these officers in opposition to the views of Daniels. In fact, Roosevelt's high-handedness nearly cost him his job during a crisis in the spring of 1913. The California legislature had just passed a law stigmatizing Japanese immigrants—who were thought to compete unfairly with American workers—as second-class citizens. A sharply worded Japanese protest brought the two countries to the brink of war. Roosevelt joined the cabal led by Bradley A. Fiske, then a rear admiral, and James Gordon Bennett of the *New York Herald* that planted a false story in the *Herald* suggesting that the United States Asiatic Squadron was about to be recalled from China to the Philippines. Their intention was that news of this retreat from an exposed position would appear to the

Japanese as a preparation for war and would prompt Japan to attack the Philippines. Roosevelt held the opinion that war with Japan was inevitable and, given that situation, was best over and done with. As it turned out, President Wilson rebuked Fiske and his coconspirators for having publicized an unauthorized plan to move the fleet provocatively, and forbade any actual naval movement during the crisis. Eventually, the trouble subsided.

In 1922, times were different, and Roosevelt was eager to stake out his new foreign policy. He accomplished this repositioning by writing an article for the prestigious *Asia* magazine in which he argued that war with Japan was now unthinkable and impossible. When Bywater read the article, the two men locked horns.

The inspiration for Roosevelt's article was an editorial in the Boston *Transcript* that he read while at his summer residence in October 1922. The editorial scored the Harding administration for having surrendered the right to fortify the Philippines and Guam. The *Transcript* also praised a hot-blooded article in *Current History* magazine by William Howard Gardiner, an author and lecturer who was then vice president of the Navy League of the United States. Gardiner's essay had likened Great Britain's struggle to gain control of the Atlantic to Japan's drive for mastery of the Pacific, and argued that sooner or later Japan was sure to take advantage of America's defenselessness in the Western Pacific by seizing her unprotected island territories.

To Roosevelt, that was the old, unnecessarily suspicious outlook. He wrote to George Marvin, an old friend and an occasional literary collaborator who had a connection with *Asia* magazine, proposing that they jointly develop an article for *Asia* challenging Gardiner's and the *Transcript*'s thesis.

Indirectly, Roosevelt was picking a fight with Bywater, for Gardiner had been deeply influenced by Bywater's *Sea Power in the Pacific*. Immediately after reading the book, Gardiner had written to Bywater commending his "really great book" as "the most vital publication to English-speaking civilization as a whole and to the United States in particular since the great works of Mahan." In a subsequent letter recommending Bywater's book to William S. Sims, who would later review it for the *Atlantic Monthly*, Gardiner told Sims he was planning to use "Bywater's argument as to the essentiality of making Guam an impregnable naval base" in a forthcoming magazine article. That was the article for *Current History* that inspired the *Transcript* editorial. Thus, Roosevelt commenced the "debate" with Bywater probably without realizing with whom he was picking a quarrel.

In a letter of October 10 to Marvin, Roosevelt outlined the article he proposed to write for *Asia*. He said he wanted to begin "by pointing out that people are still thinking in terms of war rather than in terms of trying to remove the causes of war." Next, he said he would survey some thirty years of rivalry in the Pacific between Japan and the United States, and then conclude by making the case that "a living up to the naval limitations treaty in both letter and spirit on our part will help to make Japan do so also."

Between Thanksgiving and Christmas 1922, Roosevelt wrote a rough draft with the slangy working title "The Japs—A Habit of Mind" and packed it off to Marvin for polishing. Marvin reworked the article and returned it to Roosevelt for consideration and revision.

In this manner, the article bounded back and forth several times between Roosevelt and his collaborator, and was finally submitted to *Asia* late in the winter of 1923. By July, at about the time that Roosevelt's picture appeared on the cover of *Time* magazine, showing him resolutely clenching a pipe in his prominent front teeth as an expression of determination to resume his political career despite the crippling effects of polio, Roosevelt received and approved galleys from *Asia* magazine. His political star was ascending even as he enunciated his newfound pacifism.

The article was headlined SHALL WE TRUST JAPAN? It covered six pages and was illustrated with four large photographs—pictures of Japanese troops in China and Japanese naval vessels and naval cadets. "Why do so many Americans, after witnessing the devastation and the futility of war," Roosevelt's article began, "continue to think of Japan and the Japanese in terms of war? Why have so many Japanese a similar mental attitude toward the United States? Is this mutually apprehensive habit of mind, to whatever understandable origins it may be due, justified today?"

Before answering these questions, Roosevelt reviewed the history of Japanese-American relations. Then, in order to show the futility of a Pacific war, he declared that because of the enormous distances involved, the conflict would soon result in the following "military dead-lock."

"Tableau: Japan and the United States, four or five thousand miles apart, making faces at one another across a no-man's-water as broad as the Pacific." The war might continue in this fashion "until one or the other, or both, had bled to death through the pocketbook."

Yet this madness need not occur, Roosevelt argued. He took up the causes of friction between the two nations and dismissed them one by one. In conclusion, he wrote that the people of both Japan and the United States must discard "the old habit of mind" and seize the present "magnificent opportunity" for "the quieting of troubled waters."

Among readers of this article was John Heslup Adams, the managing editor of the Baltimore *Sun*. He clipped Roosevelt's article and sent it to Bywater, asking for a comment. Bywater immediately dispatched a 2,500-word reply that Adams published in the *Sun* on July 21. Bywater began by deferentially praising Roosevelt's article for its "outstanding merit and value" and said that it "should be read in full by all who wish for enlightenment on one of the ruling problems of the day."

"While Mr. Roosevelt's conclusions are sound in the main," Bywater continued, his faith in the permanence of the present stalemate is "premature." The prospect of war between Japan and the United States was fraught with "imponderable elements." What if, Bywater asked, China or Russia intervened in a Japanese-American war? Furthermore, what prospect was there for peace in the Pacific in light of the fact that Japan had begun work on "a program of auxiliary [naval] construction so large that it transcends the collective shipbuilding effort of all the other powers," and in light of the United States' having drafted a new program of warship construction. If the American program were adopted by Congress, he continued, Japan would respond in kind and "competition in sea armaments will thus become a fact once more." Finally, Bywater observed, Japan was searching for a home for her surplus population. The British government was convinced she would attempt to plant her flag in Australia, "else the decision to develop Singapore as a great naval base would be meaningless." Even the Netherlands, he went on to say, was investing a large proportion of her national treasure in the expansion of her East India Fleet to safeguard from Japan the islands of Java, Sumatra, and the Celebes. Thus, concluded Bywater: "Two of the powers have already returned a negative answer to Mr. Roosevelt's question, 'Shall we trust Japan?'"

Adams sent a clipping of Bywater's reply to Roosevelt. "Your article in the July number of *Asia* so impressed me," Adams wrote, "that I sent a copy of it to our London correspondent, Mr. Hector C. Bywater, whom you may recall as the author of *Sea Power in the Pacific*. His comment upon the article, of which I enclose a clipping, appeared in the *Sun* of July 21st. I do not know whether there are any points in this article upon which you would care to comment, but if there are, we should like to have and print whatever you may wish to say about it."

Roosevelt accepted the challenge. "I have been much interested by Mr. Bywater's comments on my article in *Asia*," he replied to Adams. "His comment i[s] most flattering, yet I feel that the slight note of warning which he sounds is that primarily of the military circle—in other words—that he views the whole situation in the Pacific from the point of view which I am seeking to combat. I have dashed off the [e]nclosed in the form of a comment on Mr. Bywater's letter. Go ahead and run it if you want to, but if you think it is too polemic send it back and I will tone it down."

Roosevelt's two-and-a-half-page rejoinder, obviously typed by himself with many erasures, was published without alteration by Adams under the headline FRANKLIN D. ROOSEVELT ANSWERS MR. BYWATER.

I have been greatly interested in the comment of your London correspondent, Mr. Hector C. Bywater. His deep study of the whole Pacific question gives his views great weight, yet I fear that Mr. Bywater is still looking at the relationships of people and lands bordering on the Pacific Ocean from the old point of view. It is true that in the past both Great Britain and the United States have feared Japanese territorial expansion—into Australia, New Zealand, China proper, the Philippines, Hawaii, etc. He argues that Great Britain and Holland have answered "no" to the question "Shall we trust Japan?" Both nations have taken steps to strengthen their military resources in the South Pacific. By inference he approves their policy, and would approve the United States adopting a similar policy.

It is exactly that outlook which I have sought to combat. It is the old story of arming for defense because you see a threat of possible danger. The other fellow follows in order to keep up with your new armaments, and a competitive military and naval program results.

In place of the "old outlook," Roosevelt declared,

a new spirit of international relations . . . seeks new methods to
end the conditions of 1914. Materialism has not been downed—
the old order dies hard—but the more spiritual attitude gains
ground every day and year that passes. Mr. Bywater still assumes
that Japan's present and future needs for a population outlet must
force her to seek lands in the South Pacific; and that this means
inevitable clash with Great Britain and the Netherlands. I do not
grant that clash because I do not grant the Japanese necessity. . . .
The whole trend of the times is against wars for colonial expansion.
The thought of the world leans the other way.

And that, as far as Franklin D. Roosevelt was concerned, settled the
matter. As he saw it, the Pacific Ocean served as a gigantic buffer zone
to prevent Japan and the United States from coming to blows. And if,
because of the Washington Treaty, American possessions in the Western
Pacific had become indefensible, then Japan would exercise restraint
because "the whole trend of the times is against wars for colonial expansion."

The debate with Roosevelt made a lasting impression on Bywater.
He was quoting the *Asia* article as late as 1927 in his fifth book, *Navies
and Nations*. Meanwhile, almost everything about Japanese-American
relations that swam into Bywater's view seemed to challenge the conclusions Roosevelt had drawn. For example, Japanese immigration to
California had been a source of conflict between the two nations dating
back to the previously mentioned crisis of 1913. Japanese workers,
accustomed to a relatively low standard of living, accepted meager wages
when they arrived in California and in that way they took jobs from
Americans and depressed wages generally. Ill feeling was the inevitable
result.

Early in 1924, as Bywater recalled in an essay some years later, a
group of American congressmen from the West Coast proposed a revision of the immigration laws that would sharply reduce the number
of Japanese along with other Asians allowed to enter the United States
each year. It was a blatantly racist insult to a proud people. While
Congress was still considering the measure, the Japanese ambassador in
Washington handed a memorandum to the American secretary of state
that referred to "grave consequences" that might result from passage of
the bill. These words were injudicious, yet certainly innocent of the
menacing interpretation given to them by the more incendiary elements

of the American press, and they provoked a storm. As a result, a much tougher immigration bill, which by implication branded the Japanese as an inferior race, was quickly passed by a huge majority in Congress. Secretary of State Charles Evans Hughes, who had been the chief American delegate to the Washington Conference two years before, and was a vigorous opponent of the new immigration law, bewailed the action. "Our friends in the Senate have in a few minutes spoiled the work of years," he said.

Later the same year, the United States acted still more provocatively toward Japan. The government announced that the American Navy planned to conduct a major fleet exercise near Hawaii, and then sent out a feeler suggesting that Japan might receive the fleet on a goodwill visit after the maneuvers had been completed. The offer was made in the naive hope of demonstrating to Japan that the American fleet should not be regarded as a threat, but the Japanese well understood the significance of the exercise and tartly refused to act as host. It was a poor performance on the part of the United States, but the Japanese did not behave much better. The Osaka *Mainichi* declared in an editorial that if the United States went ahead with the planned fleet exercise, a Japanese-American war would become "inevitable." Bywater read the *Mainichi* editorial and wrote that it expressed "a degree of arrogance which the most swollen-headed Prussian warlord never attained."

With such portents in mind, and now determined to prove wrong those like Roosevelt who regarded a Pacific war as a practical impossibility, Bywater began to try to figure out the likely course of a future war in the Pacific. He did not do so as a lover of war, it must be said. He deplored war, but he could not accept pacifism as an alternative. Bywater regarded the pacifism of men like Roosevelt and Prime Minister Ramsay MacDonald in his own country as a palliative that might ease anxieties without curing the disease, thus giving rise to false hopes. Far better, in Bywater's view, to confront reality and try to cope with it. He had stated this philosophy in the Baltimore *Sun* at the end of 1924 as he was in the midst of writing *The Great Pacific War*, and these remarks clearly reveal his conviction at the time. "Excepting a few incorrigible militarists who continue to prate of its 'biological necessity,' war is now universally abhorred as an unmitigated curse," wrote Bywater. "The only difference of opinion concerns the best method of avoiding it in the future." Bywater's method would be to explore the course it might take, and thus reveal its horror and futility.

Already in *Sea Power in the Pacific* he had outlined the opening moves he thought best suited to Japan's strategic position—a surprise attack on the American fleet aimed at its annihilation and the simultaneous seizure of the Philippines and Guam. He would spell out all this in greater detail than before, but what then? How would it be possible to break the resulting deadlock, with Japan and the United States "making faces at one another across a no-man's-water as broad as the Pacific," as Roosevelt had phrased it? How could a United States Pacific Fleet be brought to within shooting distance of Japan?

Bywater returned to the charts of the Pacific for long hours of study, placing himself in the position of the American commander-in-chief. How to get at Japan? It would not be easy, to say the least. Could the United States build enough underwater cruisers to inflict significant damage on Japan? Could aircraft someday span the Pacific and return home safely? If naval bases could not be developed before a war started, would it be possible to build them amid hostilities?

Bywater struggled with these questions for months and eventually came up with an extraordinary answer. It was this: By means of the most careful planning and preparation, United States forces would be able to leapfrog across the Pacific from island to island, using each new base as "a stepping-stone to the conquest of the Philippines," as he phrased it. From the Philippines, the Japanese home islands would be within reach.

For Bywater to propose multiple amphibious landings in 1925 was a decidedly radical idea. Such tactics were looked upon as suicidal by most professionals. True enough, over the previous century or so there had been a bare handful of successful seaborne attacks against shore defenses. In 1801, a British army of 16,000 men intent on driving Napoleon from Egypt brazenly waded ashore in the face of fire at the Bay of Abukir—where Nelson had recently destroyed eleven French ships of the line at the so-called Battle of the Nile. The success of the British landing, however, owed a heavy debt to the incompetence of the French commanders.

In the first months of the American Civil War, the Union admiral Samuel Francis du Pont, a true believer in the combined operations of ships and troops against defended shore positions, scored a success at Port Royal Sound, South Carolina. Despite suffering heavy losses in a violent storm at sea, du Pont's fleet of seventy-seven ships bombarded two Confederate forts, compelled their evacuation, and sent ashore 10,000 troops to take possession of this strategic site from which he could control the coast and inland waterways of Florida, Georgia, and South Carolina. Two years later, however, repeated attempts by du Pont and John A. Dahlgren, the naval gun designer turned admiral, to attack the forts defending Charleston by sea were beaten back handily. The sinking of one of du Pont's ships by a mine was a taste of things to come.

In November 1915, Albert Parker Niblack, a crusty American naval officer who used to poke fun at himself as a "rampant militarist looking for trouble," had suggested to an audience of professional navy men in New York City that certain islands might be used in wartime as "stepping-stones across the Pacific." Bywater, as we have seen, quoted the lecture extensively in *Sea Power in the Pacific*; indeed, he may have heard Niblack deliver it in person. Bywater happened to be in New York City in the fall of 1915 when Niblack delivered his lecture. He was then working for British Naval Intelligence and had come to New York to investigate the fire-bombing of British merchant ships, and may have taken an evening off to attend a meeting in one of his old haunts while a reporter for the *Herald*.

Later that same year, however, all such tactics as Niblack had proposed fell into utter disrepute because of the Allied debacle at Gallipoli. It had been Winston Churchill's idea to land troops on the Gallipoli Peninsula of Turkey during the second year of the First World War. Churchill, then first lord of the Admiralty, had promoted the plan as a means of quickly neutralizing Turkey and forcing open the supply route to Russia, which was blocked in the Dardanelles. Nearly half-a-million British, French, Australian, and New Zealand troops were eventually landed at several points on Gallipoli. But the Turks defended their soil tenaciously. Allied casualties were appalling, and no fewer than three Allied battleships were sunk and three others seriously damaged in the action. Fisher, the first sea lord, resigned in protest. Churchill, however, was determined to press ahead. By January 1916, Allied forces had lost 250,000 men and were withdrawn. Churchill resigned in disgrace. The conclusion drawn by naval and military men throughout the world was that amphibious operations were bound to be a tactical nightmare and doomed to defeat.

Modern weapons, especially the mine, the submarine, and the airplane, seemed to have placed every advantage in the hands of the force resisting a seaborne attack. A single German U-boat off Gallipoli in 1915 had played havoc with British transports attempting to land troops, and professional observers agreed that if more than one submarine had been present the landings would have been impossible. It was also thought that land-based aircraft would be devastating in their attacks against troop transports, and, as a consequence, relatively weak Pacific island-nations such as New Zealand and Australia hailed the advent of air power as a "gift from the gods"—in the words of one Australian government official of the era—for prohibiting the possibility of a Japanese invasion.

So stinging was the memory of Gallipoli that even in the late 1930s, both Douglas MacArthur and Dwight Eisenhower, who headed an American military mission in the Philippines from 1935 to 1939, declared that amphibious warfare was impractical. MacArthur, who referred to the Gallipoli campaign as "that abortive undertaking," said the Philippines were safe from Japan because they could not be conquered unless Japan was willing to invest half-a-million troops, three years, and five billion dollars—an obvious impossibility. And Eisenhower, as he was departing from the Philippines in December 1939, cheered President Manuel L. Quezon with the words: "Successful penetration of a defended beach is the most difficult operation in warfare." Both generals held this belief until taught otherwise by the Japanese in 1941. Until then, neither American commander could have dreamed that in a few years' time, both would become past masters of this "impractical" type of warfare.

Bywater saw Gallipoli differently. In 1921, he had written: "After Gallipoli and Zeebrugge [the successful British raid on a German U-boat base] it would be unsafe to say that any fortified position can be made impregnable to a storming party of trained fighting men inspired with an iron will to conquer." His meaning was that the Allied forces had in fact made it ashore at both Gallipoli and Zeebrugge, and, whatever their losses, they could have held their ground if properly led and supplied. Bywater was also aware that amphibious landings had been a regular feature of Japanese Army exercises for many years, and that in their wars against China in 1894–95 and Russia a decade later, the Japanese had demonstrated great proficiency in landing large numbers of foot soldiers and heavy equipment. The Americans, he reasoned, could learn to do the job equally well.

As Bywater studied his charts, three stepping-stone routes across the Pacific seemed possible. First, there was the northern pathway via Alaska and the Aleutian Islands to the northern Japanese island of Hokkaido. Although this was the shortest of the three routes, it was the least desirable, "owing to weather conditions in the waters to be traversed," he stated in the book he had now started to write. Second, a lunge across the Central Pacific from Hawaii to Midway to Wake to Guam and then to Japan was unwise because the route would be blocked by the Japanese forces after Guam had been seized at the outset of hostilities. Further-more, Midway was "too remote from Japanese waters" and Wake Island was "a mere coral atoll without anchorage facilities for large ships." This left the southern route through the American Samoan Islands to the Marshall and Caroline islands and then to the Philippines and Japan, and it was along this route that Bywater mapped out a complex, zigzag path of leaps, feints, and bypasses that would bring American forces to the gate of Japan.

Such was Bywater's answer to Roosevelt. In both the preface and the narrative of *The Great Pacific War*, he made unmistakable references to his debate with the future American president. "It is often averred," he stated in the preface, "that war between the United States and Japan is out of the question, if only because their respective fleets, divided as they are by thousands of miles of ocean with no intermediate bases of supply, could never get sufficiently close to engage. This, however, is probably a delusion, as I have endeavored to show."

There was another reference to Bywater's intellectual sparring part-ner of 1923 when he addressed the possibility of a "strategic deadlock"—the same expression Roosevelt had used in *Asia* magazine. "It is not to be wondered at that many observers prophesied that the Pacific campaign would speedily end in stalement," he wrote. "Peace must soon be negotiated, they said, because of the physical impossibility of deciding the issue by combat. This view was widely held in the United States. . . ."

BYWATER'S THREE NAVAL ROUTES TO JAPAN

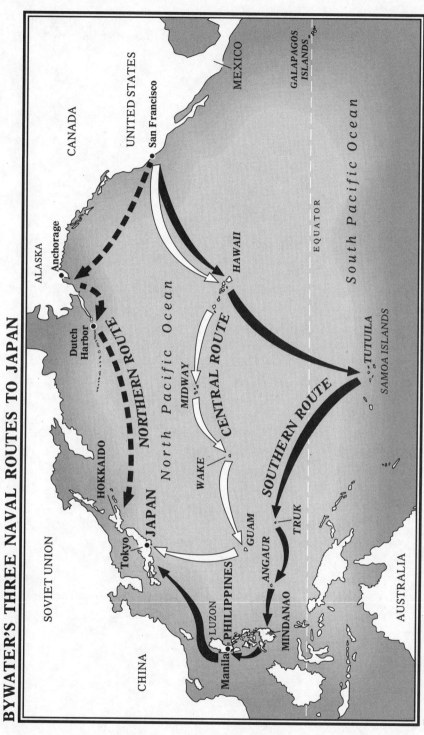

Bywater chose the Southern Route as the most practical.

CHAPTER 10

KESTON POND
MANEUVERS

THERE WAS STILL one thorny problem for Bywater to solve. Once the replenished American Pacific Fleet had leapfrogged across the ocean, how could it pin down and destroy the main body of the Japanese armada? If the Japanese force was weaker, it would not risk a major engagement. Historically, relatively weak fleets stayed within the protection of coastal defense guns, darting out now and then to inflict harm.

An inferior naval force nearly always possessed this catlike ability to slip away and avoid annihilation. The survivability of a lesser force was more certain at sea than on land. A superior army could usually track down, corner, and destroy or capture its opponent. At sea, however, the strength of a superior fleet diminished the farther it traveled from its nearest base; and since an inferior fleet could retire to the safety of a well-defended home port, decisive actions at sea were rare. In the Napoleonic wars, British and French squadrons fought only two all-out actions. In the First World War, the British Admiralty tried for two years to tempt the kaiser's relatively weak fleet to fight, and when it succeeded off Jutland, the Germans fled for safety as soon as Admiral Reinhard Scheer realized that he had met the main British force.

Furthermore, a fleet refusing to stand and fight did not lose its strategic value. So long as it existed, a weak naval force could launch a surprise attack, paralyzing offensive movements of a much stronger enemy and perhaps staving off an invasion of its homeland.

That extraordinary power of a "fleet-in-being," inferior though it might be, had been an axiom of naval strategy since the hit-and-run tactics of the British admiral Arthur Herbert, earl of Torrington, in the seventeenth century. Shying from a full fight with a stronger French force, Torrington raided the enemy often enough to keep it off balance. "Had I fought otherwise," he wrote, "our fleet had been totally lost, and the kingdom had lain open to invasion. As it was, most men were in fear that the French would invade; but I was always of another opinion, for I always said that whilst we had a fleet in being, they would not dare to make the attempt."

The principle was well illustrated in the First World War, before and after the Battle of Jutland. The existence of a German High Seas Fleet, though seldom venturing forth, made the British keep their Grand Fleet at Scapa Flow, the naval base in the Orkney Islands off northern Scotland nearest to the Germans in the North Sea. Once U-boats began to sink Allied merchantmen, it became onerous for the British to have their fleet tied down at Scapa. The British Admiralty might well have put its destroyers to good use in convoy protection, but it had to station most of them at Scapa Flow to guard the Grand Fleet against possible German raids. Furthermore, with the British fleet on sentry duty, it was not available to participate in other operations that might have hastened the end of the war. In fact, when Sir John Jellicoe, the commander of the Grand Fleet, was raised to the peerage by King George V in 1918, it prompted much guffawing in Germany when he chose the title of Viscount of Scapa. The Germans were delighted that the presence of their High Seas Fleet had caused Jellicoe to keep his superior force almost continuously at anchor at that desolate spot for four years. To the Germans, Jellicoe's choice of title was as if the exiled Napoleon had dubbed himself the Prince of Elba.

Bywater recognized that these same strategic principles would apply in a Japanese-American war. So long as Japan possessed a fleet-in-being, American forces would not risk landing troops on the Japanese home islands, nor could they compel Japan to surrender by means of a blockade.

Bywater had fretted about the problem in the very first article he wrote about Pacific strategy for the Dockyard Liar back in April 1920. At that time, when Japan was constructing a number of high-speed cruisers, the potential elusiveness of a Japanese fleet-in-being had seemed especially serious for the United States. The tonnage of the American Navy then greatly outweighed that of Japan, Bywater wrote, but "if such a force [as Japan is building] chose to avoid a general engagement it would be extremely difficult to bring to action."

There was always a possibility, of course, that the Americans could lure the Japanese fleet into battle by making a tempting target of some deliberately exposed warships, but surely the Japanese would be wary of any such trap, as were the Germans during the First World War. Another possibility was that the U.S. Navy might assemble its fleet for a demonstration off the coast of Japan. "This alternative might, or might not, bring about an action with the main Japanese Fleet," Bywater wrote in *Sea Power in the Pacific*, "[since] it is hardly to be expected that the Japanese would needlessly hazard the tremendous advantage they had won." Finally, if the Americans were brash enough to steam into Tokyo Bay and shell the capital, or make some other equally reckless stab, they might well provoke a general engagement, but such an action would be suicidal for the Americans. The Japanese fleet would attack while operating at maximum fighting efficiency in the immediate vicinity of its home base, whereas the Americans would come into action heavily loaded with fuel for the long voyage home and with their supply lines overextended. This condition would far outweigh any foreseeable differences in the strength of the two fleets.

Accordingly, the objective of the Americans had to be not merely forcing a fight but compelling one in a situation favorable to themselves. Unless the Americans could accomplish that feat, and then proceed to annihilate the Japanese battle fleet, they could not win the war. That problem haunted Bywater during the next few years. He chewed it over after hours at The Old Bell and The White Swan with members of the Fleet Street Press Gang and on the long walks he took with his friends McMurtrie and Ferraby. But his eventual solution to the problem, which was destined to have profound consequences eighteen years later in the midst of the Second World War, was accomplished, according to the last surviving members of the Fleet Street Press Gang, while war-gaming with his model ships on Keston Pond.

Like Frederick Jane and many members of the Press Gang, Bywater was an avid builder of model ships. His hobby must not be confused with that of the old tar who painstakingly constructs miniature square riggers inside bottles; Bywater's models were of the very latest fighting ships with up-to-the-minute detailing. Furthermore, they were not built for the mantelpiece. Made of a hollowed-out block of pine, either painted or in some cases sheathed with tinplate for the sake of realism, his ships had functioning engines powered by electric motors, toy steam engines, or the workings from clocks. They also had beautifully turned brass guns, which could be fired with an altogether satisfactory "bang!" Keston Pond, a couple of connected half-acre-sized lakes five miles from Bywater's home in Beckenham, served as the arena for the Saturday and Sunday afternoon maneuvers of his miniature navy.

Thanks to an article about Bywater's hobby that he wrote in 1921 for the monthly magazine the *Model Engineer and Electrician*, and to the recollections of his children and two members of the old Fleet Street Press Gang, considerable detail about his "fleet" can be learned. Bywater owned about a dozen model warships, which he kept stored on the bookshelves of his attic study at 23 Whitmore Road. These models included a four-and-a-half-foot, steam-propelled battleship that was "very heavily armed with working ordnance," according to his article; also, "an armored cruiser, steam-driven, carrying two working guns and fitted with a steel armor belt, bulkheads, and much internal subdivision; an electric torpedo boat fitted with a working model submerged gun, and various other craft."

Most of these models had been constructed by Bywater himself, using plans taken from the scale drawings published in *Jane's Fighting Ships* and Brassey's *Naval Annual*. Some of his improvisations were ingenious. He constructed miniature searchlights, for example, from the metal ends of light bulbs with wristwatch glasses used for lenses. Other parts were purchased from Stevens' Model Dockyard, at 22 Aldgate in London. This mecca for model builders, which boasted of offering "the largest and finest stock in the world," carried on its shelves everything from model hulls fitted with steam engines, turbines, electric motors, and clockworks to accessories such as miniature steam winches, propellers, rudders, stanchions, capstans, ventilators, bollards, chains, masts, flags, and functional torpedo tubes.

"These models may be called 'toys' by the scornful," Bywater once wrote in an article about the interest of naval men in model-making, "but, in reality, they are something more. They are evidence of the amount of mechanical genius and love of engineering that is latent in our country." In another article arguing the importance of his hobby, Bywater wrote that "a liberal education" could be had in London by studying the miniature warships at the Science Museum, the Royal Naval Museum in Greenwich, the Imperial War Museum, and the Royal United Service Museum. He extolled London as "easily the first among cities of the world" in terms of the number and variety of ship models on display. Especially noteworthy at the Royal Naval Museum, he observed, was "a most interesting series of models of Japanese warships, new and old, this collection having been presented in 1910 by the Japanese Government, 'as a token of their sincere gratitude for the kindness and courtesy which Japanese constructors and engineers have experienced at the hands of the authorities of the Royal Naval College on the occasion of their studies there.' " Evidently, Bywater had spent long hours poring over these exhibitions.

He had "dabbled in naval models" since 1907, Bywater related. That was the year in which he had joined his brother Ulysses in Dresden, and although the Germans were then keen model warship builders who might well have stimulated his interest, it is likely that Bywater's fascination originated even earlier. Model ship–building was popular in the United States when Bywater lived in Boston and Brooklyn. Everyone from aristocrats such as Franklin Roosevelt to blacksmiths and bank tellers seemed caught up in the hobby.

After returning to England, Bywater encountered members of the Model Engineering Club of London who went to extraordinary lengths to add realistic or interesting details to their ships. One member, for example, painstakingly constructed miniature anchors for his model from pieces of metal taken from a German Zeppelin shot down over England during the First World War. Another member decked out his vessel with functioning searchlights, range finders, circulating fans, compass, and ship's wheel—all of his own manufacture. Bywater, however, kept such detailing to a minimum. "Experience has shown," he wrote in 1921, "a multiplicity of 'gadgets' to be a nuisance in a working model, and they should therefore be reduced to the minimum consistent with the character of the ship." Clearly, Bywater was interested in performance.

To this end, his model ships possessed remarkable guidance systems that could be preset so that a considerable fleet could be made to cruise in formation or stage a sea battle. On some occasions at Keston Pond, Bywater would program his ships to reenact a classic fight such as Tsushima, with the Japanese squadron "crossing the T" at precisely the right moment. He could also reenact Jutland and have the German warships execute the famous *Gefechtskertwendung* (battle-turnabout) —the complex and risky maneuver that Admiral Scheer had employed to make a hasty exit from the scene of fighting. Other times, Bywater would use his models to experiment with fresh ideas about tactics or strategy. Partly, of course, his war games were an expression of boyish delight in working models, but they had a distinctly serious purpose as well. It was with his model warships that Bywater "invented" naval strategy.

He had learned the basic techniques of war-gaming by playing Frederick Jane's Naval War Game. Jane's invention was actually the first sophisticated modern war game to be developed. It preceded by more than a decade H. G. Wells's famous *Kriegspiel* (a land war game played with model soldiers and artillery pieces), and thus Jane's game may be considered the earliest ancestor of present-day war games played at such facilities as the Center for War Gaming at the Naval War College in Newport, Rhode Island, in which as many as 275 participants, seated at video terminals, test the latest war-contingency plans.

Jane had created his game—a parlor game as opposed to Bywater's outdoor sport—in 1899, and he marketed it in boxed sets consisting of a large supply of big, blue cards ("Sea Squares") marked with grid lines, a dozen model ships, a rule book, damage record cards, and other equipment. The Naval War Game could be purchased in several sizes, but since the least expensive set cost three guineas—about two weeks' wages in 1900—and required a table "not less than 10 feet by 8 feet," it was never popular except among professional naval officers who played it at the War College and specialists, such as the members of the Fleet Street Press Gang. In all probability, Bywater played it while searching for the way in which a superior American fleet might bring to battle the Japanese squadron.

The object of the Naval War Game, Jane explained in his last, revised rule book, published in 1912, was "to afford a means of working out any strategical problems or theories," and "to allow the working out of any particular tactical theories under conditions as nearly as possible resembling real war in miniature," and finally "to teach in the easiest and most interesting manner the guns, armor, capabilities, etc. etc. of all warships."

In one particularly instructive game that Jane described, three torpedo boats attacked four battleships. It was determined that two of the attackers were sunk immediately. The third torpedo boat got close enough to the battleships to launch two torpedoes, but both torpedoes missed. And then, all the concentrated fire from the four battleships missed the third torpedo boat as it fled from the scene. "It is not argued that such incidents are aught but abnormal," wrote Jane, "but it is just the chance of some abnormal and impossible-to-be-foreseen result that characterizes real war as opposed to tactical exercises." The lesson he deduced from this case, as well as from countless other instances when he played his game, was that "the true test of a war plan is, perhaps, its ability to succeed despite the occurrence of things outside calculation." In other words, a good war plan must be foolproof; it must bring to bear a force so overwhelming that even if many men and warships fail to carry out their missions, the plan as a whole will bludgeon through successfully.

It was a typically British approach to naval strategy, one that befitted a great power that had at its disposal the largest and mightiest navy ever built up to that time. With power to spare, British strategy made a virtue of overkill. Such thinking, of course, contrasted with that of Japanese strategists, many of whom counted on such qualities as *issho kemmei* (total commitment) to help them triumph over an opponent with a greater fleet. Bywater, it is interesting to note, understood this difference between British and Japanese approaches to strategy and was able to "think in Japanese" when he conceived of the bold and extremely risky gambit with which he thought Japan was likely to start a war against the United States.

Playing Jane's war game doubtless sharpened Bywater's naval intellect, but it was his own model-warship maneuvers on Keston Pond that helped him most to solve the problem of how an American fleet could bring to action a Japanese naval force in the Pacific. Bywater's game, like Jane's, used miniature simulation as a means of practicing the real thing, but otherwise they were as different as poker and golf. Jane's was a parlor game; Bywater's a field exercise. Furthermore, since the effect of imaginary gunfire was impossible to estimate in a fluid situation in which the distance between moving models could not be measured accurately, the emphasis of Bywater's games inevitably was on concept rather than maneuver, and thus on strategy as opposed to tactics.

When Bywater planned large-scale games on Keston Pond, he required a number of assistants. From the Fleet Street Press Gang, McMurtrie, Ferraby, and Prendergast were frequently on hand. Prendergast—tall, thin, and squinting to read lips when others spoke— often brought along a few ship models of his own. Bywater's son and daughter, Robin and Sylvia, were occasional helpers, as well. A key participant, who served as armorer, was Edward L. Goodman, a sad-eyed older man with a large, drooping mustache who was foreign editor of the *Daily Telegraph* and a great model-warship fancier. Goodman lived in Beckenham near Bywater and had an elaborate machine shop in his basement that included a precision lathe on which the miniature brass barrels of the ships' guns were turned. Goodman's guns could be set to fire at predetermined times by varying the length of the fuse that would ignite their charges.

The admiral who planned the maneuvers, of course, was Bywater himself. One of his naval war games was recorded in a story he wrote in 1923 about an imaginary battle involving a large number of model warships. Bywater's son recalls reading the typewritten manuscript that year during a brief hospitalization, but no record of it can be found. Still, one can imagine how Bywater solved the "fleet-in-being" problem in the Pacific with his model maneuvers on Keston Pond. Suppose, for example, that Prendergast and McMurtrie have been positioned on the south shore of the pond and from there release five three-foot-long cruisers powered by the workings of old clocks. In Bywater's mind, these five toy vessels represent the Imperial Japanese battle fleet, consisting of a dozen battleships and aircraft carriers, including *Mutsu, Nagato, Kaga,* and *Akagi*, some two dozen cruisers, and two destroyer flotillas plus numerous auxiliaries.

Now from the north end of the pond, Bywater, Ferraby, and Goodman launch six sleek, four-foot-long battleships, one of them a German model acquired in Dresden and the others of more recent construction. Bywater sees this group as representing a vast armada. In his mind's eye, there are the forms of ships spread across a vast sea. The aircraft carriers *Lexington*, *Saratoga*, and *Alaska* are in the van, followed by the heavyweight sluggers—the battleships *Colorado, Maryland, West Virginia, California, Tennessee, Arizona, Texas*, and *Wyoming*. Cruiser, destroyer, and submarine squadrons have formed a screen around the capital ships.

This huge American armada bears down on a patch of lily pads near the southern end of the pond, behind which the Japanese fleet is maneuvering. When the American ships are almost upon the lily pads, the Japanese fleet suddenly wheels east and, with a prolonged crackle, discharges its guns. Corks whiz through the air, and smoke from burned black powder briefly hovers over the warships and then drifts away. Now the American ships reply. Contact has been established. A fleet engagement has begun!

After *Colorado* fires her fourth three-gun salvo, as Bywater imagines it, the spotting officer in "the birdbath" on her mast reports a "straddle" of the Japanese mastodon *Mutsu*—the great warship rescued from destruction by Tomosaburo Kato at the Washington Conference. A straddle indicates that the shells in this last salvo have fallen to either side of *Mutsu* because of minute differences in the individual guns on *Colorado*. When that occurs, the order for "rapid fire" is given. Now, all nine of *Colorado*'s big guns are given identical range and bearings and come into action simultaneously. Each nine-gun salvo flings 24 tons of steel at the enemy every forty seconds. Shortly, *Maryland* and *West Virginia* join *Colorado* in visiting a storm of blows on *Mutsu*. Imagining this line of gray leviathans firing at its utmost, it seems to Bywater as if the sides of the American battleships are exploding at regular intervals in gouts of flame and brown smoke. *Mutsu* shudders as shells that have descended at a steep angle penetrate her relatively thin decks and explode with stunning force inside. Now the Japanese battleships *Nagato* and *Kaga* take hits as well.

Meanwhile, the 16-inch guns of *Kirishima* have found their mark in the American cruiser squadron. Within seconds, *Troy* becomes a shattered hulk, lying on her beam ends, with half her crew dead or wounded. *Cleveland* receives a mortal wound and *Denver* and *Wilmington* are stopped dead in the water.

Suddenly Bywater awakens from his daydream. The decisive engagement that he has been imagining, he now recognizes, might have been brought about by the American fleet's close approach to an island represented by the lily pads. What if such an island were close to the Japanese homeland—so close that it would provide a base from which the Americans could launch an attack against Japanese-held Guam, the Philippines, or indeed against Japan itself? Under no circumstances could the Japanese permit the Americans to seize any such threatening position. If faced with a naval advance of this character, and convinced that the Americans intended to land troops, the Japanese commander would be obliged to say: "This far and no farther." And then he would have no choice but to back up his defiance with the full might of the Imperial Navy.

Bywater had solved the last naval puzzle of the Pacific.

It was a novel and daring gambit because in these years, amphibious warfare—forcible entry from the ocean against a well-defended coast—was thought of by most military men as suicidal. But in this, as will be evident, Bywater had seen into the future with clarity. In the book he was now writing, he expressed the strategy thus: the American problem was "to devise a method of compelling the Japanese fleet to fight under conditions favorable to the American cause. . . . Difficult as the problem appeared to be, it was not deemed insoluble." Accordingly, the Americans should come up with a plan to threaten to seize the island of Yap in the Caroline chain, which the Japanese could not help but recognize as "a fortress which sooner or later might become an impregnable stronghold from which an American fleet could dominate their [Japan's] own waters and menace the very threshold of Dai Nippon itself."

Bywater continued:

> The [American] expedition was to sail for Yap, and not merely approach within range of the island, but so maneuver as to suggest that a landing was about to be attempted. The port was to be

shelled. . . . The sham attack was to be continued for several hours, and at a suitable opportunity three of the "transports" would move in as though about to disembark troops. . . . In the meantime, news of the attack would promptly reach Japanese headquarters at Manila. . . . There was scarcely any doubt that the Japanese battle fleet would hasten at full speed to relieve Yap. They might suspect a strategem, it was true, but having no means of verifying that suspicion they would almost certainly elect to take the risk. . . . Such, then, were the dispositions which, it was hoped, would compel the enemy to accept action in waters remote from his bases and thus enable a decisive result to be obtained.

CHAPTER
11

LES GUERRES IMAGINAIRES

ONCE BYWATER HAD solved the last tactical problem posed by a Japanese-American war, he had to decide how best to present his ideas in writing. Upon reflection, he thought it "necessary to have recourse to the medium of fiction," as he put it in the preface to his new book.

That was not such an odd choice as it may seem. Bywater had never written a novel, but had been intrigued by imaginary accounts of "the next war" popular at the turn of the century. Those books and articles—prompted by new inventions such as the torpedo, tank, military balloon, airplane, and submarine, and by a naval arms race in Europe —had come along so thick and fast that literary critics gave the genre a name: *les guerres imaginaires* or *der Zukunftskrieg*.

The most common examples were fantasies that thrilled readers with accounts of machines boring through the earth faster than a galloping horse, or of fleets of battleships cruising majestically through the clouds held aloft by Montgolfier balloons. One tale described a weapon called "controllable lightning," which in a flash reduced an ironclad man-of-war to a wisp of steam; another told of "automosinkers," motor-propelled balloons capable of mass destruction. In 1908, a German author named Ferdinand H. Grautoff described, with a mixture of outrageous fantasy and seeming clairvoyance, Japanese forces landing in California and then dealing a stunning defeat at Hilgard, Oregon, to American troops commanded by a certain "General MacArthur." Throughout the rest of the book, General MacArthur is heard exhorting his troops with the battle cry "Remember Hilgard!" until finally the "Yellow Peril" is pushed back into the sea.

What interested Bywater was a subcategory of *les guerres imaginaires* written by professional military or naval men who sought to explore the future by meticulously extrapolating present realities and trends and shaping their vision with a sophisticated political and historical analysis. What these authors lacked in literary skill they hoped to make up for with technical expertise and worldly knowledge. Many of them, like Bywater, were serious in their desire to prevent a future war by accurately conveying the horrors it would bring.

The first professional military man in modern times to try his hand at *les guerres imaginaires* was Sir George Tomkyns Chesney, a lieutenant colonel in the British Royal Engineers, who in 1871 published a short story entitled "The Battle of Dorking" in *Blackwood's Magazine*. Bismarck's unification of the German states had aroused fear in Britain, and Chesney's story plausibly foretold a German invasion of the British Isles. It so upset the British Parliament that Gladstone, then the prime minister, felt compelled to take notice of Chesney and plead for caution against "alarmism."

A later example of the genre, and one that more clearly prepared the ground for Bywater, was *The Great War of 189—, A Forecast*, written in 1893 by the widely published naval commentator Rear Admiral Philip Colomb and a team of seven British experts on warfare and international affairs. He had assembled the best brains available, Colomb told his readers, in order to forecast "the most probable campaigns and acts of policy." As it turned out, the experts couldn't have been more wrongheaded; they forecast a war in which France was allied with Russia against such unlikely bedfellows as Germany and Great Britain. Nevertheless, the book had an authoritative ring to it, being filled with technically precise descriptions of actual warships, fortifications, and weapons. All this—even Colomb's title—proved instructive to Bywater.

He also must have been familiar with the similarly titled *The Great Naval War of 1887*, written in 1886 by Sir William Laird Clowes and Commander Charles N. Robinson, later the naval correspondent of the London *Times*, whom Bywater came to know during his early days in the Fleet Street Press Gang. This fifty-eight-page broadside had the object of "waking up the British public to a consciousness of the unsatisfactory want of readiness of the Imperial Navy," according to the authors' preface. Here, too, the exact names, tonnages, and fighting capabilities of actual warships were used, but whereas Colomb and his colleagues had reassuringly arranged to have Britain gain the upper hand by defeating the French Navy in a great sea battle off the coast of Sardinia, Clowes and Robinson had the British Navy suffer a humiliating defeat at the hands of the French. They blamed the disaster on "years of indifference, mismanagement and parsimony," and they seem to have made their point because by the time the second edition of Clowes and Robinson's broadside was published in 1887, the authors cheerfully reported that "the Navy has been expanded and the danger foreseen is pretty much gone."

The most commercially successful of the genre up to its time was *The Valor of Ignorance*. Published in 1909 by Homer Lea, it was (after Grautoff) the first book-length forecast of a Japanese-American war. Because of its sensational subject and mesmerizing, high-blown rhetoric, the book sold out several editions and won a good many fervent admirers. Lea himself was what the newspapers of the day called "good copy." A boyish-looking hunchback from California, he ventured to China in 1900 in the midst of Sun Yat-sen's revolution, which would soon bring down the Manchu dynasty. Although lacking credentials (the U.S. State Department had politely demurred when Lea asked for a portfolio of some sort), he appears to have been well received, at least partly because hunchbacks were venerated in China at the time. In a few years, Lea returned to the United States wearing a heavily decorated Chinese general's uniform (of uncertain origin), and he embarked on a career as an author, military expert, Asian specialist, and all-purpose seer. His book, the first of two, was filled with harebrained ideas, including diatribes against "naturalized Americans," democracy, and individualism. Not surprisingly, *The Valor of Ignorance* became a favorite of Kaiser Wilhelm, and in 1910 the kaiser invited Lea to attend the German Army maneuvers that year. A generation later, Adolf Hitler admiringly quoted Lea in *Mein Kampf* on the supposed inability of democracies to defend themselves.

Despite Lea's pretensions to military expertise, *The Valor of Ignorance* was also replete with strategic and political nonsense. In describing the "inevitable" war between Japan and the United States, he predicted that within twenty-four hours of Japan's declaration of war, the U.S. Marines defending Hawaii would simply "disappear." Japanese immigrants in Hawaii, he explained, would eliminate the Marines and seize control. In addition, as soon as the Philippines and Hawaii were under her thumb, Japan would dispatch an army of 100,000 men to the West Coast of the United States. In three months' time, he assured his readers, Japanese forces would control California, Oregon, Washington, and Alaska, and there would be no way of shaking off the yellow horde until the American people came to their senses, recognized that their experiment with democracy had been folly, and established a monarchy.

So irritated was Bywater by *The Valor of Ignorance* that he had gone out of his way to deplore it in *Sea Power in the Pacific*. "More harm than good has been done by the well-meant efforts of writers such as Homer Lea," he declared, "whose sensational forecast of Japanese operations against the United States was so demonstrably absurd that it encouraged American public opinion to dismiss the whole subject as an idle scare."

Another example of the kind of sensationalism Bywater had no patience with happened to have been coauthored by someone he admired. In 1906, H. W. Wilson, naval correspondent of the London *Daily Mail* and author of *Ironclads in Action*, which Bywater considered "by far the most informative work on modern naval warfare" of its time, felt so frustrated by what he regarded as "our utter unpreparedness for war" that he collaborated with William Le Queux (an English writer with a French name) on a war prophecy they called *The Invasion of 1910*. In the heat of their writing, Wilson and Le Queux went overboard. Not only did they foresee the kaiser's navy defeating the Royal Navy, but they had German troops invade England, capture London, and dictate harsh peace terms before departing. Bywater would soon strike out against all such "sensational war narratives."

The book that came the closest to serving as a model for *The Great*

Pacific War was *The War Inevitable*, a 313-page novel published in 1908 that accurately forecast a general war in Europe. The author of this crudely written yet astonishingly prophetic book was Alan H. Burgoyne, a wealthy shipping agent and importer who was to become one of the Royal Navy's most ardent champions in Parliament. Bywater and Burgoyne were well acquainted. Burgoyne had been president of the Navy League at the time Bywater was living in Germany and started writing for the league's monthly publication, the *Navy*. Between 1909 and 1915, Burgoyne served as editor of the *Navy League Annual*, when Bywater contributed a steady flow of essays to those volumes. In 1911, it was probably Burgoyne who apprised Sir John Fisher, then the uniformed head of the Royal Navy, of Bywater's exceptional value as an undercover agent in Germany. Very likely Burgoyne also figured into the British Secret Service apparatus; in 1903, while on a mysterious mission to Port Arthur, he was arrested as a spy and briefly imprisoned by the Russians.

Burgoyne's novel, published at a time when most Britons were preoccupied with their golf games and lawn parties and little concerned with foreign affairs, daringly forecast a worldwide conflict in which the chief adversaries were Great Britain and Germany. In an effort to make his story as believable as possible, Burgoyne started the narrative by describing a darkening international scene. There is a period of "ever increasing friction between England and Germany," and, in a last-ditch effort to calm the situation, a marriage is arranged between a Hohenzollern prince and an English princess. Unfortunately, animosities in the two nations already run so deep that the German prince is publicly insulted when he arrives in London. In the midst of preparations for the royal wedding, a squadron of German torpedo boats makes a surprise attack on the British fleet at Portsmouth, precisely as Japanese torpedo boats had struck the Russian Asiatic Squadron at Port Arthur four years before. "Your Majesty," a messenger tells the king of England at Buckingham Palace, dramatizing what had become a recurrent nightmare in England, "the British Navy has been sunk at its moorings. Twenty minutes ago a wire came from Portsmouth stating that our finest and latest ships and in addition most of the [visiting] Japanese vessels, were torpedoed by swarms of strange craft coming from every direction. Oh, my God! My God!"

This dastardly attack sends to the bottom five British battleships and four cruisers. With lightning speed, the Germans follow up their naval success by invading England—acting out yet another British nightmare that had earlier found its way into print in Erskine Childers's 1903 novel *The Riddle of the Sands* as well as Le Queux and Wilson's *The Invasion of 1910*, among others. British resistance is stiff and spirited. "Tike that, you German sausage, and damn your cheek for comin' 'ere," cries a Cockney defender as he bayonets an invader. But within a month, the Germans have more than a million men ashore and control most of southeastern England.

The United States offers to help, but the plucky British refuse. Meanwhile, the Portsmouth Dockyard has been humming with activity. Mighty British men-of-war, most of which had been sunk in shallow water, are being raised and repaired, and soon a rebuilt British armada steams out to sea to engage the German fleet. The Germans are superior in number of ships but significantly weaker in heavy-caliber guns. "And it was these guns," Burgoyne told his readers, pressing a favorite thesis, "that told at Tsushima, when Togo placed himself on a pedestal of fame beside our own Admirals of a glorious past."

Once the opposing fleets come within sight of each other, the British commander exploits his advantage. He engages the Germans at a distance beyond the range of their medium-caliber guns. British fire power is thus overwhelming and the battle becomes "another Tsushima," except that the Germans hoist the white flag of surrender before all of their ships are lost.

Just at this moment, a Japanese squadron commanded by none other than Admiral Togo arrives on the scene, since Japan had declared war against Germany after the initial German torpedo-boat attack unwisely sunk the Japanese battleship that had just delivered the Mikado on a royal visit to England. The victorious allies then escort the battered remnant of the German fleet into captivity, and, with Britain once again mistress of the seas, the German expeditionary force on English soil quickly surrenders.

Apart from his overreaching obsession with a German invasion, Burgoyne's book contains a number of gaffes. For one thing, he diminished whatever plausibility his story achieved by including references to the supposed roles played by a number of real people. Besides Admiral Togo, there are appearances in *The War Inevitable* of the German kaiser, complete with his partially paralyzed arm; Admiral Alfred von Tirpitz, the chief of the German Navy; Sir Percy Scott, the British gunnery expert; and Field Marshal Horatio Herbert Kitchener, the army commander who would soon become Britain's war minister. Such silliness only served to remind the reader of the artificial nature of the book. Furthermore, while Burgoyne's writing style was for the most part straightforward, at moments of drama when the author decided that special effects were called for, his prose boiled madly. In describing the deadly rain of shell on the German fleet at the climatic sea battle, Burgoyne threw caution —and syntax—to the wind:

> Their contour, a moment before clear against the dawning sky, fled at a nod; a blurred, hysteric rush of choking yellow vapours, belching great gerbs of scarlet bloody tongues, groaning in travail as a mountain forge of nature, rushed to the upper skies. Out of each sweltering cauldron of boiling water spread rain-wise with fearsome spurt. Below, the calm sea gurgled, soughed and flopped; now rose in geysers high as church built spires, mountains of water bubbling, churning, spluttering; now fell again in ton-weights, sploshing the hidden decks, adding a watery inferno to a hell of fire, forcing new coils of stenchful darting smoke far over the adjacent sea. Roar on roar in a sudden quick profusion came from the stricken masses; howling shrieks rose to God through the baneful fumes as a thousand suffering souls cursed out their lives to a horror-struck Maker.

If anyone was horror-struck, it would have been Bywater, cringing at the literary huffing and puffing of his mentor. Still, setting aside its obvious faults, *The War Inevitable* had virtues that Bywater admired. The book was remarkably prophetic about the aggressive intentions of Germany and the coming of a general conflagration in Europe. In its better passages, Burgoyne's carefully detailed and knowing descriptions of actual warships and their capabilities imparted a sense of historical truth to the story. And finally, although Burgoyne lacked Bywater's gift for inventing strategy, and could only imitate the last war (the Russo-Japanese War), he had a thorough command of naval science and could foresee the long-range naval duels that would soon take place at Coronel, Jutland, and the Falkland Islands—something that even H. G. Wells completely missed in his otherwise prophetic *The War in the Air*, which was published in the same year as Burgoyne's novel.

Like Burgoyne, Bywater would produce a narrative of about 300 pages in length. Bywater's purpose, also, would be to warn the world of the danger of a possible future war. Like Burgoyne, Bywater would extrapolate recent history to set the stage for the conflict. And finally, like Burgoyne, he would employ real warships in actual geographical settings and make strategic and tactical decisions in an effort to simulate the actual course of a future war.

Still, Bywater's very first foray into *les guerres imaginaires* showed little respect for *The War Inevitable*. It was, in fact, intended to puncture Burgoyne's inflated fear of invasion, and—daringly—was written for the *Navy League Annual* which Burgoyne edited. Entitled "Possible Features of a North Sea Campaign," Bywater's object, he stated, was to figure out what might occur "if it should happen that the [British] Empire was engaged in a great European war." He, too, began by assuming a surprise attack by Germany: "Either directly prior or subsequent to the declaration of war, a determined torpedo attack will be made on some British naval base, with the dual object of reducing our capital-ship strength and of striking terror and dismay into the heart of the nation."

Next, Bywater predicted that the German Navy would stage a number of raids against the British coast in an effort to panic the public and force the Admiralty to pursue the attackers and thus divide the fleet. Naturally, such "wild goose chases" would render the British fleet vulnerable to piecemeal destruction by the smaller but well-concentrated German fleet. Here again, Bywater was prophetic. The actual German raids on Gorleston, Scarborough, and Hartlepools in the early months of 1914 were attempts to do precisely what he had foreseen.

Bywater devoted the remainder of his essay to the specter of a German invasion of the British Isles, vigorously arguing that the invasions described in many previously published "sensational war narratives" were farfetched. He did not name specific authors, but it must have been clear to the readers of the *Navy League Annual*—a hefty tome addressed to specialists—that he had in mind all those from Chesney, Childers, and Wilson to his present editor, Alan Burgoyne. To make his case, Bywater began by explaining that Germany would be extremely unlikely to risk an army that had been created "to keep inviolate the soil of the Fatherland" in an expedition that, "if it failed in the slightest degree, would probably mean the sacrifice of hundreds of thousands of the most valuable lives without any compensating advantage whatsoever." Furthermore, he went on to say, an invasion of Britain could not be undertaken without "the practical annihilation" of the British fleet—not the likeliest of eventualities. Yet even if the British Navy were completely destroyed, he continued, Germany would be prevented from launching an invasion by immense logistical obstacles, such as those posed by the difficulty of transporting three or four German army corps across the Channel. Consequently, concluded Bywater: "If war should come within the next few years and take a course devoid of supernatural phenomena, it is hard to believe that the invasion of England will be a feature of it." So much for licking the boots of his editor!

This essay went far to establish the pattern for a number of futuristic naval scenarios Bywater would write. Prophecy, as he saw it, was not a matter of giving free play to one's fancy or fear; it was a disciplined undertaking that called for a mastery of current events and political trends, a thorough knowledge of geography and national power, a sound understanding of the capabilities of modern arms, and a hardheaded, unsentimental application of all of these matters to likely circumstances.

Bywater again ventured into *les guerres imaginaires* in the midst of the First World War, following the battle of Coronel, at which the German cruisers *Scharnhorst* and *Gneisenau* sent two British cruisers to the bottom without a trace. Writing for the *Navy*, he conjured up a "mental picture" of the action, complete with a detailed description of the havoc wrought by each 8.2-inch German shell that found its mark. A comparison of this article with German accounts of Coronel, which became available after the war's end, shows Bywater's guesswork to be amazingly accurate.

A few years later, he constructed the story of an imaginary naval battle for a boys' magazine. And then, in 1921, his book *Sea Power in the Pacific* included a penultimate chapter entitled "Possible Features of a War in the Pacific," which employed techniques similar to those used in his essay "Possible Features of a North Sea Campaign." Two years afterward, he published an article in the *Navy* in which he tried to imagine the naval situation "if war had been averted in 1914." His conclusion was that Great Britain and Germany would have gone ahead building "two rival fleets, each of tremendous strength." As for the outcome, Bywater thought war would be inevitable because "the strain would have become intolerable."

This ten-year-long fascination with the possibility of examining the unknown or the future by means of meticulously extrapolating data from the present well prepared Bywater for writing his first "novel." He was, of course, aware of the pitfalls. He knew that forecasts of future wars are usually so fallacious that Burgoyne had become one of the more successful prophets simply by having named Germany and Britain as future adversaries.

There were, however, significant differences between Bywater and virtually all of the other modern Cassandras. Bywater had a genius for inventing naval strategy. It was this talent that would enable him to conceive of—among other things—an unprecedented disaster for the United States Navy, a nearly invulnerable Pacific empire for Japan, a daring yet completely successful employment of the techniques of amphibious warfare, and an ingenious means whereby a superior fleet could compel a weaker fleet-in-being to accept battle. All these would make unique the book he had now commenced to write.

CHAPTER
12

"IT MIGHT FOMENT TROUBLE"

IN THE SPRING of 1924, Bywater received two final nudges—both from unexpected quarters—to get on with the writing of his new book. In March, he became persona non grata with the Royal Navy—a state of affairs that restricted his access to news and prompted him to seek fresh markets for his writing. Two months later, something suddenly drew him to the United States. The reason for this trip remains a mystery—it may have been a final clandestine mission for the British Secret Service or Naval Intelligence—but, whatever prompted it, the visit to America put him in an advantageous position to pursue research for the book, and also to find a publisher for it.

Bywater's falling out with the navy occurred, according to his son, when he inadvertently published classified information. Although the details have long since been weeded from Admiralty records, his offense may have been revealing the exact surface and subsurface displacement of Britain's newest and largest submarine *X–1* in an article for the *Navy*.

Called to account, Bywater said he had found the information—
whatever it was—in a German newspaper, and thus had not breached
security by publishing it again. Who, he argued, was more sensitive than
he to national security, alluding to his years in the Secret Service and
Naval Intelligence? But someone in the Admiralty insisted Bywater be
made an example of. Sir Mansfield Cumming, who might have intervened, had died two years earlier, and Bywater's other friends could not
help in this instance. Consequently, the Department of Naval Intelligence
"stopped" his "facilities as a journalist," according to the huge, leather-
bound *Index of Admiralty Correspondence* for the year 1924. The result
was that Bywater could no longer enter a Royal Dockyard, board one
of His Majesty's ships, nor set foot in an Admiralty office. "They're
treating me like a leper," he told his son.

The consequences of being made an outcast seemed dire. Over the
past sixteen years, he had been earning a substantial portion of his
income by writing once a month for the Dockyard Liar and the *Navy*
—both of which depended on the goodwill of the Admiralty for their
access to news. Bywater felt he could not ask his friends in those editorial
offices to risk the wrath of the sea lords by continuing to publish his
work. His voluntary withdrawal was reported as a news item in the
Proceedings of the U.S. Naval Institute: "Mr. Hector C. Bywater, the
well-known naval critic, whose articles are so frequently quoted in the
Institute *Proceedings*, is now writing as an independent writer, having
severed his connection recently with the *Naval & Military Record*."

He continued to function as European naval correspondent for the
Baltimore *Sun*, and since 1923 had been naval correspondent for the
London *Daily News* and the weekly *Observer*, but it was an open question as to how long he could go on effectively in these positions with
official sources of information shut off. Consequently, the prospect of
devoting himself to writing about an imaginary war in the Pacific—the
idea that had obsessed him for many months now—seemed providential.

Bywater soon found himself holed up in the attic of the red-brick
house at 23 Whitmore Road in suburban Beckenham plotting the course
of the Pacific war. The first question he had to ask himself was: What
would prompt the fighting to begin? From his reading of Japanese history
and current affairs, he had come to believe that the military caste in
Japan was destined to rise to power. He gleaned indications of this
possibility from a careful reading of the *Japan Advertiser* and *Japan*

Weekly Chronicle, the two English-language weeklies published in Japan to which he subscribed. Also influential were two books in his library written by English professors who had lived in Japan—*Japan at the Cross Roads* by A. M. Pooley and *Modern Japan* by William M. McGovern. Neither scholar was anti-Japanese (McGovern, in fact, became a Buddhist priest while living in Japan), but both reported unmistakable signs of the precariousness of civilian rule and the ominous rise of the Imperial Army and Navy.

Bywater was also impressed by an essay by the Japanese naval officer Hironori Mizuno that appeared in *Chuo Koren*, a monthly review published in Tokyo. He had come across a translation of the essay in 1923 and reviewed it in the Baltimore *Sun*. Mizuno, an unusual dissident in the Imperial Navy, feared that a Japanese-American war might break out over China. The right-wing leaders of Japan, he argued, were foolhardy to seek a stranglehold on China on the theory that Japan would need immediate access to China's natural resources in case of war against a major power when that very conduct would make a clash with the United States inevitable. "Japanese militarists," Mizuno wrote, "are . . . treading in the footsteps of Germany, who drew upon herself the censure and hostility of the world by trampling upon the neutrality of Belgium." Bywater had called Mizuno's essay "a powerful indictment of the main principles on which Japan's defensive policy is now based."

With this in mind, he commenced his story of a "tremendous conflict" between Japan and the United States by imagining that a group of "military chiefs" gain control of the Japanese government. They immediately adopt a policy "aimed at the virtual enslavement of China," he wrote, and in short order find themselves on a collision course with the United States over concessions to work iron and coal fields along the upper Yangtsze Valley. A series of diplomatic notes is exchanged— "bellicose" and "truculent" on the part of the Japanese, and "courteously worded" by the Americans, who are "determined to prevent the catastrophe of war." It is in the midst of these negotiations that Japan launches a surprise attack, rendering her declaration of war a few days later "a somewhat superfluous formality."

The Japanese attack is no mere replay of the Port Arthur raid of 1904, which risked no major units of the Imperial Navy and sought only the limited goal of throwing the enemy off balance. In contrast, Bywater imagined that the Japanese commander would assemble a major fleet of capital ships so as to hurl an "overwhelming" force at the American fleet, aiming at its "annihilation" during the first hours of war.

Accordingly, Bywater described the Japanese surprise-attack fleet as a major force consisting of the battle cruisers *Kongo* (the flagship), *Hiyei*, and *Kirishima*, the aircraft carrier *Hosho*, six light cruisers, and twenty-four destroyers. (*Hiyei* and *Kirishima* were, in fact, in the Pearl Harbor striking force in 1941.)

Under the command of an imaginary Vice Admiral Hiraga, this armada steams south hoping to catch the Americans napping at their base at Manila Bay, just as Dewey found the Spanish fleet there in 1898. (When Bywater was writing, Pearl Harbor had not yet been developed as a naval base.) At the eleventh hour, Rear Admiral Ribley, the imaginary commander-in-chief of the American squadron, takes his ships to sea because, as he puts it in a letter written just before his death, "we do not know if war has been declared, but . . . there is something in the air which tells us the fight is about to begin."

Ribley also correctly guesses that the Japanese admiral who opposes him will not bring troops along "until he has disposed of our squadron." Times had changed since the days of the Chemulpo attack in 1904, Bywater explained, when Japan made "a combined naval and military attack" against Korea, brashly wheeling in her troop transports directly behind a squadron of cruisers. Bywater had well remembered the event from Willmott Lewis's account of it when he was working as a junior reporter at the *New York Herald*. The Japanese, he felt sure, would not try anything so naked in the presence of an American "fleet-in-being." To do so, he wrote, would imply "a very imperfect knowledge of the laws of strategy on the part of the Japanese." Before any invasion could take place, the American fleet would have to be eliminated. As he expressed it in the book: "The destruction of Admiral Ribley's squadron [would leave] the way open for the invasion of the Philippines."

The first shots fired, in Bywater's drama, come from carrier-based aircraft. Japanese fighter-bombers are engaged by American planes, including a number that rise from the deck of the aircraft carrier *Curtiss*—in fact, the seaplane tender *Curtiss* was in action at Pearl Harbor in 1941. But these skirmishes are indecisive, and soon the Americans spy on the horizon the pagodalike foremasts of Japanese men-of-war bearing down on them. Shortly, Japanese heavy-caliber guns find the range of their targets. Taking a page from Burgoyne's *The War Inevi-*

table, Bywater described the devastating rain of bombs and shell in the words of an American naval officer whom he calls Lieutenant Elkins. Serving as an aide to Admiral Ribley, Elkins has a bird's-eye view of the action from the bridge of the flagship *Missoula*. Elkins relates:

> All around us the sea spouted and boiled; there were half a dozen terrific explosions in as many seconds; I heard one appalling crash as if a giant redwood tree had toppled athwart our deck; then there was a blaze of light, another ear-splitting crash, and everything came to an end for me. When I recovered my senses I was being dragged into a boat from the destroyer *Hulbert*. They told me the flagship had foundered at 11:30, having been practically blown to pieces. There were only six survivors besides myself. The Admiral had gone down with the ship; probably he had been killed by the shell that knocked me senseless. . . .
>
> From our boat, we could see the Japanese sweeping up the remnants of our squadron. Shortly before the flagship went down, the *Frederick* had blown up with all hands. We could see the *Denver* lying over on her beam ends, on fire from stem to stern. Nearby was the *Galveston* in action with Japanese light cruisers, which were absolutely pumping shell into her. Even as we watched she put her bows deep under, the stern came up, and she took her last dive. . . .
>
> While watching this scene, we heard the drone of airplanes above us, and looking up saw four machines which someone in the boat said were ours. They were, in fact, torpedo planes from the *Curtiss*, which ship, seeing herself about to be attacked by Japanese cruisers, had flown off all the planes then on deck. The *Curtiss* was sunk by gunfire shortly afterwards, but meanwhile her planes were making a last try for the enemy. We could see them making straight for the Japanese battle-cruisers, which were just visible from the boat. As we heard subsequently, two were shot down before reaching their objective; but one of the remaining machines got her torpedo fairly home on the *Hiyei*, while the other, by great good luck, torpedoed and sank the scout cruiser *Tatsuta*. The *Hiyei*, though seriously damaged, appears to have returned to Japan under her own steam.

Concluding the narrative with a flash of seeming clairvoyance, Bywater has Lieutenant Elkins report: "Our squadron had been wiped out and upwards of 2,500 gallant comrades had fallen." At Pearl Harbor in 1941 the precise number of American casualties was 2,638.

Bywater's object in meticulously describing this and subsequent actions of the war was not simply to create the illusion of reality for his readers. He was not writing a novel in the usual sense, although he employed characters, a story line, and other superficial conventions of fiction. Instead, like Colomb, Robinson, and Burgoyne before him, he was using precise geographical and topographical features of the contested areas, and the exact name, tonnage, fuel range, and arms and armor capabilities of real warships and aircraft, to describe the details of a complex war game. It was a game Bywater had previously played out on paper, with model ships at Keston Pond, and in countless conversations and musings over many years. The result, he hoped, would point to the way a real war in the Pacific would *really* work itself out.

The events leading to and including the Japanese surprise attack made up the first three chapters of Bywater's new book. After completing this much, he precipitously dropped his writing and sailed for the United States. Was he prevailed upon by his old friends in the netherworld of espionage to undertake a last covert mission? One cannot be certain. However, despite Bywater's declaration after the world war that he would not "dream of taking up intelligence work again, under any circumstances whatsoever," the fact is, he did so. In 1920, working for Naval Intelligence, he translated a German analysis of naval action in the recent war, and in June 1923, he hustled off to Germany to conduct an undercover investigation of rumors (which turned out to be untrue) that the German Navy was building submarines in violation of the Treaty of Versailles. Consequently, it hardly seems unreasonable that in the spring of 1924, Bywater accepted a brief assignment from the same or a related patron to visit the United States. Much as he had come to loathe clandestine work, he may have gladly accepted an expenses-paid trip to the United States as an opportunity to pursue additional research for his new book while there, and also to try to sell the idea to an American publisher. (Bywater assumed, incorrectly, that his English publisher would have no interest in it.) Whatever prompted the trip, Bywater again traveled on a passport representing himself as an American citizen, born in Boston.*

---

* American authorities did not discover Bywater's long-standing fraud for another four years, and then made note of it in an almost-apologetic manner. In March 1928, the Office of Naval Intelligence's confidential *Monthly Information Bulletin*, vol. X, no. 9, p. 17, carried an item

Once in the United States, he found a publisher without much difficulty, and thanks to a cache of twenty-three letters and telegrams exchanged between Bywater and his new editor (preserved at the Houghton Library of Harvard University), much can be learned about his trip as well as his intentions and concerns in writing the book.

Only after arriving in New York on May 5, 1924, and checking into the Hotel Latham did Bywater write to the American publisher of his *Sea Power in the Pacific* to tell of his whereabouts and desire for a meeting. Clearly, he had left London in a great hurry. In his letter to the Houghton Mifflin Company of Boston, he said he expected to be in Boston for one or two days later in the week and asked for an appointment. The next day, Ferris Greenslet, a rising editor at the publishing company, telegraphed to say he would be "very glad" to receive Bywater.

Greenslet, an author of literary biographies who would soon become editor-in-chief of Houghton Mifflin, took an immediate liking to Bywater and was intrigued by "the war book" he said he was writing. Bywater declared he had intended to present Greenslet with "three specimen chapters" of the book, but the only copy he had brought with him was in a trunk that had mysteriously vanished. (One wonders if an American counterintelligence agency caught wind of Bywater's trip and had a hand in the disappearance of his luggage.) Pleased by Greenslet's expression of interest, Bywater departed, assuring the editor he would send him the three chapters as soon as his trunk reappeared.

On his return to New York, Bywater dined at the Hotel Latham with William Howard Gardiner, the naval writer who had been an early champion of *Sea Power in the Pacific*, leading to a correspondence between the two men. Gardiner was much in awe of Bywater and had been trumpeting his writing in the United States. About a year before

---

stating that "because of his prominence, it is of interest to note that Mr. Bywater is now definitely established as a British subject and is so recognized by the British Government." The item continued: "For some time his citizenship has been in doubt owing to the fact that his father considered himself an American citizen." There was no mention that Bywater had been lying about the date and place of his birth on passport applications for more than a decade, nor any hint of his long association with the British Secret Service and Naval Intelligence. Evidently, the U.S. Navy wanted the facts on the record, yet had no desire to pick a fight with an influential friend.

their dinner meeting, Gardiner had written to Bywater commending him for one of his *Atlantic Monthly* articles and reporting that he had brought it to the attention of "upper circles" of the government and "caused it to be brought to the personal attention of President Harding."

Bywater lost no time in putting his admirer to work. At dinner, he asked Gardiner if he could procure a table of figures comparing American, British, and Japanese light-cruiser and submarine tonnage. The desired material arrived soon after Bywater returned to England. In particular, it showed that as of February 1924, Japanese submarine construction built or authorized was nearly twice the comparable figure for the United States submarine fleet and three times that for Great Britain. Bywater used this information as the basis for his speculation in the book that when war broke out—he set his imaginary war six years ahead of the time at which he was writing—Japan would have a formidable commerce-raiding capability and would use it with telling effect against the United States.

But a much more important exchange of information may have taken place over dinner at the Latham. It may be that Gardiner disclosed to Bywater details of War Plan Orange, the nation's top-secret contingency plan for war against Japan. As vice president of the unofficial Navy League, Gardiner did not have access to Plan Orange; however, in the clubby atmosphere of the naval leadership in those days, he was close enough to men like William S. Sims to have been told the essentials of the plan and to have heard their frustration with it.

Some such leak could explain the fact that Bywater later stated in his book that the Philippines could hold out against a Japanese invasion for only about two weeks (Plan Orange assumed the same), and that he included in his narrative the description of a disastrous charge by the American fleet into the Western Pacific that was remarkably similar to the naval assault envisioned in Plan Orange. Bywater attributed his plan for the ill-fated attack to "the Bureau of Operations . . . in collaboration with the War College and the General Board of the Navy." Plan Orange, too, had been conceived by the Bureau of Operations in collaboration with the War College and the General Board of the Navy. One can imagine that Gardiner, on learning the subject of Bywater's forthcoming book, suggested that it would be helpful if somewhere in the scenario he could dramatize disaster befalling a reckless American thrust across the Western Pacific such as was then being given serious consideration by U.S. Navy contingency planners, much to the distress of Sims, himself, and others.

On May 14, Bywater traveled from New York to Baltimore, perhaps merely to pay his respects to Adams and Patterson at the Baltimore *Sun*. From the elegant old Stafford Hotel there he wrote to Greenslet to explain that his trunk was still missing and to apologize for not having delivered the first three chapters. He then returned to New York and sailed for England.

Shortly after Bywater reached his home, the trunk appeared and he sent Greenslet the chapters, provisionally entitled *A History of the Great Pacific War in 1929*. (He would eventually set the war even further off, in 1931.) In a cover letter, Bywater emphasized that the book would be written "with a scrupulous regard for the technical points of naval warfare, and with a close knowledge of the geography and topography of the localities mentioned." His care, he said, would ensure that "no naval expert will be able to put his finger on any statement or incident and say, 'that is wrong or technically impossible.' "

Greenslet was delighted with the first three chapters and lavished Bywater with praise. "I think you have begun most brilliantly," he wrote. "After the first few pages, the thing laid hold of my imagination, and I read it with an almost breathless excitement. More than any other 'future war' book that I have ever read, it has the authentic accent of past history."

But Greenslet allowed that he and his Houghton Mifflin colleagues were also troubled about the possibly provocative nature of the book. "The only doubt in our mind," he declared, "is whether it would be sound public service to publish the thing here. From one point of view, I am inclined to think that it might possibly foment trouble. Then again, I see a different set of considerations leading me to believe that it would be more likely to forestall and prevent it." One possible precaution "more likely to operate as oil on the waters rather than as gasoline on the flame," he suggested, would be to have the book manufactured in England and then exported to the United States. In any event, Greenslet concluded, he wanted Bywater to know that he considered the book's chances of being published "sufficiently bright to warrant your going ahead with it."

Bywater replied immediately, eager to champion the still-embryonic book he seemed to feel he was born to write. The finished product, he said, would represent "the fruits of long years of study." His sophisticated analysis of naval strategy, geography, and international politics would determine "the course and outcome" of the war. In contrast, he went on to say, most future war yarns are not convincing because the author invariably "resorts to sensationalism to cover up his limited knowledge of technicalities."

He then addressed Greenslet's concern that the book might "foment trouble." Bywater was hardly insensitive to the possibility. In an earlier letter, he had suggested that the book should be published anonymously. Now, however, he dropped that idea. The nationality of the author was not the issue, he believed. The question was whether or not a realistic description of a war between Japan and the United States would poison the well of international understanding and contribute to the spread of suspicion and distrust between the two nations.

He told Greenslet:

> I do not think any harm would be done by the publication of such a book in the United States. At least three books of a similar character have been published in Japan during recent years . . . , and American literature on the military aspect of the Pacific problem has already assumed imposing dimensions. There is no gainsaying the fact that the possibilities of such a war are being freely canvassed in both countries, and I cannot see that a book which attempted to forecast the incidents of the war, once issue had been joined, would have any political significance. If it were taken seriously its effect would, I think, be beneficial, for I shall try to show that an armed conflict between the United States and Japan would be a terrible affair for both countries; and since it is my profound conviction that victory must, sooner or later, incline to the American side, the data by which this conclusion is justified might not be wholly without effect on Japanese opinion. Taking everything into consideration I am sure that, so far as the will to war is concerned, the effect of the book would be deterrent rather than provocative.

Greenslet still insisted on seeing the final manuscript before guaranteeing publication, but, he said, he had read Bywater's defense "with the greatest interest." And well he might have. The author had made an eminently reasonable case that his scenario would not prove tempting to the Japanese. Surely, his argument would convince anyone willing to listen to reason.

CHAPTER

13

THE GREAT PACIFIC WAR

PICKING UP THE narrative where he left off when he sailed for
America, Bywater surmised that the Japanese surprise attack would
come "like a bolt from the blue" to the American people. The United
States is swept by "a wave of grief . . . thinking of those thousands of
gallant seamen who had gone to their doom, fighting to the last against
tremendous odds, with the old flag still flying as the waters closed above
the torn and battered hulls of their ships." For the time being, he continued, "little heed was paid to the peril which menaced the Philippines."
Nevertheless, the mood of the nation is not one of defeatism, as the
Japanese hope, but rather "a stern resolve to see this struggle through
to the bitter end." Whatever the country's disadvantage now might be,
the American people would not rest "until the sword was struck from
the enemy's grasp and he was forced to sue for peace."

Before the United States can respond, however, the Japanese follow
up the destruction of the American fleet with simultaneous moves against

Guam and the Philippines. It was, of course, simple enough to say that these territories would quickly fall into Japanese hands, but much more difficult to spell out precisely how that would happen. Bywater tackled the problem with his customary sophistication. To begin with, he explained, although amphibious operations had been given a bad name in the West because of a highly publicized disaster in the First World War at Gallipoli, this was not the case in Japan. "Landings on a supposed hostile coast had been practiced year after year as a regular feature of Japanese Army maneuvers," he wrote. "All necessary equipment— boats, barges, pontoons, and portable jetties—had been in readiness at the military depots for years."

He imagined that Guam would come under attack from "a flight of Japanese war planes, evidently from Saipan," followed a few days later by a terrific naval bombardment, including the use of gas shells, and then the landing of troops on the east and west shores of the island. Bywater anticipated the use of specially designed landing craft. "Large motor-propelled barges or pontoons," he wrote, "were carried on board the [Japanese] transports for landing tanks and artillery." The infantry makes for the shore in "motor barges." As soon as the keels of these craft ground on the beach, "little men in khaki tumbled over the side and came plunging through the surf, holding rifles and cartridge pouches above their heads, and uttering staccato war cries." The first wave of the Japanese assault is repulsed, Bywater wrote, but a subsequent attack overwhelms the island's defenders. "Here and there a handful of Marines stood their ground and opened fire as soon as the Japanese troops became visible," he said, "but their position was hopeless." After several fierce skirmishes, Bywater concluded, the Marines are compelled to surrender.

At the same time, the Philippines are assaulted. With virtually all American warships either destroyed, out of commission, or far away, the chief danger, the Japanese perceived, would come from the American aircraft. Moreover, Bywater stated, "thirty machines of a new and powerful type" had just arrived from the United States. (The parallel with the arrival of thirty-five new B-17 "Flying Fortresses" in early December 1941 is remarkable.)

He also assumed that the Japanese would have long scrutinized the topography of the Philippines. "Every yard of ground had been personally surveyed and mapped by Japanese officers," he wrote. "Not only was the site and armament of every existing battery known with exactitude, but the position where a new battery might be placed was clearly marked on the large-scale maps prepared by the Japanese Imperial Staff College in Tokyo." Provided with such excellent intelligence about the defenses of the islands, he reasoned, the Japanese invasion plan would give a wide berth to the fortress at Corregidor Island guarding Manila Bay, as well as the other heavily fortified base not far to the north at Olongapo defending Subig Bay.

> Strong batteries, equipped with 12-inch rifles on disappearing mounts, were in position on the island of Corregidor, while others crowned the headlands on either side of the 12-mile entrance to the bay. As these pieces could sweep the sea over a radius of many miles, it would have been madness to expose warships, let alone crowded transports, to their devastating fire. To silence them by naval bombardment was out of the question. Their massive concrete emplacements were shell-proof; nothing short of a direct hit on the gun itself or on its mounting would be effective, and as the piece showed above the parapet only for a few seconds at a time, it offered a hopeless target. Against bomb attack from the air the batteries were protected by strong shields of steel. . . . At Subig Bay, some forty miles up the coast, other batteries and mine fields were in position. . . .

Where, then, would Japanese forces land? Bywater supposed that they would begin with a feint. To confuse the island's defenders, he imagined, the Japanese shell Santa Cruz on the west coast of Luzon, the principal island in the Philippines. This strategem, however, is "so obviously a ruse to draw the Americans away from other parts of the coast that it failed in its purpose." Next come air strikes. A flight of Japanese interceptors attack American patrol craft between Cape Bolinao and San Fernando on the east coast of Luzon, and then bombers hit the airport at Dagupan (later replaced by Clark Field) aiming to destroy those thirty American aircraft "of a new and powerful type."

Between dusk and the next morning, the main landings take place. They come in the shape of a three-pronged attack, simultaneously throwing ashore 40,000 troops at each of two sites on Luzon, and another 50,000 at Sindangan Bay on Mindanao, the second largest and southernmost of the major Philippine islands. The landing beaches have been chosen with great care. Luzon is attacked from both east and west. On the west coast, Japanese troop transports assemble in Lingayen Gulf and send their landing barges ashore along gently sloping beaches leading directly to the lowlands of the Pampanga Plain, which extends all the way to Manila. On the east coast of Luzon, the transports make for Lamon Bay, between Cabalete and Alabat islands. Here the terrain is mountainous, but the landing site is closer to Manila. Equipped with tanks and heavy artillery, the western and eastern forces rapidly converge on the capital, obliging its defenders to divide their strength and fight on two fronts. Meanwhile, the Japanese expeditionary force on the island of Mindanao quickly overwhelms the garrisons at Zamboanga and at the port of Davao. In less than three weeks, Manila surrenders and the Philippines as well as Guam are in Japanese hands.

While much of Bywater's plan for the Japanese conquest of the Philippines was original, he appears to have borrowed a major feature —the pincers attack on Manila—from Homer Lea's book *The Valor of Ignorance*. In describing the Japanese assault on the Philippines, Lea had written: "Japan, by landing simultaneously one column of twenty thousand men at Dagupan [the largest city on Lingayen Gulf] and another column of the same size at Polillo Bight [adjacent to Lamon Bay], would, strategically, render the American position untenable." A map of Luzon accompanied Lea's text, showing the landing beaches and indicating with arrows the paths of the two invading armies as they converged on Manila.

Bywater's plan was by no means a precise duplicate of Lea's. He had more than doubled the size of the Japanese expeditionary force projected by Lea, added air strikes and a diversionary action against Luzon, and also added a third major landing on the island of Mindanao. In addition, Bywater shifted the site of the eastern Luzon landing approximately 45 miles to the south. Furthermore, if Bywater in fact adopted Lea's plan for the attack on the Philippines, he took pains to verify its practicability. In October 1924, he had written to Greenslet explaining he was having difficulty figuring out how the Japanese might best invade Luzon. He said he would be greatly aided by a map of Luzon "showing the railway system," and he understood that such a map might be procured in the United States. Could Greenslet find one for him? In a few weeks, Houghton Mifflin sent Bywater a railway map of Luzon, and it is presumably this map rather than that in Lea's book that Bywater used.

Nevertheless, it is difficult not to conclude that Bywater's concept

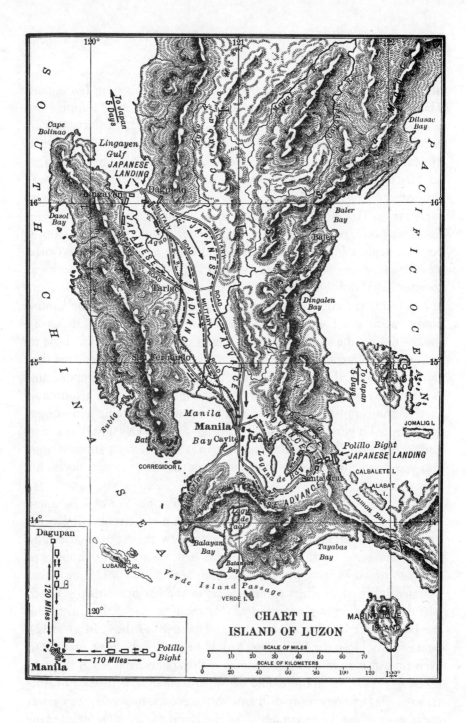

CHART II
ISLAND OF LUZON

SCALE OF MILES
0   10   20   30   40   50   60   70

SCALE OF KILOMETERS
0   20   40   60   80   100   120

of a pincers attack on Manila was derived from *The Valor of Ignorance*. There are simply too many possible landing sites in the Philippine archipelago to make it seem reasonable for Lea and Bywater to have chosen two of the same general sites purely by chance. To be sure, the capture of Manila, the capital of the Philippines, is an obvious objective for a military planner, but there are many ways of getting there. As the American officer Albert M. Jones would report more than a decade later, there are on Luzon "250 miles of possible landing beaches."

It was odd, to say the least, for Bywater to adopt an idea from a book he deplored as thoroughly as he did Lea's. In fact, having scorned *The Valor of Ignorance* in *Sea Power in the Pacific* as a "sensational forecast" that did "more harm than good," Bywater took another jab at Lea in his current book by noting that both Hawaii and the United States Pacific coast would be immune from serious military attack by Japan "despite the sensational forecasts by certain writers who chose to ignore the rudiments of strategy." Lea, it will be recalled, predicted that Japan would be able to capture California, Oregon, Washington, and Alaska. Why would Bywater borrow something from such a source as that? Perhaps he simply knew a good idea when he came across one, and adopted it without regard for its origin. Or conceivably, Lea's map with arrows marking the pincers took root in Bywater's subconscious and was later unwittingly reinvented when the time came to devise his own tactics.

Bywater made no mention in *The Great Pacific War* of a Japanese attack on the Dutch East Indies or the British naval base at Singapore, and yet it is interesting to note that he foresaw these possibilities and even commented on them in newspaper articles just as his book was going to press. Writing for the Baltimore *Sun* in May 1925, he raised the possibility of "a great conflagration in the Pacific, with the Dutch islands playing an important part." He thought that if the Celebes of the Dutch East Indies were to become Japanese (as they did in 1942), America's hold on the Philippines would be rendered "more precarious even than it is today." Furthermore, with Japanese naval bases established in Java, "Singapore would be outflanked and the defense of Australia made infinitely more difficult." Such events, he wrote, may never come to pass, yet the recent action of the Netherlands in "strengthening the defenses of her East Indian colonies" suggests that "they are not wholly impossible."

In another article written for the *Sun* the same month, Bywater observed that Japan regarded both the United States and Great Britain as "a more formidable menace" than Russia, and he discussed the possibility that "Japan intends to cultivate closer political relations with Russia and France—and perhaps even with Germany—with the view to having powerful backers should she decide to try conclusions with one or another of the Anglo-Saxon nations."

Two years later, in his book *Navies and Nations*, Bywater foresaw the Japanese surprise attack on Singapore with even greater clarity:

> Were Japan, for some inscrutable reason, to make up her mind to fight the British Empire, is it not likely that she would lay her plans for a sudden and overwhelming assault on Singapore, knowing that with this great fortress and naval dockyard reduced, the game, so far as strategy counted, would be largely in her hands? Compared with the invasion of Australia, the conquest of Singapore would be a simple operation. As a promising objective for the first great blow it might well prove irresistible. If Singapore, then, is to be converted into our naval key position in Eastern waters we must be prepared to provide it with the powerful defenses which its importance demands. If we fail in this it may become a second Port Arthur.

Real as he saw such possibilities to be, Bywater decided to limit his imaginary Pacific war for the sake of clarity and credibility. It was enough, he felt, to ask readers to believe that Japan might have the temerity to make war on America, let alone attack Great Britain and the Netherlands, too. What changed all that in 1941 was the sudden American embargo on oil and aviation fuel, the surrender of Holland to Japan's new ally Nazi Germany, and the desperation of Great Britain—all of which made Europe's oil-rich possessions in Southeast Asia seem both essential to Japan and ripe for picking.

After having captured Guam and the Philippines, Bywater was able to show that Japan had created for herself a Danube position—a central rallying point in the southwestern Pacific. "A cordon had been established across every line of approach to the waters of the South-West Pacific," he wrote, explaining Japan's formidable posture.

> At Port Lloyd, in the Bonin [Ogasawara] Islands, lay the main body of the Japanese fleet. From the Marshall, Caroline, and Mar-

iana islands Japanese cruisers, submarines, and aircraft maintained watch and ward over the South Seas. Had any large American force advanced westward from Hawaii it must speedily have been detected, whereupon the Japanese patrol craft would have been called up from every quarter to harry it like a pack of wolves. Compelled to travel at low speed in order not to outdistance its indispensable supply ships and auxiliaries, the fleet would have been exposed day and night to attack by Japanese submarines, and, as it got farther to the west, to raids by aircraft. If a ship were damaged in any way that prevented it from keeping up with the rest of the fleet, its fate would be sealed. The chances were that a considerable portion of the fleet would be destroyed on its westward voyage, and even if a greater part of the ships got through in safety there would be no friendly base awaiting them at the end of their long journey. They would find themselves in hostile waters, short of fuel, and unable to obtain fresh supplies. Every day they remained in the Western Pacific would increase their peril and bring them nearer to disaster. With their number depleted by the campaign of attrition waged by submarines, aircraft, and mine-layers, they would be liable to be brought to action by the Japanese battle fleet, which could strike at full force at its selected moment. . . . For a war with the United States, Japan's strategical position very closely approached the ideal.

This was a thesis Bywater had been propounding for at least four years, yet it was one that he doubted most Americans could accept. He knew the naive yet widespread belief in the United States, shared even by many top naval strategists, was that the U.S. Navy could whip the Japanese Navy anywhere, anytime, and without regard to bases and the length of American supply lines. Consequently, to dramatize the foolhardiness of this popular belief (perhaps at the suggestion of William Howard Gardiner), Bywater described a reckless American stab at the Bonin Islands, which lie some 600 miles southeast of Tokyo.

If successfully captured, a base so near to the Japanese home islands might lead to a speedy conclusion of the war; however, the Americans have underestimated the obstacles in their way. A Japanese raid has temporarily closed the Panama Canal, and when warships on station in the Atlantic are dispatched on the 14,000-mile voyage from Hampton Roads around Cape Horn to San Diego to reinforce the Pacific Fleet, Japanese submarines harass them all along the way. Then, as the Americans venture west of Hawaii, they encounter all of the problems of overextension that Bywater had long predicted—including, of course, a Japanese ambush. After suffering heavy losses, the American fleet limps home ingloriously. There is a public outcry in the United States followed by resignations in the high command of the navy. American leaders have now learned the hard way that the only practicable means of striking Japan is by pouncing from island to island across the Pacific Ocean, carefully retrenching after each new conquest and pausing to bring up the rear.

As described earlier, the general idea of such a campaign is one Bywater probably picked up from a lecture in 1915 given by the American naval officer Albert P. Niblack. When Bywater studied the matter further, he perceived three possible routes across this vast expanse. Of them all, the southern one seemed best. In making this choice, once again Bywater may have been influenced by a tip from someone in the leadership of the U.S. Navy. The American officer William S. Sims, it will be recalled, had praised the strategic analysis in *Sea Power in the Pacific* as "thoroughly excellent" in a review in the *Atlantic Monthly*. Sims also made the observation that although Bywater was correct in calling Guam the ideal advance naval base for the protection of the Philippines, he had neglected to mention "the possibility of utilizing the Caroline and Marshall islands as an advance base for our fleet."

It was a strange comment to be made in public by Sims, who was then president of the United States Naval War College. The League of Nations had recently awarded the formerly German Caroline and Marshall islands to Japan. Furthermore, Sims was well aware that in July 1921, after his friend John A. Lejeune took command of the U.S. Marine Corps, the latter adopted an island-hopping offensive through these very islands as the top-secret, official Marine Corps guide for war planning, training, field exercises, and equipment development.

Sims knew that his review of Bywater's book would be read in Japan, and possibly he chose this medium to hint to the Japanese that they could not seize the Philippines without a serious fight—one for which the Americans were already preparing.

Whether or not Bywater needed Sims to remind him of the existence of the Caroline and Marshall islands, he went far beyond anything Niblack or Sims had said or written publicly on the subject. Bywater conceived a complex island-hopping campaign, complete with zigzags, feints, bypasses, and other surprises, anticipating the strategy of Chester Nimitz and Douglas MacArthur in the early 1940s.

The "guiding genius" of this American strategy, Bywater wrote, was a certain Admiral Joseph Harper, the former commander of the American garrison on Guam who escaped from Guam in a submarine much as MacArthur would depart from the Philippines in 1942. Admiral Harper, whose knowledge of the various islands of the Pacific was extensive, proves crafty at playing the game of bluff and deception. He begins his campaign, as did American forces in 1942, with noisy preparations in Alaska and the Aleutians to lure the Japanese to the north. His real attack is aimed at the Central Pacific, jumping off from Hawaii to Tutuila in the American Samoans. Bywater then has Admiral Harper make a daringly long thrust to Truk in the Carolines, deep inside the Japanese defensive perimeter. But just when it seems that American forces might be cut off from their line of supply, Admiral Harper whirls around and makes simultaneous thrusts to Ponape, also in the Carolines, and to Jaluit, in the Marshalls, which opens a direct, and much shorter, line of communication with Hawaii. Then comes a feint at Guam and a leap to Angaur in the Palaus, followed by a feint at Yap in the westernmost Carolines.

By this time, it is approximately a year and a half after the Japanese surprise attack that started the war. The Americans have managed to replace all naval losses, and, thanks to Admiral Harper's brilliant tactics in the Central Pacific, American warships in the vicinity of Yap are within striking distances of the Philippines. The Philippines are the final stepping-stone in the chain of islands reaching across the Pacific from which direct attacks on Japan may be launched. Thus, the tables have turned. The United States Navy is now the superior force in the Pacific, although the Imperial Navy is a still-deadly fleet-in-being. Consequently, this is the point in the narrative at which Bywater spelled out the strategy he had devised at Keston Pond for compelling the commander of the lesser fleet—in this case, Admiral Hiraga, the Japanese commander-in-chief—to accept battle.

The commander of the American fleet, whom Bywater names Admiral Templeton, concentrates at his base a prodigious force composed of seventeen aircraft carriers and battleships as well as numerous cruisers, destroyers, and other support ships. A vanguard of this force, including the battleship *Florida*, approaches the island of Yap and commences a bombardment while troop transports "so maneuver as if to suggest that a landing was about to be attempted." When the island's defenders report to Admiral Hiraga that an invasion appears to be in progress, the Japanese commander has no choice but to employ every weapon at his disposal to block this advance—which if successful would bring American forces to the very door of Japan. The Japanese Grand Fleet, consisting of some one dozen battleships and aircraft carriers, twenty-one cruisers, and two immense destroyer flotillas, plus numerous support vessels, abandons its lair at Manila and strikes out for Yap. Bywater continued:

> The spectacle was a magnificent one as this, the greatest navy ever seen under the flag of Nippon, steamed out to meet the enemy. First went two destroyer flotillas and Rear Admiral Uyehara's Fourth Cruiser Squadron (*Myoko, Ashigara, Yonezawa,* and *Itsukushima*), the blue water of Manila Bay creaming beneath their sharp prows. They were followed by the aircraft carriers . . . , [then] the battle-cruisers under Vice Admiral Wada, headed by the colossal *Akagi,* and the smaller but still formidable *Kongo, Hiyei, Haruna,* and *Kirishima.* In the wake of these mastodons steamed the flagship *Nagato,* embodied for tactical purposes in Rear Admiral Shimizu's First Division, which comprised also the *Kaga* and *Mutsu*; and, finally, the Second Division—*Ise, Higua, Fuso,* and *Yamashiro.* Astern of the battle columns came the Second, Third, and Fifth Cruiser Squadrons, thirteen ships in all.

"Overhead blazed the sun in a vault of intense blue, unflecked by a single cloud," Bywater continued, obviously relishing the prospect of a great set-piece of naval action. "Almost as far as the eye could reach were the forms of ships . . . and each . . . left a foaming wake of vivid white as she cleft her way through the glassy sea." First contact in what was to be called the Battle of Yap, Bywater wrote, took place when some fifty torpedo planes rise from the decks of *Lexington* and *Saratoga* and are met by an equal number of Japanese aircraft. "To give any account of this scrimmage in the air would be impossible," declared Bywater, who was still baffled by the tactics of aircraft. However, after this entire flight of planes—about a third of those available to either side—is brought down in the first minutes of combat by "a hurricane of fire," it became clear, Bywater wrote, that "a decision must be achieved by weapons other than the air arm." He then proceeds to describe a naval gunfight in the classic Jutland tradition.

Shortly after the opposing fleets come within range of each other, intense firing begins. Taking advantage of his greater speed, Admiral

Hiraga attempts to cut perpendicularly across the head of the American line—to "cross the T" as Togo did at Tsushima—but Admiral Templeton foils the move by turning away as his battleships *Colorado, Maryland,* and *West Virginia* start pouring a withering fire on *Mutsu, Nagato,* and *Kaga. Mutsu* loses her second turret and *Nagato,* which has taken two 16-inch shells in her bowels, drops out of line. Now, under cover of a smokescreen, Admiral Templeton swings back toward the enemy and suddenly finds his leading division within 17,000 yards of Hiraga's center. Eight American warships are able to concentrate about ninety of the heaviest guns in the fleet on *Ise* and *Higua.* "Every minute, more of the American battleships were coming up to join in the terrible drumfire that was now smiting both the center and rear of the Japanese fleet."

An American officer hears a 1,400-pound round of naval ammunition go hissing overhead "like an express train," and the big guns of *Tennessee* fire so rapidly that "the paint on their chases rose up in blisters." This action brings the mighty *Akagi* into the fray, her huge 16-inch guns quickly wrecking four American cruisers. Soon, however, *Akagi* and *Hiyei* have received grievous wounds and, with darkness approaching, Admiral Hiraga retires to the west, thinking the Americans must be low on fuel and will not follow. But Admiral Templeton gives chase, and one by one the great Japanese mastodons are hit and destroyed.

At the very end, the crippled *Mutsu,* anticipating the suicidal sortie of the *Yamato* in April 1945, makes a kamikaze charge. Bywater picked *Mutsu* for this role deliberately. He knew how dear to the hearts of the Japanese was this ship that had been built in part with contributions from Japanese schoolchildren. Bywater had accurately forecast during the Washington Conference that the Japanese government could never agree to scrap this great symbol of national pride.

An American officer describes the scene:

> Had anyone told me beforehand that even the largest battleship could endure the converging fire of more than a hundred big guns at a range of only five miles without being sunk outright, I should have laughed at him. Yet this was the very ordeal that *Mutsu* was now enduring, and she was still above water. But as she came nearer and yet nearer, I could see her, as it were, disintegrating under the rain of sledge-hammer blows. Her massive heptapod foremast was a tangle of twisted steel. The first funnel had vanished, while the

second stack, riddled like a collander, was tilting sideways at an acute angle. Almost every second, some piece of debris flew into the air: now it was a great fragment of deck plating or casemate armour, then a boat derrick, and next a whirling mass of objects that may have been men. At this point-blank range our shells seemed to be tearing through the ship from end to end. . . . Her people had no intention of surrendering, for two guns still kept up a slow fire, so there was nothing to do but finish her off. We gave her two more salvos, and when I last saw her she was heeling over at 35 degrees, clearly on the point of sinking. Our airmen, who now came up, claim to have sunk her with their torpedoes, but it was really our guns that had done the work.

Bywater's belief that artillery remained the supreme weapon of naval war was his most serious lapse in an otherwise astonishingly prophetic book. In 1925, he could not imagine the coming importance of air power. Although he foresaw that both the opening and climactic battles of the war would be heralded by the approach of carrier-based aircraft, he thought the decisive blows would be delivered by capital ships, and thus fell back on describing old-fashioned naval gun duels. By the mid-1930s, Bywater sensed this defect in his forecasts, and in subsequent editions of this and other books, and in articles, he declared prophetically that Japan's opening stroke in the war would be delivered by her new aircraft carriers. For now, however, he remained—in this respect—a prisoner of the past.

He made one or two minor gaffes as well. In describing one particular action, for example, he told of an American submarine being rammed by a Japanese destroyer whose "sharp prow drove deep into the plating just abaft the conning tower, cutting the submarine almost in two." He of all people should have known that a destroyer's hull—approximately an eighth of an inch in thickness—would crumple like tin foil against the tough, pressure-resistant hull of a submarine. He also presumed incorrectly that "dummy" warships and poison gas—two prominent features of World War I—would play significant roles in future naval combat. But naval decoys lost favor as air reconnaissance improved, and the 1925 Geneva Convention banning the first use of poison gas was signed a month or two after Bywater's book had gone to press.

Among the minor flashes of accurate forecasting in the book, three are noteworthy. Bywater foresaw that the Japanese would attempt a carrier-borne air strike against Dutch Harbor, the principal American base in the Aleutian Islands, and also guessed the outcome. "The atrocious climate proved a staunch ally to the American cause," he wrote, since the attack caused little damage and cost the Japanese ten aircraft—much like the result of the actual Japanese carrier raid on Dutch Harbor in 1942.

He also anticipated the kamikaze philosophy if not perhaps the large-scale program under which it would be carried out. Bywater wrote that the desperation of the Japanese, after having seen their defensive ring of island-bases smashed, combined with their fanatical emperor worship, would result in Japanese aviators "never hesitating to ram when otherwise balked of their prey, preferring to immolate themselves. . . ." Also, Bywater foresaw that the torpedo plane would demonstrate its "complete superiority" over the bomber as an instrument of naval combat, since the 600-pound bombs, which he judged to be the heaviest weapon bombers would be able to lift in the short takeoff space provided by aircraft carriers, were simply not powerful enough—barring a down-the-stack freak hit—to sink a modern warship. On this point, Bywater could not have been better informed. As it turned out, the Douglas "Dauntless" dive-bomber, which carried a 500-pound bomb during the Second World War, could not compare in effectiveness with the Grumman "Avenger" torpedo plane, slung with a huge "tin fish" that accounted for the great majority of Japanese shipping sent to the bottom by aircraft during the Second World War. The rule was borne out by Japanese experience, too, whose successes at Pearl Harbor, as well as a few days later off the east coast of Malaya in sinking the British warships *Repulse* and *Prince of Wales*, were principally the work of Nakajima torpedo planes.

The Battle of Yap, like the historic Battle of Midway, is a turning point in the war, Bywater declared. Of the total of twelve capital ships engaged, Japan had lost five (she lost four at Midway), and most of the rest were seriously damaged. In contrast, American forces had only two capital ships sunk (only one at Midway—the *Yorktown*—succumbed). Thereafter, as virtually undisputed mistress of the Pacific, Bywater wrote, the Americans continue their dogged campaign from island to island, recapturing Guam and returning to the Philippines despite determined Japanese resistance at both points.

Needless to say, Bywater did not foresee the atomic bomb; and yet, he did sense that something out of the ordinary might be attempted by the United States to spare both adversaries the sanguinary horror of an invasion of the Japanese homeland. This coup de grace, he guessed, would be a "demonstration" air raid over Tokyo in which the bombs dropped contain no TNT but instead are packed with leaflets urging the Japanese to petition their government to come to terms rather than "waste more lives."

Fictional characters have always proved more adept at extricating themselves from tragic predicaments than their real-life counterparts, and Bywater's Japanese are no exception. After the demonstration air raid has made its point, Japan soberly accepts defeat. A surrender is duly arranged, and a treaty of peace is signed in which, among other things, the former German Pacific islands mandated to Japan by the League of Nations are turned over to the United States "for their future administration"—precisely as happened after the actual surrender of Japan in 1945.

On March 10, 1925, Bywater cabled Greenslet: "BOOK FINISHED KINDLY ADVISE DATE YOUR ARRIVAL LONDON." As it happened, Greenslet had just checked into Garland's Hotel, a favorite London literary haunt, and had dispatched a letter to Bywater asking if he had finished his book. Bywater delivered the manuscript to his hotel the next day, along with a letter in which he assured Greenslet he had been "careful to avoid offending Japanese sensibilities" and had scrupulously shunned "the gruesome" and "the sensational aspects of war." Greenslet took the manuscript to Scotland with him for a week of reading and salmon fishing. "It has come out uncommonly well," he wrote to Bywater on his return to London, "and we certainly want to publish it."

But Greenslet was still haunted by the possibly provocative nature of the book. Inadvertently, Bywater solved the problem for him. He had shown the manuscript to his mentor and editor, Otto Kyllmann of Constable & Company. Kyllmann had liked it, and on March 8 he and Bywater signed a contract for publication of the book in Britain. Bywater also changed the title at that time to *The Great Pacific War*.

Greenslet was delighted with the news that Kyllmann would publish the book in Great Britain. That made it possible for him to carry out an idea he had mentioned to Bywater in their early correspondence. He arranged with Kyllmann to have Constable manufacture all copies of the book for the American as well as the British market; the former would be shipped to the United States. In that way, Greenslet could conceal the fact that he had helped to originate the project. It would be much less provocative, he felt, to have *The Great Pacific War* written and published in a country that did not figure into Bywater's drama as one of the belligerents.

CHAPTER

14

WRONG END OF THE TELESCOPE

D ID BYWATER USE his position as an influential journalist to stir up a furor to help the sale of his forthcoming book? The charge is farfetched, and yet high-ranking Japanese officials and even a good many of Bywater's friends and colleagues in the Fleet Street Press Gang believed him guilty of it.

In April 1925, Western naval observers were alarmed by a news-agency report from Tokyo that Japan was starting a huge warship-building program. She aimed to construct twenty-two naval vessels, including an aircraft carrier, eight heavy cruisers, three light cruisers, and ten destroyers. All that would certainly strain the Washington Treaty to which she had become a party only three years before.

Bywater, who was then naval correspondent for the London *Daily News* and the weekly *Observer*, and European naval correspondent for the Baltimore *Sun*, naturally leapt on the story. His first move was to cable Imperial Navy headquarters in Tokyo to try to verify the report.

"I am able to state on the highest authority . . . that there is no foundation for the report," Bywater wrote in an article placed prominently on the front page of the *Daily News* on April 16. "Direct cable communication with Japanese naval authorities," he continued, "has established the fact that no new building program has been announced."

Bywater's report in the Baltimore *Sun*, filed from London four days later, was still more explicit, and delved into the reasons why the news-agency story was given little credence by well-informed naval specialists. "Seeing that Japan is on the verge of a political crisis, largely due to financial troubles," Bywater stated, "it is hardly credible that her Government should choose such an ill-timed moment for bringing forward a measure which must have involved heavy expenditures."

"For this reason," he continued, "the [news-agency] message was viewed with suspicion. In naval circles it was thought to refer not to any supplementary construction but simply to the quota of tonnage already in hand and authorized under previous enactments. Cable inquiries at Tokyo have confirmed this theory, and I am informed by Japan's representatives in London that there is 'no truth whatsoever' in a report of a new naval program."

Final as those words sound, that was hardly the end of the matter. Bywater requested another check on the situation, this time probably from his key source in Japan, Malcolm Kennedy, who had recently been appointed Reuters' Tokyo correspondent. The reply, when it arrived, was a flat contradiction of what Bywater had just published, and it provided evidence he could not ignore. Consequently, Bywater's next dispatch in the *Daily News* and the *Sun* stated that the Japanese Navy was in fact undertaking a program of new construction, and one so big it would consume no less than 35 percent of her total national budget —an enormous outlay for a country presumably scrapping warships.

Not surprisingly, this report provoked consternation in Western capitals; only a year before, Bywater had declared that the United States Navy was substantially below the tonnage level allowed by the Washington Treaty, and now he was saying that Japan was even widening the gap. The United States and Great Britain, among other signatories to the treaty, immediately demanded an explanation from Tokyo.

The Japanese were furious with Bywater—and not for the first time. He had come into conflict with them the previous year. "I have myself been attacked rather viciously by Japanese writers for daring to print the facts . . . ," Bywater had complained in 1924. This time, however, the Japanese attack came from official sources and it was more cunning than before, attempting to discredit him by suggesting that his report had been fabricated for the purpose of stimulating interest in his new book (whose forthcoming publication had just been announced by Constable & Company). "Mr. Bywater is trying to create a sensation, hinting that Japan's auxiliary ship-construction plan greatly endangers the national defense of the United States," an Imperial communiqué declared, adding that Bywater's charges "must be regarded as being made for some private end."

Bywater defended himself a few days later in the *Daily News*:

> The fact that Japan, since the Washington Conference, has actually laid down three times as many fighting ships as the British Empire and the United States together surely justifies the comment that her naval policy hardly reflects the spirit of the Treaty. At the present time, her outlay on armaments accounts for 35 percent of her total State expenditure. While it is not contended that this increase in the Japanese Navy constitutes a direct "menace" to any other Power, it inevitably reacts on naval policies the world over, and to some extent must be held responsible for recent additions to the naval budgets of this country and the United States.

In addition to what he had been able to learn about the future plans of the Imperial Navy, Bywater—thanks to the efforts of his special source in Japan—also made some extraordinary revelations about two of Japan's latest warships, which had been cloaked in secrecy. On May 2, 1925, he became the first reporter in the West to provide a full description of *Furutaka*, a new type of Japanese cruiser that had been launched only two months previously at Nagasaki. *Furutaka*, he reported, had a greater range and gun power "than any modern cruiser afloat of corresponding tonnage."

The next month, he published the first authentic details of *Akagi*, Japan's latest aircraft carrier which had been launched recently at Kure (and which would be commanded in a few years by Isoroku Yamamoto). "She is far more powerful in every way than the largest British aircraft carrier, and in actual fighting efficiency she is superior even to the giant American carrier *Saratoga*," he wrote. "In *Akagi*, as in the cruiser *Furutaka*—recently described in the *Daily News*—the Japanese have overtrumped all rivals by increasing the ratio of fighting power to tonnage, and building ships which can deliver heavier blows than the larger vessels built for other nations."

Strange as it may seem, the Fleet Street Press Gang sided with the Japanese in this dispute, challenging or scoffing at each of Bywater's revelations. "There are never wanting mischief-makers," wrote Cope Cornford, naval correspondent of the *Morning Post*, "who see in every movement of warships and in every new shipbuilding program sinister designs against the peace of the world." Writing an editorial in the *Daily Telegraph*, Bywater's one-time mentor Archibald Hurd fully accepted Japan's denial of a new naval construction program, commenting: "The financial and shipyard resources of Japan would not be adequate for such a fresh commitment in addition to the vessels which are now under construction." And the Manchester *Guardian* scolded: "There are some people who cannot contemplate the Pacific without the thought of its being given up to war, and if they continue to contemplate sufficiently they will end by bringing war apparently nearer."

The sharpest and most irresponsible attack on Bywater appeared in an article in the London *Times* by the newspaper's Tokyo correspondent. "It is a mistake to suggest, as some critics of Japanese naval matters appear to have suggested, that Japan is preparing a provocatively extensive program of naval construction," the article began. "It does not appear that the Japanese have any deliberate intention of exceeding in letter or spirit their post–Washington Conference program of 1922–1928."

The *Times* man in Tokyo then went on to scoff at the notion that the Japanese Navy could be a threat. Japanese submarines, he wrote, are "much inferior" to British boats. Japan's new cruiser *Yubari* is "a somewhat odd little ship." *Furutaka*, which had alarmed Bywater because it increased the ratio of fighting power to tonnage, was dismissed as remaining "all to be finished," and Japan's newest aircraft carrier, *Amagi*, was brushed aside for having had "her back broken on the stocks by the earthquake." There was no mention of *Akagi*. The *Times* correspondent then looked down his nose at the diminutive stature of Japanese sailors "when it comes to handling shells," and he ridiculed them for lacking "the same dash and snap that may be seen on a British ship of war." Even "the allowance of cleaning materials and paint is far below that in the British Navy, and so the Japanese sailor cannot maintain the standard of cleanliness which has made British ships famous."

Bywater could not restrain himself from replying. "In a remarkable article, bearing the stamp of [Imperial Navy] departmental inspiration," he wrote in the Baltimore *Sun*, "the Tokyo correspondent of the London *Times* shows us the Japanese fleet as it might have been seen through the wrong end of a telescope. According to this article, many of its ships are of secondary fighting power, its officers and men are below the Western standard of efficiency, and in gunnery it is fast losing ground. Those who are wise will treat such statements with the utmost reserve."

It is a sad commentary on the Press Gang that the only newspapers that lent support to Bywater were the organs of "yellow journalism"— publications Bywater would have been pleased to have had on the other side of the dispute. In the United States, the Hearst press published a lurid report about the aggressive potential of the Japanese Navy written by a writer who thrilled his readers with a preposterous cock-and-bull story about having disguised himself as "a Chinese coolie" to slip past the heavily armed guards at the gates of Japanese naval dockyards. He never explained why Chinese coolies would be admitted to these highly restricted facilities. The fact is, the Japanese were then fully as concerned about espionage conducted by Chinese as Western agents. In London, the *Daily Express* published a diatribe by Sir Herbert Russell, a celebrated former war correspondent who had spent four weeks in Japan, asserting that the Japanese naval program amounted to "unostentatious preparation for war."

Can it be said that Bywater's reports about the plans to expand the Japanese Navy had been written "for some private end"?

The evidence is clearly opposed to any such suggestion. Not only was Bywater correct in his assertion, but he had begun his investigation by defending the Japanese position. It must have been galling for him to have to retract a front-page story he had written with perfect confidence for newspapers in both Britain and the United States only a few days before, and it stands to reason that he would not have reversed himself without having strong evidence in hand.

Furthermore, in reading Bywater's dispatches about the Japanese Navy throughout this period, one can only be impressed by his moderate tone. For example, writing for the Baltimore *Sun* on June 13—in marked contrast to the tone of the *Daily Express* and the Chicago *Tribune*— Bywater stated: "Personally, I do not believe that the naval development of Japan is activated by motives of a bellicose nature. From her point of view, it is purely defensive, in a sense that Germany's naval expansion never was." A few weeks later, he was bending over backward to see Japan's side of the argument:

> There are some mitigating facts which must be stated in fairness to Japan. Previous to 1918, she had built scarcely any cruisers, most of her naval funds being invested in dreadnoughts. . . . But war experience soon demonstrated [that] . . . most of the actual fighting at sea fell to the lot of small craft, which could be risked more readily than the costly battleship. Japan, therefore, decided to make good the efficiency of her auxiliary craft, and a very large quota of the aggregate tonnage voted in the "eight-eight" scheme was accounted for by cruisers, destroyers, and submarines. . . . It is further to be noted that the end of the war found Great Britain with sixteen cruisers still unfinished, and all these ships have since been completed. . . . America, too, has built and authorized eighteen cruisers since the armistice. Japan is thus able to present a plausible case for expanding her non-capital fleet.

In addition, instead of seizing on Japanese naval construction as a pretext to call for beefing up the budget of the Royal Navy, as were the more extreme navalists of the day, Bywater opposed the navy lobby. On June 17, he deplored a proposal to build new cruisers. "The cruiser outlook, while not altogether satisfactory," he wrote in the *Daily News*, "is less serious than manipulated figures may indicate it to be. . . . The British Navy occupies an absolutely unique position." The next day the *News* supported him editorially: "To those who say 'Great Britain is dropping behind in the naval race' our Naval Correspondent has knocked these audacious statements to smithereens."

Finally, in assessing the charge that Bywater had irresponsibly riled troubled waters for purposes of personal gain, one must take into account the character of the man. Bywater was a serious journalist. The evidence of his life and writing points to that. The truth of the matter is that Bywater became the first reporter in the West to learn of an important change in Japanese naval policy simply because, after having written two books and scores of articles dealing with Japanese sea power, he was better informed about developments in this area than any of his colleagues. Bywater had scooped them on this score in the past, and he would do so in the future. It was not even pure coincidence that he should have done it on the eve of the publication of *The Great Pacific War*. After all, it was because of the Japanese-American confrontation in the Pacific that Bywater had written his book in the first place, and it was also because of this confrontation that the Japanese were once again beginning to enlarge their navy.

More serious than any doubt about Bywater's professional integrity is the question of why the other members of the Press Gang should have been so blind. The answer, it seems, is that they were beguiled by an illusion of racial superiority and could not believe that diminutive Japan would challenge the great powers by expanding her navy. The sneering indulged in by the Tokyo correspondent of the *Times* bespoke the mentality of his peers. Even as late as 1935, the British naval attaché in Tokyo cabled to the director of Naval Intelligence in London: "The Japanese have peculiarly slow brains. Teachers . . . have assured me that this is fundamentally due to the strain put on the child's brain in learning some 6,000 Chinese characters before any real education can start. . . . The inertia shows itself by an inherent disability to switch the mind from one subject to another with rapidity."

This tripe was not contemptuously dismissed, but given credence and wide circulation, distributed even at the Royal Naval Staff College. The fact that Bywater was never taken in by such racist nonsense at a time when so many of his colleagues were is further evidence that he was above the sort of mendacity of which he was accused just as his fourth book came rolling off the press.

"PROPHETIC!" "MISCHIEVOUS!" "A BUNGLE!"

"ONE OF THE few things in this world which do not come off are prophecies." So began a "Books and Authors" column in a June 1925 issue the London *Daily News*. The column continued: "A new form of prophecy will be employed by Mr. Hector C. Bywater in his new book, which Messers. Constable are bringing out. It is entitled *The Great Pacific War: A History of the American-Japanese Campaign of 1931–32* . . . , a novel in which America wins from Japan (as the racing people have it) by a short head."

That flip news item was the first announcement of *The Great Pacific War*. When the book was published about a month later, a number of newspapers considered it worth a much longer story. The *New York Evening Post*, for example, published a news story about Bywater's book on July 16 under the following stack of headlines:

U.S. DEFEATS JAPAN
IN WAR PICTURED BY
BRITISH NAVAL MAN

* * *

Book By H. C. Bywater Visualizes a
2-Year Conflict in 1933 Caused
by Unrest in Nippon

* * *

Enemy Takes Philippines:
Decisive Battle in Pacific

* * *

TROUBLE WITH CHINA, RUSSIA, AND
CLASH WITH PLANES AND SHIPS
BEAT FOE

The *Evening Post* article then described the book in detail, concluding: "What he is trying to prove is that a war in the Pacific could be fought to a decision . . . and that those who hold to the contrary view are suffering from a delusion."

The book was widely reviewed in Great Britain, the United States, and Japan. In fact, no major newspaper in any of these three countries failed to comment on the book, and most did so prominently. In the West, praise was generally glowing; in Japan, the book was received with scorn and derision. Indeed, Japanese authors soon made the writing of "answers" to Bywater a minor publishing genre.

Most Western naval experts who reviewed *The Great Pacific War* found it convincing from a technical point of view. *The New York Times*, for example, published a laudatory review by Nicholas Roosevelt, a cousin of Franklin's* and then a member of the editorial board of the newspa-

---

* No record of Franklin Roosevelt's reaction to the book exists, although it seems likely that he read it. Apart from the fact that he had a serious interest in Pacific naval strategy, Franklin Roosevelt was in close touch with Nicholas during 1925 and would have been alerted to the existence of the book by seeing his front-page review in the *Times*.

In any case, it is certain that Franklin Roosevelt became familiar with at least the *ideas* in *The Great Pacific War*. In 1936, then-president Roosevelt purchased a thinly veiled copy of Bywater's book called *War in the Pacific* by Sutherland Denlinger and Charles B. Gary. This book may be found today along with President Roosevelt's personal copy of Bywater's *Sea Power in the Pacific* in the Franklin D. Roosevelt Library at Hyde Park, N.Y., inscribed on the flyleaf "Franklin D. Roosevelt, The White House, 1936."

per, in which he declared: "If there is going to be a war between Japan and the United States this volume may prove to have foretold accurately many of the most important incidents in it." The review appeared on the front page of the Sunday Book Review under a large, dramatic picture of American destroyers laying a smoke screen while on maneuvers in the Pacific. A one-inch-high headline read: IF WAR COMES IN THE PACIFIC.

Charles N. Robinson, naval correspondent of the London *Times* and author of the broadside *The Great Naval War of 1887*, which probably influenced Bywater's book, declared that *The Great Pacific War* had "the ring of truth" and that the lessons Bywater drew "are worthy to be borne in mind, and for them alone Mr. Bywater's interesting book is well worth reading." The American periodical *Booklist* commented that Bywater's scenario had been "drawn with such convincing realism, the strategic moves and countermoves of the suppositious campaign so accurately presented, that the book has excited Japanese criticism," and the British magazine *Punch* saluted Bywater for conveying "an amazing impression of historic truth."

Reviewers who found *The Great Pacific War* implausible were a small minority. A writer for the British magazine *The Nation and The Athenaeum* derided Bywater's fictional war as "happily improbable." Especially outlandish, this reviewer thought, was the notion that "a [Japanese] army of 100,000 men, with all their impedimenta," could be transported to the Philippines and supplied there.

Many reviewers commented on whether the book would serve to incite war or warn against it. "One of its best points," wrote the reviewer for the American magazine *Outlook*, "is that it emphasizes the wicked folly of a war between Japan and this country." The *New Republic* agreed: "Surely anyone who finds in *The Great Pacific War* an incentive to the war spirit must have considerably more than the common measure of stupidity." And the *Saturday Review of Literature* praised the book for "emphasizing the futility of an American-Japanese war." The Boston *Independent*, however, concluded a favorable review with the words: "Unfortunately, the dramatic side of the tactical excitement of war so overshadows the horrors of the losses sustained on both sides that one would almost wish to see Mr. Bywater's drama acted."

Some regarded the book as an amusement. The playwright Eugene O'Neill obtained a copy in July 1926 while he and his family were summering in Maine. O'Neill was then struggling to write *Strange In-*

terlude, but, for relaxation, he, his wife, his son, and a friend devised a game based on Bywater's book, which they played throughout the summer. A humorous reference to "witch doctors from the Solomon islands" in *Strange Interlude* may have been inspired by *The Great Pacific War*.

Virtually all members of the Fleet Street Press Gang, some of whom had been hostile to Bywater only a few weeks earlier, recognized *The Great Pacific War* for the minor masterpiece it was. Writing for the *Daily Telegraph*, Archibald Hurd, the dean of the Press Gang, declared: "On naval strategy, Mr. Bywater speaks with authority, and this dramatic narrative could hardly be bettered as a means of driving home his views." Hurd added that the book is "far more interesting than the average novel." The review in the British service monthly, the *Navy*, was an unabashed love letter, spun out at such length that it appeared in two installments in the magazine. Written by the now nearly blind Maurice Prendergast, Bywater's friend who had drawn the chart of warship silhouettes to illustrate *Sea Power in the Pacific*, the review stated: "One can, hardly put the book down without feeling that this is history as it may yet be written. . . . We sincerely congratulate Mr. Bywater on the production of the best 'future war yarn' yet penned."

In the United States, a writer for *Proceedings of the U.S. Naval Institute* echoed the praise Bywater had received from his professional colleagues in England. He was hailed for his "surprising insight into the problems of the Pacific, and the strength of the Japanese and American navies," and commended for presenting "an accurate impression of modern naval warfare."

There was one dissenting voice among the Western service writers who commented publicly on *The Great Pacific War*. This criticism afforded Bywater an opportunity to defend his book and, in so doing, to spell out a fundamental concept that underlay *The Great Pacific War*. His critic in question was Sir Frederic Maurice, a British Army officer who had served as director of military operations of the Imperial General Staff during the First World War. Writing for the *Empire Review*, Maurice dismissed Bywater's imaginary war as highly unlikely. A few months later, Henry Goddard Leach, the editor of the *Forum*, an American magazine that specialized in "giving both sides" of controversial issues, invited both Maurice and Bywater to participate in a literary debate under the heading: "Is a War with Japan Possible?" Both accepted the commission, and their essays appeared in the June 1926 issue.

Maurice's contribution, entitled "The Factor of Raw Materials," was presented first. He argued that there were no conceivable circumstances in which a war against the United States would "appear to the statesmen of Japan to offer advantages commensurate with its risks." The reason, Maurice declared, was that the Japanese were well aware that a war against the United States would be a fight between a colossus that has "the largest supply of raw materials and the most highly developed industries applicable to the purposes of war" versus a nation that has "the least of both."

Bywater's rejoinder, entitled "The Russo-Japanese Precedent," contended that those who believed Japan "would never dream of going to war with America" were captives of the delusion that all future wars must follow the course of the First World War. The precedent of the Russo-Japanese War must also be considered, he said.

Japan had seemed to be "courting destruction" when she attacked the Russian Empire in 1904, Bywater wrote. She had practically no reserves of coal, iron, and other essential war materials. All of her major warships and heavy artillery pieces were of foreign construction, and her industry was not yet capable of replacing any lost in battle. Financially, too, Japan was at a disadvantage with a depleted treasury, whereas czarist Russia had command of abundant cash and credit. As a result, Western observers regarded a Russo-Japanese war as "impossible." When the impossible took place, he continued, these same observers insisted that "everything would be over in a few weeks, owing to the exhaustion of Japan's resources." Nevertheless, the war lasted for almost two years, and although toward the end Japan was approaching the limit of her endurance, she was able to keep her navy and army supplied with all necessities until the cease-fire.

"The error into which the prophets had fallen," Bywater wrote, "was in confusing potential with actual resources." Russia was "never able to deploy more than a relatively small part of her strength in the war zone," which lay at an immense distance from her industrial heartland. Japan, on the other hand, fighting almost on her own ground, was "able to throw into the contest every ounce of weight she possessed. Russia fought with one hand tied, Japan with both hands free."

"A future war in the Far East with Japan and the United States as belligerents," he went on to say, "would be waged under conditions not very dissimilar." He then provided a summary of the conflict envisioned in *The Great Pacific War* and concluded: "We see, therefore, that in relation to a conflict between Japan and the United States, the question of material resources is less important than it is often assumed to be. To count upon Japanese inferiority in this respect as a positive guarantee against war in the Pacific would surely be unwise."

If *The Great Pacific War* aroused considerable interest in the West, that was mild compared to its reception in Japan. On the one hand, the Japanese were fascinated by Bywater's application of the principles of naval strategy to the Pacific, but on the other hand, they felt angry and humiliated by his making Japan the loser. The notion that Japan would be defeated was "mistaken" and "illogical," thundered Soho Tokutomi, editor of *Kokumin*, a newspaper that emphasized military and naval news. Tokyo's two major daily newspapers, *Asahi* and *Nichi Nichi*, which were read throughout Japan, scored Bywater's book as "provocative" and, in portraying Japan the loser, insulting.

Nichi Nichi went a step further and declared in an editorial that *The Great Pacific War* apparently had been inspired by the British Government. "That Britain is obliged to work for the estrangement of feeling between Japan and America," this editorial stated, "is the natural result of her abrogation of the Anglo-Japanese Alliance at the Washington Conference on her own initiative . . . [but] it is absurd for Britain to try to influence the situation in the Far East by means of such petty tricks as are illustrated by Mr. Bywater's new book."

Writing for *Chugai Shogyo*, a newspaper that catered to the business community, Komatsu Midori, the former Japanese governor-general of Korea, vigorously seconded the view that Bywater had served as a tool of the British government. *The Great Pacific War*, Midori wrote, was "a bungle hardly meriting comment" except that it illustrated, as did a recent speech by former prime minister Lloyd George, the lengths to which Britain would go in order to "bring ruin to Japan."

Equally savage was the attack on Bywater launched by A. Morgan Young, the British editor of the English-language *Japan Weekly Chronicle*, published in Kobe. *The Great Pacific War* was a "second-rate work of fiction," wrote Young in a blustery editorial. He continued: "This is a thoroughly mischievous work . . . chiefly because of the tendency it has to get people into the habit of thinking that a war between Japan and America is inevitable, while, being written for American consumption, it panders to the Anglo-Saxon conceit of always winning the last battle."

Young also castigated Bywater for having "somewhat restored the idea of a good gentlemanly war." While acknowledging that Bywater had said that a Japanese-American war would cause great destruction and loss of life, Young declared: "Mr. Bywater certainly does make his war as pleasant as possible. . . . In short, this book is sheer propaganda of the usual base quality that is issued in war-time—but it comes out in time of peace."

Still irked by the book, Young cabled London and asked Joseph M. Kenworthy, a retired naval officer then a member of Parliament, to review *The Great Pacific War* for his newspaper. Kenworthy replied with a review that attacked the book for its "distinct anti-Japanese bias" and argued—perhaps giving Young more than he bargained for—that "a much more likely war would be a Japanese-Russian combination against England." Japanese diplomats in the United States and Great Britain also condemned the book as "provocative" and destined to stimulate ill feeling between the two countries.

Bywater bore all this in stoic silence, except on one occasion when he wrote in the Baltimore *Sun* in August 1926:

> From time to time I have been singled out for attack [by an unnamed pro-Japanese magazine] on account of my articles in the *Sun* and as the author of a book portraying an imaginary war in the Far East. My writings are held up as evidence of a deep-laid plot to "railroad" America and Japan into war, with the object of relieving Europe of its war debts. With those two countries involved in a mutually ruinous struggle, Britain, as a purveyor of munitions to both belligerents, would do a thriving trade, and might even succeed in converting her American debt into a credit balance.

Bywater had little difficulty showing the absurdity of that accusation. A war between the United States and Japan would hardly benefit Britain, he declared. If the United States won, she would displace Britain in the Far East. If Japan emerged the winner, Britain's "open door" to China would be slammed shut. Furthermore, wrote Bywater, his projection of a possible war showed Japan suffering a crushing defeat—"not precisely the line that would be taken if the object were to encourage Japan to go to war."

In contrast, he went on to write, forecasts of a war with America were so common in Japanese newspapers, books, and periodicals as to "defy enumeration," and they "almost always show their country triumphing in a duel with the American colossus." He cited a couple of Japanese authors and quoted a few samples of their overheated prose. "There is nothing exceptional about these quotations," he declared. "If space allowed, I could fill pages of the *Sun* with similar excerpts from the Japanese press."

He concluded:

> That any Englishman in his senses would try to promote a Japanese-American war is inconceivable. Apart from ethical considerations, it would be an act of crass folly. The maintenance of peace in the Far East is quite as much a British as an American interest. . . . For this country [Britain], a Japanese-American war would be an unmitigated curse, because it would raise in the most acute form those racial issues which every statesman of the British Empire, with its vast Oriental population, strives for obvious reasons to keep in the background. Munition contracts would be a poor recompense for the troubles which might beset the Empire if Japan and America came to blows.

About the only favorable voice within Japan concerning Bywater's opus was that of B. W. Fleisher, the American publisher and editor of the English-language newspaper the *Japan Advertiser* and the weekly review called *Trans-Pacific*. Bywater's book was written "with skill and painstaking care," Fleisher declared in an editorial, and those in Japan who said it did more harm than good could not be taken seriously because "it was patent to anyone who read the book that its author's object was, in part, to emphasize the futility of Japan and the United States contemplating a war of such nature, owing to the disastrous consequences likely to befall victor and vanquished alike."

Despite all the condemnation heaped upon *The Great Pacific War*, the Japanese were eager to read it and had ample opportunity to do so. Bywater was aware of several Japanese editions and expressed annoyance to his son that he never received a royalty from Japan. Just a few weeks after it had been published in England, *Kokumin* had *The Great Pacific War* translated into Japanese and ran the entire book in installments. Two months later, *Kokumin* brought out *The Great Pacific War* in book form with a preface by Tokutomi repeating his assertion that it was perverse of Bywater to have concluded his scenario with the defeat of Japan.

A month later, Hakuho-sha, a Tokyo book publisher, had *The Great Pacific War* rendered into Japanese by a translator named Kyoji Kitagami and offered for sale under the title *Taiheiyo no Soha-sen, 1931–1933 (The Great Pacific War, 1931–1933)*.

Two months after that, *The Great Pacific War* was translated and published yet again, this time by Bummei Kyokai, the Waseda University Press, under the title *Taiheiyo Senso to sono Hihan (The Pacific War and Comment)* with a long, argumentative preface by Tota Ishimaru, an officer in the Imperial Navy.

Virtually all contemporary Japanese commentators insisted that Bywater had unfairly stacked the cards against Japan, devising a war situation in which Japan was bound to be the loser. If at first this opinion was expressed in reviews and editorials, it would not be long before complete books were written expressly to refute Bywater's prognostication.

Among the more widely discussed of these "answer books" were scenarios for a Japanese-American war written by Seijiro Kawashima, one of the most popular naval writers in Japan, and Teisuke Akiyama, a writer with close ties to the political establishment. Both their future-war accounts were copies of *The Great Pacific War*, differing from it chiefly in that they made Japan the victor at the war's end.

Kawashima's imitation, which first appeared early in 1926 in two installments in the magazine *Naikwan (Introspection)*, began by shrilly branding the United States "an evil spirit menacing the existence of Japan," and went on to assert that war with the United States is "an absolute necessity" and has been "decreed by Heaven." Kawashima then provided a detailed description of the war that, according to an editorial in *Trans-Pacific*, the English-language review, demonstrated that "Kawashima must not only have read that extraordinary book [*The Great Pacific War*] but . . . studied it closely." Akiyama, the other Japanese scenarist who came under Bywater's influence that year, also regarded a war against the United States as inevitable, and justified the conflict because war would "whip up the present somnolent Japan into a state of spiritual awakening." Akiyama, too, followed Bywater's narrative closely, departing from it only at the end when he had the Japanese smash the American Navy in a climactic sea battle patterned after Togo's victory at Tsushima.

The most thoughtful of the Japanese writers who attacked Bywater soon after the publication of *The Great Pacific War* was Tota Ishimaru, a naval officer who wrote a long preface for his translation of the book published by the Waseda University Press in February 1926. Ishimaru, who signed his preface with a flourish reminiscent of Earl Brassey—"Written by the translator temporarily aboard the *Sugamo* in Tokyo Bay"—acknowledged that Bywater's narrative possessed "a certain degree of rational probability," although the outcome is "insulting to the Ministry of Foreign Affairs of Japan and to our brave and loyal Army and Navy men." Bywater's book, he declared, is not a genuine attempt to forecast the course of a future war but "a format calculated to show how Japan might be defeated." He supported this interpretation by arguing that Bywater put Japan at a disadvantage by having her adopt an "intentionally irrational" strategy—that of seizing Guam and the Philippines at the outset of the war.

"But despite these propagandistic distortions," Ishimaru concluded, "Mr. Bywater's book contains many suggestions and prophetic observations which are extremely valuable. If one discounts the author's falsehoods and twists of fact and puts to good use his strategic analysis, the people of Japan may turn a misfortune into a blessing."

A great many Japanese naval theorists took Ishimaru's advice, freely borrowing from Bywater's scenario only to tack on a happy ending for Japan. Such books and articles continued to be written over the next sixteen years. The last and most widely read of them was Kinoaki Matsuo's *The Three Power Alliance and a United States–Japanese War*, a book popularly referred to as "the Japanese *Mein Kampf*," published in 1940. The author, a Japanese Naval Intelligence officer and member of the ultranationalist Black Dragon Society, appropriated Bywater's ideas extensively, always carefully crediting him by name. As in *The Great Pacific War*, Matsuo had Japan make a surprise attack against the U.S. Pacific force and launch simultaneous invasions of Guam and the Philippines (landing on the latter at Lingayen Gulf and Lamon Bay, as Bywater had specified).

"As Bywater has pointed out," Matsuo wrote, "if Guam and the Philippines fall into . . . [Japanese] hands, the United States will be confronted with a serious problem, the solution of which will be almost impossible." But that was as far as Matsuo followed Bywater. As carefully as he read the opening chapters of the book, he ignored the last 155 pages.

CHAPTER

16

"ATTACK AMERICANS AT HAWAII"

WHILE CRITICS AND commentators were having their say about *The Great Pacific War* in the public press, Japanese agents stationed in the United States discreetly sent reports about Bywater's latest book to their superiors in Tokyo. There was nothing underhanded about such communications. All nations maintain agents in foreign countries to keep themselves informed about developments in the host countries.

The Japanese military, naval, and diplomatic traffic concerning *The Great Pacific War* was unusually heavy, and it is of interest for two reasons. First, it is another indication of the seriousness with which Bywater's book was taken by high officials of the Japanese government. Second, and most important, it reveals the fact that a boyish-looking navy captain named Isoroku Yamamoto, while serving as naval attaché at the Japanese embassy in Washington, was among those who reported to Tokyo about *The Great Pacific War*. When Yamamoto returned to

177

Japan two years later, he delivered a lecture in which he adopted By-water's ideas as his own. His exposure to—and acceptance of—By-water's strategy for Japan is important because years afterward, when commander-in-chief of the Combined Fleet of the Imperial Navy, Ya-mamoto would face down nearly universal opposition in the navy in order to be allowed to put into practice a war plan astonishingly similar to that spelled out for Japan in *The Great Pacific War*.

Born in 1884—the same year as Bywater—Yamamoto was small, fine boned, and slightly built even by Japanese standards. He dressed immaculately, and whether emerging from a submarine or the cramped cockpit of a navy bomber, his clothes invariably seemed spotless and smartly pressed. Even his blemishes inspired awe. His scarred left hand, missing the first two fingers, was the most visible of his many wounds received at the Battle of Tsushima in 1905. "Whenever I go into a public bath," he would quip, "people think I'm a gangster." But he was being modest. Throughout his life, countrymen would stare at Yamamoto's maimed left hand and feel a surge of emotion and closeness with Japan and her destiny.

In later years, Emperor Hirohito, mindful of Yamamoto's injury, presented him with two false fingers, beautifully fashioned from leather, to go with formal dress. Mostly, the leather fingers stayed in their san-dalwood box.

Yamamoto never played the war hero. Unpretentious and childlike, at a party he would suddenly strip off his trousers, wrap a towel around his waist, and, still wearing his naval officer's jacket, perform what he called "an African king dance"—a frenzied jig during which he would juggle two dinner plates. On other occasions, he would stand on his head, leap somersaults in the air, or get down on all fours and blow against an egg so as to roll it successively to each corner of a room. He adored playing charades; his friends said they could never forget the night he acted out a vintage airplane taking flight, and then, as a crown-ing performance, the Big Dipper.

While playful on the surface, Yamamoto's love of games—especially gambling and all sorts of endurance contests—had a serious purpose. These were the means with which he civilized an aggressive nature. Throughout his adult life, he was almost continuously engaged in one contest or another, whether poker, bridge, mah-jongg, chess, shogi, go, billiards, roulette, or some challenge of his own invention. On many occasions, he was the ringleader of a poker game that might last thirty to forty hours nonstop. While at sea, he customarily played five games of chess every day. He seemed to relish every contest, and every aspect of each contest. He once mesmerized an opponent who had casually agreed to play a game of chess by sending him an elaborate scroll in the manner of a samurai invitation to a duel to the death.

After recovering from the wounds he received at Tsushima, Yamamoto narrowly qualified as physically fit for service. His rise was then rapid. Because the Imperial Navy regarded the United States as its most likely future opponent, the brightest young naval officers were sent there on various tours of duty. Yamamoto visited several ports on the West Coast of the United States aboard a training ship in 1909, studied English for a year at Harvard in 1919, returned for the Washington Conference on Naval Limitation in 1921, and finally took up his duties as naval attaché at the embassy in March 1926.

He understood, in his new capacity, that his most important task was to keep a close watch on the United States Navy. He was to report immediately to the Navy General Staff in Tokyo any indication he might detect of preparations for war, or other activities that might affect Japan. This surveillance—sanctioned espionage—was, and remains, the essential work of naval and military attachés. It is accepted on the theory that tolerating some limited spying by the uniformed attachés of potential adversaries helps to keep the peace; when the attachés' reports indicate that no unusual activity is taking place, international tensions are soothed.

An enterprising attaché can also use his privileged access to the military or naval establishment of the host country to gather all sorts of potentially useful information, and Yamamoto appears to have exploited this opportunity with his customary diligence. For example, in July 1926, accompanied by a U.S. intelligence officer, he inspected the devastation at the naval ammunition depot at Lake Denmark, New Jersey, which had blown up, perhaps triggered by an electrical storm. A score of lives had been lost and damage totaled $50 million. Yamamoto also visited airports, harbors, and factories, but always—so far as is known—on officially approved trips.

His most important means of gathering information, according to former Japanese naval attachés who served in Washington before the war, was his careful reading of American newspapers, magazines, and books. "America being what it is with freedom of the press et cetera, a great deal of material comes out in magazines and newspapers," one former Japanese naval attaché told an interrogator in 1945. "By this method, we picked up much information. Accordingly, that is where I laid my primary stress."

Being a voracious reader, Yamamoto was well chosen for this work. While at Harvard, he had raced through four or five biographies of Abraham Lincoln before pronouncing Carl Sandburg's the finest of the lot. At the Washington Conference, Yamamoto scanned as many as forty newspapers and periodicals every day for any comment about Japan or the Japanese proposals.

It is hardly surprising, therefore, that he should have pounced upon Bywater's *The Great Pacific War* as a genuine find when he encountered the book soon after arriving in Washington. A Western expert's view of a future Pacific war was precisely the sort of material he had been sent to the United States to be on the lookout for. Moreover, the author was not just any Western expert. Bywater, after all, had written the important *Sea Power in the Pacific* and was the correspondent who, during the Washington Conference, had found out what the Japanese delegates were going to say even before they opened their mouths.

The obvious place to find proof that Yamamoto read and reacted to *The Great Pacific War* would be among the reports from the naval attachés now in the archives of the Military History Department of the National Defense College in Tokyo (Boeicho Boei Kenshujo Senshibu Shiryoko). Yamamoto is known to have written a quantity of such reports between March 1926 and March 1928. Unfortunately, all attaché reports written after 1921, and most records of the Navy General Staff (Gunreibu), which kept copies of these documents on file, were destroyed either by the American bombing of Tokyo on May 25, 1945, which burned out half of the Navy Ministry building, or by the Japanese themselves just before American occupation troops arrived at the war's end. Early in 1945, the Potsdam Declaration had announced to the Axis nations that "stern justice shall by meted out to all war criminals," and that prompted fearful Japanese officers to begin the wholesale destruction of Imperial Navy records.

Consequently, one must look elsewhere for confirmation of Yamamoto's exposure to *The Great Pacific War*. Fortunately, the Diplomatic Record Office (Gaiko Shiryokan) in Tokyo proves a treasure house of revealing documents from the 1920s. These files show that during the time Yamamoto served as naval attaché, quite a number of Japanese officials living in the United States sent home reports about articles in the press and periodicals relating to *The Great Pacific War*. Significantly, two of the officials who sent home such material happened to be close friends of Yamamoto, and, in the opinion of former members of the Japanese diplomatic corps, they would not have failed to mention information about Bywater's book to their navy colleague and friend, if indeed it was not *he* who first brought these items to their attention.

Furthermore, two top-level military briefing papers dealing predominantly with *The Great Pacific War*, and the controversy surrounding it, have survived in the Diplomatic Record Office. Both documents are based on information that was obviously supplied by the uniformed attachés at the Japanese embassy in Washington during the first seven months of Yamamoto's tenure there. These papers remove all reasonable doubt that Yamamoto followed the controversy over *The Great Pacific War* and reported extensively about it.

One of Yamamoto's best friends in the diplomatic service who sent home information about *The Great Pacific War* was Hiroshi Saito, a slightly built, sad-eyed man who, like Yamamoto, was a graduate of the Nagaoka Middle School and a member of the Nagaoka clan. According to Yamamoto's son, the two men were close not only because they hailed from the same provincial city and school but because they served together on two overlapping tours of duty in the United States and held similar views about the formidable power of America as a potential enemy. So firm was their friendship that when Saito died in 1939 while Japanese ambassador in Washington and his ashes were sent home aboard the American cruiser *Astoria*, Yamamoto put great store in meeting the American warship at the pier at Yokohama. When he did so, the ship's captain, Richmond K. Turner, presented him with a signed photograph of the *Astoria*, which Yamamoto kept prominently displayed on his library desk.

It was while serving as consul general in New York City in 1926 that Saito's attention was caught by Bywater's *The Great Pacific War*. On June 4, he sent the Foreign Ministry in Tokyo a copy of the debate between Bywater and Sir Frederic Maurice, which had appeared in the *Forum* headlined "Is a War with Japan Possible?" This literary debate, as Saito pointed out, had been prompted by the publication of Bywater's

The Great Pacific War. In the view of several former Japanese naval attachés who served in Washington before the war, Saito would have alerted Yamamoto to any such material before dispatching it to Tokyo.

Another good friend of Yamamoto in the diplomatic corps who informed his superiors about the debate over *The Great Pacific War* was Tsuneo Matsudaira, a patrician with a pencil-like mustache who served as Japanese ambassador to the United States throughout Yamamoto's term as naval attaché. Although Matsudaira publicly dismissed talk of a possible Japanese-American war with remarks such as "One does not fight one's best customer," he sent home a different message. On August 28, 1926, he wrote to Foreign Minister Kijuro Shidehara: "I have frequently reported to you about the possibility of the outbreak of a Japanese-American war, and this issue is still being discussed in certain quarters with considerable interest. The Baltimore *Sun*, dated August 13, 1926, carried an article by Bywater entitled 'England Craves Peace Between U.S. and Japan.'" Matsudaira then gave a complete translation of this article in which Bywater defended *The Great Pacific War* against the accusation that his motive in writing it had been to provoke conflict.

Rather than include the newspaper clipping from the Baltimore *Sun*, Matsudaira enclosed a three-page, single-spaced typewritten copy of Bywater's article in English. Former Japanese naval attachés said that in this case, too, Matsudaira would have shared such an article with the naval attaché whose office was just down the hall.

Saito and Matsudaira were only two of a number of Japanese diplomats who reported home about Bywater's book. Others who did so included Masanao Uehara, who had succeeded Shidehara as ambassador to the United States; and Toshihiko Taketomi, the consul general in San Francisco. Such frequent mention of a foreign journalist by name was unusual in Japanese diplomatic correspondence from the United States. Even so prominent a commentator as Walter Lippmann is mentioned only once in the years between 1921 and 1926. The fact that Bywater's name appears as often as it does suggests the potency of his writing in Japanese thought. And if Japanese diplomats, who had a wide range of concerns, were impressed by what Bywater wrote, one feels certain that a navy man such as Yamamoto was drawn even more strongly to his writing.

Still more compelling evidence to suggest Yamamoto's familiarity with Bywater's book is contained in the previously mentioned briefing papers. These documents were issued by the Army General Staff (Sanbo

Honbu), the highest peacetime council of the Imperial Army, which was headed by a member of the emperor's family and composed of officers of the highest rank. Mimeographed copies of these extraordinary twenty-two- and twenty-nine-page papers were sent to a small circle of officers and diplomats—hence their survival in the Diplomatic Record Office—in order to inform them about a book that contained novel ideas of obvious importance to Japan.

Although it is unlikely that the Tokyo headquarters of the Army General Staff and the Navy General Staff exchanged information in 1926 (they did so later on), the reverse is true, in the view of former attachés, of the army and navy attachés in their small office in Washington. On so weighty a matter as the possibility of a future war, the attachés worked as a team and shared virtually everything they came across. Thus, it appears that the material in the two briefing papers reflects contributions from both Yamamoto and his army counterpart, Colonel Noburu Morita, the military attaché.

The first of these documents is a twenty-two-page, handwritten mimeographed report from the Army General Staff dated June 20, 1926, entitled "The Debate Concerning a Japanese-American War" and addressed to top-ranking service and diplomatic personnel. It begins with a complete translation of the debate between Bywater and Sir Frederic Maurice in the *Forum*. The paper then notes that the May 1926 issue of an American service publication, the *Coast Artillery Journal*, had summarized an essay by Maurice that appeared previously in the *Empire Review*, a British magazine. It was there that Maurice had reviewed *The Great Pacific War*. "Sir Frederic has evidently read Bywater's recent book, but will have none of it," the *Coast Artillery Journal* was quoted in the document as stating. "He [Maurice] thinks Japan is secure in the Western Pacific and will never risk war with . . . [the United States]."

The fact that the information in the briefing paper came from two American publications, instead of directly from the British magazine, marks the source of this material as a Japanese agent in the United States. Of course, virtually any such agent might have sent the *Forum* articles to Tokyo (as did Consul General Saito, for example), but most would have sent them to the Foreign Ministry because all those in the diplomatic service, from the ambassador to the lowliest assistant consul, reported to that office. Since the briefing paper was issued by a military agency rather than the Foreign Ministry, however, the source must have been someone reporting through service channels. And what uniformed Japanese agent in the United States at this time would have been reading the *Coast Artillery Journal?* It was, without doubt, either Yamamoto, Morita, or both.

Yamamoto and Morita's fingerprints are also plainly visible on the second General Staff paper in the diplomatic files concerned with Bywater's *The Great Pacific War.* Dated September 16, 1926, this twenty-nine-page, handwritten, mimeographed document is entitled "The Debate Concerning a U.S.-Japanese War and Observations About Japan That Recently Appeared in the U.S. Press."

Four articles from American newspapers and magazines published during the summer of 1926 are extensively quoted and paraphrased. The first, entitled "The Situation in the Pacific," which appeared in the *Coast Artillery Journal*, argued that "Japan will ultimately resort to the use of force." The second was Bywater's article in the Baltimore *Sun* in which he defended *The Great Pacific War* against the charge of war-mongering. (Matsudaira had sent this same article to the Foreign Ministry.)

The third article quoted and paraphrased was a report in the Baltimore *Sun* on a conference on Japan held at Williams College in Williamstown, Massachusetts, and the fourth was a report in the *Literary Digest* about two widely discussed Japanese prophets of a Japanese-American war. Both of these Japanese writers were said to have been "careful reader(s) of Mr. Hector Bywater's recent novel, *The Great Pacific War.*" Since all of the articles had appeared in American newspapers and magazines, here again the material appears to have been provided by someone living in the United States. One may be confident, therefore, that Yamamoto was involved in the the the procurement and transmission of these articles to Tokyo.

When Yamamoto returned to Japan in March 1928, he was given the command of the light cruiser *Isuzu.* A relatively new vessel of 5,170 tons, she was armed with seven 5.5-inch guns plus antiaircraft weapons and, what must have delighted Yamamoto, a brand-new catapult and reconnaissance plane. It was while serving as captain of *Isuzu* that he delivered the lecture that reveals that Yamamoto had adopted Bywater's war plan.

Being captain of a light cruiser was something of a comedown for one who had been rubbing elbows with President Calvin Coolidge and the international diplomatic corps in Washington. However, Yamamoto's taking command of *Isuzu* was intended as a brief warm-up for his assignment as captain of the 34,000-ton *Akagi,* the new flattop

Bywater had described as "more powerful in every way" than the largest British and American aircraft carriers. The assignment gave Yamamoto time to think—and play.

From all reports, he was unusually permissive as a ship's captain in at least one respect. In the Imperial Navy, if a commanding officer was sighted heading for the wardroom or junior officers' lounge while a game of go, shogi, or mah-jongg was in progress, the young officers would quickly disperse. It was not that gaming was against regulations but that it was considered undignified. Yamamoto, of course, had no such compunction and thoroughly enjoyed joining the young officers in whatever sport was afoot.

But more sober thoughts were also on the mind of the young captain. Shortly after returning to Japan, he articulated them in a lecture about the course of a possible future war between Japan and the United States delivered at the Imperial Navy Torpedo School at Yokosuka. No text of Yamamoto's lecture exists. It was, after all, only the brash talk of a promising young officer freshly returned from a two-year tour of duty in the United States. Nevertheless, the postwar Compilation Committee on the History of the Japanese Naval Air Force, which published a four-volume history in 1970, found and interviewed a former naval officer named Ichitaro Oshima, who recalled having attended Yamamoto's lecture at the torpedo school. "It seems," Oshima told the committee, "that the attack on Pearl Harbor originated during Yamamoto's stay as naval attaché in the United States." Sadamu Sanagi, who served on the Compilation Committee and also knew Yamamoto personally, shared Oshima's conviction.

"In the event of a future war between Japan and the United States," Oshima recalled Yamamoto's having said, "Japan will lose if she adopts the traditional defensive strategy. Japan's only chance of victory would be to attack American forces at Hawaii." Yamamoto then went on to predict, according to Oshima, that aircraft carriers would soon replace battleships as the supreme weapon of naval war, and therefore the attack on Hawaii should be made by naval aircraft.

The meaning of Yamamoto's words requires careful analysis. To begin with, when he said Japan should attack American forces "at Hawaii" he cannot have meant engaging the handful of U.S. troops stationed there—a mere constabulary that could in no way menace Japan or Japanese interests in the Pacific. Did he mean, instead, that Japan should attack the Pearl Harbor naval base? That, too, seems unlikely when one considers that in 1928 Pearl Harbor was only a navy yard and supply depot with no commissioned warships based there. The U.S. Navy's battle fleet was stationed at the San Pedro–Long Beach roadstead near Los Angeles on the California coast, and the Asiatic Fleet—which consisted of only three destroyer squadrons—called Cavite in the Philippines its home port.

What, then, did Yamamoto have in mind? It appears he was looking to the future of Hawaii. In December 1926—ten months after his taking up residence in Washington—the U.S. Navy announced that it had awarded two contracts to dredge 9 million cubic yards of coral from the channel and anchorage at Pearl Harbor so that the base could accommodate a fleet of the largest warships. This information was published in the daily press as well as in naval and trade journals freely available to the public; as with *The Great Pacific War*, it is inconceivable that the Japanese naval attaché in Washington was not well informed about the matter and did not take pains to keep Tokyo abreast of it as well. Furthermore, by the time Yamamoto returned to Japan, he must also have learned that the dredging at Pearl Harbor was progressing rapidly and that the United States was spending a phenomenal $50 million to develop the base as a first-class naval station. Yamamoto thus understood that at some point in the not-too-distant future—sooner rather than later if relations between Japan and the United States became tense—a sizable American fleet would be present at Pearl Harbor. That must have been the target he had in mind when he said Japan should "attack American forces at Hawaii."

But why attack an American fleet 3,374 miles from Tokyo? There can be only one explanation. Yamamoto envisioned Japan boldly extending the boundaries of her empire into the South Seas, planting her flag on the Philippines and perhaps Guam. An effective, preemptive strike against American warships concentrated at Pearl Harbor would prevent them from interfering with highly vulnerable landing operations. Indeed, the Japanese conquest of the Philippines would be impossible so long as a powerful American "fleet-in-being" existed at Hawaii. That fleet would have to become the first casualty of a successful Japanese offensive in the South Sea islands. In short, Yamamoto was proposing the strategy for Japan that he had read about in Bywater's *The Great Pacific War*.

CHAPTER

17

WAR PLAN ORANGE

BYWATER'S BOOK ALSO influenced the leaders of the United States Navy. In fact, it appears that *The Great Pacific War* played an important role in demolishing the navy's remarkably amateurish contingency plan for war against Japan, and in substituting a far more sophisticated strategy that, in general outline, is the course pursued by American forces after war broke out in December 1941.

Like their Japanese counterparts, American navy and military men began to think seriously about the possibility of a Pacific war at about the turn of the century. The United States had extracted Guam and the Philippines from the clutches of Spain at the conclusion of the Spanish-American War in 1898, and only afterward did American leaders come to the full realization that their new acquisitions were situated perilously close to Japan and distant from the United States. Manila, the capital of the Philippines, is only 1,700 miles from the Japanese port city of

Yokosuka but almost 7,000 miles from San Francisco. Guam is closer to Japan than Manila. Even Hawaii, America's mid-Pacific outpost since it was annexed in 1898, is 4,800 miles from Manila—almost three times as far away as Yokosuka.

From these figures, it was obvious to American strategists that if Japan set out to capture Guam and the Philippines, she would have an enormous geographical advantage. The only way to guard against her preemptory seizure of these territories, it became clear, would be with the creation of substantial army garrisons, coastal fortifications, and a powerful naval force ready to meet the invader wherever he chose to strike. In short, there would have to be a major *combined* effort by the army and the navy—something unprecedented in American history. To meet that need, the interservice Joint Army and Navy Board, a predecessor of the current Joint Chiefs of Staff, was established in 1903. For the next thirty-seven years, the Joint Board devoted most of its energies to devising and updating War Plan Orange—a contingency plan for war against Japan. (Japan was always designated as "Orange.")

The first of these plans, as the military historian Louis Morton has pointed out, was only "a statement of principles which, it was piously hoped, could be followed in the event of war." But even as principles, the plans were amazingly naive. Their fundamental notion was that of a naked American thrust across the hostile Pacific. Not even the demonstration of Japan's naval power at Tsushima in 1905 prompted a reconsideration of this rash idea. For example, the version of War Plan Orange approved by the Joint Board in June 1907 stated innocently: "The battle fleet should be assembled and dispatched for the Orient as soon as practicable."

There seemed no appreciation of the fact that with a determined effort, Japan could seize Guam and the Philippines well before reinforcements from the United States could possibly arrive on the scene. Once the United States had lost her footholds in that quarter of the globe, it would be almost suicidal for the American fleet to venture into the Western Pacific in the hope of recapturing the lost territories. There were no fuel depots, no repair docks and supplies along the line of advance, nothing to compensate for the reduced fighting efficiency of warships heavily laden with fuel, no adequate means of defending troop transports in hostile waters, and no plan for the protection of lines of communication. There was not even, it seems, any awareness of the danger of enemy naval action, which would almost certainly include harassment by submarine packs and, at some point, a Tsushima-like ambush.

As late as 1924, War Plan Orange—which had been touched up every few years since 1903—continued to specify a headlong dash by U.S. forces across the Western Pacific to relieve Manila. The seven-page Plan Orange approved by the Joint Board in August 1924 is an extraordinary document. "Operations should be conducted with boldness from the earliest stage of the war," the plan stated. And bold indeed was the operation imagined. Within ten days of the outbreak of war, an army corps consisting of "at least 50,000 troops" was to be dispatched to Hawaii. Four days later, this force was expected to push off from Honolulu (Pearl Harbor was not yet developed) on a 4,800-mile voyage across the Western Pacific. "It [was] understood," the authors stated, "that the promptest possible reinforcement of Manila Bay is of the greatest military and naval importance." It was a prescription for disaster.

Not every strategist in the United States Navy was a captive of this thinking. Shortly after the end of the First World War, men like James H. Oliver, director of the navy's Plans Division, were arguing that an American naval force striking out across a hostile Western Pacific would have to make intermediate stops before liberating Guam or the Philippines. Even earlier, a group of forward-looking navy and Marine Corps officers centered around William S. Sims, president of the U.S. Naval War College, had been privately discussing ideas similar to those in the mind of Hector Bywater. As early as 1913, a student at the Naval War College named Earl "Pete" Ellis, a brilliant but eccentric Marine officer given to bouts of drunkenness, outlined a radical war-contingency plan for the Pacific. Ellis* imagined that after the outbreak of a Japanese-American war, amphibious American forces could use a chain of Central Pacific islands as stepping-stones to Manila. The daring idea won advocates such as Sims, then an instructor at the college; John A. Lejeune,

---

* Ellis died in 1923 while exploring the military possibilities of Micronesia. Contrary to popular myth, alcohol, and not Japanese skulduggery, was responsible for his death. (See Ballendorf, PER.)

the future commandant of the Marine Corps; Alfred P. Niblack, who became director of the Office of Naval Intelligence; and William V. Pratt, who served on the General Board of the Navy and later became chief of naval operations.

Strangely, these officers were careless about keeping their ideas under wraps, and because their plans occasionally surfaced in public, the American visionaries and Hector Bywater seem to have reinforced each other's thinking over a period of years. As we have seen, at a meeting of the Society of Naval Architects and Marine Engineers in New York City in 1915, Niblack talked openly about the possibility of a Pacific island–hopping campaign. Bywater was either in the audience or later read Niblack's remarks in the society's *Transactions*. And although he declared in the preface to *Sea Power in the Pacific* that he alone must accept "full and undivided responsibility" for all of the strategic ideas presented in his book, Bywater acknowledged the value of Niblack's lecture.

Also, in the fall of 1921, when Sims reviewed *Sea Power in the Pacific* for the *Atlantic Monthly*, he let slip—or perhaps deliberately leaked—"the possibility of utilizing the Caroline and Marshall islands as an advance base for our fleet."

Whatever Sims's motives for writing as he did, Bywater may have received a useful hint from his review and thus, when composing *The Great Pacific War* four years later, followed Sims's lead and spelled out a zigzag, island-hopping campaign through the Caroline and Marshall islands.

But why were Niblack and Sims so open about matters of such obvious sensitivity? Perhaps they wanted to alert the Japanese to the fact that the United States would stop at nothing to protect her possessions in the Western Pacific. Or maybe they were using their forums as platforms from which to persuade their fellow naval officers of the need to develop a capability in amphibious warfare.

Still, as far as War Plan Orange was concerned, prior to the publication of *The Great Pacific War*, Niblack, Sims, Lejeune, and the others were voices crying in the wilderness, and the official intention of the Joint Army and Navy Board remained that of launching a 4,800-mile-long charge across the Western Pacific. It may have been frustration with this scheme that moved William Howard Gardiner, the vice president of the United States Navy League and a confidant of Sims, to

Left, James Gordon Bennett (*Brown Brothers*).
Above, torpedo practice in 1904.
Bottom, Japanese battleships in action during the Russo-Japanese War (*U.S. Navy photo*).

Hector Bywater, standing right, with his family in 1892. It was at about
this age that Bywater discovered that visiting the Royal Dockyards was
his "nearest conception of heaven" (*courtesy of Jeffrey Holman*).

Left, Togo as a celebrity in Japan. No admiral had come as close to matching Nelson
at Trafalgar as Togo at Tsushima (*The Bettmann Archive/BBC Hulton*).

Churchill and Fisher at about the time they dubbed Bywater their
"splendid spy in Germany" (*courtesy of Mary Soames*).

Bywater and his wife in Dresden at about the time he was recruited
by the British Secret Service (*courtesy of Gladys E. Bywater-Calnan*).

Top, Bywater in 1915 (*U.S. State Department*); bottom, masthead of the "Dockyard Liar."

Top left, Archibald Hurd; top right, H. C. Ferraby; center left, Francis McMurtrie; center right, Oscar Parkes; bottom, Fred Jane playing his naval war game (Hurd *courtesy of Ian Bremner*; Ferraby, *The Bettmann Archive/BBC Hulton*; others *courtesy of Jane's Publishing Co., Ltd.*).

Left top, Earl Ellis (*U.S. Department of Defense photo*).
Left bottom, Homer Lea in his Chinese general's uniform (*Brown Brothers*).
Below, the pocket battleship *Graf Spee* (*Topham*).

Bywater at about the time he wrote *The Great
Pacific War* (*courtesy of Rev. Hector W. R. Bywater*).

Franklin D. Roosevelt, left, with his Navy Department Chief, Josephus Daniels, shortly before his "debate" with Bywater (*Franklin D. Roosevelt Library*).

TTERS TO HE EDITOR

The Schools Provided With ble Fire Escapes? Have chool Commissioners Per- y Inspected Them?

E EDITOR OF THE SUN—*Sir:* s questionable whether any of the Board of School Com- s inspected personally the fire a the public school buildings, er they relied on reports of tes, who might be anxious to some serious neglect in this ant matter.

school people consider fire b be safe that are constructed covered partly by corrugated so, then the whole inspection t may be largely unreliable.

these wooden structures is a the northern side of school orner of Biddle and Patterson ue. Can it be true that such are considered good enough any children in that section? re, Sept. 1.   JUSTICE.

FRANKLIN D. ROOSEVELT ANSWERS MR. BYWATER

Problems That Focus In The Pacific Do Not Justify Fear Nor The Armaments To Which It Leads.

By FRANKLIN D. ROOSEVELT.
Former Assistant Secretary of the Navy.

HYDE PARK, N. Y., Aug. 13.
I have been greatly interested in the comment of your London correspond- ent, Mr. Hector C. Bywater, on my article in the July Number of *Asia* on American-Japanese relations. His deep study of the whole Pacific question gives his views great weight, yet I fear that Mr. Bywater is still looking at the relationships of people and lands bor- dering on the Pacific Ocean from the old point of view.

It is true that in the past both Great

Indies—these are gestures not in accord with the spirit of the day.

Why this new arming? It is not fear of Russia or China or the United States. It is for fear of Japan. It will result in the same old vicious circle. Mr. Bywater still assumes that Japan's present and future needs for a "population outlet" must force her to seek lands in the South Pacific; and that this means inevitable clash with Great Britain and the Netherlands. I do not grant the clash because I do

Yamamoto during his tenure as naval attaché in Washington, with Navy Secretary Curtis Wilbur (*U.S. Navy Historical Center photo*). Below, the "debate" in the Baltimore *Sun* (Reprinted from the Baltimore *Sun* © 1923, The Baltimore Sun Co.).

「バイウォータ」（Hector C. Bywater）不可能
論ニ対スル駁論ヲ掲載レタルガ右萬座官種ヲンジ
要譯センノ何事氏参ヲ遙本読切提ホ候
義ニ報告ス
本信送付先　在米英大使

Consul General Hiroshi Saito, inset, spelled out Bywater's name in English (circled) on the last page of a communiqué reporting on the debate over *The Great Pacific War* (*Gaiko Shiryokan*).

Yamamoto in London in 1934 when he met Bywater (*AP/Wide World*).

By 1936, Bywater was a sought-after author and speaker. Above, a
London Press Club program (*courtesy of Gladys E. Bywater-Calnan*).

Above left, Dudley Knox (*U.S. Navy Historical Center*); right, Melville Cox (*AP/Wide World*); bottom, the monstrous *Yamato* nears completion at Kure (*U.S. Navy photo*).

Left, Bywater in 1940.
Below left, Yamamoto's official portrait (*Kaigun Bunko*).
Right, Chester W. Nimitz (*National Archives*).

suggest to Bywater over dinner in 1924 that he dramatize the folly of such an undertaking in his war scenario. Whether prompted or not, Bywater devoted two chapters of *The Great Pacific War* to just such a plan and its tragic result.

Although briefly alluded to in chapter 13, it will be useful here to spell out in detail Bywater's account of this American naval charge in order to show how persuasive were his arguments.

In his narrative, Bywater wrote that shortly after the outbreak of a Japanese-American war, "the popular clamor for energetic naval action" in the United States forces the American government to attempt a daring—and foolhardy—attack. It is not aimed at Manila; in Bywater's view, the garrison in the Philippines could not possibly hold out until even the speediest reinforcements arrive from the United States. By the time the U.S. Navy's battle fleet could make it there, American soldiers in the Philippines, no matter how brave and well led, would have long since been killed or captured by Japanese forces. Consequently, Bywater imagined an equally bold transpacific venture seeking to capture Port Lloyd in the Japanese Bonin, or Ogasawara, Islands, which lie about 600 miles southeast of Tokyo.

This plan is no "spur of the moment" improvisation, he declared, but "one among several Pacific war plans which the Bureau of Operations had studied in collaboration with the War College and the General Board of the Navy, long before hostilities were in sight." Although many experienced naval officers regard it as "unsound and dangerous," the plan well suits the political needs of the administration in Washington, and an imaginary Admiral Morrison, the chief of naval operations, wins over the president and the cabinet by providing "a plausible answer" for every criticism offered.

The "very audacity" of the plan, Morrison declares, holds out the best promise of success. Japan, he argues, "would never anticipate so daring an operation as the seizure of islands that lay within a day's steaming distance of her great naval arsenals." Furthermore, as Morrison sees it, the establishment of an American base in the Bonins will force the Japanese to accept a decisive fleet action and in that way bring a quick end to the war.

Surprise, always difficult to achieve in combat, is the essence of Morrison's plan. The assault, aimed at Port Lloyd, a harbor formed by a huge volcanic crater in the Bonin Islands, will commence with a gas attack delivered by American carrier-borne seaplanes. This is sure to overwhelm the defenders, who will be taken unawares, Morrison believes. As soon as the gas has cleared, 20,000 elite American troops will storm ashore and quickly seize the base. By the time the Japanese fleet arrives, Port Lloyd will be in American hands. The Japanese warships will then begin to shell the American positions ashore. After they have expended most of their ammunition, a superior American fleet, which has been hiding just over the horizon, will attack the Japanese force "and so end the war at a blow."

When Morrison attempts to put the plan into action, however, nearly everything that can go wrong does go wrong. The American expeditionary force encounters a gale as it makes its way across the Western Pacific. Two troop transports collide and sink with heavy loss of life. Perhaps even worse, a number of landing craft intended to bring artillery pieces ashore at Port Lloyd are also lost in the gale. The expedition is then intercepted by Japanese submarines, and although the Japanese are unable to torpedo any American vessel, the submarines immediately report the presence of the American fleet approaching Port Lloyd, thus eliminating any possibility of surprise. It is not long before the Americans detect heavy radio traffic on the frequencies used by the Imperial Navy, and although they cannot comprehend the Japanese code, they understand full well that a huge Japanese force is being rushed to the defense of the Bonins.

To further complicate the American predicament, a missed rendezvous brings the troop transports close to the Bonins ahead of their escorts. Quickly realizing the gravity of the situation, the American commander cancels the Port Lloyd invasion, orders the transports to withdraw at their best speed, and sends his battle fleet racing to their aid.

"But the evil fortune which had dogged the expedition almost from the start had not yet deserted it," wrote Bywater. A Japanese cruiser squadron overtakes the retreating Americans and a pitched battle ensues, with the American force severely handicapped by being obliged to maintain a protective screen around the troop transports. In the course of the withering exchange of fire, the Japanese lose three of their four cruisers, but the Americans' losses are even greater. The expeditionary force suffers two cruisers sunk and one seriously damaged, eight destroyers lost and three left scarcely seaworthy, and—most grievous of all—three transports sunk. The total loss of life for the Americans amounts to some 5,000, as compared to Japanese losses of 1,200.

Even so, wrote Bywater, the devastation suffered by the Americans is mild compared to what might have happened. The commander of a squadron of Japanese battle cruisers bearing down on the retreating invaders inexplicably abandons his pursuit. Furthermore, the homeward-bound Americans are relatively successful in beating off a Japanese submarine attack, losing only one cruiser in the night. And finally, as the survivors limp home, the weather is fair; had another gale arisen, it would have claimed some of the battered ships that were barely floating. At last, the bedraggled Americans make it back to Honolulu. "The ill-starred expedition was over," wrote Bywater, "and to this day its survivors still marvel that any one of them lived to tell the tale."

"Mahan, Colomb, and other authoritative historians of sea power," he reminded his readers, "had all demonstrated by numerous precedents the importance of gaining command of the sea before embarking on military expeditions against hostile territory. Yet in this instance no such command had been gained."

Bywater then described the humbled leaders of the American Navy rethinking their situation and eventually deciding to carry out the revolutionary idea of an amphibious advance across a bridge of islands in the Marshall and Caroline chains. "The plan adopted by the U.S. Bureau of Operations," he declared, "was to advance step by step to a position from which an invasion of the Philippines could be launched." Then, in a tour de force of dazzling strokes, Bywater described American forces making a series of bold leaps from Tutuila in the American Samoan Islands to Truk in the Carolines; next, zigzagging back simultaneously to Ponape in the eastern Carolines and Jaluit in the Marshalls in order to open a direct line of communications to Hawaii; then a feint to Guam and a pounce ahead to Angaur in the Palaus followed by a feint to Yap in the westernmost Palaus and finally on to the Philippines and, if need be, the Marianas. (While the actual American moves were not a duplicate of these, all of the above-named islands were in the thick of the fighting in the 1940s, and Bywater's principle of deception and surprise was at the heart of American strategy.)

"By a succession of bold yet well-considered moves the Americans had contrived to modify the whole strategical outlook to their advantage," he wrote. "At the beginning of the war, they had been confined

THE 'HIGHWAY' TO JAPAN

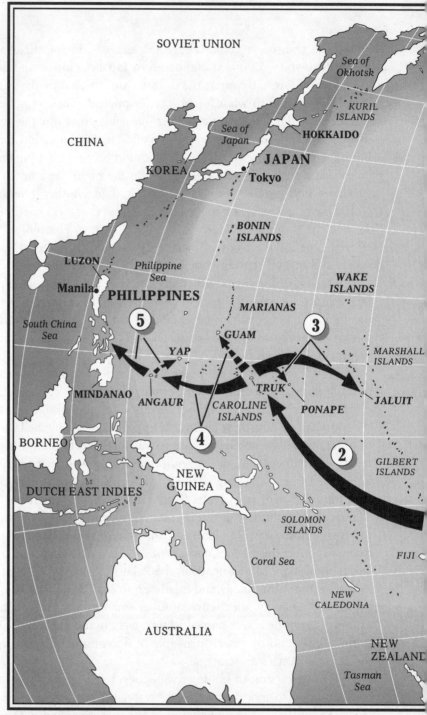

Bywater's plan featured the zigzagging, feinting and bypassing that characterized American strategy over a similar route two decades later.

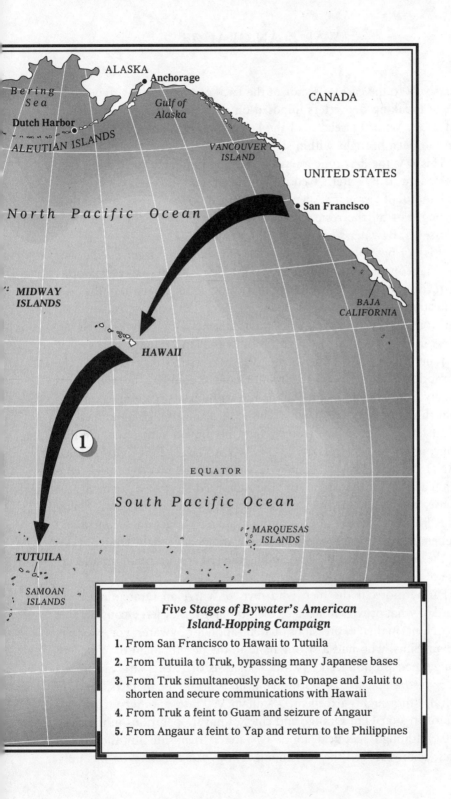

ALASKA
Anchorage

Bering Sea

Dutch Harbor

Gulf of Alaska

CANADA

ALEUTIAN ISLANDS

VANCOUVER ISLAND

UNITED STATES

North   Pacific   Ocean

● San Francisco

MIDWAY ISLANDS

BAJA CALIFORNIA

HAWAII

①

EQUATOR

South   Pacific   Ocean

MARQUESAS ISLANDS

TUTUILA

SAMOAN ISLANDS

Five Stages of Bywater's American Island-Hopping Campaign

1. From San Francisco to Hawaii to Tutuila

2. From Tutuila to Truk, bypassing many Japanese bases

3. From Truk simultaneously back to Ponape and Jaluit to shorten and secure communications with Hawaii

4. From Truk a feint to Guam and seizure of Angaur

5. From Angaur a feint to Yap and return to the Philippines exclusively to the eastern sector of the Pacific, apparently with no prospect of breaking the fetters imposed on them by geographical circumstance. . . . With the seizure of the Pelew [Palau] group, the end of the war had been brought within sight."

This was the first time a naval expert had publicly spelled out such a campaign. If Bywater's Central Pacific strategy was not entirely new to a handful of visionary American officers, it powerfully seconded their thinking. For all the rest, who had not been privy to their top-secret discussions, Bywater's book opened a new world.

It is not possible to prove conclusively that *The Great Pacific War* was what convinced the authorities in the U.S. Navy to make the wholesale revision of War Plan Orange that came about fifteen months after publication of Bywater's book. These men were diligently secretive about their work and left scant record of what influenced their thinking. Nevertheless, it is a fact that the revision of War Plan Orange approved by the Joint Board in October 1926 was the first to dispense with the assumption of earlier plans that reinforcements could be shuttled almost casually from Hawaii to the Philippines without first gaining command of much of the Western Pacific. The 1926 Plan Orange announced in capital letters that before troops could be moved across the Western Pacific, it would be necessary "TO GAIN AND TO EXERCISE COMMAND OF THE SEA." The new revision also adopted Bywater's conviction about the importance of "the Advanced Fleet Base, or bases, for defense, and for the maintenance and supply of the United States Forces in the Principal Theater of Operations" and also "the establishment and maintenance of secure lines of Communication between the United States and the Advance Fleet Base, including the seizure, occupation, and defense of Subsidiary Bases."

Furthermore, if the men who revised War Plan Orange made no record of what or who influenced their thoughts, they left a considerable trail of hints in their expressions of admiration for Bywater. For example, William Sims, who had a strong hand in the development of War Plan Orange, had pronounced Bywater's analysis of Pacific strategy in *Sea Power in the Pacific* "authoritative in its assemblage of facts" and, in general, "thoroughly excellent." William V. Pratt, another major contributor to War Plan Orange and chief of naval operations in the early 1930s, although skeptical about Bywater's friendship for the United States, acknowledged the very month *The Great Pacific War* was published that many of his fellow officers "saw a champion in him" and looked upon Bywater "as something [of] a prophet." Gardiner, the influential naval publicist and vice president of the United States Navy League, rhapsodized that Bywater's *Sea Power in the Pacific* was "the most vital publication to English-speaking civilization as a whole and to the United States in particular since the great works of Mahan." And a future commander-in-chief of the United States Navy—one whose name Bywater never revealed—wrote to him after reading *The Great Pacific War*, exclaiming: "You've said it!"

By April 1935—a decade after the publication of *The Great Pacific War*—the latest updating of War Plan Orange included an even more sophisticated description of an island-hopping campaign similar to the one Bywater had spelled out. At that time, the director of the navy's War Plans Division termed his proposal "an entirely new line of action" for the fleet's "progressive movement through the Mandates." The first of the operations envisioned was "the ejection of Orange [Japan] from the Marshall and Caroline Islands, and development in these areas of such subsidiary outlying advanced bases as are necessary for the establishment of a secure line of communications to the Western Pacific."

The Joint Planning Committee considered the proposed changes as "sound, in that they attempt to provide at the beginning of operations a secure line of communications to the Western Pacific prior to any immediate general advance to that area."

By 1938, the Joint Planning Committee was developing even more elaborate plans—and even more than previously an echo of the language of *The Great Pacific War*. In November of that year, these strategists considered four possible routes across the Pacific, giving preference to "the 'Step by Step' Route" from Pearl Harbor and including "the capture, occupation, and use of the Marshalls, Carolines, and possibly Marianas, Yap, and Pelews [Palaus]" leading to the recapture of Guam. It was a plan that could have been lifted directly from the pages of *The Great Pacific War*.

CHAPTER

18

WORLD'S LEADING AUTHORITY

COPIES OF *The Great Pacific War* sold so well in England and the United States that the author and his family could consider themselves, for the first time in their lives, comfortably well off. With an unexpected surplus of cash, Bywater purchased a car—a Morris "Bullnose"—which looked like a Model-A Ford except that it had a sleekly streamlined radiator grille. He took pleasure in mastering the smooth shifting of the gears and in motoring into the country on a warm Saturday morning with Emma and the two children, Robin and Sylvia. Picnicking on a meadow alongside the road, he would fall asleep with a copy of *Marine Rundschau*, the semiofficial publication of the German Navy, folded like a tent over his head.

The success of his latest book had attracted the attention of editors around the world, and Bywater suddenly found himself inundated with more offers of free-lance writing assignments than he could accept. That meant he could pick and choose. Eventually, it led to a prestigious job.

The result was that the late 1920s were the years when Bywater established himself as the successor to Alfred Thayer Mahan as the world's leading authority on naval affairs. So celebrated did his name become that by 1934, Bywater had four of his books in print and was invited by the French Admiralty and Benito Mussolini to inspect their new navies.

Bywater readily found his way around the restrictions the Admiralty imposed when his "facilities as a journalist" were canceled in 1924. And once he discovered he could get along without the assistance of the sea lords, he felt perfectly free—indeed, he seems to have relished every opportunity—to remind them of precisely with whom they had trifled. In February 1926, when the Admiralty became involved in a budget dispute with Winston Churchill, then chancellor of the Exchequer, Bywater declared in the Baltimore *Sun*: "If they [the sea lords], on their part, desire to resign in a body by way of protest, the country will remain unmoved." The next year, after the collapse of the Geneva Naval Conference, Bywater laid the blame on the British Admiralty in a stinging attack: "Since 1921," he wrote for the London *Daily News*, "blunder after blunder has been committed [by the sea lords], each betraying an astonishing ignorance both of psychology and the rudiments of statecraft."

At least once, Bywater touched on the source of his personal pique. In an essay for the periodical *Nineteenth Century and After*, he denounced the Admiralty's postwar obsession with secrecy as a "typical example of bureaucratic ineptitude." Without a doubt, he had in mind his own run-in with the sea lords in which, as Bywater saw it, they had decided to punish him for having breached some perfectly idiotic application of their hush-hush policy. Bywater added, almost as a threat: "Excessive official secrecy is . . . a direct encouragement to criticism because it suggests that there are damaging facts to be hidden."

No records survive to reveal the Admiralty's reaction to these periodic thunderbolts, but it was not long before the sea lords had had enough. Inked in after Bywater's name in the huge, leather-bound *Index of Admiralty Correspondence* for the year 1927 are the words: "Facilities as journalist restored." Bywater's exile was ended.

There was lots for a naval expert to write about at this time. For one thing, the rapid development of aircraft was thought to threaten the existence of the battleship and had given rise to an emotional debate between big-ship defenders and air-power enthusiasts. As Bywater saw it, the debate was a recycling of an old controversy. Almost as soon as ironclad turret ships began to dominate the seas following the duel between *Monitor* and *Merrimac* in March 1862, critics argued that the torpedo would put an end to their reign. And, sure enough, at the Yalu in 1894 and at Port Arthur in 1904, daring Japanese torpedo boats had made short work of several Chinese and Russian men-of-war. During the First World War, German U-boats wreaked havoc with Allied shipping, and while no battleship was sunk on the high seas by a submarine, it appeared that all vessels were potentially vulnerable to underwater attack. Nevertheless, the battleship held its own by such means as the "bulge" or "blister," an exterior hull added to serve as a shield against underwater attack; honeycomb construction to limit flooding if the hull were breached; and the development of submarine-tracking techniques.

The airplane was thus only the latest challenge to the supremacy of the great surface ship. Some air enthusiasts, including William "Billy" Mitchell, the much-decorated American World War I ace, began preaching that the battleship was a thing of the past. To prove it, Mitchell staged a series of publicity stunts in which his aircraft bombed and sank the former German battleship *Ostfriesland* and later the obsolete United States battleships *Alabama, Virginia*, and *New Jersey*. Big-ship proponents argued with justice that Mitchell's demonstrations were unrealistic because the target ships were all stationary and undefended. Consequently, nothing was resolved, although the furor did help to promote the aircraft industry and also the development of a naval hybrid, the aircraft carrier.

Bywater, who had been almost viscerally attracted to the biggest ships with the biggest guns ever since his youth, naturally championed the battleship. He was ideally suited for the job. He was, as he once expressed it, "an old admirer of the battleship" who would sorely "lament its passing." In fact, Bywater had been defending the battleship for almost as long as he could remember. Some of his earliest signed articles, written from Germany in 1909, had held up the dreadnought as a thing of awe, wonder, and even beauty. A few months before the First World War, when Sir Percy Scott shocked the Royal Navy by declaring that the battleship had outlived its usefulness, Bywater sprang to the defense, arguing that it seemed "almost sacrilegious to impugn its primacy."

The fact that three British battle cruisers had been blown to bits by single well-placed shots at Jutland was, to Bywater's mind, only an illustration of the fact that heavily armored battleships probably would have survived the blows where the more lightly armored battle cruisers had not. After the war, when the battleship came under attack by a French military analyst, Bywater replied with a long, sharply worded essay entitled "Future of the Mastodon" for the old Dockyard Liar.

"Theory is one thing, fact another," he wrote. "If we look round we find every important naval state building, or preparing to build, mastodons of dimensions and power unthought of a few years ago. As it is not usual to build battleships, costing several millions apiece, simply for fun, one can only conclude that the capital ship is still universally regarded as lord of the sea."

Scarcely a year went by thereafter when Bywater did not speak up for the man-of-war. "The only vessel capable of fighting a battleship on equal terms is another battleship," he wrote in 1924 in a two-part article for the Baltimore *Sun*.

This pair of articles was well received, and consequently, after finishing *The Great Pacific War*, Bywater expanded the *Sun* articles into what he intended as a definitive defense of the battleship. He submitted the article to the annual essay contest of the United States Naval Institute, the semiofficial organization of navy supporters with its headquarters on the grounds of the Naval Academy at Annapolis. In a few weeks, he received a letter informing him that his essay had won the contest! A check for $200 was enclosed, and Bywater was told that his article would be published in the March 1926 issue of *Proceedings* of the U.S. Naval Institute, the most prestigious American journal on naval affairs. Exultantly, Bywater joked with his children about having "hoodwinked" the U.S. Naval Institute into giving its first prize to a foreigner.

It was only the second time that a foreign writer had won the Naval Institute's first prize, and so the Baltimore *Sun* lost no time in trumpeting the honor. Bywater's picture appeared at the top of the *Sun*'s front page over the headline: AMERICAN MEDAL GIVEN BRITISH NAVAL WRITER.

His twenty-page essay sought to spell out "the status of the battleship under existing conditions" and explore "what it is likely to be ten or twenty years hence, assuming a normal rate of progress in the science of naval warfare." Despite the low-key title, and the densely reasoned style, Bywater's essay was, in fact, a bell-ringing rejoinder to battleship critics ranging all the way from pacifists and budget-cutters to airmen and submariners, not to mention pro-army publicists who wanted a larger share of the defense budget for tanks and guns. It is an important document because it highlights Bywater's deep and lasting commitment to the old ways of naval combat, and also because this, too, may have influenced Isoroku Yamamoto in the coming war at sea.

Bywater began by noting that "critics assure us that the battleship is a slothful, clumsy, and feeble giant, an emasculated Goliath, impressive only because of its bulk, and entirely at the mercy of the punier but more agile opponents who would swarm about the inert monster and sting it to death." He then proceeded to demolish that statement. Far from being slothful, he said, a modern 30,000-ton battleship could step along at the equivalent of 35.7 miles per hour. At slower speeds, these vessels could make nonstop voyages of 10,000 miles. And, armed with eight guns, each of which weighed a stupendous 105 tons, they could hurl 37 tons of steel and high explosives at an opponent every three minutes.

Bywater then reviewed the presumed vulnerability of the battleship. The danger of mines and torpedoes, he maintained, had been greatly exaggerated. It was true that the British dreadnought *Audacious* had foundered after striking two German mines during the First World War, but she was "a battleship of the older class." The more modern British monitor *Terror* had made it back to port after having taken three German torpedoes. On another occasion, a sister ship, *Erebus*, was hit by a remote controlled German motorboat carrying 500 pounds of TNT that detonated amidships. Her exterior hull absorbed the shock so effectively that *Erebus* did not even spring a leak! These exterior hulls, called "bulges" in the Royal Navy and "blisters" in the United States Navy, which were being added to battleships to serve as shields against underwater attack, "proved successful beyond all anticipation." In fact, he observed, "Many bulged ships were torpedoed during the war, but not a single one was sunk." Furthermore, honeycomb construction to limit flooding if the hull was breached was so effective that "no outside explosion would be likely to inflict disabling injury."

The danger of air attack, Bywater continued, was far less menacing than many aviation publicists had made it out to be. The largest bombs capable of being lifted by ship-borne aircraft could inflict "only superficial injury on a battleship." Bombs of 1,000 pounds or more, which could be carried by land-based aircraft, "most certainly constitute a real danger to the battleship," he conceded, but the way to cope with that threat was to keep battleships out of range of "the enemy's airdromes on shore" and to recognize that "a well-directed cannonade from the numerous 3-inch high-angle guns—eight per ship—of a battleship division would scarcely conduce to accuracy of aim on the part of the bombers."

He concluded with a prophetic statement: "When the torpedo has acquired the range and precision of a 16-inch gun; when submarines have become as swift, as seaworthy, and as habitable as big surface vessels; when the radius and carrying power of aircraft have increased tenfold, and bomb dropping is as accurate as gun practice: then, but not till then, will the primacy of the battleship be endangered."

It is almost inevitable that a British naval writer of this era should champion the battleship. A nation's choice of weapons, after all, is not haphazardly determined but is a direct expression of the realities of geography, industrial capacity, and recent experience. Every Briton knew that as an inhabitant of an island-nation with a worldwide empire, his survival depended upon saltwater arteries. Great Britain had to defend these ocean passageways the way other empires in different eras had thrown up insurmountable walls around their cities or built impregnable fortresses to guard strategic mountain passes. The only way for Britain to provide that kind of defense for its vital interests was with an unexcelled fleet of warships.

At the time Bywater was writing, Great Britain had sixteen battleships afloat, and although the five *Queen Elizabeth*–class vessels had been designed as long ago as 1912, they were recognized by experts throughout the world as masterpieces of naval architecture that had provided exemplary service in the world war. Furthermore, Britain's economic and industrial power to bolt up still more and even better mastodons was legendary (the 35,000-ton *Nelson* and *Rodney* were due for completion the next year), and, even though the supremacy of the Royal Navy was being challenged by the United States, as late as 1927 the British battle fleet was nearly 100,000 tons heavier than the U.S. fleet. Thus, a British writer such as Bywater had every reason to keep faith in a weapon that seemed to have sprung from his country's native genius, seemed ideally suited to her needs, and had reached a state of near perfection, harnessing every conceivable ounce of speed, endurance, impregnability, and destructiveness that modern science and technology could provide.

Likewise, it was no accident that forward-looking Japanese leaders such as Yamamoto were banking on air power. Once Japan's capital-ship construction had been fixed in inferiority by the ratios of the Washington Treaty, it was only a matter of time before her strategists would emphasize the development of new technologies that offered hope of overcoming superior surface fleets. Since aircraft were the most likely means of filling that prescription, Japan was bound to develop her air arm at a rapid rate. The battleship, of course, was still the dominant preoccupation of her navy, as with every other major navy in the world, and although Japan's Third Replenishment Program in 1936 included an enormous investment in superbattleships, it also funded the construction of two heavy aircraft carriers, *Shokaku* and *Zuikaku*. Furthermore, by then Japan already led the world in the development of shore-based and carrier-borne naval aircraft. Had the aircraft option not existed, Japan would certainly have invested her energies in submarines, as had Germany and, in more recent times, the Soviet Union.

Viewed from today's perspective, Bywater was both right and wrong about the battleship. He erred in his failure to recognize that the contest was not one to decide whether aircraft could destroy battleships or vice versa. The real issue—obscured by Billy Mitchell's histrionics, and indeed by some of Hector Bywater's arguments, too—was which of the two weapons could project armed might the farthest. The outcome of that contest should have been foreseeable. Naval gunfire was limited to a maximum range of twenty-odd miles whereas the aircraft carrier could send planes many times that distance. Furthermore, Bywater overlooked the factor of cost. Aircraft carriers, as well as their complement of airplanes, were comparatively cheap in both money and in the investment of human life they required. One could dispatch a carrier against a target and put at risk only a small percentage of the money and lives that would have to be gambled on the sortie of a capital ship. In addition, aircraft carriers and airplanes could be produced in a fraction of the time it took to build a battleship.

Bywater was right in understanding that the battleship possessed profound advantages in certain tactical situations. It was not dependent on fair weather as was air power; it could brazenly steam into harm's way in order to show the flag, intimidate an adversary, or enter restricted seas where the aircraft carrier, unarmored and loaded with combustible aviation fuel, would never dare to venture; and finally, the battleship could remain on the scene indefinitely, unlike aircraft, which must deliver their punches and then streak homeward. These important advantages were lost sight of during the Second World War. So effective were the air-power publicists that in the aftermath of Pearl Harbor, aircraft became the universal weapon no matter how ill-suited to a particular tactical situation. Ignominiously, battleships were relegated to service as oilers, limousines for three-star admirals, and—a far cry from the heroics of Tsushima or Jutland—for shore bombardment.

Bywater's honor from the U.S. Naval Institute was not overlooked on Fleet Street. Soon after the publication of his fifth book, *Navies and Nations*, an analysis of naval issues of the postwar era in which he continued to stress the paramount importance of Japanese-American rivalry in the Pacific, Bywater became the envy of every member of the Fleet Street Press Gang. He was invited to succeed his old boss, Archibald Hurd, as naval and shipping correspondent of the London *Daily Telegraph*. Hurd suggested in his memoirs that his retirement at the age of fifty-nine was due to poor health, but his private papers at Cambridge University make it clear that his departure resulted from a long and painful squabble with the publisher of the *Telegraph*. Furthermore, Arthur Watson, the newspaper's top editor, feared that Hurd had become more friendly with the Admiralty than was prudent for a "disinterested" reporter. After Bywater's three years as persona non grata with the sea lords, no such question could be raised about him. Bywater accepted a salary of 700 pounds per anum and started work on January 1, 1928.

The job on the Old Telewag, as the newspaper was affectionately dubbed on Fleet Street, was a plum not only because Hurd had made it important in naval circles over the twenty-eight years he had handled naval and shipping news, but also because the *Telegraph*—one of Britain's major daily newspapers—traditionally devoted more space, and a more generous travel allowance, to its naval correspondent than did any of its competitors. Furthermore, the *Telegraph*'s correspondent was granted a byline, something newspapers such as the London *Times* withheld from their writers in those days. These advantages made the job at the Old Telewag an opportunity to achieve prominence, and that was a chance Bywater would seize with gusto. For the next few years, he would focus his attention on Europe, and his extraordinary revelations about the secret expansion of the German and Italian navies established his reputation throughout the world.

After just a few weeks at the *Telegraph*, Bywater proved his worth to Watson, the stern, teetotaling, and devout managing editor nicknamed "The Old Bottle of Ink." Bywater became the first reporter to tell the world about a revolutionary new type of warship that was being secretly built by the German Navy, and that aroused battleship proponents even more than the threat of air power.

Bywater had continued to be a serious reader of German newspapers, magazines, and technical publications even after leaving Germany in 1910. One day in February 1928, he spotted an item in the *Berliner Tageblatt* detailing the extraordinary sums of money the German government was lavishing on a new 10,000-ton cruiser—the maximum size permissible for Germany under the terms of the Treaty of Versailles. A less knowledgeable reader might well have passed over the figures without detecting their significance; Bywater, however, was immediately struck by such facts as that the guns alone of the new cruiser were going to cost the equivalent of 750,000 pounds. Before the war, he recalled, a completely fitted-out German cruiser cost only 500,000 pounds. The *Berliner Tageblatt* article contained a number of other surprising figures as well, and Bywater reasoned that since there was no evidence to suggest that Germany was exceeding the 10,000-ton limit in violation of the Treaty of Versailles, it must be that German engineers and naval architects were developing "new naval weapons of unprecedented power."

Watson, who had once interviewed the kaiser and was intrigued by all things German, splashed Bywater's story with the headlines FABU-LOUS COST OF GERMAN WARSHIPS—MYSTERY OF MILLIONS—REPORTS OF NEW NAVAL WEAPONS. The next morning, Bywater began pursuing the mystery with all his energy and resourcefulness. It was, after all, the perfect story to suit his talents, offering the opportunity to use the expertise and contacts he had developed while living in Germany. He began by scouring every German publication he could lay his hands on, and then contacted old sources in Germany. Within a week of his first story, he was able to report in the *Telegraph* that not one but four cruisers of the new type were "in conception," and that the German Navy had designated them *Panzerschiffe* (armorclads). Furthermore, the new warships would be powered solely by diesel engines—an important innovation since up to that time diesels had been used only as auxiliary engines in vessels of such size. The next month, Bywater revealed that the new cruisers would have a type of hull combining "great strength with extraordinary lightness" since the hull plates would be electrically welded together rather than riveted.

In August, Bywater seized upon the occasion of a routine visit to Germany to cover the launching of the North German Lloyd twin liners, *Europa* and *Bremen*, to scout the *Panzerschiffe* with his own eyes and ears. From an article he later wrote for the Baltimore *Sun*, and from a reference in one of his books, we learn that as the giant 52,000-ton Atlantic liner *Bremen* slid down the ways into the waters of the Elbe, Bywater stood shoulder to shoulder with "a vast concourse" and joined in the emotional singing of "*Deutschland Über Alles*." The aging Field Marshal von Hindenburg presided at the launching, and Bywater some-how managed to exchange a few words with the bewhiskered president whom he regarded as "a fine old veteran." Soon afterward, perhaps employing the wiles he perfected while working as a Secret Service agent in Germany, Bywater slipped into the top-secret Deutsche Werke Kiel, formerly the Imperial Dockyard at Kiel, where the first *Panzerschiffe* was under construction. He picked up a wealth of information.

On August 28, the *Daily Telegraph* and the Baltimore *Sun* simul-taneously published Bywater's detailed description of what he termed Germany's new "pocket battleship." He described the ship's "formidable qualities of attack and defense," including an unusually shallow draft and extensive honeycombing of the underwater hull, which would reduce the danger of torpedo attack, especially heavy topside armor for resis-tance to air attack, and formidable 11-inch high-velocity turret guns that could heave a shell 20 miles. Although Bywater stated that the pocket battleships would be "for their tonnage, the most expensive warships ever built," he assured his readers that there was no reason to be "perturbed" by their construction.

He was a good deal less reassuring a few months later when he published another exclusive—and this time definitive—description of the by-then famous pocket battleships. While introducing a long list of specifications the German Admiralty had provided him with—evidently to demonstrate that the new ship was not in violation of the Treaty of Versailles—Bywater declared that Germany's new warship "has the fighting power of a battleship, the speed of a cruiser, and the radius of the biggest ocean liner." Nevertheless, her greatest threat, he predicted, would be as a commerce raider. The appearance of such warships on the trade routes "would introduce an entirely new factor into war strategy." A month later, after mulling over the extraordinary innovations incorporated in the design, Bywater caused a stir in naval circles by stating that Germany's pocket battleships "may eventually produce a revolution in the whole scheme of armament restriction," because, as he later phrased it, they had "upset conventional calculations of tons and guns."

Bywater may have been able to grasp the importance of the pocket battleships as quickly as he did because the concept was not really new to him. Writing for the Dockyard Liar back in 1919, he had happened to interview a German naval architect who predicted something very much along the lines of the *Panzerschiffe*. That year, it was expected that the victorious Allies would impose on Germany a 10,000-ton limit on warship construction. The German expert Bywater talked to did not seem greatly distressed about that. He said: "We should have no difficulty in designing an ocean cruiser fast enough to overhaul or to escape from anything but the swiftest battlecruiser, carrying a battery stronger than that of any but ships of the line [battleships], and having a 15,000-mile radius of action. All these qualities could be combined in a ship of 10,000 tons. In the late war, a dozen such cruisers might have been more useful to us than the entire High Seas Fleet."

In the long run, Bywater was mainly right about the pocket battleships. Their chief value was as commerce raiders. Early in World War II, *Graf Spee* sank nine British merchantmen in the South Atlantic, and later *Scheer* accounted for the destruction or capture of seventeen Allied merchant ships. But Bywater was wrong in implying that only battle cruisers or full-scale battleships could sink them. In December 1939, *Graf Spee* was set upon by the heavy cruiser *Exeter* and the light cruisers *Ajax* and *Achilles* and was so damaged that she retired to a neutral port and then was blown up by her crew rather than risk capture. Of the remaining two pocket battleships, *Lützow* survived the war only to be scuttled like her predecessor, and *Scheer* was sunk by British bombers in 1945.

Although his exposure of the German pocket battleships won Bywater praise around the world, it led to his being branded a "propagandist" in the Baltimore *Sun*. And that prompted his indignant resignation. Shortly after Bywater's definitive story about the *Panzer-*

schiffe appeared in the *Sun* on December 28, Dudley W. Knox, the feisty American naval correspondent of the *Sun* who frequently crossed swords with Bywater, published an essay in which he asserted that Bywater had greatly overestimated their potential power. Knox, a naval historian of repute but also a curmudgeonly Anglophobe who was convinced that it was the British, not the Japanese, who bested the United States at the Washington Conference, went on in his article to suggest that Bywater had heaped undeserved praise on the pocket battleships in order to "cast doubt" on the wisdom of the U.S. Navy's request for funds to build fifteen new cruisers, which was just then before the U.S. Senate.

The timing of Bywater's exposé may have been unfortunate, but there was nothing to Knox's suspicion. Bywater, being a competitive journalist, broke the news the moment he discovered it. Still, his report did indeed cast shadows that were impossible to ignore. Why go on building 8-inch-gunned cruisers, Bywater would ask the following year, which an 11-inch pocket battleship "could blow out of the water at her first salvo?" Knox's counterargument was that the relatively small American cruisers were still viable because they would be fast enough to keep a safe distance from the pocket battleship, could successfully gang up against one, or, if need be, keep tabs on it until a first-class battleship could be brought to bear. His position was not without merit, yet the same could be said of Bywater. There simply was no justification for impugning Bywater's integrity.

It was not the first time Knox had locked horns with Bywater, although recently his attacks had become increasingly shrill and personal. The relationship between the two men had started with almost chummy mutual admiration after Knox became the *Sun*'s American naval correspondent at the end of 1924. One of his early assignments had been to review *The Great Pacific War*, and Knox praised Bywater's book as "a carefully studied analysis by a man who is well versed in . . . naval affairs besides being a most entertaining writer." A few months later, Bywater tossed a bouquet to Knox by commending the lucidity of one of his essays. But these were years of growing animosity between the British and American navies; many American officers were infuriated to learn that at the Geneva Naval Conference of 1927, the British battle fleet had unexpectedly become 96,000 tons heavier than the U.S. fleet. Even William Sims, the president of the U.S. Naval War College and an Anglophile, remarked that the British fleet was so superior to its American counterpart as to possess an "overwhelmingly decisive advantage should by any chance the two fleets come to battle." Not a few American officers agreed with Frank H. Schofield, director of the Naval War Plans Division, that a British-American war had become inescapable because throughout history the world's two leading powers had always fought it out "to decide superiority and relieve trade competition."

In this atmosphere, it was only natural that Bywater and Knox should tangle. And so they did—repeatedly. One day Bywater asserted in the *Sun* that it was "difficult to reconcile" President Coolidge's homilies on the evils of foreign militarism with the fact that the United States led the world in a naval arms race between 1918 and the Washington Conference in 1921. Knox replied that Bywater's "extremely misleading" article was "open to grave dispute" because everyone knew that America's postwar surge of naval construction had come about because it had been "manifestly impossible" to cancel shipbuilding contracts that had been written during the war. Bywater responded that, no, it wasn't the fulfillment of wartime contracts that had bloated the size of the U.S. Navy but the fact that an entirely new fleet, consisting of sixteen battleships, ten cruisers, seventy-seven destroyers, and thirty submarines, "was begun *after* the Armistice."

So heated did their dispute become that in 1927 Knox wrote to John H. Adams, the managing editor of the *Sun*, to urge that Bywater's articles be censored. Adams replied with a rebuke to Knox.

The temperature of the conflict shot up in June 1929 when Knox, flushed with anger over mounting opposition to the so-called Butler cruiser-construction bill, published a broadside in the *Proceedings* of the U.S. Naval Institute in which he lashed out against "intellectual foreign propagandists" who would cripple the U.S. Navy's cruiser flotilla. He did not mention Bywater by name, yet so pointed was his reference that when the *Sun* published on its front page a news account of Knox's diatribe, the editors felt obliged to insert an "Editor's Note" stating that "for several years he [Dudley Knox] has carried on a running debate in the *Sun*'s columns with Hector C. Bywater, an English writer specializing in naval matters, who also is a *Sun* special correspondent."

The Butler bill authorizing fifteen new cruisers was finally passed in the closing days of the Coolidge administration, but hatchets kept flying back and forth between Bywater and Knox for another couple of years. Then Bywater inadvertently triggered the showdown when he published an article in the *Sun* arguing that relatively small warships—15,000- to 20,000-ton battleships and 6,000-ton cruisers—would be just as suitable for the U.S. Navy as for the Royal Navy, which favored them. By this time, Knox had resigned from the *Sun* as a regular correspondent, but the very next day the newspaper published an unsigned article headlined: BYWATER'S IDEAS DRAW FIRE OF NAVY, which stated that the U.S. Navy had reacted "vigorously to the contrary" against what Bywater had written, and quoted an unnamed American naval officer as having characterized the article as "clever British propaganda." It was obvious that the Anglophobic Knox was the officer quoted, and more than likely it was he who had inspired the article in the first place. "British propaganda" had become Knox's favorite slander for any of Bywater's opinions he disagreed with.

As a professional journalist, Bywater never considered himself above criticism. Indeed, a year after Knox had questioned his motive in reporting on the pocket battleships, Bywater was able to make light of the episode in an article for the *Sun*: "It's amusing to recall that several of your big-navy stalwarts saw in this 'beat' a subtle piece of foreign propaganda aimed against the 15-cruiser bill then before Congress," he wrote, adding modestly: "But the responsibility for releasing details of the *Ersatz Preussen* at that particular juncture lay not with my humble self, but with the German Admiralty." The *Reichsmarine*, as we have seen, responded to Bywater's early revelations about the pocket battleships by giving him an exclusive in the hope of demonstrating that the Versailles Treaty had been honored.

However, the charge of writing "clever British propaganda" could not be laughed off. One can imagine Bywater's reaction. After settling into an easy chair to peruse his latest ship-borne copy of the *Sun*, he comes across his name in a headline, sees the phrase "clever British propaganda," and explodes like a naval mine. How dare they, he must have thundered, publish such a scurrilous attack on a staff member without granting him the right of reply? Surely, such an abuse would never have been tolerated by his old friends John Heslup Adams, the managing editor who had journeyed to London to hire him in 1921, and Van Lear Black, the chairman of the board of the *Sun* who had become a close friend through his frequent trips to London. But Adams had died in 1927 and Black had been lost at sea in a yachting mishap in 1930. Paul Patterson, who had met Bywater in London with Adams, never became a close ally of Bywater and probably had come under increasing pressure from his father-in-law—an American admiral—to remain aloof. As a result, Bywater felt friendless in the newsroom, much as he had at the *New York Herald* after the death of James Gordon Bennett. It was time to move on.

If Bywater wrote to the editor of the *Sun* telling him where to go, so to speak, the letter has not survived; all that is known is that Bywater's familiar byline would never again grace the pages of the *Sun*. But a man of his renown was unlikely to go begging for work. And sure enough, Bywater was taken on as a contract writer almost immediately by *The New York Times*. He was to provide a series of 1,200-word articles on naval subjects for 10 guineas (10 pounds and 10 shillings) each—an arrangement that continued, with appropriate raises, for the rest of his life. It is interesting to note that as the fortunes of Britain and the United States became drawn together over the next decade, Knox and Bywater were able to patch things up. By 1938, Bywater was referring to Knox in the *Telegraph* as "the most eminent naval historian and critic in the United States," and was applauding him for having abandoned isolationism and recognized Britain as one of America's "allies."

One day in 1930 when Bywater and his son Robin were test-firing a miniature brass cannon for one of their model warships while Emma was putting out the wash to dry, the discharged cork came perilously close to scoring a hit on Mrs. Bywater's backside. She was "most distressed," Robin recalled, and gave her husband a tongue-lashing.

The near miss, the younger Bywater believes, was no accident but expressed unconscious hostile intent. The stress and strain of these years had taken a toll on the Bywaters, and life was not harmonious in their household. Emma Bywater, once radiant and charming, was now heavy in both body and spirit. She had become a domineering mother not greatly popular with her children and "a real battleax" to one of their suitors. Bywater had largely retreated to his attic workroom, and to the pubs where he caroused with the Fleet Street Press Gang and such newfound friends at the *Telegraph* as the military correspondent Basil Liddell Hart. Gradually, the bonds that had held the family together dissolved. Bywater deserted 23 Whitmore Road where he had written both *Sea Power in the Pacific* and *The Great Pacific War* and took an apartment about six miles away in suburban Sidcup. Within a year he remarried. His sixth book, which concerned naval intelligence during the world war, was dedicated to Francesca Bywater (the former Mrs. Francesca Dorothy Gross), a divorcée eleven years his junior, who had become his second wife.

Thereafter, Bywater became a distant figure to his children, seeing them only occasionally—for lunch in the dining room at the *Daily Telegraph* or at the Norwegian Club, or perhaps for a quick nip at a Fleet Street pub. One could lay the blame for the breakup on the domineering Emma, or on tensions arising from the long, drawn-out debate with Knox, which pitted Bywater against his many American friends. In addition, the drastic cutbacks in navies around the world had rendered Bywater something of a beached sailor—frustrated, irritable, and perhaps less able than before to bear the normal friction of family life.

His anguish over the shrunken size of the Royal Navy during this period (Britain's decision "to abdicate the viceregal throne of Neptune," as he expressed it rather grandly in 1933) is plainly evident in his correspondence that year with Rudyard Kipling, Britain's first literary Nobel laureate. At that time, Bywater was in despair over what he regarded as the ominous rise of Hitler and Mussolini while Britain's defenses were being allowed to wither. Accordingly, he decided to write a series of articles for the *Telegraph* that would dramatize the "parlous plight of our Navy today." Bywater wrote to Kipling asking the poet-statesman "to usher this series in with a few lines"—a not unreasonable request since Kipling was a champion of the navy and had frequently contributed feature articles to the *Daily Telegraph*. But the great man begged off, explaining that he was "jammed up with belated engagements and work," although he went on at length to express "being very interested in your proposed series of articles on what used to be the Navy." Because of the political intricacies of financing the services, Kipling warned, "what is ahead of you will be rather like target practice at a fog bank." But, he declared, "if sympathy and interest are any use, you have mine."

It was then that Bywater bared his feelings. After thanking Kipling for his "most kind and encouraging letter," Bywater went on to say: "To be a naval correspondent today is a rather thankless task, for the Fleet has become a mere skeleton. Some of the effects of consistent malnutrition are obvious enough, but the worst are hidden from public view. It is tragic to one who, like myself, knew the Navy at the zenith of its power."

Ironically, Bywater's prominence seemed to rise in inverse proportion to the strength of British sea power. In 1932, the prominent American historian Charles A. Beard referred to him in an article as "that towering naval expert." The same year, Houghton Mifflin arranged to have *The Great Pacific War* reissued with a "Publisher's Note" declaring that the situation in the Pacific "renews in stunning degree the interest and significance of Mr. Bywater's story." And, in 1934, Bywater had three more books in the shops for sale. In addition to his latest volume, *A Searchlight on the Navy*, which was a study of naval issues throughout the world, his publishers reissued both *Sea Power in the Pacific* and *Strange Intelligence*, his 1931 book about the British Secret Service. These titles sold well throughout the world.

In fact, so great had Bywater's reputation become that in 1934, he was invited by both the French and Italian navies to personally inspect their fleets. The Italian invitation is especially interesting because it appears to have emanated from Mussolini himself and included a personal audience with Il Duce. Two years earlier, Bywater had angered the Italian dictator when he revealed the fact that Italy was building fourteen warships, which until then had "remained unknown to the outer world." Like his exposure of Germany's pocket battleships, this "startling revelation," as Bywater termed it, made headlines around the world. Mussolini immediately denied the report as "a ridiculous invention," but the Italian naval attaché in London got his signals crossed, admitted that the ships were under construction, and said there had never been any "secret" about them. All this seems to have won Mussolini's grudging admiration, and thus, when he felt the time ripe, his eagerness to show off his new warships to the man who had unmasked them.

Although Bywater shared British prime minister Arthur Balfour's view of Mussolini as "a strutting lunatic" (in contrast to the Italian dictator's self-image as a latter-day Caesar who would restore the Roman Empire), he was evidently flattered by the invitation to meet Mussolini. Furthermore, Bywater could not pass up the chance to be conducted through highly restricted Italian naval bases that he had not visited since his days with the Secret Service before the war.

He sailed in early April and by the end of the next month filed a dispatch with the dateline "On board the Cruiser *Cadorna*, VENICE." By then, he had visited several Italian naval bases and been taken aboard one of Italy's new *Condottieri*-class fast cruisers. Except for the German pocket battleships, no foreign fighting ship had excited greater interest than these sleek and speedy greyhounds of the sea. Bywater provided a meticulous description of the vessel that he considered "a picture of beauty and power." On a trial run, he reported, *Cadorna* had attained a speed of 41 knots—an "almost fabulous speed for a ship of the cruiser type."

Two weeks later, Bywater was ushered into Mussolini's imperial office in the Palazzo Venezia in Rome. According to a colleague at the *Daily Telegraph*, when Bywater returned to Fleet Street, he described the scene, and the way he pulled Mussolini's leg, this way:

> The dictator's office was an enormous room obviously intended to intimidate visitors. You had what seemed like a quarter-mile walk to get to his desk. As soon as the flunkies opened the door, I made a beeline to his desk and before Mussolini invited me to sit down, he said in English: "Well, Mr. Bywater, how do you like my navy?" I replied: "Duce, it's magnificent!" Mussolini then leaped to his feet and began pounding his chest saying: "I made it! I made it!" Well, the truth is, apart from the cruisers, I'd never seen so many old tubs in my life.

Among the obsolete "old tubs" Bywater mischievously singled out for praise and recommended for modernization were the prewar dread-noughts *Conte di Cavour* and *Giulio Cesare*, both laid down in 1910. A short while later, very likely influenced by what Bywater had told him, Mussolini spent a small fortune attempting to update these ancient and useless warships.

The *Daily Telegraph* spread Bywater's exclusive interview with Mussolini across the top of its front page, accompanied by a picture of the scowling dictator. "All of Italy is on the sea," Bywater quoted Mussolini as telling him. "Thirty capitals of its provinces are on the sea. Even Rome itself is on the sea. Geography is an unchangeable fact that determines the destinies of people." And such, said Bywater, was Signor Mussolini's justification for accelerated naval building.

Back in London, Bywater regaled the Fleet Street Press Gang with jokes about Mussolini and his new navy. He took particular pleasure in describing how he had bamboozled the Duce by assuring him that a couple of old rust buckets could be made to strike terror into the hearts of his enemies. Bywater also enjoyed telling the sarcastic riddle: "Question: What's the shortest book ever written? Answer: Great Victories of the Italian Navy."

CHAPTER

19

"WE SAILORS GET ON ADMIRABLY TOGETHER"

IF EUROPE'S LEADERS were in Bywater's thrall, the same could be said many times over for those in Japan where for so long British seagoing traditions had aroused admiration and envy. In particular, Bywater's proposal for naval arms limitation published in the *Telegraph* in 1933 struck a responsive chord in Japan. Eventually, the Imperial Navy adopted his proposal as its official position, and it was none other than Isoroku Yamamoto who turned up in London in October 1934 to present the idea to representatives of the Western powers gathered for the Preliminary Naval Limitation Conference. Listening to Yamamoto make the case, one might say that the script he recited had been virtually written by Hector Bywater. It is not possible to know whether Yamamoto was aware of the origin of the proposal he was urging, but if he was, it can only have raised his estimation of Bywater and in that way perhaps heightened his respect for the British expert's ideas about what steps Japan might take if arms limitation failed.

Toward the end of the conference, at which Yamamoto's proposal was ultimately rejected by the Western powers, Bywater and Yamamoto met face to face and whiled away the better part of an evening discussing international relations in the Pacific.

That meeting was amiable. But by this time the major powers had become dissatisfied with the state of naval arms limitation. The Washington Treaty of 1922 had held battleship size to 35,000 tons and restricted the total weight of capital ships of the great powers to a 5-to-5-to-3-to-1.75 ratio (Britain and the United States each could have battleship fleets weighing a total of 525,000 tons compared to Japan's 315,000 tons and France's and Italy's 175,000 tons). As a result of a last-minute impasse, cruisers of 10,000 tons or less had not been covered by the treaty, and thereafter Britain and Japan began building them at a breakneck pace. That competition threatened to upset the balance of naval limitation, and so President Calvin Coolidge called on the leading naval powers to meet at Geneva to resolve what was euphemistically called "the auxiliary craft problem." The Geneva Conference was a failure. France and Italy, suspicious in one case and belligerent in the other, refused to attend. Germany, presumably held in check by the Treaty of Versailles, which sharply limited her navy, was not invited. And the United States and Britain fell to wrangling over what should be the proper size of a cruiser. The conference broke up in August 1927, unable to stem the cruiser-construction frenzy. The entertainer Will Rogers remarked: "Two more disarmament conferences and there won't be enough ocean to hold all the cruisers they all want to build."

Three years later, Britain, the United States, Japan, France, and Italy were ready to try again, and delegates met at the London Conference of 1930—where, in fact, Bywater and Yamamoto first briefly met. This conference brought results, although the more closely they were scrutinized, the less salutary they appeared to be. Japan improved her relative position in capital-ship tonnage by having the 5-to-5-to-3 ratio changed to 5-to-5-to-3.5. In addition, quotas were established for smaller ships, and there Japan secured a higher ratio in destroyer and cruiser size and equality on submarine size. France and Italy, however, stood aloof from these agreements, thus prompting the other signatories to fear they had put themselves at a disadvantage. Furthermore, the news about Germany's pocket battleships, not to mention the rapid development of air power, suggested that the old formulas of tons and guns might now be meaningless.

By the early 1930s, Bywater viewed an ominous scene. Every major power had lost faith in the Washington Treaty as amended in 1930. A rising generation in Japan fiercely resented the fact that their leaders had accepted any restrictions at all on the size of their fleet. Several officials who had supported the treaty were assassinated by young, ultranationalist naval officers, and although the killers were brought to justice, many Japanese thought that there would be no end to violence in their country until the treaty was drastically revised or repudiated. Moreover, seething with anger at being censured by the League of Nations for invading Manchuria, Japan had withdrawn from the League. It was evident she felt that the world was against her and now had little interest in efforts at international cooperation.

In Britain, it was thought that the Socialist government of 1930 had been reckless in agreeing to naval limitations that Britain's most powerful neighbors, France and Italy, had not accepted. And the United States, regarding Japan's expansion of her cruiser fleet as threatening, countered with a cruiser-construction program of her own.

The failure of each of the great maritime powers to see itself on the international stage as perceived by others was well illustrated in August 1933 by an exchange between Bywater and his new employer, *The New York Times*. Bywater had written in the *Telegraph* that America's new shipbuilding program was "a death blow to naval limitation by agreement." The *Times* then lambasted him in an editorial for having failed to take into consideration such factors as that the United States was building new warships largely as a method to "relieve unemployment." That must have been worth a good laugh on Fleet Street—were it not for its dire implications.

Still, Bywater had not given up on diplomacy. Writing for the *Telegraph* in 1933, he tried a new tack. Since naval arms limitation conferences were likely to fail because each nation tried to impose on the others a formula reflecting its own needs, he wrote, "why not lay down a maximum tonnage allowance to all?" Such an agreement, he continued, "would have the supreme advantage of placing all the Powers concerned on the same level. . . . It would put an end to the invidious distinctions which affront national pride and have notoriously rendered the conclusion of disarmament agreements more difficult."

The "common aggregate tonnage" limitation, he went on to say, would have to be sufficiently large "to provide for the needs of the leading Powers"—perhaps 1.2 million tons. It would leave each signatory "free to invest" the lion's share of its tonnage in submarines, or indeed battleships, if it wished; however, that need be no cause for concern since recent history shows that all nations, given complete freedom to build, have invariably preferred "a well-balanced fleet to a lopsided armada composed mainly of one special type of vessel." Furthermore, Bywater argued, a common-aggregate-tonnage treaty would help the world's ailing economy because "the contingency that one or another of the countries . . . would actually build to the full tonnage limit is so remote as to be negligible." The alternative, he concluded, "is a reversion to the pre-War situation, when each Power built such warships as it wanted and asked nobody's leave."

An article of this nature by Bywater did not take long to reach Tokyo. The files of the Foreign Ministry, although incomplete, reveal that in 1933, Tsuneo Matsudaira, then Japanese ambassador to Great Britain, sent home two of Bywater's *Daily Telegraph* articles in just the space of two months. The Japanese naval attaché in London must have sent a good many more. We have the word of Malcolm Kennedy—that keen observer who acted as the eyes and ears of both Reuters and Bywater in Japan—that Bywater's essay proposing a common-aggregate-tonnage treaty "met with a ready response in Japan," and, by early 1934, was "being reflected in the Press and by comments in the Diet." Soon, it would become Japan's basic negotiating position.

One historian, evidently unaware of Bywater's article, has suggested that the Imperial Navy's adoption of what came to be translated as the "common-upper-limit" proposal stemmed from a paper written in the 1920s by the militantly antitreaty Kanji Kato, then chief of the Navy General Staff. Doubtless, Kato's ideas carried weight. The Imperial Navy may also have been prompted by somewhat similar ideas put forward in France and Italy after the 1930 London Naval Conference. However, all of these possible promptings had had a number of years in which to work their influence without notable result; it is the close timing of Bywater's proposal and the decisive change in the Imperial Navy's diplomatic strategy that makes persuasive Malcolm Kennedy's belief that Bywater's essay exerted the critical influence.

Yamamoto probably learned that Japan would press for a common upper limit at a meeting of the Military Council at the official residence of Navy Minister Mineo Osumi on June 8, 1934. At that gathering, attended by the entire upper echelon of the Imperial Navy, Nobumasa Suetsugu, the hawkish commander-in-chief of the Combined Fleet, threatened a coup if the group did not consent "to abrogate the existing treaties and have no treaties and no restrictions" or, as second best, propose at the coming international conference "a common upper limit on naval tonnage." Suetsugu was not merely reciting Bywater's proposal by rote but had seized the idea because it meshed with his own belief that Japan was finally ready to challenge the United States in virtually unrestricted naval building. He, like other hard-liners in the navy, took courage from the fact that Japan continued to make economic progress while the United States seemed inextricably mired in the depression.

Furthermore, Suetsugu saw such new weapons as aircraft, long-range submarines, and the so-called long-lance torpedo as greatly favoring the defense of Japan against intruders from afar. He also thought that the strictures of the Washington Treaty had forced Japan to attempt costly and unsound naval construction, such as the experimental light destroyer *Tomotsuru*, which had capsized in a storm with great loss of life. Finally, if Suetsugu and his colleagues had been impressed with Bywater, they were also disciples of Mahan, and were convinced, as Mahan taught, that trade follows the flag. Just as Japan's expansion into Manchuria had been made possible by a strong navy, Suetsugu maintained, so her progress elsewhere would depend upon a fleet second to none. By the end of the meeting, the military councillors agreed to adopt Suetsugu's second proposal—the common upper limit.

Yamamoto was not a major player in these deliberations, and yet, once he had been chosen as the navy's chief delegate and been given his instructions, he had a remarkably free hand in the manner and force with which to present his country's positions. In addition, although his civilian counterpart Tsuneo Matsudaira, the Japanese ambassador to London, was technically the representative of the emperor, Yamamoto, as spokesman for the navy, held the ultimate veto power. In order to impress the militants like Suetsugu and Kato of his solidarity with them, Yamamoto declared just before sailing from Yokohama: "My departure today is just the same to me as a departure for actual warfare."

Yamamoto and his staff arrived at Liverpool on the Cunard liner *Berengaria* in October 1934. The Western nations saw it as portentous that while their own delegations were led by civilians assisted by admirals, Yamamoto, newly promoted from rear admiral to vice admiral, appeared to play a more commanding role than Matsudaira. At the first meeting at 10 Downing Street, Yamamoto denounced the concept of naval ratios and proposed in its stead that the five major powers "fix a common upper limit" of naval tonnage. When Ramsay MacDonald, the British prime minister, asked Yamamoto to explain his idea in greater detail, Yamamoto replied that a common upper limit would be "a figure which the country feeling most vulnerable deemed necessary for herself"—precisely Bywater's idea.

The Western diplomats kept their faces wreathed with cordial smiles but privately scoffed at the proposal as either Oriental obfuscation or gross naivete. Sir Ernle Chatfield, the British first sea lord, called the common upper limit "quite impossible," and Sir Robert Craigie, then a representative of the Foreign Office but later the British ambassador to Tokyo, privately ridiculed the proposal as a "very theoretical plan evolved by someone in Tokyo who had evidently not the least idea of conditions either in Europe or the United States." How surprised Chatfield and Craigie would have been to know its true source!

Later, Yamamoto urged the abolition of "offensive weapons," by which he meant aircraft carriers, capital ships, and heavy cruisers. He also asked for agreement on the principle of "non-aggression and non-menace." The talks dragged on through the autumn of 1934 with each side calling the other intransigent. Meanwhile, Yamamoto kept his distance from the press. The no-comment policy he established when he arrived in Seattle at the end of the first leg of his journey was maintained throughout his stay in London. Apart from the initial press conference, which he held a day after arriving in England, Yamamoto in general refused to speak to the press. He made only one or two exceptions. One of these was for the well-known naval journalist and author whose book about a possible future war in the Pacific had deeply impressed him while serving as naval attaché in Washington eight-and-a-half years before. Perhaps Yamamoto's desire to meet and converse with Bywater simply got the better of his discretion—which until now had fairly well shielded him from the press—or perhaps, inveterate gambler that he was, he sought to match wits in some fashion. Whatever his motive, he agreed to the interview. Bywater recorded their meeting in the *Daily Telegraph* the next day. From this article and other sources, it is possible to piece together much of what transpired—and to make some informed guesses as to what else may have taken place when the leading Pacific strategist met one of Japan's rising samurai.

Bywater visited Yamamoto at his hotel suite at Grosvenor House on the evening of December 3. One can imagine Yamamoto's eagerness to ask Bywater about *The Great Pacific War*. Did Mr. Bywater believe that the strategic concepts expressed in that most interesting book were still valid? What made him think Japan would seek to expand her empire by advancing south by sea rather than north by land, marching up through Manchuria to the Soviet Union? What were his sources of information when he covered the Washington Conference? But Yamamoto would never utter such blunt questions. He would not wish to signal too great an interest in the possibility of war against the United States. Also, being a cultivated Japanese, he would think it impolite to ask if naval strategies had changed since that might imply Bywater had been wrong originally. It would be more in character for him to wait for an opportunity to present his questions with subtlety and with a well-meaning display of tact and flattery.

Even though the two men had met previously at the 1930 conference, and had perhaps nodded to each other over the past few weeks when their paths crossed during the current conference, their meeting would begin formally. Bywater, after all, was coming on business, looking for a news story.

After he had been admitted to Yamamoto's rooms and been guided to an easy chair, and once the two men had exchanged pleasantries, Bywater asked the vice admiral how he viewed the possibility of a naval arms race in case the Washington Treaty were allowed to expire. Yamamoto replied that it would be "an international calamity" that Japan would "go to any reasonable length to avoid." He also said that termination of the treaty might be more to the disadvantage of Japan than any of the other signatories. "Japan recognizes," he said, "that denunciation of the Washington Treaty would restore to the other Powers liberty to develop fleet bases within Japan's strategical sphere of interest."

What about naval bases in the Pacific, as, for example, the British base at Singapore? he was asked. "I and many other Japanese naval officers," Yamamoto responded, "do not regard [the British base at] Singapore as a menace. It is too far away from our country to cause us worry. We should, however, be seriously perturbed if the United States were to create a powerful base in the Philippines."

Yamamoto then remarked that his common-upper-limit proposal still under consideration at the conference was not only intended to reduce current naval construction programs but to scrap many existing warships. He insisted that Japan sought to get rid of all capital ships and reduce navies to the status of coastal defense forces.

He went on to acknowledge that his plan—there is no indication that he knew it was originally Bywater's—had not sparked enthusiasm among the other delegates. But, he said, he had an alternative. If capital ships could not be abolished by treaty, he would favor continuing the battleship-building moratorium by extending the life of already-existing ships.

At this point, perhaps observing an indication from Bywater that he had enough in his notebook to make a story, Yamamoto signaled to his butler to roll out a portable bar and offer his guest a drink. Although Yamamoto himself did not imbibe, Bywater would have asked for a Scotch, that being the customary beverage on such occasions. Now in a more convivial tone, Yamamoto expressed his appreciation of William H. Standley, the American chief of naval operations, and Ernle Chatfield, the British first sea lord, for their kindness and especially for putting up with "my imperfect command of English." He might also have mentioned that Chatfield had proved an agreeable host a few days back when Yamamoto relieved him of 20 pounds in a game of bridge. "No matter what our differences of opinion may be," Yamamoto told Bywater, "we sailors get on admirably together."

But chummy though Yamamoto's personal relations were with the other delegates, that could not alter the cold facts of power politics. Throughout the coming sessions, Yamamoto would steadfastly refuse to accept any suggestion of an inferior naval strength for Japan, and his British and American colleagues would not seriously consider any alternative such as a common upper limit. When Standley and Chatfield argued that their countries required relatively large navies because they had vital sea lanes in every ocean whereas Japan was purely a Pacific power, Yamamoto would quip: "I am smaller than you, but you do not insist that I eat three-fifths of the food on my plate." Thus, the conference was soon to end in stalemate.

This same bleak outlook was also evident during Bywater's interview. In fact, so unyielding was Yamamoto on the subject of naval ratios that Bywater took the unusual step of withholding from publication one of his most important remarks. A year would go by, and Japan would have to make certain her determination to let the Washington Treaty expire, before Bywater would divulge in the *Telegraph*: "It can now be disclosed" that in December 1934 Yamamoto told him Japan would simply refuse to be party to any treaty that did not cast aside the ratios once and for all and instead "embody the principle of a common upper limit."

"Well, Mr. Bywater, I enjoyed reading your latest book—*A Searchlight on the Navy*," Yamamoto might continue, raising a glass of seltzer in a toast to good health. "I found it illuminating!"

His object would be to introduce the subject of Bywater's books, thus affording an opportunity to bring up *The Great Pacific War* with seeming casualness. If this gambit did not succeed, Yamamoto might approach the subject somewhat more directly by expressing admiration for the way in which Bywater had skillfully insinuated his ideas about naval strategy into the narrative of *The Great Pacific War*.

By one such means or another, he would seek to draw out Bywater on whether or not he thought either power in a Japanese-American war would adopt a different strategy in 1934 than the one described in 1925. Presented with such a question, Bywater would unhesitatingly respond in the negative. A few months previously, he had commented on *The Great Pacific War* in his preface to the 1934 reissue of *Sea Power in the Pacific*. "The moves on a war-game board arranged for a Pacific campaign in the near future," he had written, "must needs follow very closely those which the players would have made thirteen years ago."

Furthermore, a few weeks after this meeting with Yamamoto, Bywater would be asked to update *The Great Pacific War* in an article for the scholarly journal *Pacific Affairs*. On that occasion, he would spell out "the hypothetical case of a war between the United States and Japan" as he had nearly a decade before but with a few minor yet intriguing changes. Japan, he would declare, "might choose to strike first" with her new aircraft carriers instead of with a surface fleet. The Philippines and Guam would "no doubt be gobbled up by Japan in the first weeks of war." In addition, he would say, American aircraft carriers could raid Tokyo and long-range Japanese submarines could harass Hawaii and the Pacific coast of the United States. Human nature, of course, would remain unchanged, and consequently a public demand for victories would probably force both adversaries to launch ill-advised expeditions, and these would result in "reverses, defeats, perhaps disasters." The outcome would depend in large measure on whether or not the United States could find a way to project her immense power into "the decisive zone" in the Western Pacific, and how effectively Japan could exploit her geographical position and strong fleet to prevent that intrusion.

He would go on to say that despite her tremendous industrial power, the United States would by no means have it easy in such a war. "Some years ago, in a book dealing with Pacific strategy," he would write for *Pacific Affairs*, "I observed that the man least to be envied was the admiral destined to command the United States fleet in a war with Japan. Not long afterwards I received a letter from an American officer—who subsequently became commander-in-chief—which began with the words: 'You've said it!'"

All this, Bywater would freely expound for Yamamoto. These were, after all, remarks he had already published or would soon be putting into print, and why not share his thoughts with a bright, rising star of the Imperial Navy? If Bywater, in fact, expressed such thoughts, one can imagine Yamamoto taking them in with the utmost gravity. It may well be that in this interview, the die was cast for the shape of the greatest naval war the world has ever known.

CHAPTER 20

THE MONSTER
BATTLESHIP CRISIS

IN NOVEMBER 1937, Bywater scored a newsbreak that easily topped in importance his prophetic revelations during the Washington Conference and exposure of Germany's pocket battleships. He became the first reporter to tell the world authoritatively that Japan was secretly building four "monster" battleships. So fearsome did these seagoing fortresses appear that even though he considerably underestimated their actual size, the news of their existence threw open the starting gate for the naval arms race that led to Pearl Harbor.

A flurry of diplomatic activity—frequently reported and commented upon by Bywater—preceded the crisis of the monster battleships. After the Preliminary London Conference of 1934, at which Yamamoto took a defiant stand against the continuation of naval ratios, there was hope in Western capitals that even if Japan would no longer accept a smaller navy in principle, she might at least agree to make public any planned expansion so that the other powers would not fear to be caught napping.

In fact, when the British delegation made this very proposal at the outset of the next London Conference, Bywater reported that the Japanese delegates "appeared to welcome it." But he misread the signals from the militant Osami Nagano, who succeeded Yamamoto as the navy's chief delegate to the conference. The truth was that Nagano's object was to wind up the talks as speedily as possible and hurry home in order to take advantage of Japan's new freedom to build the superships he had long dreamed of.

Ironically, it was not Nagano but his more peace-minded rival, Yamamoto, who sounded the death knell for arms limitation at the 1935–36 London Conference. Shortly after Nagano arrived in London, Yamamoto, back in Tokyo, happened to be testifying before the National Diet. When asked by a member how the just-convened London Conference might affect the Imperial Navy's budget, Yamamoto replied that if Japan's demands for equality were not met, she would "break up the conference." Melville Cox, the Tokyo-based Reuters correspondent, who had succeeded Malcolm Kennedy as Bywater's principal informant in Japan, was in the Diet's press gallery and quickly dashed off a cable for Reuters reporting what Yamamoto had said.

Bywater typified those stunned by Yamamoto's remark. Only the day before, he had written that it was "now practically certain" that the conference would effect "a substantial reduction in the size and cost of future warships." But now he had to take it all back. He wrote that Reuters quoted Yamamoto as declaring that Japan "would press for a common upper limit, even if it meant the breakup of the conference." He added that if this report were confirmed, "the Conference might as well break up at once." And well it might have. Yamamoto's remark cast a pall over the diplomatic minuet that dragged on for another month. Then, as Nagano withdrew from the conference, thus allowing the expiration of the world's first, briefly successful international treaty to limit the means of warfare, he pledged that his country would not be the one to start a naval arms race. The Western powers believed him, thinking Japan too poor to attempt to outbuild nations with a much greater industrial capacity. And thus, after Nagano's departure from London, the Western powers agreed among themselves to continue to observe the 35,000-ton limit for capital ships, assuming that Japan, even without having renewed the treaty, would docilely follow their lead.

Nagano, of course, had deceived the West. Only a few weeks after returning to Tokyo, he was named navy minister and promptly made the construction of two monster battleships a top priority of the Imperial Navy's so-called Third Replenishment Program, the first major expansion of the Japanese Navy unfettered by treaty obligations.

Gigantic battleships had long had a special appeal to Japanese naval planners. Ever since the opening of the Panama Canal in 1914, which had given the U.S. Navy the great advantage of being able to quickly gather its forces in the Atlantic or Pacific Ocean, Japanese strategists recognized that the canal also imposed a limit on its owner. It was only 110 feet wide. In August 1935, Imperial Navy architects drew up a table of the major ships of the world, listing all those that could and those that could not pass through the Panama Canal. For example, it was a tight squeeze for Britain's 42,000-ton *Hood*, the biggest warship afloat in the period between the two world wars, which measured 105.25 feet in beam. It was tighter still for more modern battleships fitted with antitorpedo "bulges" or "blisters," such as the 35,000-ton *North Carolina* and *Washington*, which were to have beams of 108 feet when completed in 1941. The 42,000-ton German dreadnoughts *Bismarck* and *Tirpitz*—squat craft of 118 feet in width—were simply out of the question for the canal, as were such commercial liners as the French *Normandie* (117 feet, 9 inches) and the British *Queen Mary* (118.5 feet).

This study, which included vessels of all practical sizes and shapes, convinced the Japanese that the largest warship capable of making the transit would displace 63,000 tons. Since it was fair to assume that the United States would not build battleships too big for her cherished canal, the way for Japan to turn an American advantage into a disadvantage —it occurred to these naval architects—would be to build a squadron of monster battleships so large, strong, and powerfully armed that they could handily defeat a fleet of 63,000-ton American men-of-war.

Between 1921 and 1936, Japan was prevented from any such exercise in gigantism by the Washington Treaty, which pledged the signatories to limit the size of their warships to 35,000 tons. But virtually the day the treaty expired, the Imperial Navy, in great secrecy, began to construct battleships the likes of which the world had never seen. Specifically designed to outclass any American fighting vessel that could pass through the locks of the Panama Canal, Japan's superships were to displace a phenomenal 72,000 tons, making them nearly twice the size of the mighty *Hood*.

In terms of the extreme secrecy and vital resources applied, the construction of the first two monster battleships—*Yamato* and *Musashi*, as they were named—became a kind of Japanese Manhattan Project. Part of the slip at the Kure Naval Yard where *Yamato* began to be built was roofed over to prevent observation from the air, and at the Mitsubishi Yard at Nagasaki, where *Musashi* was under construction, the entire slip was covered with a 408-ton rope curtain. So much sisal was used in making this curtain that there was a serious shortage of rope for fishing nets throughout 1938. Numerous screens prevented workers occupied in one section from seeing other sections and thus comprehending the overall size of the ship.

By every measure, the *Yamato*s boggled the mind. Just the weight of their gunnery installations was 2,000 tons greater than the total displacement of a German pocket battleship. The main batteries were engineered to mount stupendous 18.11-inch guns that could heave a 3,220-pound explosive bullet—more on the order of a meteorite than an artillery shell—26 miles, outreaching the 16-inch guns of the biggest American battleships by at least five miles. These Japanese shells could slam through any known armor. A full nine-gun salvo from one of the *Yamato*s would weigh 14.5 tons—approximately the weight of a small switching locomotive engine—in contrast to *Maryland*'s 8.5 tons and *New Jersey*'s 9.5 tons. And the *Yamato*'s armor—all 34,000 tons of it, 2 feet thick in places—was built to withstand direct hits from innumerable bombs, torpedos, and 16-inch armor-piercing shells. If ever such monsters came up against the American battle line in the Pacific, one could readily imagine American shells bouncing off of them like Ping-Pong balls while the *Yamato*s methodically ripped the U.S. fleet to bloody shreds. Such a horror show might well lead Americans to regard the Panama Canal as the naval equivalent of the ill-fated Maginot Line—a fixed structure whose chief effect was to tempt one's opponent to devise a way to overcome it.

Bywater had long been aware of Japan's fascination with superships. In *Sea Power in the Pacific*, he pointed out that the Imperial Navy had been the first to build a modern "all-big-gun" battleship, although the claim of priority was usually granted to Britain. The fact was, Bywater explained, that Japan's 19,000-ton dreadnoughts *Aki* and *Satsuma* had been laid down early in 1905, "many months before the *Dreadnought* [which gave its name to the class] was commenced in England." Also in *Sea Power in the Pacific*, and in an article for the *New York Herald*, he reported many particulars of Japan's four planned 43,500-ton superdreadnoughts (to be named *Akagi, Amagi, Atago,* and *Takao*), which would mount main batteries of 18-inch guns, greatly outranging the 16-inch guns to be carried by the American *Indiana*-class battleships. These Japanese monsters were never completed due to the signing of the Washington Treaty in 1921, but Bywater suspected that the heady notion of trumping the United States Navy with a fleet of overwhelmingly superior battleships was never consigned to oblivion by diehards in the Imperial Navy. He expressed this belief in *The Great Pacific War* when he imagined Japan building a 40,000-ton superdreadnought and an immense 44,000-ton battle cruiser. "Each in its own way," he wrote, "was a more powerful ship than any unit of the United States Navy." Nevertheless, in Bywater's drama, the Japanese were not able to build enough of these monsters to give themselves a decisive edge, and, in the climactic sea battle, which he called the Battle of Yap, the Imperial Navy's superdreadnought is blown to bits and the gigantic battle cruiser heavily damaged.

In 1930, when reporting the completion of "the greatest naval drydock in the world" at Kure, Bywater recalled the never-completed Japanese superdreadnoughts of 1920. The Kure drydock had been planned in 1921 to accommodate the *Akagi*, he wrote. It was then abandoned but later resumed and finally finished in 1930. What was the purpose of such an immense drydock? he asked himself. The Kure facility, he answered, could accommodate "the largest battleship, or four of the new 10,000-ton cruisers at once." Still, he found no direct evidence that Japan was building warships of unusual size.

Six years later, following the expiration of the Washington Treaty, Bywater took note of the moment at which the Japanese government "decided henceforth to observe complete secrecy over new naval construction." Secrecy, naturally, aroused suspicion. And writers for the jingoistic Hearst press gave free rein to their nightmarish anxieties. Bywater never stooped to any such mendacity himself and in fact took particular pains in February 1936 to refute a Hearst-inspired fantasy that told of Japan's clandestine building of a "gigantic" armada. He investigated the particulars and wrote the next day in the *Telegraph* that the story was nothing but "tendentious fiction."

Throughout 1936, Bywater maintained that there was no compelling reason to believe that Japan was "laying down monster ships." Japan would be ill-advised, he wrote, to start a building race in which "she would infallibly be defeated by the superior financial and technical resources of this country and the United States." By April 1937, however, he traced rumors about major warship construction in Japan to plausible sources and almost simultaneously discovered that the Imperial Navy's latest annual appropriation took up 24 percent of the entire national budget. These findings prompted him to express concern. "It is doubtful whether anyone outside the Ministry of Marine in Tokyo knows what is going on in the Japanese dockyards," he wrote, "or what the approximate strength of the Japanese Navy will be two or three years hence."

After further study of the Imperial Navy's budget, he concluded in early June that a striking 65 million pounds would be spent during the next five years for "new ships, over and above the normal provision of the naval budget." What this meant, he declared, was that "a new fleet is being built in complete secrecy." He quoted Yamamoto's mentor, Mitsumasa Yonai, who had succeeded Nagano as navy minister, as having stated that any new battleships under construction would be of "less than 40,000 tons." But Bywater expressed his doubts about Yonai's veracity and reminded readers that if Japan persisted in refusing to reveal the tonnage and armament of her new battleships, the 35,000-ton limit observed by Britain, the United States, and France "may have to be dropped." Otherwise, "those Powers might find their latest ships overshadowed in fighting value by Japanese contemporaries."

He repeated this warning once again, and then, as the brisk winds of autumn began to rattle windows at the office of the *Daily Telegraph*, Bywater picked up a scent as unmistakable as that which had led him to unmask the German pocket battleships a decade before. The first indication was a bulletin in the *Telegraph* on November 8, written by the newspaper's Rome correspondent. "Some observers," the correspondent wrote, "see a naval alliance between Germany, Italy, and Japan foreshadowed in [a] long and enthusiastic article in [a] newspaper extolling the size and fighting efficiency of the Japanese Navy."

Whether Bywater cabled the *Telegraph*'s Rome correspondent to ask for a clipping of the article referred to, or asked his brother Ulysses, a longtime resident of Rome and Milan, to scout up a copy for him, he soon received the clipping of a long article entitled JAPAN AND HER FLEET.

It had appeared simultaneously in two government-controlled Italian newspapers, *Giornale d'Italia* and *Il Messaggero*. The article contained a surprising amount of information about new naval construction in Japan. By 1941, the article stated, Japan would possess a fleet of 289 warships with a total displacement of 1,109,150 tons. These figures— all well within the realm of possibility—were alarming. The U.S. Navy projected at best 1,418,895 tons by that date. But then came the real shocker. Of the sixty-six vessels now under construction in Japanese shipyards, "three are battleships of 46,000 tons," the article stated. Here it was in black and white that the much-rumored superships were actually being built.

What lent particular credence to this report was its timing. Apart from the fact that identical articles had appeared simultaneously in two different newspapers that regularly acted as spokesmen for the Italian government, the articles had appeared the day after Italy announced she had joined Germany and Japan in the so-called Anti-Comintern Pact, the anti-Communist alliance formed by the Fascist powers.

One by one during the 1930s, the nations that chose the path of aggression had backed out of the international organizations and treaties that might restrain them. Then they formed their own alliance. The process had begun in 1931 when Japan invaded Manchuria and was censured by the League of Nations. Indignantly, she withdrew her membership. In October 1935, Mussolini defied the League with his conquest of Ethiopia, and Italy, too, soon quit the international body. The following March, Hitler scoffed at the League's censure when he remilitarized the German Rhineland, which had been established by the Treaty of Versailles as a demilitarized zone.

With the formation of the Axis alliance, it stood to reason that the Japanese, eager to impress their new allies, might have divulged information about their secret naval construction to the Italian government—information suggesting that the Japanese Navy would soon be powerful enough to draw a sizable British counterforce into the Pacific, thus reducing naval pressure on Italy in the Mediterranean. Italy's invasion of Ethiopia, coupled with the possibility of Mussolini's joining an alliance with Hitler, had prompted Britain to move a large naval force into the Mediterranean, and the Italians, no doubt, would be gratified to learn that a huge Japanese naval construction program might soon attract British attention elsewhere.

If Bywater now accepted as a fact that Japan was building monster battleships, he remained skeptical about certain details in the Italian newspaper account. For purely technical reasons, the 46,000-ton figure seemed an unlikely displacement for a battleship; 43,000 tons would have made more sense and been closer to what the Japanese had had on their drawing boards back in 1920. For the time being, therefore, Bywater decided not to specify the size of the monsters. Also, the notion that three giant battleships were under construction seemed wrong; new naval construction almost always proceeded in pairs to ease the procurement of replacement parts and make possible cannibalization in an emergency. Furthermore, Japan's known expenditure of 55 million pounds—Bywater now realized that the figure used in his earlier report had been too high—would suggest four, not three, 10-million-pound superships, plus auxiliaries. Despite these reservations, however, Bywater decided it was time to speak out.

On November 22, 1937, under the headline JAPAN'S SECRET NEW FLEET, he announced to the world: "A new fleet is being built [in Japan] under the cloak of secrecy. There is nothing to show that Japan's new ships will be restricted to the tonnage and gun calibre fixed by existing treaty, to which all the other leading naval Powers except Italy are signatories." In fact, he went on to write, "there is some evidence that it [the new fleet] includes four battleships of unknown size, two of which are already in hand."

This was a daring and provocative statement for the world's leading naval authority to make. Even so, the reaction was not immediate— perhaps because his assertions did not appear to be based on firsthand observation. Whatever the reason, two-and-a-half weeks elapsed before Hanson W. Baldwin, the renowned military editor of *The New York Times*, published a front-page story headlined: 3 GREAT WARSHIPS REPORTED IN JAPAN. Baldwin did not mention Bywater but rather cited the *Giornale d'Italia* article, which he called "semi-official confirmation of the construction of 46,000-ton Japanese ships." The reason for Baldwin's avoidance of Bywater's name even though he knew and admired him is not difficult to imagine. Anti-British feeling in the United States had increased considerably since 1931, when Dudley Knox branded Bywater a "propagandist." By 1937, many American isolationists feared that Britain was trying to drag the United States into a war against Germany or Japan, and therefore any suggestion from a British writer about war preparations in either of the major dictatorships would be suspect.

Although the figure Baldwin gave for the size of the Japanese monsters was 26,000 tons short of the actual fact, it was startling enough. And coming on the heels of Bywater's pronouncement, it stimulated a series of hurried conferences in Western capitals. In Washington, President Roosevelt (Bywater's old debating partner, who must have been having second thoughts by now about the physical impossibility of a Pacific war) summoned his chief of naval operations, Admiral William D. Leahy. Whatever the Japanese were up to, it seemed evident to Roosevelt and Leahy that *North Carolina* and *Washington*—the two 35,000-ton, 14-inch battleships the U.S. Navy had started to build earlier in the year—were being rendered obsolete. But, as for specific facts about the Japanese superships, Leahy told the president, the navy had not been able to gather reliable information. Embarrassingly, he said, he had to rely on reports published in the press.

Roosevelt decided on two courses of action. First, he instructed the State Department to cable the British Foreign Office to find out if the British government had managed to gather any hard facts about Japan's monster battleships. Second, without even waiting for a reply from Britain, Roosevelt announced at a press conference on December 29 that he would soon urge Congress to authorize funds for an expanded naval building program.

Roosevelt's request for information about Japan's superships arrived in London just as the British government was preparing to ask for the very same assistance from the United States. British naval attachés investigating Bywater's report of monster-battleship construction had also run into a blank wall, but the British Admiralty, like its American counterpart, was convinced of the accuracy of what Bywater, and now Hanson Baldwin, had reported. And, the British Admiralty had as much reason to be alarmed as Roosevelt and Leahy, for it now appeared that the five 35,000-ton, 14-inch *King George V*–class battleships under construction in Britain were being outmoded long before they could be completed.

Moreover, within a few days, the sea lords were given a new report based on the best information their naval attachés and diplomats could glean from foreign capitals. This memorandum confirmed their worst fears. Hard facts and firsthand observation were still frustratingly absent, but the consensus of opinion was that Japan "probably intends to build ships carrying 16-inch guns of a size of 42,000 or 43,000 tons." Here again, a Western estimate fell far short of what the Japanese were actually constructing, yet the report aroused grave concern. On January 13, First Lord of the Admiralty Alfred Duff Cooper presented this latest report to Britain's highest military policy council, the Committee of Imperial Defense (CID). At the meeting, Duff Cooper suggested that the best way to deter Japan from proceeding with the construction of monster warships would be to have Britain, the United States, and France jointly inform Japan that if she did not own up to the size of the battleships she was building and "inform us what are her intentions," the Western democracies would feel free to build monsters of their own. The Committee of Imperial Defense approved Duff Cooper's proposal and forwarded it to Prime Minister Neville Chamberlain.

At that point, a breach of security occurred that reveals how the Admiralty collaborated with the press when it suited its interests. The sea lords, perhaps in order to signal the Japanese that they were on to their game, as well as to exert pressure on their own government to consult poste haste with the United States and France, leaked to Bywater everything Duff Cooper had told the Committee of Imperial Defense. It was his second major scoop of the monster-battleship crisis. Obviously, by 1938, the strained feelings between Bywater and the Admiralty had healed, or at least were able to be overlooked when paramount common interests arose.

Under the headline JAPAN BUILDING WORLD'S BIGGEST BATTLESHIPS, Bywater declared in the *Telegraph* that his earlier report that Japan was building "the largest battleships in the world" was "now confirmed." These monster warships would displace "about 43,000 tons," he wrote, and would mount twelve 16-inch guns. It is "not improbable," he went on to say, adopting a speculative tone in order to conceal the authoritative nature of his source, "that conversations will be initiated at an early date between the Governments interested, to consider a revision of the Treaty restrictions."

Four days later, Bywater reported that if definite confirmation was obtained of the report that Japan had several 43,000-ton battleships under construction, "an early consultation will be arranged between Britain, the United States, and France." He went on to say that his earlier report about 43,000-ton vessels under construction had been "accepted as authentic in unofficial naval quarters." His use of the phrase "unofficial naval quarters" was a well-known euphemism for *official* naval quarters, the euphemism being a requirement to spare the government possible embarrassment in sensitive situations such as this. It was evident, however, that Bywater had been talking to officials in the Admiralty. Apart from the rapidity with which he divulged information from Britain's highest and most secure defense council, it would have been scarcely worth his reporting whether or not "unofficial" circles believed his previous story. Furthermore, when Bywater stated that confirmation of the existence of Japan's monster warships would lead to "an early consultation" between Britain, the United States, and France, it was evident that no "unofficial" source could have told him that.

Bywater's acceptance of the 43,000-ton figure may seem credulous in view of the fact that the ships were actually 72,000 tons; however, the highest authorities in both the United States and Britain also believed this estimate. By the standards of the day, 43,000 tons represented a phenomenally huge warship. Indeed, even after the U.S. Navy had actually sunk both *Yamato* and *Musashi* in 1945, U.S. Naval Intelligence *still* believed them to be 45,000-ton battleships armed with 16-inch guns.

Bywater's revelations would soon—at least indirectly—bring him into contact with Yamamoto once again, but first their respective governments would interact. Duff Cooper's proposal that identical notes be sent simultaneously to Japan was endorsed by Chamberlain and met with almost immediate acceptance in Washington and Paris. Thus, within a matter of days, the ambassadors of all three governments were handing notes employing most of Duff Cooper's language to Japanese foreign minister Koki Hirota in Tokyo.

Hirota's reply to the Western powers on February 12 dashed all hope for continued arms limitation. In the absence of a treaty, Hirota declared, "the mere communication of information concerning the construction of vessels will . . . not contribute to any fair and equitable measure of disarmament." Then, giving expression to years of hostility, he could not resist getting in a final dig. "It is not a matter which should concern this Government," he stated tartly, "if your Government, on the basis of whatever reason or rumor, should exercise the right of escalation provided in any treaty to which Japan is not a party."

This stinging rebuff unleashed the long pent-up naval arms race, and huge battleships were at the center of the building program of every first-class navy. The British Admiralty laid down two 40,000-ton *Lion*-class battleships—the biggest vessels that could be accommodated at British docking facilities. The Soviet Union announced construction of a 44,190-ton capital ship. In the United States, Congress adopted the Second Vinson–Trammell Naval Act, which authorized a record $1.1 billion in naval construction over a period of several years, including authorization for the first two 45,000-ton *Iowa*-class battleships. Germany had already announced that she was building *Bismarck* and *Tirpitz*, although no one in the democracies knew that they would prove to be 42,000-ton superships. Thus, engines of war preparation began to hum throughout the world; what was unknown in the West was that heroic exertions by the Japanese were forging leviathans beside which even this new class of superbattleship would seem as dwarfs.

At this moment, Melville Cox—either with or without Bywater's prompting—sought out Yamamoto. Was the Imperial Navy really building the stupendous new battleships Bywater had described? Cox wanted to know. And if not, then why the secrecy?

"Japan wanted a force only sufficient to defend herself, and had no intention of threatening other countries," Yamamoto replied. "But," he continued, weaving a skein of misleading suggestions,

> it is quite natural for a country like Japan, with a small navy to rely upon for her security, to need special armament, and I believe it is patent to everybody that the necessity of keeping her armaments secret is far greater than it is for Powers with larger navies. . . . And yet, they [Britain, France, and the United States] request in these Notes [that we] reveal the content of our naval program, and would dogmatically assume in case of our failure to comply, that we are building beyond the limits of the treaty. This attitude cannot be called reasonable or fair.

So tortured was the logic of this statement that the London *Times* devoted an editorial to denouncing Yamamoto. "Admiral Yamamoto, Vice Minister of Marine," the *Times* declared, "in one breath expresses Japan's need for secrecy and 'special armament,' and in the next castigates the unreason and unfairness of foreign Powers who, as a result of her secrecy, conclude that the special armament is actually being provided." Bywater, in particular, must have shaken his head in dismay as he read this exposure of thinly veiled hypocrisy.

For his part, Yamamoto cannot have been pleased with this turn of events, and if his annoyance needed an outlet, there could be no better targets than Cox and Bywater. Melville Cox, Bywater's eyes and ears in Japan for the past four years, had begun to provoke Yamamoto in December 1935 when he broadcast to the world the admiral's chance remark that Japan intended to break up the arms conference. Now, Cox had backed Yamamoto into an uncomfortable corner on the superships, resulting in blistering press reactions in the West. As for Bywater—the recipient of many of Cox's cables—Yamamoto could remember how during the Washington Conference he had seemed to know what the Japanese delegates were going to say even before they confided their thoughts to the other delegates. It was also Bywater, with his persistent questioning, who had stirred up the monster battleship crisis. And, of course, it was Bywater who had made an intrusive study of Japanese naval strategy and set the world to thinking about how Japan might employ her naval strength to expand her empire.

If Japan were to undertake preparations for the sort of war Yamamoto had conceived after reading *The Great Pacific War*, Bywater and Cox might be quick to detect it. Yamamoto had good reason to wonder if, with the possible approach of hostilities against the United States, something should be done about these two Englishmen.

CHAPTER

21

THE MOST VIOLENT
DAY

AUGUST 16, 1940, dawned bright and clear over London, giving no hint of the savage air battle soon to begin. The Second World War had been in progress in Europe for almost a year, and German air marshall Hermann Goering's bombing campaign against Britain— widely believed to be the prelude to an invasion—had reached its climax. By midmorning, one of the mightiest fleets of aircraft ever assembled came roaring over the English Channel to strike targets in the south-western outskirts of London. Defenders quickly rose to meet them, and much of the combat took place at low level, treating onlookers to a hair-raising air show in which planes were seen chasing and dodging each other over rooftops and behind clumps of trees.

Within earshot of this melee, in the dormitory town of Richmond, Hector Bywater lay on a bed lingering between life and death. One wonders how his semiconscious mind reacted to the whine of racing aircraft engines and the thunder of exploding bombs—and indeed how

241

he would have taken the news that one of these insolent missiles had demolished the offices of Sampson Low, Marston & Co., the publisher of *Jane's Fighting Ships*. Only a few weeks before, Bywater had assured his fellow Britons that their faith in the Royal Navy was not misplaced because sea power, not air power, remained the decisive weapon of war for the British Empire.

His words had appeared in the London *News-Chronicle*, the daily newspaper he now served as naval correspondent. The year before, he had left the *Daily Telegraph* as precipitously as he had severed connections with the Baltimore *Sun* eight years before. There is no written record of the exact circumstances of his departure, but E. A. Harwood, the newspaper's former chief librarian, recalled that just before Bywater left the *Telegraph*, he had been summoned to the office of Arthur Watson, the tall, sober-faced managing editor known as "The Old Bottle of Ink." When Bywater emerged from Watson's office, according to Harwood, he entered the library where he frequently used to stop for afternoon tea. On this occasion, however, Bywater "just stood there," according to Harwood, and said nothing. He was "pale and shaking like a leaf." Harwood added: "I'll never forget that because the idea that a man like Bywater could go into a flat spin [lose control] was unbelievable. After standing there for a minute like that, he just walked out without saying a word and never came back to the office. I saw him after that, but he never explained what happened."

It had been evident for some time that Bywater's relations with the *Telegraph* had become strained. In February 1939, one of his articles scoring the British government for failing to strengthen the Royal Navy at a time of deepening international crisis had been preceded by an unusual, seemingly apologetic "Editor's Note." Bywater persisted in criticizing the government of Neville Chamberlain for its blindness to the aggressive intentions of Nazi Germany, adopting an editorial tone in one article in which he declared that Britain "would seem to have the right to denounce" the Anglo-German Naval Agreement of 1935 because Hitler had violated it. Over the succeeding months, his warnings about the threat posed by Nazi Germany grew increasingly vehement, and consequently embarrassing to the management of the *Telegraph*, which supported Chamberlain and his policy of appeasement. In February 1939, Watson had fired his veteran Central European correspondent, George Gedye, for having ridiculed Chamberlain as "*Monsieur J'aime*

Berlin." Bywater continued to write for the newspaper until a few days before war broke out, but managed to remain on the company payroll until the year's end. At that time, the clerk in the company secretary's office entered the date of Bywater's last paycheck in red ink—the office code for a dismissal or resignation under fire.

The *Telegraph* issued the story that Bywater had resigned because of "failing health," but many in the Fleet Street Press Gang refused to believe it. George Bryant, the naval and shipping correspondent for *Lloyd's List and Shipping Gazette*, recalled having been told that Bywater was either fired by Watson or resigned because "The Old Bottle of Ink" had refused to publish one of his articles. "I heard he got a bowler hat," recalled David Woodward, a colleague on the *News-Chronicle*. Woodward's jargon derives from the story about a reporter who once saved up his money and bought a bowler only to be fired the next day.

"The statement in Bywater's obituaries that he left the *Telegraph* because of poor health was euphemistic—in the tradition of 'never speak ill of the dead,' " said Harwood. "The fact is he left because of a dispute with Watson, although I never learned exactly what it was."

Bywater was out of work for about two months, and started drinking heavily at this time, according to his son. He had done so during other periods of stress. In fact, alcohol consumption was a subject that frequently crept into Bywater's writing, suggestive of personal involvement. At one time or another, he went out of his way to write about drinking practices in the German, British, and American navies, and once, in an unusual and personally revealing essay about Prohibition for the Baltimore *Sun*, he wrote: "I think it will be conceded by many that, outside the ranks of incorrigible topers, drink is taken more often than not either to relieve the nervous strain incidental to modern life under our hyper-civilized conditions or to introduce a note of color into the drab background of everyday existence." One suspects he was not so much analyzing a social condition as rationalizing a personal habit.

In March 1940, he was hired by a former employer, the London *Daily News*, which had become the *News-Chronicle* following a merger. His first column for the *News-Chronicle* appeared on March 8, accompanied by a photograph that showed him to be increasingly bald and perhaps a bit heavy, yet still possessed of his characteristic look of firmness and determination. Over the next five months, he covered or commented on the Dunkirk evacuation; the fall of Paris; Hitler's "anti-

Jewish frenzy," which, Bywater declared, "robbed Germany of one of her most formidable assets"; the Royal Navy's capture of the French fleet; and the sinking of the British aircraft carrier *Glorious* by the German battle cruisers *Scharnhorst* and *Gneisenau*—which confirmed his faith in the superiority of the big gun. But the frequency of his articles declined markedly. Between March and August 1940, Bywater wrote fewer than thirty articles for the *News-Chronicle*, averaging about an article and a half per week when other service correspondents were writing at double or triple that rate.

On July 2, 1940, Bywater wrote his last essay about Japan. It was a brief article in the *News-Chronicle* that was as clear-sighted and clairvoyant as anything he had ever written. "Japan, for all her pledges of non-involvement in the European war, intends to take advantage of Allied preoccupations to spread war to parts of Asia other than her immediate field of operations in China," Bywater wrote.

He continued:

> The war in China is only a cover for her claims on French Indochina and now for her claims on the British Empire. What remains to be seen is whether concerted [Allied] action can be taken against the Japanese claims or whether once more "appeasement" will be tried to stave off the final clash. The situation is reminiscent of Europe from 1936 to 1938—but with this difference. Japan has laid all her cards on the table. She has stated her ambitions *en bloc* and at one time—not piecemeal, with false promises of "no more territorial ambitions" in Asia.

After this, Bywater wrote only half-a-dozen more articles for the *News-Chronicle*. One of the last was a spirited, firsthand account of the sinking of a German U-boat as observed from the spray-showered bridge of a British destroyer. He described the detection of the German submarine by means of an early type of sonar, and then reported the tremendous explosion of a depth charge, which caused the bow of the unfortunate U-boat to shoot out of the water at a steep angle "like a harpooned whale." It was "a good morning's work," he wrote.

The day after the great German air raid of August 16, 1940, Goering's planes did not return to England. Mrs. Margaret Perrin, who had become Bywater's housekeeper after the breakup of his second marriage two years before, rose early to start her chores. At 10 A.M., as was her custom, Mrs. Perrin knocked on her employer's bedroom door. Hearing no response, she entered the room and found Bywater "still sleeping but perspiring freely," as she later told the coroner. Mrs. Perrin opened the bedroom windows, positioned just a few feet above a pleasant grass and flagstone courtyard, and then departed, returning several times to see whether or not Bywater had awakened.

For the past two years, Bywater had been living in this comfortable ground-floor flat in Selwyn Court, a modern, five-story brick apartment building in suburban Richmond. Just a minute's walk from spacious Richmond Park and a graceful arc of the grass-banked Thames River, the apartment was ideally situated for a man like Bywater whose chief recreation was taking long walks. It was conveniently near London; the commuter train could put him on Fleet Street in twenty minutes. Also, his apartment was close to a congenial watering hole, The Park Road Arms (known affectionately as "The Hole in the Wall"), which was precisely 200 paces from 2 Selwyn Court. Bywater was drinking heavily, according to his personal physician, and was well known at The Hole in the Wall as "a commanding presence and a great talker," according to several old-timers who remembered him.

By 1:40 P.M., Mrs. Perrin became concerned that Bywater was not yet up, and again she entered his room. She caught her breath as she saw that he had "gone pale." Mrs. Perrin felt for his pulse. She could find none. She rushed to the telephone and called Bywater's personal physician, a certain Dr. Brunton. Then she called Bywater's brother Ulysses at his home in suburban Esher some five miles away and told him to come at once. In less than ten minutes, Bywater's physician was ringing the doorbell. After a brief examination, he drew the sheet over his distinguished patient's head. The Royal Navy, and indeed navies throughout the world, had lost one of their most eloquent champions. Hector Bywater was dead at the age of fifty-five.

As the next of kin were being told the news, Dr. Brunton pondered the cause of death. He had seen his patient only the day before in connection with his phlebitis—a painful but not life-threatening inflammation of the veins. But what could explain this sudden passing? Based on what he learned from Mrs. Perrin—that Bywater had fallen into a deep sleep—and from his own observation and knowledge of his patient, Dr. Brunton stated on the medical report he was required to fill out: "Consider death due to Alcoholic Poisoning."

The next morning, the London *News-Chronicle* declared Bywater to have been "one of the greatest living authorities on naval affairs." Other British newspapers and periodicals echoed this assessment. Both *The New York Times* and the *New York Herald Tribune* published a United Press obituary that called Bywater "the successor of the late Admiral Mahan, U.S.N., as the greatest authority on naval theory and practice during his lifetime." Bywater's lifelong friend and one-time coauthor, H. C. Ferraby, wrote an obituary for the Manchester *Guardian* ending with the statement: "Few men have ever given such single-minded devotion to a calling as Hector Bywater gave to the Navy." The *Daily Telegraph*, which Bywater had served so brilliantly for twelve years, published only a sixteen-word notice of his death.

Since Bywater's passing had been sudden and unexpected, the Surrey County Coroner ordered an inquest. Dr. R. Donald Geare, a Harley Street physician, was asked to conduct the autopsy, and he commenced it at the public mortuary at Richmond at 5:40 P.M. on August 18. The exact time, place, and date are significant because they happen to coincide with the climax of the single most violent day of the air battle in the skies over Great Britain. Early in the afternoon, the Luftwaffe resumed its attacks on the RAF airfields at Croydon and Kenley, and a tremendous air battle developed directly over Richmond. At 5:30 P.M., just as Dr. Geare was starting his work, a fresh force of some 250 German planes converged on the RAF bases at Hornchurch and North Weald fifteen miles east and southeast of where the autopsy was being performed. One hundred and forty British aircraft screamed aloft to challenge the invaders, and a furious air battle ensued, with dogfights and the pursuit of crippled and stray planes spreading the action over much of southeastern England. All told, sixty-nine German aircraft and sixty-eight British fighters plunged to the earth that day.

Those on the ground were expecting the worst. For weeks, British newspapers had been filled with warnings that a German invasion was imminent. Signposts had been removed from highways throughout the country so that invaders would have no help in finding their way, and motor-vehicle owners had been urged to remove the rotor arms from the distributors mounted on their engines to render them useless to German paratroops. Bywater himself had sought to calm his fellow countrymen, writing the previous May: "We cannot be 'invaded' as long as we retain command of the sea. The parachutists . . . may create local havoc and confusion, but such sporadic operations cannot, according to all the teachings of history, be decisive." By the middle of August, however, the prevailing voices were less reasoned.

Conducting the autopsy under these circumstances was hardly conducive to painstaking inquiry, and it would be understandable if Dr. Geare simply decided not to challenge the findings of the dead man's personal physician. Dr. Geare noted in his postmortem report several conditions consistent with alcoholism. He observed "chronic gastritis" in the stomach and found that the liver was "slightly enlarged," but he made no mention of cirrhosis—the orange-yellow appearance of a typical alcoholic's liver. His conclusion was that Bywater had died of "Myocardial Degeneration [heart attack] consistent with chronic Alcoholism," but Dr. Geare's report was far from complete in terms of the then-prevailing practice of postmortem examinations. Apart from the fact that he made no mention of cirrhosis, he ordered no toxicology studies, no laboratory tissue studies, and no detailed anatomical studies.

At the inquest the following day at the Richmond Police Court, the coroner accepted Dr. Geare's opinion and jotted down: "Sudden death. No suspicion of foul play." Then, in accordance with the wishes of the deceased, as made known by Ulysses Bywater, the remains were cremated at the Mortlake Crematorium, thus foreclosing the possibility of further scientific inquiry.

It may be that Dr. Geare would not have reached a different conclusion if working in perfect tranquility, and that the cause of Bywater's death was no more than it appeared to be. There is, however, another possibility that cannot be lightly dismissed; namely, that in his haste, Dr. Geare overlooked evidence that Bywater had been murdered. The late E. A. Harwood of the *Telegraph*, a friend and admirer of Bywater, said in an interview at his home prior to his death in September 1987 that he believed Bywater was killed by a Japanese agent possibly acting on instructions from Isoroku Yamamoto. Harwood, who became a student of naval history after his retirement, acknowledged that he had only circumstantial evidence to support his theory.

What chiefly aroused his suspicion, Harwood said, is that nineteen days before Bywater's death, his principal informant in Japan, Melville Cox, was either pushed or driven to leap from the third-floor window of police headquarters in Tokyo. Harwood believed the two deaths were related.

The Japanese claimed Cox jumped while being interrogated on suspicion of espionage, but most Britons and Americans at the time refused to accept the story that Cox had committed suicide. The presumption was that he had been beaten in an effort to force a confession of espionage, and then, after the beating had gone too far, was thrown out a window so that his injuries might appear to have been caused by the fall. Shortly after Cox's death, Lord Halifax, the British foreign secretary, drew cheers in the House of Lords when he declared that his government was "entirely unable to accept" the Japanese explanation about Cox. Over the years since, numerous theories have been put forward in an attempt to explain Cox's death and none has yet satisfied Reuters, according to Shahe Guebenlian, a spokesman for the news agency.

A big, hearty Englishman in his early forties, Cox had spent most of his adult life as a correspondent for Reuters in China. When Malcolm Kennedy vacated the Reuters post in Tokyo in 1934, Cox was assigned to replace him. In that capacity, it was natural for Cox to inherit Kennedy's free-lance or special-assignment work, such as answering requests for information from writers like Bywater. Thus, over a period of six years, Cox and Bywater developed a working relationship.

Cox was arrested on July 27, 1940, by two Japanese officers wearing red arm bands and a holstered revolver on each hip—the uniform of the special political arm of the police, the *Kempei-tai*. They said they had orders to take him "for questioning" to their headquarters. No specific charge was mentioned. A newspaper colleague chanced to see Cox as he was being led away. He was "pale and worried-looking," buttoning up his coat as he went, but managed to make a strained jest about going off to see "the Lord High Executioner." Later, his home was searched and Cox was charged with having violated the Military Secrets Law for possessing, among other things, "a record of Japan's naval building plan and its progress."

Three days after his arrest, Cox's wife was summoned to police headquarters. When she arrived, she was taken to a dying man. Cox, suffering from numerous injuries, was unconscious. In a few minutes, he was dead. A Western doctor who later examined his body counted some thirty-five injection marks. The Japanese contended the injections had been administered in an effort to revive him after his fall. Others suspected the injections had been made during his interrogation.

Harwood theorized that Yamamoto ordered the deaths of Bywater and Cox shortly after he committed himself to the Pearl Harbor attack and feared that these two Englishmen might discover his plans. After all, said Harwood, Bywater had conceived a similar attack fifteen years earlier and would be particularly alert to any indication that such an operation was actually being rehearsed. Furthermore, if the team of Bywater and Cox could bring to light the top-secret *Yamato*s, they might well be able to unmask the even-harder-to-conceal preparations for a large-scale surprise attack involving six aircraft carriers, two battleships, two heavy cruisers, numerous support ships, and thousands of men.

There was, in fact, sufficient time for events to have proceeded in the way Harwood imagined. Yamamoto had been named commander-in-chief of the Combined Fleet (the battle fleet) in the fall of 1939 and was charged with responsibility for preparing it for war. Quite naturally, he gravitated to the ideas outlined in his torpedo school speech in 1928, formulated after having read, and become immersed in, the controversy surrounding *The Great Pacific War*. In April or May 1940, he confided his thinking about a surprise attack on the American fleet to Shigeru Fukudome, his chief of staff. A few weeks later, the United States Pacific Fleet, which had been on maneuvers in Hawaiian waters, shifted its base from the San Pedro–Long Beach roadstead near Los Angeles to Hawaii. It then became clear to Yamamoto that the attack he was contemplating would be aimed at Pearl Harbor—a target that would require special equipment (shallow-running aerial torpedoes, for instance) and special pilot training. He immediately assigned studies and initiated preparations for what came to be called the Hawaii Operation, and, according to Fukudome, soon became intensely security conscious. He remarked repeatedly that secrecy and surprise were the vital elements of his plan and that everything possible must be done to maintain absolute confidentiality. It was then, according to Harwood, that Yamamoto decided Bywater and Cox endangered the whole operation and would have to be eliminated. At least two months would pass before their deaths.

Harwood also pointed out that after war broke out in Europe, Bywater came to believe that his life was in danger. He took the precaution of carrying a revolver for the first time since his days in Naval Intelligence. He showed the weapon to Harwood, and once exhibited to his prospective son-in-law, John Newland, the leather webbing he had paid a tailor to sew into his jackets to support the weight of the revolver without distorting the appearance of his clothes. Bywater joked to Newland about "fools who carry their guns in holsters," explaining: "If you ever really need a gun, you'd never have time to draw it. The skill you must master is to fire accurately from inside your jacket pocket since it's far better to have a hole in your jacket than in you."

It would have been a simple matter, Harwood observed, for an assassin to steal into Bywater's bedroom at night by stepping from the courtyard through the ground-floor window left open on a hot August night to administer an injection while his victim slept. The findings of Drs. Brunton and Geare in connection with Bywater's death are consistent not only with alcoholic poisoning but with a lethal injection of insulin (a relatively new murder weapon in 1940) or strychnine (a favorite of Japanese agents).

But, tantalizing as is such speculation, it remains only guesswork and seems more the stuff of thrillers than history. Hard evidence of foul play, as Harwood was the first to admit, is simply lacking. Bywater's sense of personal jeopardy toward the end of his life may well have been a case of alcohol-induced paranoia. Furthermore, not only Bywater's physician but also his brother and son were of the opinion that he had become alcoholic by the end of his life.

Finally, apart from the medical reports, there is the fact that while the outbreak of war afforded Bywater a greater opportunity than ever before to write and publish on his specialty, his output in 1940 was surprisingly meager. That may best be explained by mental and physical decline.

As for Yamamoto, he may well have had good reason to wish Bywater and Cox dead, but there is no evidence that he was ever in contact with the ultranationalist *Kempei-tai*. Indeed, considering how Yamamoto had antagonized the far right in his country by opposing the proposed alliance with Hitler and Mussolini, he seems a more likely *target* of the *Kempei-tai* than the mastermind of one of its schemes.

Still, Bywater's death—like so much of his life as an undercover agent and investigative reporter—raises questions that cannot be answered. Whether or not his death had any connection with that of Melville Cox must remain a matter of conjecture. About all that can be said with assurance is that the sudden deaths of these two Englishmen within the space of about a fortnight in the summer of 1940 came as a gift from heaven for Isoroku Yamamoto—considering the course he was now embarked upon.

CHAPTER

22

"I CAN GIVE THEM HELL"

I N SEPTEMBER 1940, well after Yamamoto had begun preparations for his opening gambit in the coming conflict, Prime Minister
Fumimaro Konoye asked him what the Imperial Navy's prospects would
be if it came to war with the United States. Yamamoto had no illusions
about the endurance of Japan in such a conflict—in marked contrast to
the other leaders of the navy who had just assured the high-ranking
privy council of the navy's ability to fight and win a protracted war
against the United States. According to Konoye's diary, Yamamoto replied: "If you insist on my going ahead, I can promise to give them hell
for a year or a year and a half, but can guarantee nothing as to what
will happen after that." It was as if he had cribbed his answer from *The
Great Pacific War* in which Bywater wrote: "The war had been in
progress a year and a half. How much longer could Japan afford to
continue a struggle which had already taxed her strength to the utmost?
She might, at a liberal estimate, carry on for a further six months."

This is but one of many indications that Yamamoto relied on the teachings of Hector Bywater in the Pacific war; however, the case that he did so rests on more than a miscellany of such similarities. After all, the strategic options in the Pacific were not unlimited, and at least some of the correspondence between Bywater's imaginings and Yamamoto's words and deeds could have been purely coincidental. If Newton and Leibnitz invented calculus independently ("polygenesis," scholars call it), Yamamoto could have hit upon at least some aspects of a war plan similar to Bywater's without reference to his writing.

What makes Yamamoto's dependence on Bywater's blueprint unmistakable is a body of evidence. It begins with the fact that virtually all Imperial Navy officers had the deepest regard for British naval expertise—which Bywater certainly represented. It goes on to include Yamamoto's thorough and repeated exposure to *The Great Pacific War* when stationed in Washington in 1926; his reaction to this exposure in a lecture he delivered soon after his return to Japan; his repeated contacts with Bywater over a number of years (including a personal meeting in 1934), which reinforced his exposure to Bywater's ideas; and finally— most important—the fact that Yamamoto's strategy and tactics in launching war in the Pacific were strikingly similar to the plans formulated by Bywater. Yamamoto's actions mirror Bywater's writing in matters ranging from overall objectives and strategy down to such small but critical details as the exact beaches on which invading forces were to land.

The matchup is not always precise. Yamamoto was no craven copyist but a skilled practitioner of that quintessentially Japanese form of cultural jujitsu whereby the Japanese absorb from others only that which suits their particular needs. In addition, Yamamoto drew upon the rich military culture and inventiveness of his own people. For instance, in planning the Pearl Harbor attack, he adopted Bywater's overall strategy but carried it out with the daring tactical innovation of his air chief Minoru Genda, employing massed aircraft carriers as an offensive force. Indeed, Yamamoto's sophisticated process of adaptation is reminiscent of Togo at Tsushima, where the latter artfully melded the Western naval concept of "crossing the T" with an ancient Japanese practice known as *Otsuji sempo*, meaning to embrace the enemy in an enveloping curve.

Yet we should not be surprised to learn that much of Yamamoto's strategic thinking was derivative. Necessity is only rarely the mother of invention; more often the nurturing force is leisure. And the commander of a great navy, whether engaged in actual war or preparation for war as was Yamamoto in 1940 and 1941, has precious little of that. Given his lack of leisure at the time he conceived of the Japanese offensive, it was only natural for Yamamoto to have fallen back on ideas that entered his mind when he was a young officer stationed in the United States.

Yamamoto's grand strategy for the commencement of the Pacific war was essentially twofold. First, he believed, Japanese forces must destroy the American Pacific Fleet outright. Second, Japanese forces must quickly move into the resulting power vacuum and seize those territories that would expand the Japanese Empire so as to render it nearly invulnerable to outside attack. These objectives are spelled out in two documents—a collection of notes about his plans, which Yamamoto gave for safekeeping to his friend and naval academy classmate Teikichi Hori in January 1941, and "Combined Fleet Top Secret Operation Order Number 1," the 118-page document that Yamamoto and his staff prepared aboard the flagship *Nagato* and issued to the fleet on November 5, 1941. The notes deal with strategy while Order Number 1 concerns tactics ranging from such minutiae as reinforcing the mooring cables of mines laid in the San Bernardino Straits of the Philippine Islands "to withstand strong tidal current," to detailing a sweeping series of attacks against American, British, and Dutch forces and possessions throughout the Central and Western Pacific.

In deciding on the Pearl Harbor attack, Yamamoto was obviously influenced by the Port Arthur raid of 1904 as well as the undeclared fighting that started the Sino-Japanese War in 1894. Nevertheless, he was not simply following historical precedent, as has been frequently suggested. On the contrary, in his notes, Yamamoto was highly critical of the Port Arthur attack. He stated that "lessons must be learned" from Togo's failures in that action, and "utmost efforts should be made" in planning and executing the Pearl Harbor assault so as "to decide the issue of the war" in that single action.

The Port Arthur raid put at risk no major Japanese warship and was intended only to throw the enemy off balance at the outset of hostilities. In fact, only three of the fourteen Russian vessels present at Port Arthur were damaged, and two of those were quickly returned to service. In contrast, Yamamoto's Pearl Harbor attack would employ six of Japan's ten heavy aircraft carriers, two battleships, and two heavy cruisers plus numerous auxiliaries. This huge force was to *"thoroughly destroy* the main body of the enemy fleet in the first moments of the war" (italics added), according to Yamamoto's notes. He did not seek to destroy the naval base at Pearl Harbor, burn up the tank farm, wipe out the garrison, or, certainly, land troops and attempt the conquest of Hawaii, as several of his more zealous aides had urged. Order Number 1 specifies the target solely as "the American fleet," which was "supposed to be in Hawaiian waters." He left no doubt that he intended to attack that fleet no matter whether it should be found at Pearl Harbor, the Philippines, or cruising in the open ocean on the predetermined day of the attack.

Japan had to eradicate the American naval presence, he explained, because as long as it existed, any large-scale movement of Japanese troops across water would invite disaster. Accordingly, he wrote, once the American fleet had been disposed of, Japan could pursue her second objective, namely, "to occupy strategic places in East Asia [Guam, the Philippines, British Malaya, and the Dutch East Indies] to secure an invincible position." With these territories under her control, Japan could develop "a defensive posture" behind which she "might be able to obtain her goals and secure the peace in the Greater East Asia Co-Prosperity Sphere."

And that was precisely Bywater's trademark conception. The Japanese surprise attack, he declared in *The Great Pacific War*, was not to be a harrying, Port Arthur–style venture; on the contrary, an "overwhelming" force was dispatched with the aim of completely "wiping out" the American fleet. The total destruction of that force, Bywater explained, "left the way open for the invasion of the Philippines." And that conquest, plus the taking of Guam, would allow Japan to surround herself with a virtually impregnable ring of island bastions.

As indicated earlier, Yamamoto fully accepted Bywater's conclusion that even such an island empire could eventually be crushed by a determined United States. But once war had seemed inevitable, Yamamoto believed that his carrying out of Bywater's strategy would place Japan in a formidable stronghold. From that position, she might be able to insist on favorable terms in a negotiated settlement of the war.

Obvious as was the need to eliminate American naval power in the Pacific, given Japan's other objectives, it did not seem compelling to the Navy General Staff, the final authority on naval strategy, when one of

Yamamoto's aides formally presented his plan in April 1941. Hostile questions flew thick and fast. "How can Japan afford to divide her strength over such wide areas?" asked Nobutake Kondo, a true Mahanist. Yamamoto's former chief of staff, Fukudome, argued that the plan to attack the American fleet was an extremely risky sideshow that, if it failed, would jeopardize the conquest of the vital oil-producing Dutch East Indies. Others raised practical problems, such as that midocean refueling techniques on which the strike would depend were not yet perfected, that there was no guarantee the U.S. fleet would be present at Pearl Harbor when the Japanese surprise-attack fleet arrived, and that the surprise-attack fleet itself might be surprised, in which case Japan, with six of her ten precious aircraft carriers exposed, might "lose the war in an afternoon," as Churchill would say. Most perceptively of all, Takijiro Onishi argued that since Japan could never defeat a colossus like the United States, her only hope would be for a negotiated settlement on favorable terms, and that a surprise attack on the fleet at Pearl Harbor would drive America "so insanely mad" that a negotiated settlement would be out of the question. It is remarkable that although having studied the fundamentals of what Yamamoto was proposing through their reading of Bywater's books at the Naval War College, every officer of flag rank who learned of Yamamoto's plan, including all those who would be obliged to carry it out, were resolutely opposed to it.

While the Japanese were not about to ask the Americans what they thought of Yamamoto's plan, anyone who troubled to consult the public record would have found no more comfort there for Yamamoto than among his fellow naval officers in Japan. To be sure, many in Washington considered the Philippines indefensible, but prominent leaders with personal knowledge of the islands, such as MacArthur and Eisenhower, had long been saying that an invasion of the Philippines was next to impossible. Moreover, William D. Puleston, one of the leading American experts on Pacific strategy before the war, had written in 1941: "If the Japanese High Command decide to invade Luzon and Guam . . . [and] obligingly scatter her light [naval] forces, submarine and aircraft across the middle Pacific, the American Commander-in-Chief should be grateful to his opponent. The quickest way to win the war would be to destroy the Japanese Fleet, and if it were sent into action piecemeal it could be destroyed more easily."

In sum, Yamamoto was not docilely following the Port Arthur precedent, and he was not pursuing an obvious course that any seasoned commander might have taken. He was planning something wholly new, something that conventional wisdom on both sides of the Pacific considered foolhardy, and something—not incidentally—that Hector Bywater had spelled out sixteen years before.

In mid-September 1941, Yamamoto attempted to demonstrate the feasibility of his plan at the annual Table Top Maneuvers at the Imperial Naval War College—the institution at which Bywater's *Sea Power in the Pacific* and *The Great Pacific War* were still being read. Presided over and dominated by Yamamoto, this dress rehearsal in miniature showed that the simultaneous conduct of many far-flung operations throughout the Pacific was theoretically possible. Nevertheless, six weeks before the Table Top Maneuvers were held, a new and even stronger reason for their opposition to Yamamoto's plan was given to conservatives like Kondo, Fukudome, and Osami Nagano, chief of the Navy General Staff. The United States, angered by Japan's advance into French Indochina and a subsequent attack on the American gunboat *Tutuila*, placed an embargo on the sale of oil and high-octane aviation fuel to Japan. The Imperial Navy had recoiled in horror, calculating that it had only enough liquid-fuel reserves to last for two years at the most, and only a year to eighteen months in time of war. Consequently, the leaders of the navy were now looking at the Dutch East Indies—Japan's most likely, nearby source of oil—the way a man sprawled on the desert contemplates an oasis. Furthermore, if still greater temptation were needed, the Netherlands had surrendered to Japan's new ally Nazi Germany the year before, and the Dutch East Indies seemed ripe for plucking. Thus preoccupied, the upper echelon of the navy had little interest in far-off Pearl Harbor.

Yamamoto, however, was determined. So passionate was he about his plan that when the Navy General Staff finally balked at accepting it, he sent an emissary to Tokyo to declare that he and his entire staff would resign if not permitted to carry it out. Nagano and his staff shook their heads in dismay. Yamamoto's plan called for approximately simultaneous attacks against Pearl Harbor, Guam, Wake Island, the Philippines, British Malaya, the Dutch East Indies, and other islands of the South Pacific—enough frittering dispersal of forces to make Mahan cry out from his grave in protest. But Nagano said that the navy simply had to put its trust in the commander-in-chief of the Combined Fleet who, after all, had been living with the problem longer than anyone else—a truer statement than he was aware. Authorization from the highest councils of the government and the emperor followed quickly. Thereupon Yamamoto and his staff commenced final preparations and began spelling out the grand design in what was to become Top Secret Operation Order Number 1.

Although specific contingency plans to invade Guam and the Philippines had been drawn up at least as early as 1926 and either approved or modified by the Navy General Staff every year thereafter, the final plan was not determined until the Table Top Maneuvers in September. Back in the 1920s, very likely bowing to Bywater, Japanese strategists had plotted simultaneous main landings on the west and east coasts of Luzon, coming ashore at Lingayen Gulf and Lamon Bay and converging on Manila. Over the years, the landing sites were frequently changed, and by 1941, Lamon Bay had been stricken because of the difficult inland terrain and the likelihood of encountering poor weather conditions. According to Nagano's forty-seven-page "Imperial Navy Operation Plan," which he drafted in 1940 and updated in 1941, if war should break out with the United States and it became necessary for Japan to capture the Philippines, "the landing site of the main force will be the coast of Lingayen Gulf." No other landing site for the main force was specified; almost the entire army of invaders would find its way ashore along this immense, unobstructed coastline. But by September 1941, after having gained control of naval planning by means of his threat to resign, Yamamoto called the tune. It was unusual for a fleet admiral to become deeply involved in tactical planning, but Yamamoto had virtually usurped Nagano's position and could do as he pleased. At the Table Top Maneuvers in September, he had Nagano's plan for the invasion of the Philippines revised so as to conform in astonishing detail to the tactics Bywater spelled out in *The Great Pacific War*.

The plan approved by Yamamoto called for three simultaneous main landings—at Lingayen Gulf, at Lamon Bay between Cabalete and Alabat islands, and at either Davao or Dumanquilas on Mindanao, the second largest and southernmost of the major Philippine islands. (Because of one delay or another, the main landings were only approximately simultaneous, taking place between December 20 and 24.) Bywater, too, had prescribed three simultaneous main landings—at Lingayen Gulf, at Lamon Bay between Cabalete and Alabat islands, and at Sindangan Bay

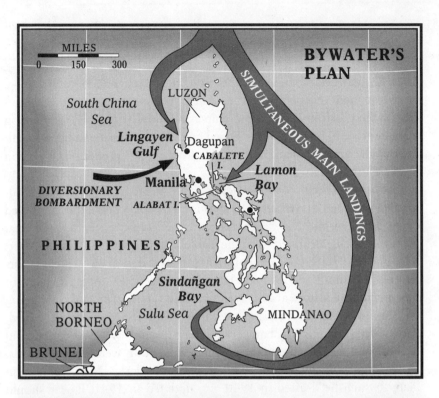

BYWATER'S PLAN

MILES
0   150   300

South China Sea

LUZON

SIMULTANEOUS MAIN LANDINGS

Lingayen Gulf

Dagupan
CABALETE I.

Manila

Lamon Bay

DIVERSIONARY BOMBARDMENT

ALABAT I.

PHILIPPINES

Sindañgan Bay
Sulu Sea

NORTH BORNEO

MINDANAO

BRUNEI

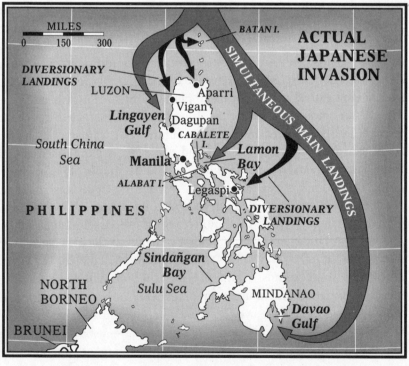

ACTUAL JAPANESE INVASION

MILES
0   150   300

BATAN I.

DIVERSIONARY LANDINGS

LUZON

SIMULTANEOUS MAIN LANDINGS

Aparri

Vigan

Lingayen Gulf

Dagupan
CABALETE I.

South China Sea

Manila

Lamon Bay

ALABAT I.

Legaspi

DIVERSIONARY LANDINGS

PHILIPPINES

Sindañgan Bay
Sulu Sea

NORTH BORNEO

MINDANAO

Davao Gulf

BRUNEI

on Mindanao (not far from Dumanquilas, where an airstrip had been built since the time of his writing).

Yamamoto prepared for the invasion with several preliminary diversionary raids on Luzon and Mindanao, thinking that the small parties thrown ashore might not only distract the island's defenders but could "prepare air bases quickly." Bywater, also, had specified a diversionary bombardment of Luzon aimed at Santa Cruz in the north plus air strikes against the airport at Dagupan (later replaced by Clark Field).

Could it be that the topography of the Philippines dictated these same landing sites to any experienced commander planning an invasion? If what MacArthur told his official biographer, Frazier Hunt, is to be believed, Bywater's prediction of the exact Japanese landing sites was not remarkable. MacArthur, according to Hunt, regarded Lingayen Gulf and Lamon Bay as the logical places for the Japanese to aim their large-scale amphibious assaults, and he fully expected the Japanese to land there.

But MacArthur's boast has long since been exploded. According to both the official United States Army history *The Fall of the Philippines* by Louis Morton and the more recent biography of MacArthur by William Manchester, the general was taken by surprise by the landings at Lamon Bay. The area was not defended by a single heavy artillery piece on Christmas Eve 1941 when the twenty-four transports bearing the Japanese 16th Division steamed between Cabalete and Alabat islands and sent troops ashore virtually unopposed. Despite repeated requests from the local commander in the area, MacArthur had refused to send to Lamon Bay a single one of the six 155-mm or sixteen 75-mm guns at his disposal. He had concentrated them at Batangas, Balayan, and Nasugbu bays on the west coast of Luzon where, evidently, he expected to meet the invaders.

Furthermore, far from being inevitable, the choice of Lamon Bay flew in the face of sound professional judgment. Spacious Lingayen Gulf, offering any number of superb landing beaches leading directly to the lowlands of the Pampanga Plain, which extended all the way to Manila, was certainly an ideal invasion route; however, a landing at Lamon Bay would face serious hazards. In the monsoon season during the winter months, the weather conditions are foul at Lamon Bay. Just before the war, Albert M. Jones, the American officer who commanded the South Luzon Force, made a survey of potential landing sites on Luzon and excluded Lamon as a possibility because of the "monsoon factor." Furthermore, although it may have looked like an easy trek from Lamon Bay to Manila on the railway map of Luzon that Ferris Greenslet had sent Bywater, the better-informed Americans and Japanese knew that this route lay across the rugged Tayabas Mountains and several marshy areas.

Puleston also considered the Bywater-Yamamoto plan the least likely of all possibilities. "Wind and weather conditions are rarely suitable for simultaneous landings on the east and west coasts," Puleston wrote, "and along the roads to Manila from the beaches there are several difficult passes and marshy areas that would enable a small force to delay the advance of the Japanese on Manila." Furthermore, the Japanese Navy General Staff, which was probably as well informed on the matter as the Americans, rejected Lamon Bay in 1941 for similar reasons.

There were many favorable spots for an invading army to come ashore. Jones reported that Luzon "included 250 miles of possible landing beaches." Puleston listed Lingayen Gulf, Subic Bay, and Batangas Bay as the most likely points of attack. And, as far back as 1923, Franklin Roosevelt had stated that when serving as assistant secretary of the navy he had been told authoritatively that there were "innumerable" practical landing sites on the coast of Luzon.

Thus, both Bywater and Yamamoto selected one of the landing sites most authorities accepted as likely (Lingayen) and one that they regarded as least likely (Lamon). Given the many alternatives, the mathematical odds are heavily weighted against any such accidental occurrence, and the negative odds become greater still when one considers that both men added a third simultaneous main landing on southern Mindanao.

Furthermore, Yamamoto's plan for the occupation of Guam also bears a close resemblance to the tactics Bywater laid out in *The Great Pacific War*. In the operation approved by Yamamoto, the island was first bombed by warplanes from Saipan with the special objective of destroying the radio tower at Mt. Machanao in the north. Next, several warships were brought in to shell the defenses of Guam, and finally the island was seized by a force of 5,000 men that divided and landed simultaneously on the west and east coasts. Bywater, too, envisioned commencing the assault with an air strike by planes from Saipan with the principal aim of knocking down the radio tower at Machanao, then a naval bombardment, and finally the seizure of Guam by a force of "several thousand" men that divided and landed simultaneously on the west and east coasts.

Impressed as Yamamoto was by Bywater's tactics, he cannot have been pleased, as he read the account of the battle of Guam in *The Great Pacific War*, to find Bywater describing an action in which the armored cruiser *Nisshin*—the venerable ship on which Yamamoto served at the Battle of Tsushima—strays too close to shore, gets hit by an American shell, and is ignominiously blown to bits.

There are, of course, significant differences between the war plans devised by Bywater and Yamamoto. In the first place, by the time Yamamoto had folded into his master plan all the agreed-upon objectives of the Imperial Army together with those of the Navy General Staff, he had immensely expanded upon Bywater's original conception. As Yamamoto's final strategy had it, Japan, already at war with China, was to attack the territories and forces of the United States, Great Britain, and the Netherlands. She would continue her progressive occupation of French Indochina and soon subject Thailand and Burma to her rule. All this was an enormous undertaking, even if two of the countries on the list of enemies had already been brought to their knees by Germany, and Britain was near exhaustion. One marvels at Japan's daring in seeking to remake the map of Asia as profoundly as Hitler had altered Europe the year before. Nevertheless, the far-flung attacks on Pearl Harbor, British Malaya, and the Dutch East Indies—the seaward side of Japanese expansion—were essentially an extrapolation of one guiding idea: namely, that of pushing Japan's defensive perimeter deep into the South Seas by means of a preemptive attack on U.S. forces in the Pacific, coupled with a series of unorthodox amphibious assaults and occupation of territories throughout the Western Pacific so as to create a nearly impregnable empire. That, one might say, was vintage Bywater.

The other important difference between the two plans, of course, is that Yamamoto prescribed the daring and unprecedented use of massed aircraft carriers to surprise the U.S. Navy, whereas Bywater had written that the attack would be conducted by a conventional surface force accompanied by only a single carrier. By the mid-1930s, Bywater was no longer blind to the coming importance of naval air power. In his mature view, if the battleship remained mistress of the seas, the aircraft carrier was superior for projecting a long-range offensive thrust. But Yamamoto needed no prompting to put the aircraft carrier to effective use at Pearl Harbor; that was his (and Minoru Genda's) contribution to naval science. Yet even Yamamoto, the man who was about to become famous—or infamous—for demonstrating the awesome power of the collective use of aircraft carriers, would, at a critical moment in the war, forsake his belief in the primacy of aeronaval power. In this, he may have been inspired, once again, by Hector Bywater.

Throughout the early months of 1942, Yamamoto was haunted by the belief that the only way for Japan to "win" the war was by means of a negotiated settlement. Successful as had been his bold initiatives at the outset—Yamamoto destroyed more ships at Pearl Harbor than had been lost by all sides in the world war up to that time—he realized he had not been able to "decide the issue of the war" in his opening stroke as he had hoped. The United States was not remotely interested in sitting down at the conference table. To bring that about, Yamamoto believed, he needed one more spectacular triumph that would convince the United States of the futility of continuing the war. With this aim in mind, he conceived the Battle of Midway, an all-out clash of forces in which he hoped to decisively destroy American naval power in the Pacific.

"The Midway venture," wrote Mitsuo Fuchida and Masatake Oku-miya in their authoritative study of the battle from the Japanese side, "was inspired by his [Yamamoto's] conviction that the balance of military strength between Japan and the United States would shift in the latter's favor within two years at the most from the start of hostilities. Because of this pressing time factor, he felt that Japan's only hope lay in seeking a quick decision which might induce the enemy to come to terms." Yamamoto confided to a few friends, Fuchida and Okumiya continued, that if he succeeded in decimating the U.S. fleet in the Midway operation, he intended "to press the nation's political leaders to initiate overtures for peace."

Once again, Yamamoto's thinking strongly resembles the way in which Bywater analyzed an identical situation described in *The Great Pacific War*. Even after a smashingly successful attack on the U.S. naval force in the Pacific and capture of Guam and the Philippines, Japan could not rest on her laurels, Bywater declared. "Nor could . . . [the Japanese] be under the illusion that the blows already administered were severe enough to compel the United States to sue for peace," he contin-ued. "Much more would have to be done before this desirable result was attained. . . . Were it possible to achieve some undeniable success, decisive enough to impress American public opinion with the futility of going on with the war, all might yet be well [for Japan]."

The problem Yamamoto faced was how to bring the full force of his Combined Fleet into contact with what remained of the American naval force in the Pacific so as to bring about its annihilation. It was the old "fleet-in-being" conundrum, familiar to all navy men. In contrast to land warfare, on the sea, a weaker force usually need not accept battle with a superior foe; the lesser fleet can almost always avoid complete destruction by slipping away or retiring to an anchorage protected by shore-based weapons. So how could the Japanese smoke out the Americans?

Yamamoto had a brainstorm. He would use amphibious forces to effect a landing somewhere within the defensive perimeter of the United States too dear to the Americans to be given up without a major fight. That would bring out what was left of the American fleet, and then Yamamoto could pound it to death with his superior force.

He selected as his target one of three islands nominated by his chief of staff. It was called Midway, a barren, windswept pair of atolls 1,100 miles west of Hawaii. Yamamoto knew the Americans could not tolerate a base that close to Hawaii falling into enemy hands. To allow that would expose Hawaii to constant attack from Midway. According to Fuchida and Okumiya, "Admiral Yamamoto and his staff were convinced that the move against Midway, because it would pose a threat to the safety of Hawaii, would virtually compel the enemy fleet to react with all its available strength."

It was a brilliant conception, but it was not Yamamoto's own—nor did he get the idea from one of his countrymen. In the early years of the century, the Japanese strategists Tetsutaro Sato and Saneyuki Akiyama contemplated attacking the Philippines as a means of provoking the U.S. fleet to make a rash attack on Japan, but there was an enormous difference between that plan and Yamamoto's Midway campaign. Unlike Midway, the Philippines were hardly a jumping-off base from which to attack the United States, or even Hawaii. And even if the Philippines had been located much closer to Hawaii, the Mahanists Sato and Akiyama were not seeking an advance base since that might bring about a fatal division of the fleet. Their idea of attacking the Philippines was more on the order of executing hostages to outrage the United States.

In contrast, Bywater, while war-gaming with his model ships at

Keston Pond in the 1920s, used the threat of an amphibious invasion of an island close to the enemy's vitals as a means of inducing an all-out engagement. In his narrative, while the Japanese manage to attain a powerful "Danube position" in the Pacific, the Americans employ their incomparable industrial resources to build a mighty fleet. With this force in hand, they pursue an island-hopping campaign across the Central Pacific, and, after about a year and a half of fighting, they are ready to try to bring to battle a lesser Japanese force with the expectation of destroying it and thus ending the war. Bywater had the Americans select the island of Yap in the Caroline chain as the landmass the Japanese would risk everything to defend. Yap is roughly 1,100 miles from Manila, or about the same distance as Midway from Hawaii, and thus perilously close to a vital part of the expanded Japanese Empire. Consequently, wrote Bywater, Japan would have no choice but to do everything possible—even gamble the survival of the Imperial Navy—to repel the Americans at that point.

In *The Great Pacific War*, he wrote:

> The expedition was to set sail for Yap, and not merely approach to within range of the island, but so maneuver as to suggest that a landing was about to be attempted. . . . At a suitable opportunity three of the "transports" would move in as though about to disembark troops. . . . It was probable that the expedition would have been sighted and reported by . . . scouts while on its way to the island. There was scarcely any doubt that the Japanese battle fleet would hasten at full speed to the relief of Yap. They might suspect a strategem, it was true, but having no means of verifying that suspicion they would almost certainly elect to take the risk.

From today's perspective, it may seem that Bywater's solution to the problem of drawing out a weaker fleet-in-being should have been almost second nature to an experienced naval commander; however, the fact is, it was a daring and wholly unorthodox gamble at the time he dreamed it up. Even as late as 1942, amphibious warfare—forcible entry from the ocean—was thought by most Western experts to be a tactical nightmare no sensible military leader would undertake. As in so many other respects, Bywater had been ahead of his time.

At the actual Battle of Midway, it appears that Yamamoto followed Bywater's plan to a fault. Essentially, what happened at this engagement—the greatest sea battle the world has ever known—is that the Americans learned of Yamamoto's trap, thanks to the advanced state of their cryptanalysis and radio intelligence, and set a trap of their own. This plan, helped immeasurably by good luck, enabled United States forces to destroy four Japanese aircraft carriers while losing only one, *Yorktown*. With that outcome, Japan lost the cutting edge of her offensive strength and the tide of war turned in favor of the United States.

Yamamoto lost the battle for many reasons, including the fact that the Americans were able to read his cryptograph messages, overconfidence, bad luck, and lack of sufficient air reconnaissance, but the biggest mistake of all by common agreement of Japanese and American historians was his baffling decision to try to fight what he hoped would be the decisive engagement of the war as an old-style naval artillery slugging match. Historians have been at a loss to explain why the man who demonstrated to the world at Pearl Harbor the tremendous power of the collective use of aircraft carriers, and who became acutely aware of their vulnerability from observing the fate of *Lexington*, *Shokaku*, *Glorious*, and *Hermes*, should expose his carriers in the van of his armada and waste their strength bombarding Midway Island while holding back his monster battleships to deliver the decisive blows against the American fleet. The ideal disposition of Japanese forces at Midway would have been the exact opposite. He should have positioned the battlewagons, which were built to take punishment, in the van and used them to draw fire and bombard Midway, and hold back the carriers at a safe distance to be employed in the destruction of the American fleet as soon as it had been located. In fact, a similar plan had been proposed to Yamamoto by his friend Tamon Yamaguchi, then commander-in-chief of the 2d Carrier Division, but Yamamoto rejected it.

His disposition of forces, Fuchida and Okumiya declared, "could be considered satisfactory only from the viewpoint of those who persisted in regarding the battleship, with its big guns, as the main striking force of the Fleet. Despite the important roles assigned to the carrier and submarine forces, they were still to act primarily as an advance guard and shield for the battleships, softening up the enemy so that the battleships could step in to deliver the decisive blow." Fuchida and Okumiya go on to say: "From a tactical standpoint, the Midway plan evidenced an adherence to the outmoded doctrine of the battleship advocates, which was difficult to reconcile with Yamamoto's supposed understanding of the role of air power. It seems strange, to say the least, that the man who conceived the carrier strike on Pearl Harbor was not quicker to institute sweeping changes in fleet organization and tactics so as to make air power the central core of the combat forces. . . . It is hard to find any logical explanation."

Paul S. Dull, author of *A Battle History of the Imperial Japanese Navy*, seems equally mystified as he notes: "Yamamoto, although a proponent of carrier attack warfare, still showed signs of being battle-ship-bound, for the disposition of his forces suggests that he believed the decisive battle would be fought by his and Kondo's forces at night, in ship-to-ship battle."

After the war, Toshiyuki Yokoi, who commanded the carrier *Hiyo*, wrote scathingly of Yamamoto's reluctance "to cast away [his] conventional battleship doctrine until . . . completely defeated at Midway." More recently, Saburo Toyama, a former officer in the Imperial Navy who now teaches at the Japanese Defense Academy, agreed that "Yamamoto's disposition of forces in large part determined the outcome of the [Midway] battle."

How can Yamamoto's action be explained? The American historian Gordon W. Prange speculated that Yamamoto's failure at Midway may have resulted from his being caught between "the battleship coterie" and the "airminded" among his own staff, and that he sought "to reconcile both concepts in toto instead of extracting the best of each." It seems unlikely, however, that Yamamoto, who was now at the height of his prestige and had twice in the space of a few months fought to the point of offering his resignation to get his way (the second threat came when his Midway plan encountered opposition), would be so passive with his own staff. It would have been more in character for Yamamoto to run like a bull through all who stood in his way. Professor Toyama points to the possible influence of Mahan and the "overcommitment of resources to the battleship navy" as possible explanations for Yamamoto's lapse. The former, however, seems hopelessly old-fashioned (Mahan, after all, died in 1914) and the latter had never affected Yamamoto previously.

Still others have suggested that Yamamoto himself was not responsible for the disposition of forces at Midway but delegated the matter to Kameto Kuroshima, his brilliant senior staff officer and strategist. However, Zenshiro Hoshina, who worked with Yamamoto as chief of the Naval Planning Section of the Naval Ministry, said he knew for a fact that Yamamoto "personally determined the order of ships and told Kuroshima what to do" in planning the Midway operation.

The best possible explanation for Yamamoto's curious conduct at Midway is to be found in *The Great Pacific War*. There, Bywater's description of the disposition of forces at what he calls the Battle of Yap is precisely that employed by Yamamoto at Midway—aircraft carriers in the van and battleships to the rear. Bywater described the Japanese formation as having "the heavy ships in three short columns, the airplane carriers ahead, and the cruisers and destroyers forming a complete screen around [them]." The battleships ("the heavy ships"), not the aircraft carriers, were the center of the fleet, as Bywater saw it. The opposing American armada, in Bywater's description, adopted a similar order of battle, with the aircraft carriers *Lexington, Saratoga, Alaska, Montauk*, and *Curtiss* in the lead—serving as naval picadors.

Bywater imagined that the climactic battle would begin with "a violent and reciprocal air offensive," and that aircraft would inflict some damage on both surface fleets. Nevertheless, he wrote, "a decision must be achieved by weapons other than the air arm." At that point, opposing cruisers make contact and Bywater goes on to describe an old-fashioned naval artillery duel.

Apart from Bywater's plan, a great many naval exercises drawn up in the 1920s might have described a similar disposition of forces and dependence on heavily gunned surface ships for casting the decisive blows, and Yamamoto could have been influenced by one just as well as another of them. What makes significant the similarities between Bywater's disposition and use of forces in the imaginary Battle of Yap, and Yamamoto's tactics at Midway, is that they are part and parcel of Bywater's overall battle plan (based on the threat of an amphibious assault) that became encoded in Yamamoto's mind in 1926. In this instance—although usually more independent minded—Yamamoto copied the cracks as well as the dam.

It is tempting to wonder what course events might have taken if Bywater had never written about strategy in the Pacific—or if Yamamoto had not been affected by his thinking. Quite possibly, the war would have assumed a very different shape and left a far different mark on history.

The military historian Louis Morton has written that if the Japanese had never conceived of the Pearl Harbor attack, had bypassed the Philippines and concentrated their aggression on the Dutch East Indies and British Malaya, "it is possible that the United States might not have gone to war, or, if it had, that the American people would have been more favorably disposed to a negotiated peace."

Roosevelt was prepared to ask Congress to declare war if Japan attacked Singapore; however, no one could be certain how Congress might respond. Many Americans were still deeply isolationist; many others perceived the chief danger as being in Europe. In February 1941, a Gallup poll found that although 56 percent of the American people favored efforts "to keep Japan from seizing the Dutch East Indies and Singapore," only 39 percent were willing to risk war in the attempt. The notion of sacrificing American lives and treasure to help beleaguered European empires cling to their colonies in Asia was not an appealing call to arms. "I don't know," Secretary of State Cordell Hull remarked after the Pearl Harbor attack, "whether we would have been at war yet if Japan had not attacked us."

What effect did Bywater have on the American conduct of the war?

Back in 1926, the Joint Army and Navy Board approved a revised War Plan Orange—the contingency plan for war against Japan—that appears to have been profoundly influenced by *The Great Pacific War*, which had been published fifteen months previously. The reckless 5,000-mile charge from Hawaii to Manila that had been central to all previous plans was at last abandoned, and in its place was substituted a carefully planned, step-by-step advance to Manila across a bridge of islands in the Marshall and Caroline chains. This plan was every bit as much a copy of Bywater's book as was Yamamoto's strategy. And yet, on the American side of the Pacific, there was a more complex set of influences at play, making it difficult to sort out the precise springs of thought and action.

Indeed, historians are hard put to show that even War Plan Orange guided those who plotted America's Pacific strategy once the nation entered the war. In the heat of combat, strategists rarely take time to expound on their intellectual antecedents. Arleigh Burke's assertion that his plan for the Battle of Vella Gulf in 1943 was inspired by the tactics of Scipio Africanus in the Punic Wars of the third century B.C. was hardly typical! Most commanders react viscerally, living day by day and week by week, and whatever influenced their actions lies buried in their subconscious minds.

Furthermore, although there were striking similarities between *The Great Pacific War*, War Plan Orange, and America's actual wartime strategy, there were also disparities. For example, both *The Great Pacific War* and Plan Orange envisioned an American invasion of Truk in the Caroline Islands, whereas, in actuality, Truk was bombed and bypassed. Nevertheless, if Bywater could not precisely claim paternity for every detail of American Pacific strategy, it cannot be doubted that his writing was influential in terms of broad overall planning. Just as most of the naval strategists working for the Joint Chiefs of Staff in Washington, and for Chester W. Nimitz, the commander of the Central Pacific theater of operations, had had Plan Orange drummed into them through training and exercises year after year, most of them were familiar with *The Great Pacific War*—or one of its imitations, such as Sutherland Denlinger's *War in the Pacific*. By the time the war started, Bywater's ideas had become part of the naval culture.

This is not to say that he stood alone as the single influence on the men who conceived the U.S. Navy's transpacific campaign. Those strategists sharpened their appreciation of what William Manchester called the "dance of Pacific strategy" by studying the masterful way in which the Japanese bypassed MacArthur's forces on Luzon and encircled Java before seizing it. They may have been influenced, too, by observing their own forces stumble on the tactic of military leapfrog in the Aleutian Islands in May 1943, bypassing the heavily defended island of Kiska and seizing the more distant Attu. When American troops finally stormed Kiska, they found it unoccupied, since their capture of Attu had cut off Kiska's line of supply and Japanese forces had then abandoned it.

All this was doubtless taken in by Nimitz and his staff as well as by the Joint Chiefs and their planners in Washington. Yet it seems undeniable that they also drew their inspiration—even if unaware of its origin—from the writing of Hector Bywater, the man who invented the Pacific war.

EPILOGUE

IF IT IS true that Yamamoto, and a number of American strategists, were influenced by Hector Bywater, why has this fact remained a virtual secret for nearly half a century? Why is Bywater's name all but absent from the literature of the Pacific war?*

To begin on the Japanese side, the most obvious explanation is that Yamamoto, who after the war might have told the world where he found his inspiration, was killed in 1943 in the Solomon Islands by an American fighter plane. Furthermore, although a sociable man, Yamamoto characteristically kept his fellow officers in the dark as to what might have influenced his thoughts. Sokichi Takagi, one of his biographers who

---

* An article by the author about the possible significance of Bywater appeared in *American Heritage* in December 1970, but apart from that, Bywater's name crops up in the literature of the Pacific war only in a footnote to John Toland's *The Rising Sun* and in several sentences in Gerald Wheeler's *Prelude to Pearl Harbor*.

knew him well, observed that Yamamoto "never let others know what
he was reading or studying." Conceivably, Yamamoto himself was unaware of how deeply Bywater had affected him, or, more likely, he had
no desire to advertise his indebtedness to a foreign strategist.

When Yamamoto's close friends and associates who could be interviewed after the war were questioned about Bywater, all but one
recognized his name and most said they had read his books and vol-
unteered the Japanese titles. However, when asked about Bywater's
possible influence on Yamamoto, the reaction was mixed. Sadatoshi
Tomioka, former chief of the Operations Section of the Navy General
Staff, felt "sure that our military circle was not influenced by H. C.
Bywater . . . though similarities appeared between the events of December 1941 and Bywater's proposals." But then, Tomioka had strenuously
opposed every major strategic initiative Yamamoto proposed and was
never personally close to him. On the other hand, Mitsuo Fuchida, a
confidant of Yamamoto who commanded the air attack on Pearl Harbor
and later coauthored the definitive Japanese account of the Battle of
Midway, declared that he had studied both *Taiheiyo Kaiken Ron* (*Sea
Power in the Pacific*) and *Taiheiyo Senso* (*The Great Pacific War*) while
a student at the Naval War College, the highest-level training school in
the Imperial Navy. He added in his imperfect English that "both of these
books gave a great influence for our study of the strategy."

Takagi came close to the truth when he guessed that in planning the
opening moves in the Pacific war, Yamamoto "took a hint from the
strategic concepts of the American army and navy during his stay in the
States." Takagi speculated that the book that inspired Yamamoto was
not *The Great Pacific War* but William "Billy" Mitchell's *Winged Defense*. Mitchell's book, published in 1924, a year before *The Great Pacific
War*, was still causing a stir when Yamamoto was stationed in Washington, and while it may have stimulated his thinking about air power,
it cannot be said to have shaped his vision of the coming campaign in
the Pacific. In *Winged Defense*, Mitchell had much to say about how
air power had transformed the science of war, but he also proclaimed
that aviation had made large-scale amphibious invasions such as the one
Yamamoto planned for the Philippines "an impossibility," and declared
that "there is little use for the retention of airplane carriers in the general
scheme of armaments."

Another who might have called attention to the similarity between what Bywater wrote and the way the war turned out was, of course, Bywater himself. Had he lived, he certainly would have been outspoken about where the Japanese and the Americans had found their ideas—and surely Bywater's voice would have commanded attention.

Yet even without Bywater's presence, there was a brief flurry of interest in *The Great Pacific War* in the United States immediately after the Pearl Harbor attack. None of this discussion, however, did justice to Bywater, and paradoxically it seems to have had the effect of eclipsing further consideration of his significance. On December 9, 1941, *The New York Times* published a review of the book, which started out by declaring that *The Great Pacific War* was certainly timely even if sixteen years old. After describing the book, the review concentrated patriotically on Bywater's conclusion that the United States was bound to win the conflict. Two weeks later, perhaps prompted by the *Times* review, *Life* magazine published an abridged version of *The Great Pacific War*, billed, with remarkable understatement, as "the most current book of the week." Soon after, Ferris Greenslet, the Houghton Mifflin editor who had encouraged Bywater to write *The Great Pacific War* back in 1924 and who was now editor-in-chief of the Boston publishing firm, brought out a new hardcover edition of the book with the subtitle *A Historic Prophecy Now Being Fulfilled* and an introduction by Hanson W. Baldwin, chief military correspondent of *The New York Times*. Baldwin described the book as "deeply prophetic."

Unfortunately, all of these publications came too soon (Baldwin dated his preface just six days after the Pearl Harbor attack) for anyone outside the high command of the Japanese Navy to grasp what had taken place and was about to unfold in the Pacific. The only observation possible in the *Times* review, the *Life* presentation, and Baldwin's introduction to the new edition of *The Great Pacific War*, was that Bywater seemed to have been correct in guessing that Japan would attack without warning. Details about the invasions of Guam and the Philippines, and an awareness of the overall Japanese offensive and the American counterattack, which would reveal striking similarities with Bywater's writing, would not emerge for months, and in some cases, not until the war's end. Thus, the attention given Bywater's book immediately following Pearl Harbor was premature, although it gave the appearance of having extracted from the book everything of consequence. In that way, further inquiry was precluded.

At least one Japanese military expert also wrote prematurely. Writing for the newspaper *Nichi Nichi* on December 9, 1941, Yahei Oba, a retired major general, declared that the Pearl Harbor attack had defied the predictions of "even Hector Bywater." He, too, was writing much before he had all the relevant facts in hand.

Bywater also escaped notice because his close professional colleagues and personal friends—those who might be expected to have had special insight into the correspondence between what he had written and what was happening in the Pacific—were simply too stunned and baffled to comprehend and articulate what seems so obvious today. The cases of Francis McMurtrie and H. C. Ferraby, Bywater's closest friends in the Fleet Street Press Gang, illustrate how incapacitating the outbreak of war in the Pacific was to many of those who had made a lifetime study of naval theory and practice.

McMurtrie's inability to speak out was compounded by a bitter personal rivalry with Bywater that had developed. In the late 1930s, McMurtrie began to claim credit for having cowritten *The Great Pacific War*. He had, in fact, helped Bywater in writing the book and had been given generous acknowledgment in the preface for contributing "maritime knowledge" and material on "the trade war and other subsidiary but instructive operations beyond the principal zone of hostilities." However, that was not enough for McMurtrie. Perhaps inspired by the manner in which Bywater had sought to set matters straight with Archibald Hurd concerning the authorship of *The Fleets at War*, McMurtrie stated in the biographical information about himself he submitted to the British *Who's Who* for 1938 that he was the author "with H. C. Bywater" of *The Great Pacific War*. At about the same time, he went to the Admiralty Library, asked for the registered copy of the book, and there, on the title page under the lines that read "By Hector Bywater," he wrote: "and Francis E. McMurtrie."

But soon after succeeding Bywater as naval correspondent of the *Daily Telegraph* in the fall of 1939, McMurtrie began to repudiate the book's conclusions. Nine months before the Pearl Harbor attack, he wrote that the presence of the United States fleet at Pearl Harbor "precludes Japan from making any decisive stroke against an opponent." Furthermore, McMurtrie declared, the distance between Pearl Harbor and Yokohama "is too great for any fleet to cover with the prospect of having to fight an action at the other end." In contrast, Bywater at that time was prophetically warning in the *News-Chronicle* that Japan "intends to take advantage of Allied preoccupations to spread war to parts of Asia other than her immediate field of operations in China."

When the Pearl Harbor attack finally took place, McMurtrie all but fell to pieces. His dispatches in the *Telegraph* became not merely terse, but feeble. In one of his articles, after the Japanese reported that their aircraft had sunk the British warships *Prince of Wales* and the *Repulse* in the South China Sea, McMurtrie could not bring himself to accept the fact that aircraft had been responsible for the sinking of a British battleship and battle cruiser. These men-of-war must have "encountered the bulk of the Japanese fleet," he insisted in the *Telegraph*, despite all indications to the contrary.

Then, as the reality of the Japanese successes became undeniable, McMurtrie reasserted his claim to coauthorship of *The Great Pacific War*. Writing for the November 1942 issue of the *Navy*, he stated: "In 1925, forcasting the probable course of a future war in the Pacific, I ventured to write: 'The remote islands of the Western Pacific could not be held against a hostile Japan, and must inevitably be forfeited soon after the outbreak of war.' " In a footnote, he gave the source as *The Great Pacific War*, the authors of which he listed as "H. C. Bywater and F. E. McMurtrie."

By this time, McMurtrie was a confused and pathetic man. He had become "a gaunt figure" and "a little dotty," according to those who knew him. His wife had become addicted to morphine, and he, too, may have succumbed to the drug. McMurtrie was replaced as the *Telegraph*'s naval correspondent in 1942 but continued as editor of *Jane's Fighting Ships* until his death from throat cancer in 1949 at the age of sixty-four. Afterward, his wife, who had grown to loathe his obsession with naval matters, burned his books and extensive files in a bonfire behind their home in Hoddesdon, thus destroying much of the record of an extraordinary chapter of British naval history.

Bywater's other close friend in the Fleet Street Press Gang, H. C. Ferraby, was equally befuddled by events in the Pacific and seemed incapable of comprehending what his longtime friend and one-time collaborator had been preaching for two decades. After the fall of the Philippines in 1942, Ferraby wrote that the Allied taking of Madagascar had built "a containing wall round Japan" that "may be expected to serve until such time as the accumulating pressure of Allied sea-power forces drive back the buccaneering expeditions" of Japan. He seemed blind to Bywater's insistence that it was Japan, not the Allies, that would be building a containing wall rendering her greatly expanded empire close to invulnerable. His death in 1942 was a drunken accident.

Ulysses Bywater was also incapable of explaining his brother's impact on world events. In 1940, he tried his hand at journalism, but with sorry results. After visiting Germany, he wrote a couple of articles for the London *Daily Express* in which he assured his readers that Germany had no intention of bombing England and that "anti-Jewish drives in Germany seemed to have died down in [their] more ferocious manifestations." Uly hardly displayed his brother's gift for prophecy.

A few years later, the FBI grew suspicious of Uly's association with Nazi Germany and investigated him as a possible enemy agent. He was found innocent but the report characterized him as a "shiftless, never-do-very-well" drifter who had led a "precarious, wandering existence in various European countries since the last war."

Were there not others—readers of the original *Great Pacific War*—who could have recognized that Bywater was either a latter-day Nostradamus or else someone who had exerted an extraordinary influence on future war planners? One searches for them in vain. Possibly, their silence is explained by the fact that events moved so swiftly—and catastrophically—during the war years that virtually anything written or said about the war before it started seemed hopelessly naive or old-fashioned. If Bywater was remembered at all during and after the war, it was as one of the many benighted proponents of battleship supremacy—no one to be taken seriously by a world in awe of the wonders and horrors wrought by the airplane.

Still another reason for the neglect of Bywater is that to date, most historians who have analyzed the Japanese offensive have concentrated on tactics rather than strategy—perhaps understandably so. After all, the dramatic shock of a "bolt from the blue" (as Bywater phrased it) and the spectacle of racing aircraft blasting, burning, and turning belly-up gargantuan warships could not help but mesmerize the world. This fascination, naturally, led to the investigation of such influences on Yamamoto as the American war games at Hawaii in 1932, which demonstrated that carrier aircraft might be able to inflict serious damage on warships at Pearl Harbor, and the remarkably effective British carrier-borne attack against Italian warships at anchor at Taranto in November

1940. All of this has its place, but Yamamoto, as we have seen, was not just staging an air show at Pearl Harbor. He regarded the attack on the American fleet as part of a broad strategy, and it is not until one focuses on that larger vision that the importance of Bywater's work becomes apparent.

As for the American island-hopping campaign, the credit for its inception has rightly been assigned to Earl Ellis and John A. Lejeune, yet no one seems to have noticed that Hector Bywater independently invented the plan and mightily helped convince a reluctant U.S. Navy to accept amphibious warfare as the only sound means of projecting its power into the Western Pacific.

But who would have imagined that the Japanese and American war plans had been spelled out in such detail in a book published in the West sixteen years before Pearl Harbor? Even when this truth is grasped in all its complexity, and Yamamoto's actions together with the American counteroffensive are seen as driven by a subtle mix of influence and innovation, it seems bizarre.

Then, too, Bywater has been overlooked simply because *much* in human events is glossed over. "History with its flickering lamp stumbles along the trail of the past," said Winston Churchill, "trying to reconstruct its scenes, to revive its echoes, and kindle with pale gleams the passion of former days."

Finally, now that the story is out, one hopes it will, in at least a small way, help lay to rest the old canard about the Pearl Harbor attack as a characteristic expression of the "treacherous and deceitful" Japanese. When one considers that that historic event—possibly the greatest event of the twentieth century—was conceived by an Englishman and encouraged in its conception by an American publisher who took pains to conceal his involvement, it appears it was, in reality, as English as plum pudding and as American as apple pie.

ACKNOWLEDGMENTS

HECTOR BYWATER'S CHILDREN, the Reverend Hector W. R. Bywater and Sylvia Newland, have been unfailingly helpful and hospitable throughout the preparation of this book. I am also particularly grateful to John Newland, who not only shared with me his personal recollections of his father-in-law but also made free with his detailed knowledge of maritime and naval affairs.

In addition, Hector Bywater's nephew and his wife, Mr. and Mrs. John A. Bywater, and Jeffrey Holman of New Zealand, have kindly supplied me with photographs and reminiscences.

Others who knew Hector Bywater personally, and generously put themselves at my disposal, were Raymond Blackman, George J. Bryant, E. A. Harwood, Malcolm Kennedy (through his daughter Mrs. Aline Buxton), Donald McCormick, Stephen Roskill, and David Woodward.

The staff of the London *Daily Telegraph* was as helpful as possible in giving me access to everything from their cuttings files to personnel records. I am especially grateful to H. W. Stephen, former managing director. Shahe Guebenlian, the former publicity manager of Reuters, was also of great assistance, as was Gordon Phillips, archivist of the Times Newspapers Ltd.

A number of libraries and archival institutions in the United States, Britain, and Japan were of great help.

In the United States, the institutions and individuals in them I wish to thank are the Library of Congress; the National Archives; the Washington Navy Yard; the Still Photo Branch of the Navy Department; Rodney G. Dennis and the Houghton Library of Harvard University for permission to quote from the letters of William Howard Gardiner to Bywater and to William S. Sims and from the correspondence between Ferris Greenslet and Bywater, and to make use of the papers of Joseph C. Grew; the Franklin D. Roosevelt Library in Hyde Park, New York, for access to files, the use of photographs, and permission to quote from presidential correspondence; the Naval Historical Collection of the U.S. Naval War College in Newport, Rhode Island, and Evelyn Cherpak, director of the collection; the Harry Ransom Humanities Research Center at the University of Texas at Austin, especially to John Kirkpatrick, for assistance and permission to quote from Bywater's correspondence with J. L. Garvin and Compton Mackenzie; the Special Collections and Programs Department of the Samuel Paley Library of Temple University in Philadelphia and especially Thomas M. Whitehead for assistance and permission to quote from Bywater's correspondence with Constable & Co.; and finally the British Information Service in New York.

I am indebted to Professor Ross Lamont of the University of New England, Armidale, Australia, for helpful advice and especially the tip that the Fisher-Churchill correspondence of 1911 might refer to Bywater's activities as a secret agent. Also to Professor Robert B. Davis of Moorhead State University in Moorhead, Minnesota, for the lead about the Bywater-Greenslet correspondence at the Houghton Library at Harvard University in Cambridge, Massachusetts. Edward S. Miller, who has specialized in the study of War Plan Orange, spoke so interestingly about his subject that I decided to amplify material in the first (British) edition of this book to include a separate chapter on War Plan Orange. Professor William Braisted of the University of Texas at Austin was another who provided much helpful advice; also, Stanley Weintraub, director of the Institute for the Arts and Humanistic Studies at Pennsylvania State University. I want to thank Barbara Chevins, the daughter of Hugh Chevins of the London *Daily Telegraph*, and the British Library of Political and Economic Science for allowing me to read Hugh Chevins's unpublished autobiography; Rear Admiral Philip W. Snyder, USN, Ret., for details about capital-ship construction; Rear Admiral D. H. Kane, Jr., director of Naval History and curator for the Navy Department; Dr. Dean Allard of the Naval History Department; Ms. Hannah Zeidlik and Dr. Young Gil Chang of the Historical Records Branch, U.S. Army Center of Military History, Washington, D.C.; Elaine Everly of the Navy and Old Army Branch of the National Archives, Washington, D.C.; Heather Bradley Lowder, formerly of *The New York Times* London Bureau, for valuable introductions and countless favors over many years; Alice Klingsberg, former manager of *The New York Times* Archives; Paul Greenfeder, former chief librarian of the *Times*; Linda Amster, research manager of the *Times* and Marilyn Annan of the *Times* library; Lonnie Schlein, Culture Department photo editor of the *Times*;

Donald H. Patterson, Sr., publisher of the Baltimore *Sun*, especially for sending me copies of the correspondence and diary of his father, Paul Patterson, and permission to quote from this material; August J. Janos, assistant to Mr. Patterson; Gary Black, the son of Van Lear Black; and Clement G. Vitek, chief librarian of the Baltimore *Sun*. I am also grateful to three very special people who served as my secretary during the years I was writing this book—Gwin Chin, Dolores Dolan, and Ruth Strauss.

In Great Britain, the institutions I wish to thank include the Public Record Office; the British National Library; the National Maritime Museum in Greenwich; the masters, fellows, and scholars of Churchill College, Cambridge University, who granted me permission to refer to the papers of Sir Archibald Hurd; the Imperial War Museum; the Liddell Hart Centre for Military Archives at King's College, London; the Manuscript Section of the University of Sussex Library, Brighton, England; and the National Trust for Places of Historic Interest or Natural Beauty, which granted me permission to quote from the Bywater-Kipling correspondence.

I was fortunate to be able to travel to Japan in 1982 thanks to a grant from the Foreign Press Center/Japan, a nongovernmental, nonprofit, independent foundation established in 1976 to assist foreign journalists in Japan. I am indebted to Peter Grilli, formerly of the Japan Society, for his recommendation for the grant and for a constant flow of sound advice. On the staff of the Foreign Press Center/Japan, I wish to thank Shizuo Saito, former president, and Kinji Kawamura, former managing director, for their support throughout my visit to Japan.

Seiichi Soeda, former assistant to the managing director of the Foreign Press Center/Japan, deserves a separate paragraph of acknowledgment. With consummate patience and skill, he guided me through the intricacies of research in a land quite strange to me, and he has generously continued to serve as my eyes and ears in Japan over a period of years.

Also of great assistance in Japan were my friends Akio and Emiko Namekata and Junnosuke Ofusa of *The New York Times* Tokyo Bureau.

Among the former officers of the Imperial Japanese Navy who graciously gave up their time to submit to my questions were, at the outset, Mitsuo Fuchida, Shigeru Fukudome, and Sadatoshi Tomioka. Then came Ichiro Yokoyama, Sadamu Sanagi, Minoru Genda, Atsushi Oi (a fellow alumnus of the University of Virginia!), and finally the sprightly Admiral

Zenshiro Hoshina, who at the age of ninety-one, could run down a flight of stairs like a boy and taught me how to pay my respects to Admiral Togo at a shrine dedicated to his memory.

Yamamoto's most recent biographer, Hiroyuki Agawa, graciously received me at his home and offered a number of useful suggestions. And finally, I shall never forget my visit with the venerable Zengan Hashimoto, the then-ninety-six-year-old Zen priest who sat with me on the veranda of his *Kensho-ji* temple outside Nagaoka where he had so often passed the time of day with his friend Admiral Yamamoto half a century before. He spoke of those bygone days, vividly recalling Yamamoto's insistence that he could hold out against the United States for only a year and a half—a notion I suspect he got from Bywater.

Among the institutions in Japan of assistance were Boeicho Boei Kenshujo Senshibu Shiryoko (the Military History Department of the National Defense College, National Defense Agency). I am especially indebted to Minoru Nomura, IJN, Ret., chief of the second history division of the Military History Department of the college, who was a masterful, tireless, and delightfully wry-witted guide over many days. Another institution that was of great service was Gaiko Shiryokan (the Diplomatic Records Office).

I also wish to thank my translators, including Kay H. Kim, Bunji Omura, Fukuko Yorifuji, Masahiko Umekita (IJN, Ret.), Hiroshi Yoshida, Keizo Ohashi (IJN, Ret.), Masako Tanaka, and Wakako Mitsui.

This book has been made possible through the commitment and support of a number of editors. Oliver Jensen, while editor of *American Heritage*, responded with enthusiasm to my proposal to investigate Bywater back in 1967, and he advanced me the funds that made possible my early work leading to the publication of an article in his magazine in 1970. Nine years later, when I decided to seek the answer to questions about Bywater that had eluded me, and to attempt a book-length biography, Tom Wallace, then editor-in-chief of Holt, Rinehart & Winston, provided the faith and capital necessary to extend my research to England, Texas, and other distant parts of the United States. His successors—Don Hutter, Jennifer Josephy, and Richard Seaver—continued to be supportive.

It was, however, the determination and drive of Robert Weil of St. Martin's Press and Peter Lavery of Macdonald & Company Publishers,

Ltd., that proved decisive in bringing about publication of the book, and to them I am deeply grateful.

I also wish to express my appreciation for the editorial, production, and marketing contributions of a number of friends at St. Martin's Press, including Barbara Andrews, Mark H. Berkowitz, Josh Marwell, Al Reuben, Richard Romano, and Bill Thomas.

My agent, Roslyn Targ, has spent years encouraging me to pursue this subject, and I want to thank her most affectionately.

Park Honan, a gifted biographer, gave perceptive and painstaking assistance with the final manuscript, along with plenty of advice and encouragement along the way. Jeannette Colin Honan and Corinna and Nicholas Inge were lifesavers during my visits to England.

Finally, my wife Nancy has encouraged this project from the moment she discovered a mildew-covered copy of *Sea Power in the Pacific* in a used bookstore in Old Mystic, Connecticut, and my dedication of this volume to her and to our children Bradley, Daniel, and Edith is only the smallest measure of my deep appreciation for their loyalty and support.

NOTES

In the following notes, books are generally referred to by the author's last name only. Exceptions are in cases of common last names where a first name or initial is added, and in cases of an author with more than one book listed in the bibliography where a condensed title is added. References to periodicals, papers, and government documents are also cited by the author's last name or the title, with the above exceptions, and the word or words PER (for periodicals), PAP (for papers), or GOV DOC (for government documents) to indicate their appearance in a subsection of the bibliography that follows these notes. Other abbreviated forms of citation are:

DT	*Daily Telegraph*, London
DN	*Daily News*, London
NC	*News-Chronicle*, London
LT	London *Times*
BS	Baltimore *Sun*
NYT	*New York Times*
NYH	*New York Herald*
NMRRDG	*Naval & Military Record and Royal Dockyards Gazette*
N	*Navy*, London
USNIP	United States Naval Institute *Proceedings*
WHH	Author's interview
WHHC	Author's correspondence
HCB	Hector Charles Bywater
SPP	Bywater's *Sea Power in the Pacific*
GPW	Bywater's *The Great Pacific War*
SI	Bywater and Ferraby's *Strange Intelligence*
CFTSOO	Combined Fleet Top Secret Operation Order Number 1
RJB	Records of the Joint Army and Navy Board

PREFACE

xiv, "remain obscure"—Spector, 79.
xv, Kaiser Wilhelm II—Tuchman, *Proud Tower*, 133.
xv, Heinz Guderian—Barnett, 101, 203; Liddell Hart, *Memoirs*, I, 269–70.
xv, John F. C. Fuller, Charles DeGaulle—Elting, 217.

1 TORPEDO ATTACK

1, torpedo attack—"The Russo-Japanese War," GOV DOC; Benjamin, PER; NYH, 2/10/1904 and 4/24/1904.

2, Trafalgar significance—WHHC, Rev. Hector W. R. Bywater, 12/12/80 and 12/22/80.

3, "nearest conception . . ."—SI, 14–19; WHH, Rev. Hector W. R. Bywater, Derby, England, 1979, in which he confirmed that "x" in SI is autobiographical.

3, "first occasion"—SPP, 140.

4, *Ironclads in Action*—SI, 16.

4–5, Kipling—see Kipling, PAP.

4–5, *A Fleet in Being*—Kipling, 46, 65.

5, HCB details—WHH, Rev. Hector W. R. Bywater, Derby, England, 1979; WHHC, John Newland, 5/31/1967, and PAP, a memoir about his father-in-law written in 1967 and given to author in 1979.

6, U.S.S. *Connecticut*—West, J., 30–39; Mitchell, D. W., 150–51.

6, *Marine Journal*—NYH, editorial, 5/6/1911.

6–7, HCB and *Herald*—WHH, Rev. Hector W. R. Bywater, Derby, England, 1979; Bywater's "Application for Appointment," GOV DOC.

7, James Gordon Bennett details—Seitz; O'Connor; Redding, PER.

7, editor marooned—O'Connor, 215–16.

7, Bennett editing—Redding, PER.

7, Morse code—WHH, Rev. Hector W. R. Bywater, Derby, England, 1979.

8, J. D. Jarrold Kelley—Cook; NYT, 5/1/1922, 17; Seitz and O'Connor both incorrectly spell the name "Kelly."

8, HCB's survey—NYH, 2/10/1904, 6.

8, "foul bottom"—HCB, *Cruisers in Battle*, 83.

2 "WAR WHEN JAPAN IS READY"

9–10, McCullagh's report—NYH, 2/10/1904, 2, and 4/24/1904, 4.

10–11, Lewis's report—NYH, 3/17/1904, 2.

10–11, more on Chemulpo—"The Russo-Japanese War," GOV DOC; Warner, 193.

11, Uriu—NYH, 2/14/1905, 5; Sweetman, 102, 156.

12, "shell passed between the arm"—San Francisco *Chronicle*, 5/2/1909, 5.

13, HCB in *Herald*—"Surgery for the Steel Skins . . . ," NYH, 3/27/1904, *Magazine*, 12; "Liners Here Like Polar Icebergs," NYH, 2/18/1904, 6.

14, HCB departs for London—HCB's U.S. Passport Application dated 9/22/1915 declares applicant last in U.S. 2/12/1905.

16, Tsushima and "Goddess of Victory"—BS, 5/27/1925; DT, 5/30/1934; SI, 99–101; SPP, 143–49; N, 8/1909, 230.

16, *Herald* on centennial—NYH, 10/21/1905, 9.

17, Royal Albert Hall—LT, 10/23/1905.

17, William Packenham—"Report of the Committee on Designs," 27, GOV DOC.

17–18, HCB on Tsushima—N, "German Naval Notes (From H.C.B., Our Own Correspondent)," 8/1909, 230.

18, *Aki* and *Satsuma*—SPP, 148.

18, HCB "got the message"—*Navy League Annual*, 1913–1914, 224.

18, Bennett "for many years has been convinced"—Redding, PER.

18, Bennett hostile to Japan—NYH editorials 9/8/1897 and 9/10/1897 are suggestive, although Bennett did not specifically name Japan until 1/20/1898.

18, 1897 crisis—Tate, 282–83; Bailey, PER, 46–61.

19, Bennett fears attack—NYH, 1/20/1898.

19, special code books—Redding, PER.

19, "sympathies . . . with white race"—NYH, 3/10/1904.

19, "a dozen reporters"—Redding, PER.

19, Homer Lea "earliest prophet"—see, for example, William Manchester's *American Caesar*, which cites Lea but makes no mention of Bennett or HCB.

19, *Herald* hails Lea's book—NYH, 11/12/1909, 5; 12/20/1909, 10; 12/26/1909, 4.

3 "OUR SPLENDID SPY IN GERMANY"

22, HCB apprehended—SI, 56–58. Identified as autobiographical passage in WHH, Rev. Hector W. R. Bywater, Derby, England, 1979.

22, "Naval Baedecker"—SI, 167.

23, "splendid spy in Germany"—Churchill, Randolph S., ed., 1352 and 1365. The unnamed agent referred to by Fisher as a "splendid spy in Germany" is obviously HCB. Fisher said the agent uncovered details about how "the Germans drew 2 feet too much water in four [early dreadnoughts] and tried to sell them to the Turks!" This reference matches information in signed articles by HCB in the *Navy*, 3/1910, 54, and 9/1910, 241, and the *Navy League Annual*, 1910–11, 191. Three weeks later, Fisher wrote to Churchill again referring to an unnamed "first class spy in Berlin" associated with the Navy League, Alan Burgoyne, and Patrick J. H. Hannon. Burgoyne or Hannon, wrote Fisher, could supply Churchill with the spy's name if he wished to have it. Once again, it is clear the reference is to HCB since all of those mentioned, including HCB, were closely associated with the Navy League. Burgoyne was then president of the Navy League and editor of the *Navy League Annual*, a publication to which HCB had been a regular contributor since 1908. Hannon was then the new general secretary of the Navy League and editor of the *Navy*, for which HCB wrote a weekly column. Although HCB's actual residence was in Dresden, the *Navy* date-lined his articles "Berlin," and thus it would be natural for Fisher to refer to him as a "first class spy in Berlin."

23, *United Service Magazine*—1/1910, vol. 40, no. 974, 441.
23, Alfred von Tirpitz vs. HCB—N, 2/1909, 36; 6/1909, 161.
23, agent like reporter—SI, 31.
24, Uly's career—Bywater, Ulysses John Victor, GOV DOC.
24, language ability—Bywater, Hector C., "Application for Appointment," GOV DOC.
24, Uly's ability—WHHC, John and Gladys Bywater, 4/27/81.
24, Anthony Trollope—Anthony Trollope, *Phineas Redux*, I, 118–19.
24, German Navy fascination—Braisted, I, 189–90.
25, Germans experimenting—SI, 2, 10–11.
25, Ulysses as American—Gaffney, GOV DOC, Gaffney to Robert Bacon, 9/6/1906, #21-3563/28.
25, *Daily Record*—Bywater, Hector C., "Application for Appointment," GOV DOC.
26, *Frederick the Great* and conversion—SI, 17–18.
26, "affable and entertaining"—Bywater, Hector C., letter of support by Rev. Moore for "Application for Appointment," GOV DOC.
26, "Big Bertha"—SI, 61–67.
26, Uly's marriage—Bywater, John A., U.S. Passport Application, 4/9/1952; Passport Application Files, Record Group 59, National Archives, Washington, D.C.
26, Hector's marriage—Bywater, Hector C., Certificate of Registration of American Citizen with 8/1914 U.S. Passport Application, GOV DOC.
27, "piece together [HCB's] career"—HCB's 8/3/1932 to Compton Mackenzie, Mackenzie PAP; HCB "Application for Appointment," GOV DOC; SI, 14, 16–19; DT, 9/24, 9/25, 9/26, and 9/29/1930; and WHH, Rev. Hector W. R. Bywater and John and Sylvia Newland, 1979 and 1980.
27, "large and airy"—SI, 5.
27, "a large role"—HCB's 8/3/1932 to Compton Mackenzie, Mackenzie PAP.
27, "Foreign Section"—West, Nigel, 34.
27, HCB on Cumming—DT, 10/27/1932.
27, "C was completely unknown"—DT, 10/27/1932.
28, C speaks—SI, 3–4; John Newland, PAP; and WHH, John Newland, 1979.
29, certifies Hector's citizenship—Gaffney, GOV DOC, Ulysses Bywater to assistant secretary of state, 2/10/1909, #11011-156/168.
29, pay of lieutenant commander—John Newland, PAP.

4 CRUEL YEARS

31, "Secret Service activities . . ."—HCB, trans., *Spies Break Through*, Introduction.

31–36, "six-month-long adventure"—SI, 132–46.

32, "[HCB's] own experience"—Ferraby confirms in general way in his obituary, Manchester *Guardian*, 8/19/1940.

32, "spy fever"—SI, 130.

36, returns to England—HCB, "Affidavit to Overcome ..." GOV DOC.

36, John Burke—Williams, W., 12.

36, "$125 a month"—HCB, "Application for Appointment," GOV DOC.

36, Togo's press conference—NYH, 7/30/1911, 11.

37, J. L. Garvin—Scott, 393–99.

37–38, HCB–Garvin correspondence—Garvin, J. L., PAP, HCB's 11/11, 11/24, 12/15, 12/29/1910 and 3/4/1911.

38, HCB works for DT in 1910—HCB, "Affidavit to Overcome ... ," GOV DOC.

39, "C urged [HCB] to apply ..."—HCB, "Application for Appointment," GOV DOC.

40, "letter of reference"—ibid.

40, 1914 application—ibid.

40, "My God, it's happened!"—WHH, Rev. Hector W. R. Bywater, Derby, England, 1979.

41, 1915 mission—SI, 252–62; ibid.

42, turns down OBE—WHH, John and Sylvia Newland, Cornwall, England, 1979.

42, "Needless to say ..."—SI, 36.

42, "Nearly every valuable ..."—SI, 40.

5 THE FLEET STREET PRESS GANG

43, " 'Ding Dong' and 'The Mucky Duck' "—WHH, E. A. Harwood, David Woodward, 1979.

43–53, Fleet Street Press Gang in general—WHH, Hanson W. Baldwin, former military correspondent of NYT, New York, 1969; David Divine, former *Sunday Times* defense correspondent, London, 1979; Cyril Ray, former *Sunday Times* war correspondent, London, 1979; Donald McCormick, naval writer, London, 1979; Robert Cooper, former LT foreign correspondent; Carlos Largo, naval architect and longtime London resident, London, 1979; WHHC, George J. Bryant 6/6/1967 and Bryant, "The Anchorites" (pamphlet, 1974); Blackman, PER; and Hurd, *Who Goes There?* 52–53.

44, "the Britten that rules the waves"—BS, 12/27/1928, 9.

44, parrot joke—WHH, E. A. Harwood, Godalming, Surrey, England, 1979.

44, Lord Bolingbroke—HCB, "Lord Brassey," PER.

45, HCB tribute to Brassey—ibid.

45, "the three most beautiful things ..."—WHH, Raymond Blackman, London, 1979.

45–46, Kipling—Kipling, *A Fleet in Being*, 83–84.

46, "their favorite recreation" was "seagoing"—listings in *Who's Who*, 1940, for Francis E. McMurtrie, H. C. Ferraby, and others.

46, Admiralty aloof—WHH, Captain Stephen W. Roskill, Cambridge, England, 1980; Rodger, 122–40.

46, Fisher's friendships—Fisher, PAP, Garvin to Fisher, 11/26/1916 (3/13/2776).

47, "prayers"—Godfrey, PAP; WHH, Raymond Blackman, London, 1979, and George J. Bryant, East Horsley, Leatherhead, Surrey, 1979.

47, Raymond Blackman—WHH, Raymond Blackman, London, 1979.

47, "gin glasses shook or shattered"—see, for example, Benedict Nightingale, "He Makes the Ordinary Extraordinary," NYT, 12/19/1982, 2, 1.

48, Terence Lewin on gin pennant—DT, 12/22/1978.

48, Thomas Woodroofe—WHH, Rev. Hector W. R. Bywater, Derby, England, 1979.

48, Ferraby's death—WHH, George J. Bryant, East Horsley, Leatherhead, Surrey, 1979; David Woodward, Oxford, 1979; also obituaries in the Manchester *Guardian* and *Daily Express*, 1/1/1943.

49, Jane's Naval War Game—Jane, *Naval War Game*.

49, played at War College—Blackman, PER.

50, "alike as peas"—SI, 15.

50, Emden's disguise—Robinson, PER, 212.

50, Archibald Hurd—Hurd, *Who Goes There?* 22–29; obituaries LT and DT, 6/22/1959; Hurd, PAP; WHH, George J. Bryant, East Horsley, Leatherhead, Surrey, 1979; Raymond Blackman, London, 1979; David Woodward, Oxford, 1979; and E. A. Harwood, Godalming, Surrey, 1979.

50, "too-cozy friendships"—Hurd, PAP, Hurd to Lord Burnham, 10/28/1910, Folder 1/12.

51, H. C. Ferraby—obituaries in Manchester *Guardian* and *Daily Express*, 1/1/1943; WHH, David Woodward, Oxford, 1979; and George J. Bryant, East Horsley, Leatherhead, Surrey, 1979; British *Who's Who* for 1940.

52, McMurtrie on *Formidable*s,—WHH, George J. Bryant, East Horsley, Leatherhead, Surrey, 1979.

52, McMurtrie lectures—WHH, Raymond Blackman, London, 1979.

52–53, Francis E. McMurtrie—obituaries in DT and LT, 2/24/1949; WHH, E. A. Harwood, Godalming, Surrey, 1979; Raymond Blackman, London, 1979; David Woodward, Oxford, 1979; George J. Bryant, East Horsley, Leatherhead, Surrey, 1979; WHHC, S. Mervyn Herbert, 3/6 and 4/13/1981.

53, McMurtrie's letter—DT 1/14/1939.

6 SEIZE THE DANUBE POSITION

55, "U.S. AND THE PACIFIC"—NMRRDG, 4/7/1920, 222.

57, "might well prove insoluble"—NMRRDG, 4/28/1920.

57, U.S. and Japanese superdreadnoughts—NMRRDG, 6/9/1920, 355.

58, "Pacific Armaments"—NMRRDG, 403.

58, William H. Seward on Pacific—Falk, 133.

58, Alfred Thayer Mahan on Pacific—ibid., 142.

59, "strategical situation"—SPP, 1, 27.

60, Maurice Prendergast's praise—Prendergast, PER, 260.

61, preface quotes—SPP, vi.

61, comparing navies—SPP, 67, 68, 148, 229.

62, "great discretion" and "prudence"—SPP, 188–89.

62, Guam—SPP, 262–66.

63, "terminate negotiations with Russia"—SPP, 280.

64, "well-nigh insolvable"—SPP, 287–88.

64–66, Mahan on Danube—Mahan, *Naval Strategy*, 22–25, 58.

66, "concentration"—ibid., 6.

66, "between Port Arthur and Baltic"—ibid., 40, 126.

67, "worse than useless"—ibid., 127.

67, Eisenhower on Philippines—Manchester, 185.

68, Kyllmann—Arnold, 26–29.

68, Kyllmann's "stable"—Mumby, 386–87; Arnold, 89–90.

68, HCB's letters to Constable & Co.—Constable & Co., PAP.

68–70, correspondence with Kyllmann, contract—HCB, Constable & Co., PAP.

70, Sims's review—*Atlantic Monthly*, 11/1921, 8.

7 AN EXHILARATING POSSIBILITY

71, publication SPP in Japan—HCB, *Taiheiyo kaiken ron*; Preface contains publishing history and reference to "heavy requests."

71, "household word"—WHHC, Mitsuo Fuchida, 6/29/1967; Shigeru Fukudome, 4/29/1967; Sadatoshi Tomioka, 7/3/1967; and WHH, Ichiro Yokoyama, Tokyo, 1982; Kazutaka Niimi, Tokyo, 1982; Zenshiro Hoshina, Tokyo, 1982; Atsushi Oi, Tokyo, 1982; and Sadamu Sanagi, Tokyo, 1982.

71, Homer Lea—O'Connor, *Destiny*, 321.

71, translation of Mahan—Dingman, 14, 235.

72, "an authority"—Sato, *If Japan and America Fight* (English edition), 179–80.

72, "Island Empire"—SPP, 314.

73, "well-nigh insolvable"—SPP, 288.

73, Sato and Akiyama plan—*Senshi Sosho*, GOV DOC, vol. 91, 115, 124, 189, 214; Minoru Nomura, "*Tai-Bei-Ei Kaisen to Kaigun no Tai-Bei Shichiwari*

Shiso" in *Gunji Shigaku*, no. 2, 1973; WHH, Minoru Nomura, then chief, Second History Division, Military History Department, National Defense College, Tokyo, 1982; Dingman, 60, 125–26; Asada in Jordan, ed., 145–47.

73, "the Japanese Mahan"—Asada in Jordan, ed., 145.

73, Akiyama details—Peattie, PER, 60–69; Asada in Jordan, ed., 147.

73, Akiyama's Tsushima plan—Peattie, PER, 60–69; Marder, *Old Friends*, 319.

74, vicinity of Bonins—WHH, Minoru Nomura, op. cit.

74, attack on Philippines—Pelz, 28.

75, "sufficient to defend"—Asada in Jordan, ed., 147.

75, "intelligence reports"—Takagi, 65; R. E. Coontz to Edwin Denby, 2/27/1920, P.D. 198-2, Rec. Gp. 80, National Archives; Asada in Jordan, ed., 148; NYT reports on Farnsworth trial on 7/16 and 8/12/1936.

76, Mizuno's novel—Mizuno, *Tsugi*; Peattie, PAP, "Forecasting," 9–10, 51.

76, Kojiro Sato—Sato, *If Japan and America Fight* and *Japanese American War Fantasy*.

76, "no great sacrifice"—Sato, *If Japan and America Fight*, 20–25, 35.

76, Guam and Philippines indefensible—ibid., 22.

77, "If the American expeditionary force . . ."—ibid., 24–26.

77, Shirokita and Oto—Peattie, PAP, 5–8.

77, Toru Hattori, etc.—Akira, *Pacific Estrangement*, 38–59.

77, Peattie and Evans—PER.

77, Kato and Philippines—WHH, Minoru Nomura, op. cit.; Dingman, 60, 125–26.

77, Murofushi Takanobu—Yano, 151.

8 "SPECIAL LINE ON JAPANESE INFORMATION"

80, "wisely guided and crystallized"—Patterson, PAP, Paul Patterson to J. R. Scott, 9/5/1921.

81, "with romantic devotion"—BS, H. L. Mencken, 10/14/1927.

81, Patterson's London diary—Patterson, PAP.

81, H. G. Wells, Strachey, and Massingham—Johnson et al., 412–13.

82, "three printings"—see opposite title page of 1934 American edition of SPP.

82, "tiresome profundity"—BS, 8/19/1921.

82, USNIP review SPP—USNIP, 9/1921, 1486–1504.

83, Patterson's London diary—Patterson, PAP.

83, NYH details—O'Connor, *Mr. Bennett.*

83, Bywater given space—NYH, "Japan Soon to Stage Costly Naval Maneuvers," 8/7/1921; "Japan Speeding Up Naval Program," 8/28/1921; and "Japan's Naval Plans Dominate Pacific Question/Essential to Complete the Eight-Eight Programme, H. C. Bywater Finds . . ." 9/4/1921.

84, Keynes invitation—Patterson, PAP, Keynes to J. H. Adams, 9/9/1921.

84, "Some of my friends have told me"—Johnson et al., 411.

85, HCB's first *Sun* article—BS, 11/11/1921.

86, Washington Conference—Dingman, *Power in the Pacific.*

86, "dismantle existing forts"—BS, 11/18/1921.

87, "America . . . on her guard"—BS, 11/22/1921.

87, HCB on *Mutsu*—BS, 11/14 and 12/3/1921.

87, "submarine cruiser"—BS, 11/30/1921, 1.

87, Japanese submarines—HCB, PER, "Japanese and American Naval Power," 708.

88, Seizo Kobayashi—DT, 8/2/1933; pro-British reputation, FO 371/21044, Public Record Office, Kew, England.

88, Japanese newspapers—BS, 4/1/1925.

88, Malcom Kennedy's recollection—WHHC, Mrs. Aline Buxton (his daughter), Longmeadow, Woodlane, Neston, South Wirral, Cheshire, England, 10/15 and 11/17/1982.

89, Kennedy–Young squabble—*Japan Weekly Chronicle*, 12/3/1925, 720.

89, "complimentary references to Bywater"—Kennedy, *The Military Side of Japanese Life*, 312–13, 336; *Some Aspects of Japan and Her Defense Forces*, 55, 77, 119, 121, 211, 221; *The Changing Fabric of Japan*, 261; *The Estrangement of Great Britain and Japan*, 1917–35, 111, 303, 347; and *A History of Japan*, 317.

Also, according to Hugh Byas, the dean of foreign correspondents in Tokyo during the 1920s and 1930s, Kennedy was obliged to seek supplementary work while employed by Reuters. "Reuter only pays him a half salary, so he supplements his income by working hard in various fields of correspondence which do not conflict with his Reuter duties," Byas wrote to his editor in London, recommending Kennedy for a job. See Byas letters to London *Sunday Times*, 4/13/1929 and 12/26/1929, Archives of the London *Sunday Times*, London, England.

89, "greatest diplomatic triumph"—BS, 12/12/1921.

90, "new epoch"—BS, 12/15/1921.

90, "splendid work"—BS, 12/23/1921, 6.

90, *Sun* recognized for coverage—Garrison, chapter on "The Baltimore *Sun*s: A Notable Journalistic Resurrection."

91, "conceded here"—J. H. Adams to HCB, 1/3/1922, in files of Rev. Hector W. R. Bywater, Derby, England.

9 BYWATER VS. ROOSEVELT

95, Dewey could have been stranded—Braisted, I, 230.

95, Sperry induced dealers—ibid.

95, Japan invulnerable—HCB, PER, "The Limitation of Naval Armaments," 269.

96, HCB "wrestled"—BS, "Stopped War in the Pacific," 2/7/1922; "What Japan Thinks of the Naval Treaty," 3/11/1922; "Arms Conference Was a Triumph for Japan," 3/31/1922; "Japan Happy," 4/14/1922; "Events Foreshadow Big Changes in Japan," 4/16/1922; "Naval Treaty Has Not Had Hoped For Effect," 5/1/1922; "Did Japan Outwit U.S. at Naval Conference?" 10/13/1922; and "Brighter Outlook Beyond Pacific," 12/31/1922.

97, "fallacious"—HCB, PER, "Japan: A Sequel to the Washington Conference."

97, "prove irresistible"—HCB, PER, "The Spirit of the Treaty: Recent Naval Developments in Japan."

97, infantile paralysis—Freidel, II, 98.

97, Roosevelt influenced by SPP and Pitkin—copies of the first edition of SPP and *Must We Fight Japan?* in Roosevelt's personal library at the Franklin D. Roosevelt Library, Hyde Park, New York. Both books are also cited as having influenced Roosevelt by Dallek, 16, and Freidel, II, 31.

98, Roosevelt's comment—Dallek, 16

98, Roosevelt's fascination, Daniels—Freidel, II, 28–29, 155.

98, Roosevelt pro-big-Navy—Freidel, II, 220–25; Daniels, J., 107.

99, Roosevelt to George Marvin—Roosevelt, PAP, FDR to Marvin, 10/10/1922.

99, Boston *Transcript* editorial—"Sea Power in the Pacific," 10/6/1922, pt. 2, 2.

99, William Howard Gardiner essay—Gardiner, PER; also Gardiner obituary, NYT, 6/22/1951, 69.

99, Gardiner letters—Gardiner, PAP, Gardiner to HCB, 4/27/1921, *52M–295, Item 32, Box 3, "Political & Military Miscellany," manila folder labeled Bywater, Hector C.; Gardiner to William S. Sims, 9/27 and 10/10/1921 and 2/19/1922; and Sims to Gardiner, 8/19 and 9/29/1921, Box 2, "Political & Military Miscellany," manila folder labeled Sims, William S.

100, Roosevelt outlines article—Roosevelt, PAP, Roosevelt to Marvin, 10/10/1922.

100, "The Japs—A Habit of Mind"—ibid., Roosevelt to Marvin, 11/12/1922.

100, galleys sent to FDR—ibid., Marietta Neff of *Asia* magazine to Roosevelt, 5/8/1923; Roosevelt on cover of *Time*, 5/28/1923.

100–101, Roosevelt's article—Roosevelt, Franklin D., PER.

101, Adams sends Roosevelt article—Roosevelt, PAP, J. H. Adams to Roosevelt, 7/23/1923.

101, HCB's comment—BS, 7/21/1923.

102, "whatever you may wish to say"—Roosevelt, PAP, J. H. Adams to Roosevelt, 7/23/1923.

102, "I will tone it down"—ibid., Roosevelt to J. H. Adams, 8/13/1923.

102–103, Roosevelt on HCB—BS, 9/3/1923.

103, HCB's fifth book—HCB, *Navies and Nations*, 152.

103, HCB essay some years later—SPP, 1934 edition, preface to new edition, xx–xxii.

104, Hughes quote—Link and Catton, 347.

104, "swollen-headed Prussian"—BS, 1/3/1925.

104, "best method of avoiding it"—BS, 9/27/1924.

105, "stepping-stone"—GPW, 153.

105, Abukir—Robinson, 439.

105–106, du Pont, Dahlgren—ibid., 598–602, 642–43.

106, Albert Parker Niblack's "stepping-stones"—Niblack, PER, "The Maintenance of the Fleet," 107–15; HCB credits this essay in Preface, SPP.

106–107, Gallipoli—Robinson, 849–50.

107, "gift from the gods"—Brodie, 174.

107, Dwight Eisenhower—Ambrose, I, 117.

107, Eisenhower and Douglas MacArthur—Manchester, 184–85. Some historians have dismissed MacArthur's statements about the invulnerability of the Philippines as bluff calculated to intimidate the Japanese, but the fact that he deeply believed what he was saying is evident from the verbatim transcript of his meeting with the British Admiral Tom Phillips on 12/5/1941. MacArthur confidently declared that his "ace units" of B-17 bombers, along with his Filipino militia and a dozen light tanks, would stop a Japanese invasion force "on the beaches." Phillips's fleet, MacArthur said, could then use Manila Bay as the "Scapa Flow of the Far East." See Costello, PER, 61.

107, "iron will to conquer"—SPP, 299–300.

108, HCB aware Japanese proficiency—GPW, 42.

108, HCB's three routes—GPW, Alaska, 183; Midway–Wake, 75; southern, 75, 185–239.

108, HCB's references to Roosevelt—ibid., v, 101, 150.

10 KESTON POND MANEUVERS

112, Arthur Herbert Torrington's letter—Mahan, *Lessons of the War with Spain*, 76; Rodger, 35–39.

112, Viscount Jellico of Scapa—HCB, *The Two White Nations*, 41.

113, "difficult to bring to action"—NMRRDG, 4/20/1920.

113, "tremendous advantage"—SPP, 289.

114, HCB's model collection—WHHC, Rev. Hector W. R. Bywater, 8/20/1980, and WHH, Rev. Bywater, Derby, England, 1980, identify "Barbette's" article "Model Naval Construction" in *Model Engineer and Electrician*, London, 9/29/1921, 264–65, as the work of HCB containing an accurate description of his collection of model ships.

114, Stevens' Model Dockyard—see advertisement in Percival Marshall's *Model Steamer Building: A Practical Handbook for the Design and Construction of Model Steamer Hulls and Fittings* (Percival Marshall & Co., London, 1902), 74.

115, "latent in our country"—N, 1/1922, 19.

115, "a liberal education" N, 4/1922, 95–96.

115, "German Zeppelin"—*Model Engineer and Electrician*, London, 4/27/1933, 400.

115, model detailing—ibid., 235.

116, H. G. Wells's *Kriegspiel*—Wells, *Little Wars.*
116, Naval War College—Honan, PER, "Return of the Battleship."
116, cost of Jane's game—Jane, "How to Play the Naval War Game," 26.
117, objectives of Jane's game—ibid., 8.
117, "things outside calculation"—ibid., 10.
118, HCB's model maneuvers—WHH, Rev. Hector W. R. Bywater, Derby, England, 1980; WHHC, Rev. Bywater, 5/9/1967 and 8/20/1980; WHH, Sylvia and John Newland, Cornwall, England, 1980, and New York City, 9/1980; George J. Bryant, East Horsley, Leatherhead, Surrey, England, 1979; E. A. Harwood, Godalming, Surrey, England, 1979; WHHC, Harwood, 8/5/1980; Donald McCormick, Beckenham, 4/9 and 6/16/1981. E. L. Goodman is mentioned in Archibald Hurd's *Who Goes There?* 31, 39.
119, HCB's imaginings—GPW, 282–84.
120–121, "a decisive result"—GPW, 246, 262–64, 265.

11 *LES GUERRES IMAGINAIRES*

123, *Les guerres imaginaires*—Clarke, I. F., 79.
124, William Ewart Gladstone—Clarke, I. F., PER, 309–28.
124, Philip Colomb—Colomb et al., *The Great War of 189—.*
125, William Laird Clowes—Clowes, *The Great Naval War of 1887.*
125–126, Lea—O'Connor, 300–329; Lea, Introduction by Clare Boothe.
126, Marines "disappear"—Lea, 173.
126, 100,000 men invade—ibid., 178.
126, HCB on Lea—GPW, 74–75, 149.
126, H. W. Wilson—*The Invasion of 1910.*
127, HCB on Wilson—SI, 16.
127, Burgoyne in Secret Service—see Chapter 3, "Our Splendid Spy in Germany," note 3.
127, Burgoyne details—DT obituary 4/27/1929 probably written by Bywater.
127, *Navy League Annual—Navy League Annual*, 1909–15, Alan H. Burgoyne, ed. Navy League, London.
127, messenger tells King—Burgoyne, 55.
128, "Tike that, you German sausage"—ibid., 119.
128, "And it was these guns"—ibid., 221.
129, "Their contour . . ."—ibid., 225.
130, "Possible Features"—HCB, "Possible Features of a North Sea Campaign," PER, Chap. 10, 197–209.
131, Coronel—HCB, "Coronel and the Falklands: Some Reflections," N, 1/1915, 8–10.
131, "boys' magazine"—WHHC, Rev. Hector W. R. Bywater, Derby, England, 5/9/1967.
131, "if war had been averted . . ."—N, 5/1923, 122–24.

12 "IT MIGHT FOMENT TROUBLE"

133–134, X–1—HCB, "Mastodons of The Deep," PER, 39.

134, facilities (as journalist) stopped—Index, GOV DOC (ADM 12/1673).

134, "like a leper"—WHH, Rev. Hector W. R. Bywater, Derby, England, 1979.

134, "severed his connection"—USNIP, 9/1924, 1535.

135, Pooley and McGovern—Preface to SPP, numerous newspaper articles, and especially HCB's "Japanese Naval Policy."

135, Mizuno essay—BS, 8/17 and 8/18/1923; Peattie, PAP, 9–10, 51; Dingman, 210, 279.

135, Japanese in China—GPW, 1–70.

135, "superfluous formality"—ibid., 21.

136, "hurl an 'overwhelming' force"—GPW, 34.

136, American fleet destroyed—ibid., 40.

136, *Kongo, Hiyei, Kirishima, Hosho*—ibid., 34.

136, "something in the air . . . tells us"—ibid., 32.

137, Elkins—ibid., 39–43.

137, 2,500 fallen—ibid., 42.

138, not "dream of taking up intelligence work again"—SI, 37.

138, 1920 translation—HCB, trans., *The Two White Nations*: date of translation, HCB as trans., and Naval Intelligence Division imprimatur appear on title page.

138, HCB's 1923 mission—BS, 12/14/1923; DT, 9/29/1930.

139–140, HCB–William Howard Gardiner—Gardiner to HCB re Harding, 2/6/1923; HCB to Gardiner, 5/9/1924; and Gardiner to HCB, 6/1/1924, Gardiner, PAP.

139–142, HCB–Greenslet correspondence—letters and cables exchanged 5/5/1924 to 10/31/1925. See Greenslet, Ferris, PAP, 89–22ll; Greenslet obituary in NYT, 11/20/1959.

140, Philippines hold out two weeks—GPW, 62.

140, "Bureau of Operations . . ."—ibid., 160–61.

140, parallels with Orange—RJB; also Morton, PER, "War Plan Orange."

13 *THE GREAT PACIFIC WAR*

143, "bolt from the blue"—GPW, 31.

144, "at the military depots for years"—ibid., 42

145, defenses of Manila and Subig Bay—ibid., 43.

146, Lea's Philippines invasion—Lea, 253.

146, HCB requests map—Greenslet, Ferris, PAP.

148, "250 miles of possible landing beaches"—Manchester, 185.

148, "ignore the rudiments"—GPW, 74–75, 149.

148, invasion of American mainland—SPP, 261.

148, Dutch East Indies and Singapore—BS, 5/1/1925, 5/25/1925.

149, "Were Japan, for some inscrutable reason"—HCB, *Navies and Nations*, 96–97.

150, "closely approached the ideal"—GPW, 60–61, 67–68.

150, "reckless American stab"—ibid., 163–79.

151, Sims suggestion—*Atlantic Monthly*, 11/1921, 8.

152, Harper's tactics—ibid., 183, 185, 229, 239, 240–41, 245, 254–55.

152–154, Battle of Yap—ibid., 278–96.

154–155, *Mutsu's* charge—ibid., 291–92.

155, destroyer's sharp prow—ibid., 58.

156, air attack on Dutch Harbor—ibid., 205–07.

157, Kyllman, March 8—Constable & Co., PAP.

157–158, Bywater–Greenslet correspondence—Greenslet, Ferris, PAP.

14 WRONG END OF THE TELESCOPE

159–160, "I am able to state . . ."—DN, 4/16/1925

160, "For this reason . . ."—BS, 5/9/1925, 9

160, Malcolm Kennedy—Kennedy's letter to *Japan Weekly Chronicle* of 12/3/1925, 720, reveals he alone among Tokyo correspondents was filing stories parallel to those HCB now began to write.

160, 35 percent—DN, 5/6/1925, 8; NYT, 4/28/1925, 23.

160, demanded explanation—NYT, 5/18/1924, II, 2.

160, "I have myself . . ."—BS, 6/18/1924.

161, "trying to create a sensation"—NYT, 4/28/1925, 23; DN, 5/5/1925, 8.

161, defended himself—DN, 5/5/1925, 8.

161, *Furutaka*—DN, 5/2/1925, 7.

161, *Akagi*—DN, 6/1/1925, 9.

162, *Post, Telegraph*—Trans-Pacific, 6/20/1925, 7.

162, *Guardian*—Trans-Pacific, 7/11/1925.

162, London *Times*—5/15/1925, 15a.

163, HCB replies—BS, 6/13/1925, 9.

163, Curtis and Russell—Trans-Pacific, 6/6/1925, 7.

164, "Personally, I do not believe . . ."—BS, 6/13/1925, 9.

164, "bending over backward"—BS, 7/12/1925, 11.

164, cruiser outlook—DN, 6/17/1925, 9.

164, editorial support—DN, 6/18/1925, 6.

165, "as late as 1935"—Roskill, II, 188–89.

15 "PROPHETIC!" "MISCHIEVOUS!" "A BUNGLE!"

167, announcement—*New York Evening Post*, 7/16/1925, 9.

168, Nicholas Roosevelt—NYT, 9/13/1925, *Book Review*, 1.

168n, FDR close to Nicholas—FDR offers to send Thomas G. Frothingham ms. to Nicholas in 1925, Roosevelt, PAP, "Papers Pertaining to Family, Business and Personal Affairs, 1882–1945," Box 84.

169, Charles N. Robinson—LT *Literary Supplement*, 7/30/1925, 502.

169, *Booklist*—1/1926, 143.

169, *Punch*—9/1925.

169, *The Nation and The Athenaeum*—8/29/1925, 653–54.

169, *Outlook*—10/14/1925.

169, *New Republic*—10/21/1925.

169, *Saturday Review of Literature*—12/5/1925, 385.

169, *Boston Independent*—10/17/1925, 451.

169–170, Eugene O'Neill—Gelb, 610.

170, Archibald Hurd—DT, 8/11/1925.

170, Maurice Prendergast—N, 9/1925, 260–63, and 10/1925, 282–83.

170, USNIP—10/1925, 1988–90.

170, Frederic Maurice—*Empire Review*, 1/1926.

170–172, *Forum*—6/1926, 808–19.

172, *Kokumin*—Japan Weekly Chronicle, 9/24/1925, 395.

172, *Asahi* and *Nichi Nichi*—Kennedy, *Changing Fabric*, 180–203.

172, *Nichi Nichi* and *Chugai Shogyo*—Japan Weekly Chronicle, 9/17/1925, 350.

173, A. Morgan Young and Joseph M. Kenworthy—*Japan Weekly Chronicle*, 9/17/1925, 349–50.

173, "Japanese diplomats"—*New Republic*, 10/21/1925.

173, "from time to time . . ."—BS, 8/13/1926, 9.

174, B. W. Fleisher—*Trans-Pacific*, 9/3/1927, 1.

174, *Kokumin* (Tokutomi)—*Japan Weekly Chronicle*, 9/24/1925, 395.

175, Kyoji Kitagami—Japanese translator, GPW.

175, Seijiro Kawashima and Teisuke Akiyama—*Trans-Pacific*, 6/5/1926, 4.

175–176, Tota Ishimaru—Japanese translator, GPW.

176, "Japanese *Mein Kampf*"—Matsuo.

16 "ATTACK AMERICANS AT HAWAII"

177–179, Isoroku Yamamoto career and personality—Agawa, Kuzuoka, Sorimachi.

179, Yamamoto's arrival—Isoroku Yamamoto, Record Group 59 (701.9411/504), Sub-Group 1910–29, Decimal File, National Archives and Records Service, Diplomatic Branch, Civil Archives Division, Washington, D.C.

179, Lake Denmark arsenal—NYT, 7/18/1926, 13.

180, "America being what it is . . ."—U.S. Strategic Bombing Survey (Pacific), Interrogation no. 455 with Rear Admiral Ichiro Yokoyama; also, WHH, Yokoyama, Tokyo, 6/10/1982.

180, Sandburg's *Lincoln* biography—WHHC, Seiichi Soeda, 3/23/1985, recounting interview with Yoshimasa Yamamoto; see also Agawa, 84.

180, Forty newspapers per day—Sorimachi, 1, 248; also, BS, 12/18/1921, 17:3.

181, Yamamoto and Turner—WHHC, Seiichi Soeda, 3/23/1985 letter recounting interview with Yoshimasa Yamamoto.

181, Richmond K. Turner—obituary, NYT, 2/14/1961.

181, Hiroshi Saito reports on HCB—Saito to Foreign Minister Shidehara, 6/4/1926, Collection of Miscellaneous Documents Concerning Japan and Other Countries (Japan and Britain), 1902–1923, classmark 1/1/4/1-7, *Gaiko Shiryokan*, Tokyo.

182, "One does not fight . . ."—NYT, 1/2/1926, 5:1.

182, Tsuneo Matsudaira reports on HCB—Matsudaira to Foreign Minister Shidehara, 8/28/1926, Collection of Miscellaneous Documents Concerning Japan and Other Countries (Japan and America), vol. 5, classmark 1/1/3/3-1, *Gaiko Shiryokan*, Tokyo.

182, Masanao Uehara reports on HCB—Uehara to Count Koya Uchida, 7/2/1923, Collection of Miscellaneous Documents Concerning Japan and Other Countries (Japan and Britain), 1902–1923, classmark 1/1/4/1-7, *Gaiko Shiryokan*, Tokyo.

182, Toshihiko Taketomi reports on HCB—Taketomi to Foreign Minister Shidehara, 6/11/1926, Collection of Miscellaneous Documents Concerning Japan and Other Countries (Japan and America), vol. 5, classmark 1/1/3/3-1, *Gaiko Shiryokan*, Tokyo.

183, Yamamoto communicated directly to 3rd Division of Navy General Staff and other details about work and practices of the naval attaché—U.S. Strategic Bombing Survey (Pacific), Interrogation no. 455; also WHH, Ichiro Yokoyama, Tokyo, 6/10/1982; Atsushi Oi, 6/9/1982, Tokyo.

183, "The Debate Concerning a Japanese-American War"—Collection of Miscellaneous Documents Concerning Japan and Other Countries (Japan and America), vol. 5, classmark 1/1/3/3-1, *Gaiko Shiryokan*, Tokyo; also *Coast Artillery Journal* (Fort Monroe, Va.), 5/1926, 532.

183–184, Noburu Morita as Yamamoto's opposite number—United States, State Department, *Diplomatic List* (Monthly) (NY Public Library classmark XBKA), 1926, 1927. See also U.S. State Dept. correspondence on Yamamoto in National Archives, which frequently mentions Morita.

184, "The Debate Concerning a U.S.-Japanese War and Observations About Japan That Recently Appeared in the U.S. Press"—Collection of Miscellaneous Documents Concerning Japan and Other Countries (Japan and America), 1923–1926, vol. 5, classmark 1/1/3/3-1, *Gaiko Shiryokan*, Tokyo.

184, third article quoted—ibid.; also BS, 8/7/1926, 7.

184, fourth article—ibid., plus *Literary Digest*, 7/17/1926, 13–14; see also *Trans-Pacific*, 6/5/1926, 4.

184, *Isuzu*—Service record of Isoroku Yamamoto, Historical Record Branch, U.S. Army Center of Military History, Washington, D.C.; see also Agawa, 87.

184, details about *Isuzu*—Jentschura et al., 107–08.

185, mah-jongg, etc.—Agawa, 87–88.

185, Sadamu Sanagi on Oshima—WHH, Sadamu Sanagi, Tokyo, 1982.

185, Oshima's recollection—Compilation Committee, GOV DOC, Japanese, vol. 1, 278. Note that John J. Stephan in *Hawaii Under the Rising Sun*, 74, translates Oshima's statement as meaning "invasion" rather than "attack" on Hawaii. Since Oshima used the word *"shinko"*(meaning attack by advancement) rather than the more precise *"koryaku"* (invasion) or *"kogeki"* (attack), his meaning is ambiguous. However, Oshima went on to say that Yamamoto's lecture suggests the origin of his plan to raid Pearl Harbor, and thus it seems evident that he intended *"shinko"* to mean raid or attack, not invasion.

186, Pearl Harbor in 1928—U.S. Navy Directory, 1927–28.

186, Pearl Harbor dredging—NYT, 12/2/1926; Dillingham, USNIP, 410.

17 WAR PLAN ORANGE

188, "it was piously hoped"—Morton, PER.

188, 1907 Orange—RJB, 6/18/1907.

189, 1924 Orange—RJB, 8/15/1924.

189, James H. Oliver—Secretary of Navy to President, 1919, National Archives, R. G. 45, Subj. file 1911–27, Naval Records Collection of the Office of Naval Records and Library, WA-5, Japan and the Allies, Box 604, P. D. 198-2.

189, Earl "Pete" Ellis—Ballendorf, PER; Reber, PER; Earl Ellis file, Reference Section, History Branch, History and Museum Division of the Marine Corps Historical Center, Washington Navy Yard, Washington, D.C.

189, William S. Sims, John A. Lejeune, Alfred P. Niblack, et al.—Millett, 321–27; Isely and Crowl, 26–29.

191–192, HCB's Port Lloyd plan—GPW, 134–54.

192, "evil fortune"—GPW, 169.

193, "ill-starred expedition"—GPW, 179.

193, Mahan, Colomb—GPW, 171.

196, 1926 Orange—RJB, 11/10/1926, File 325, serial 280.

196, Sims on HCB—*Atlantic Monthly*, 11/1921, 8.

197, William V. Pratt on HCB—Pratt, PAP.

197, Gardiner on HCB—Gardiner, PAP.

197, "You've said it!"—HCB, PER, "Japanese and American Naval Power in the Pacific."

197, 1935 Orange—RJB, Joint Planning Committee to Joint Board, 4/23/1935.

197, HCB's island-hopping—GPW, 183, 185, 229, 239, 240–41, 245, 254–55.

18 WORLD'S LEADING AUTHORITY

199, Morris "Bullnose"—WHH, Sylvia Newland, Cornwall, England, 8/1979.

200, "country will remain unmoved"—BS, 2/7/1926, 11.

200, "blunder after blunder"—DN, 8/7/1927; BS, 8/7/1927, 9.

200, "damaging facts to be hidden"—HCB, PER, "The British Navy To-Day," 639.

200, "facilities as journalist restored"—Index of Admiralty Correspondence from the Admiralty Secretariat, 1927, Hector Chas. Bywater, Naval journalist, Public Record Office, Kew, England (ADM 12/1689) N.I.D., 0349/27.

201, "lament its passing"—BS, 4/20/1930, 9.

201, "almost sacrilegious"—HCB, PER, "The Limitation of Naval Armaments," 261.

202, "lord of the sea"—NMRRDG, 3/15/1919, 151.

202, "is another battleship"—BS, 10/9 and 10/10/1924.

202, check for $200—H. A. Baldridge, secretary treasurer USNI to HCB, 1/29/1926, files of Rev. Hector W. R. Bywater.

202, "hoodwinked"—WHH, Sylvia Newland, Cornwall, England, 6/1979.

202, prize announced—BS, 1/30/1926, 1.

202–204, prize-winning essay—HCB, PER, "The Battleship and its Uses," 407–26.

206, Hurd's resignation—memorandum written by Hurd to the new management of the *Daily Telegraph* and undated draft letter to Arthur Watson, folder 1/12, Hurd, PAP.

206, 700 pounds per anum—Staff Records Book, Hector C. Bywater, Office of Company Secretary, DT, London.

207, "new naval weapons"—DT, 2/18/1928.

207–208, *Panzerschiffe* details—DT, 2/23 and 3/29/1928.

208, *Bremen, Europa* launching—DT, 8/21/1928; SI, 76.

208, Paul von Hindenburg—BS, 9/29/1928, 13.

209, pocket battleships—DT, 8/21/1928.

209, more on pocket battleships—DT, 8/28/1928; BS, 8/28/1928.

209, definitive description—DT, 12/28/1928; BS, 12/28/1928; see also recapitulation in DT, 1/17/1929.

209, "whole scheme of armament restriction"—BS, 1/22/1929.

209, "tons and guns"—HCB, *A Searchlight on the Navy*, 299.

209, "We should have no difficulty"—NMRRDG, 5/23/1919, 262.

210, Knox on pocket battleships—BS, 1/24/1929, 13.

210, Knox reviews GPW—BS, 9/21/1925.

210, HCB praises Knox—BS, 1/13/1926, 9.

210–211, Sims and Frank H. Schofield on war with Britain—William R. Braisted, "On the American Red and Red-Orange Plans, 1919–1939," in *Naval Warfare in the Twentieth Century, 1900–1945*, Gerald Jordan, ed., 171.

211, "difficult to reconcile"—BS, 7/15/1926, 13.

211, "open to grave dispute"—BS, 7/21/1926, 11.

211, "an entirely new fleet"—BS, 8/22/1926, 7.

211, Knox urges censoring—Davies, PER, 165.

211, "intellectual foreign propagandists"—Dudley W. Knox, "The Navy and Public Indoctrination," USNIP, 6/1929.

211, "Editor's Note" on HCB and Knox—BS, 6/4/1929.

212, HCB on small warships—BS, 5/13/1931, 11.

212, "clever British propaganda"—"Bywater's Ideas Draw Fire of Navy," BS, 5/14/1931, 13. **Note:** This article appears only in D edition of vol. 188 microfilm in morgue of the *Sun*; it does not appear in C edition preserved on the Bell and Howell microfilm held by the Library of Congress, the New York Public Library, and others.

212, HCB makes light of Knox—BS, 12/30/1929, 13.

212, Van Lear Black—WHHC, Hector W. R. Bywater, 12/22/1967; HCB's memoir "By a Personal Friend," DT, 8/20/1930, 11.

213, HCB moves to NYT—letters and cables between Charles A. Selden and Frederick T. Birchall, 1/1931 to 5/1931, *New York Times* Archives, 229 W. 43rd Street, New York, N.Y.

213, HCB praises Knox—DT, 6/17/1938.

213, "tongue lashing"—WHH, Rev. Hector W. R. Bywater, Derby, England, 1979.

213, HCB and Basil Liddell Hart—Liddell Hart Centre for Military Archives, King's College, London. See Liddell Hart correspondence, PAP.

213–214, HCB's second marriage—DT, 12/7/1931.

214, "viceregal throne of Neptune"—DT, 12/30/1933, 10.

214, HCB's "series"—DT, 7/4/1933.

214, Kipling's frequent contributions to DT—DT, 1/18/1936, 9.

214, HCB–Kipling correspondence—Bywater to Kipling, 6/9/1933; Kipling to Bywater, 6/12/1933; Bywater to Kipling, 6/15/1933. Kipling, PAP.

215, Charles A. Beard on HCB—Beard, PER, 264.

215, HCB invited to inspect French and Italian navies—HCB, "Italy's War Gamble," London *News-Chronicle*, 4/20/1940; *A Searchlight on the Navy*, 290, 294.

215, Italy's secret construction—DT, 7/25/1932; NYT, 7/25/1932, 1; Italian denial, NYT, 7/26/1932, 9. See also, Arthur Brisbane in *New York American*, 7/26/1932.

215, *Cadorna*—DT, 4/30/1934.

216, HCB meets Mussolini—WHH, E. A. Harwood, Godalming, Surrey, England, 1979; Dulin and Garzke, *Axis*, 383.

216, HCB interviews Mussolini—DT, 5/14/1934, 1.

19 "WE SAILORS GET ON ADMIRABLY TOGETHER"

218, Will Rogers—NYT, 7/7/1927, 27.

218, HCB and Yamamoto first met in 1930—DT, 2/3/1930, HCB reports meeting all Japanese delegates.

219, "relieve unemployment"—NYT, 8/25/1933, 14:1.

219–220, HCB's common-aggregate-tonnage proposal—DT, 2/13/1933; reprinted in *A Searchlight on the Navy*, 232–39.

220, Tsuneo Matsudaira sends HCB articles—Reports Prior to the London Naval Disarmament Conference of 1935 (1933–34), B/10/4/0/2-2, Report from Ambassador Matsudaira to Foreign Minister Koki Hirota in Tokyo, 10/21 and 10/31/1933, *Gaiko Shiryokan*, Tokyo.

220, Malcolm Kennedy reports HCB's influence in Japan—Kennedy, *Estrangement*, 303. Also, HCB essay echoed by *Jiji* and *Chugai* reported in *Japan Advertiser*, 12/13 and 12/15/1933. See also Yamamoto statement in FO 371/18732, 1, Public Record Office, Kew, London.

220, Kanji Kato's paper—Pelz, 27–88.

220, France and Italy on common upper limit—HCB, *A Searchlight on the Navy*, 237.

221, Military Council of 6/8/1934—Pelz, 39–40.

221, "departure for actual warfare"—*Trans-Pacific*, 9/27/1934.

222, Yamamoto's proposal—CAB 29, 149; XCIA 1301, 282, Public Record Office, Kew, London.

222, "quite impossible"—Roskill, II, 296.

222, Craigie's reaction—FO 371/18732, 39–40, Public Record Office, Kew, London.

222, HCB and Yamamoto meet—DT, 12/4/1934.

223–226, HCB's account of Yamamoto meeting—DT, 12/4/1934.

225, "It can now be disclosed"—DT, 1/11/1936, 11.

226, update GPW—HCB, PER, "Japanese and American Naval Power in the Pacific," 168–75.

20 THE MONSTER BATTLESHIP CRISIS

228, "appeared to welcome it"—DT, 12/18/1935, 15.

228, Osami Nagano's object—Pelz, 159.

228, "a substantial reduction"—DT, 12/18/1935.

228, "might as well break up at once"—DT, 12/19/1935.

228, Nagano pledged—Pelz, 164.

229, Canal width 110 feet, Hood 105.75 feet—Hoyt, *Hood*; DT, 4/6/1937.

229, 63,000 tons—Friedman, 40; Dulin and Garzke, *Axis*, 45.

230, details on *Yamatos*—W. David Dickson, "*Yamato*," in *Warship International*, no. 4, 1975, 294–318 (Naval Records Club, 726 North Reynolds

Road, Toledo, Ohio 43615); Jentschura et al., 38–39; "The Design and
Construction of the *Yamato* and *Musashi*," USNIP, 10/1953; and Dulin
and Garzke, *Axis*, 43–125.

230, *Aki, Satsuma*—SPP, 148.

231, four 43,500-ton superdreadnoughts—ibid., 204–05; HCB, NYH, 9/4/1921.

231, 40,000-ton battleship and 44,000-ton battle cruiser—GPW, 259, 287, 290.

231, "greatest naval drydock"—DT, 1/4/1930.

231, "observe complete secrecy"—DT, 4/16/1936.

231, "tendentious fiction"—DT, 2/6/1936.

232, not "laying down monster ships"—DT, 6/24, 7/22, 9/3, 10/6 and 12/17/
1936.

232, "superior financial and technical resources"—DT, 7/22/1936.

232, "two or three years hence"—DT, 4/6/1937.

232, "overshadowed in fighting value"—DT, 6/4/1937.

232, DT reports Italian article—DT, 11/8/1937, 13.

233, "three are battleships of 46,000 tons"—"Japan and Her Fleet," *Giornale
d'Italia*, Rome, 11/7/1937; *Il Messaggero*, Rome, 11/7/1937.

233, "two of which are already in hand"—DT, 11/22/1937, 7.

234, Hanson W. Baldwin knew Bywater—WHH, Hanson Baldwin, New York,
6/1967.

234, "semi-official confirmation"—NYT, 12/12/1937, 1.

235, William D. Leahy relied on press reports—U.S. Congress, GOV DOC,
American.

235, British believe Japan exceeding 35,000-ton limit—memorandum, XCA
1359, CAB 4/27, Public Record Office, Kew, London.

235, Britain to ask U.S. for information—FO 371/20650, Public Record Office,
Kew, London.

236, Admiralty report on 42,000- or 43,000-ton Japanese ships—CAB 4/27,
XCA 1359, Public Record Office, Kew, London.

236, Alfred Duff Cooper proposal to CID—CAB 2/7, XC/A 001356, Public
Record Office, London.

236, "JAPAN BUILDING . . ."—DT 1/15/38, 13.

236, "Four days later . . ."—DT 1/19/38.

237, U.S. Navy believed only 45,000 tons—Dulin and Garzke, *Axis*, 51.

237, Koki Hirota's reply—*Tokyo Gazette*, no. 8, 2/1938, 23–27.

238, Yamamoto statement to Cox—LT, 2/14/1938, 11.

238, LT on Yamamoto—LT, 2/14/1938, 13.

239, unleashed naval arms race—Pelz, 188; Roskill, II, 419.

21 THE MOST VIOLENT DAY

241, low-level air battle—NC, 8/19/1940, 1.

242, Jane's office bombed—*Jane's Fighting Ships*, 1/1941, v.

242, "just stood there"—WHH, E. A. Harwood, Godalming, Surrey, England, 1979.

242, "apologetic Editor's Note"—Watson's note stated that although Bywater's article pointed out "certain deficiencies [in the Royal Navy] which cannot immediately be remedied," it also emphasized "the heartening effect of the new increase in fighting power on the spirit and zeal of the personnel." DT, 2/10/1939.

242–243, Arthur Watson fires George Gedye—*Curtain Raiser*, the unpublished autobiography of George Gedye, vol. 21, 48, Papers of George Eric Rowe Gedye, Imperial War Museum, London.

243, HCB's last paycheck—HCB entry, Telegraph Staff Records Book, Office of the Company Secretary, DT, London, England.

243, "failing health"—LT, 8/21/1940, 7; *Engineer* (London), 8/23/1940, 123.

243, George Bryant recalls—WHH, George J. Bryant, East Horsley, Leatherhead, Surrey, England, 1979.

243, David Woodward recalls—WHH, David Woodward, Randolph Hotel, Oxford, England, 1979.

243, E. A. Harwood recalls—WHH, E. A. Harwood, Godalming, Surrey, England, 1979.

243, "I think it will be conceded . . ."—BS, 9/3/1924; NYH, 10/2/1921, 3; N, 2/1914, 37.

243–244, "anti-Jewish frenzy"—NC, 3/16/1940, 7.

244, "no more territorial ambitions"—NC, 7/2/1940.

244, "like a harpooned whale"—NC, 8/2/1940.

244, Mrs. Perrin—Coroner's Officer's Report Concerning Death 19th August 1940, Hector Charles Bywater, Surrey County Hall, Kingston-upon-Thames, England.

245, "The Hole in the Wall"—WHH, Mrs. Margaret Savage, former proprietor; Denis Bryant; Cecil Riley, The Hole in the Wall, Park Road, Richmond, 1979. The Park Road Arms was known for two centuries by its patrons as "The Hole in the Wall" and changed its name to that in 1966.

245, Dr. Brunton, R. Donald Geare, Ulysses Bywater, Surrey County Coroner—Coroner's Officer's Report Concerning Death 19th August 1940, Hector Charles Bywater, Surrey County Hall, Kingston-upon-Thames, England.

246, HCB obituaries—NC, 8/19/1940, 2; NYT, 8/18/1940, 37; *New York Herald-Tribune*, 8/18/1940, 34; DT, 8/19/1940, 3; Manchester *Guardian*, 8/19/1940; LT, 8/21/1940, 7; *Engineer* (London), 8/23/1940, 123; N (London), 8/1940, 300; and BS, 8/18/1940, 12.

246, most violent day—Price.

246, action near Richmond—ibid, 31–32.

246, "all the teachings of history"—NC, 5/21/1940, 4.

247, autopsy . . .—Coroner's Officer's Report, as above.

247, HCB's remains cremated—telegram from Ulysses Bywater to Rev. Hector W. R. Bywater, 8/19/1940, from the latter's personal files. Mortlake Crematorium mentioned in obituary notices in DT, 8/22/1940.

247–248, Harwood's theory—WHH, E. A. Harwood, Godalming, Surrey, England, 1979.

248, Lord Halifax on Cox—LT, 7/30/1940, 4d.

248, *Kempei-tai*—Johnson, Chalmers, footnote, 8; Farago, 180.

248, Cox charged with possessing naval building plan—NYT, 8/16/1940, 4:5.

248, Cox as HCB's informant—WHH, Shahe Guebenlian, a longtime Reuters executive, Reuters, London, 1979; E. A. Harwood, Godalming, Surrey, England, 1979.

248–249, Melville Cox case—DT, 11/27/1940; London *Star*, 10/4/1940; *New York Sun*, 9/12/1940; *Singapore Free Press*, 11/22/1940; *Time* 9/16/1940, 43; Tolischus, 335; Hughes, 51–52; Fleisher, 307; Hygh Byas file, *Sunday Times* Archives, *Sunday Times*, London; WHH, Shahe Guebenlian, Reuters, London, 1979. See also, letter from Foreign Minister Yosuke Matsuoka to Ambassador Shigemitsu in London, 1/28/1941, Miscellaneous Documents of Japan-British Diplomatic Relations, 1940s, *Gaiko Shiryokan*, Tokyo.

249, Yamamoto takes command—service record of Yamamoto, Isoroku, History Records Branch, U.S. Army Center of Military History, Washington, D.C.

249, Yamamoto confides to Shigeru Fukudome—Fukudome memoir, Stillwell, 59.

249, Pacific fleet base—Beigel, PER.

249, security conscious—Stillwell, 60–61.

249, HCB believed life in danger—WHH, E. A. Harwood, Godalming, Surrey, England, 1979.

249, leather webbing—WHH, John Newland, Cornwall, England, 1979; WHHC, John Newland, 1967.

250, strychnine a favorite—Nishimura case, NYT, 12/8/1934, 9; DT, 12/6, 12/10, 12/11, 12/13 and 12/14/1934.

22 "I CAN GIVE THEM HELL"

251, Navy tells privy council—Pelz, 218.

251, Yamamoto to Fumimaro Konoye—Agawa, 232. Yamamoto also spoke of "a year and a half" as the limit of Japan's endurance to his friends Masahiro Yasuoka and Zengan Hashimoto, WHH, Zengan Hashimoto, *Kensho-ji* temple outside Nagoaka, Japan, 1982.

251, HCB's "a year and a half"—GPW, 256.

252, Newton and Leibnitz—For a lively putdown of the extravagant interpretation of coincidences, see Gardner, ed.

252, Togo's adaptation—*Brassey's Naval Annual*, 1906, 105–06. *Otsu* is a Chinese character similar to the letter "L" and thus implies an enveloping movement.

253, Yamamoto's notes—Tsunoda and Uchida, PER.

253, Top Secret Operation Order Number 1—GOV DOC, British and American.

253, six of ten carriers at risk—Jentschura et al., 40–58.

254, "supposed to be in Hawaiian waters"—ibid.; Prange, *At Dawn We Slept*, 332.

254, "overwhelming"—GPW, 34.

254, "wiping out"—ibid., 40.

254, "left the way open"—ibid., 41.

254–255, Yamamoto presents plan in April 1941—Prange, *At Dawn We Slept*, 104.

255, Nobutake Kondo opposition—ibid., 283.

255, Fukudome's opposition—ibid., 298.

255, Takijiro Onishi's "so insanely mad"—ibid., 261.

255, William D. Puleston—Puleston, 234–38.

256, HCB's books studied—WHHC, Mitsuo Fuchida, 6/29/1967.

256, Yamamoto dominates Table Top Maneuvers—WHH, Sadamu Sanagi, Tokyo, 1982; Prange, *At Dawn We Slept*, 223–31.

256, Yamamoto offers to resign—Prange, *At Dawn We Slept*, 297–99.

257, earliest Philippine invasion plan in 1926—"Naval Headquarters and General Fleet: Until the Opening of the War," *Senshi Sosho* (Official War History), vol. 91, 213–14.

257, Lingayen, Lamon, and Guam—"Operations to Attack and Occupy the Philippines," ibid, vol. 2, 10–76.

257, Nagano's plan—"1940 Imperial Navy Operation Plan by Chief of Naval Staff" (with pencil corrections for 1941). (*"Showa jugo-nando teiku kaigun sakusen keikaku kaigun gunrei-bu"*), Military History Department of the National Defense College, National Defense Agency, Tokyo (Boeicho Boei Kenshujo Senshibu Shiryoko).

257, Yamamoto's main and diversionary landings—CFTSOO, 2/33–2/38 and 36–38; Morton, *Philippines*, 57.

257, Between Cabalete and Alabat—Japanese Monograph no. 2, Philippines Operations Record, Phase 1, 11/1941–4/10/1942, 14th Army Operations, vol. 2, Office of the Chief of Military History, Dept. of the Army, Washington, D.C., 11.

257–258, HCB's three main landings—GPW, 56–59.

259, "prepare air bases quickly"—CFTSOO, 44.

259, MacArthur's predicted Philippine landings—Hunt, 6.

259, MacArthur's failure to defend Lamon Bay—Morton, *Philippines*, 141.

259, Albert M. Jones on Lamon Bay—Manchester, 185.

260, disadvantages of Lamon—Puleston, 136; Morton, *Philippines*, 139.

260, Puleston's analysis—Puleston, 136; Morton, *Philippines*, 50–53.

260, Roosevelt on Luzon—Roosevelt, PER.

260, invasion of Guam—Morton, *Strategy*, 133.

260, HCB on Guam—GPW, 79–95.

261, fate of *Nisshin*—ibid., 91.

261–262, HCB on air power—*Sea Power in the Pacific: New Edition* (Constable, London, 1934), xxi–xxii; also HCB, PER, "Japanese and American Naval Power in the Pacific."

262, Mitsuo Fuchida and Masatake Okumiya on Yamamoto's hopes for Midway—Fuchida and Okumiya, 76.

262, Fuchida and Okumiya quote Yamamoto on Midway—Fuchida and Okumiya, 64, 77.

262–263, "before this desirable result was attained"—GPW, 98.

263, "all might yet be well"—ibid., 257.

263, "react with all its available strength"—Fuchida and Okumiya, 78.

264, Battle of Yap—GPW, 263–64.

265, Tamon Yamaguchi proposal—Prange, *Midway*, 29, 34.

265, "to deliver the decisive blow"—Fuchida and Okumiya, 90.

266, "hard to find any logical explanation"—ibid., 77.

266, "in ship-to-ship battle"—Dull, 138.

266, Toshiyuki Yokoi on Yamamoto—USNIP, 10/1960.

266, Saburo Toyama on Midway—USNIP, 9/1982.

266, Gordon W. Prange on Midway—Prange, *Midway*, 380.

267, Zenshiro Hoshina on Kuroshima—WHH, Zenshiro Hoshina, Tokyo, 1982.

267, HCB's disposition of forces—GPW, 273, 278–80.

267, HCB describes air action—GPW, 281.

268, Morton speculates—Morton, *Strategy*, 125.

268, Gallup Poll and Cordell Hull—ibid, 126.

EPILOGUE

272, senior officers familiar with HCB—WHHC, Shigeru Fukudome, 4/4/1967; Mitsuo Fuchida, 6/29/1967; Sadatoshi Tomioka, 7/3/1967; WHH, Sadamu Sanagi, Tokyo, 1982; Ichiro Yokoyama, Tokyo, 1982; Kazutaka Niimi, Tokyo, 1982; Zenshiro Hoshina, Tokyo, 1982; and Atsushi Oi, Tokyo, 1982.

272, Sadatoshi Tomioka on HCB—WHHC, 7/3/1967.

272, Mitsuo Fuchida on HCB—WHHC, 6/29/1967.

272, Sokichi Takagi's belief—Agawa, 72.

272, William "Billy" Mitchell's beliefs—Mitchell, William, 5, 126.

273, interest in GPW in 1941–42—NYT, 12/9/1941; *Life*, 12/22/1941; HCB, *The Great Pacific War: A Historical Prophecy Now Being Fulfilled*.

273, Yahei Oba—*Japan Times and Advertiser*, 12/10/1941.

274, McMurtrie shied away—DT, 2/21/1941.

275, McMurtrie on *Prince of Wales* and *Repulse*—DT, 12/11/1941.

275, McMurtrie claims authorship GPW—N, 11/1942, 296.

275, McMurtrie "a gaunt figure"—WHHC, S. Mervyn Herbert, formerly on the staff of the *News-Chronicle*, 3/6/1981; and "a little dotty," WHH, David Woodward, former staff correspondent of *News-Chronicle*, Oxford, England, 8/13/1979.

275, McMurtrie's wife addicted to morphine; burned McMurtrie's papers—WHH, George J. Bryant, East Horsley, Leatherhead, Surrey, 1979; other details in George J. Bryant, "The Anchorites," 1974, pamphlet in author's collection.

275, Ferraby's death—WHH, David Woodward, Oxford, England, 1979; also Ferraby's obituaries in *Daily Express* and Manchester *Guardian*, 1/1/1943.

275–276, Ulysses's decline—WHH, E. A. Harwood, Godalming, Surrey, England, 1979.

276, Ulysses's articles—*Daily Express*, London, 7/17/1940.

276, FBI report on Ulysses—files on Ulysses J. Bywater and John A. Bywater, Diplomatic Branch, Civil Archives Division, National Archives, Washington, D.C.

277, Churchill quote—House of Commons, 11/12/1940.

BIBLIOGRAPHY

BOOKS

Agawa, Hiroyuki, *The Reluctant Admiral: Yamamoto and the Imperial Navy* (Kodan-sha International, New York, 1979).

Akira, Iriye, *Pacific Estrangement: Japanese and American Expansion, 1897–1911* (Harvard University Press, Cambridge, Mass., 1972).

——, ed., *Mutual Images: Essays in American-Japanese Relations* (Harvard University Press, Cambridge, Mass., 1975). See Shoichi Saeki and Miwa Kimitada.

Ambrose, Stephen E., *Eisenhower: Soldier, General of the Army, President-Elect, 1890–1952*, vol. 1 (Simon & Schuster, New York, 1983).

Andrew, Christopher, *Her Majesty's Secret Service* (Viking, New York, 1986).

Arnold, Ralph, *Orange Street and Brickhole Lane* (Hart-Davis, London, 1963). Memoirs of the young publisher who bought his way into Constable & Co.

Asada, Sadao, "Japanese Admirals and the Politics of Naval Limitation: Kato Tomasaburo Vs. Kato Kanji," in *Naval Warfare in the Twentieth Century, 1900–1945: Essays in Honor of Arthur Marder*, edited by Gerald Jordan (Croom Helm, London, 1977).

——, "The Japanese Navy and the United States," in *Pearl Harbor as History: Japanese-American Relations, 1931–1941*, edited by Dorothy Borg et al. (Columbia University Press, New York, 1973).

Barnett, Correlli, *The Desert Generals* (Kimber, London, 1960).

Bauermeister, A.—See Hector C. Bywater, translator.

Beard, Charles A., *President Roosevelt and the Coming of the War, 1941: A Study in Appearances and Realities* (Yale University Press, New Haven, Conn., 1948).

Beesly, Patrick, *Room 40: British Naval Intelligence, 1914–18* (Harcourt Brace Jovanovich, New York, 1982).

Borg, Dorothy, et al., eds. *Pearl Harbor as History: Japanese-American Relations, 1931–1941* (Columbia University Press, New York, 1973). See Sadao Asada.

Braisted, William Reynolds, *The United States Navy in the Pacific, 1897–1909* (University of Texas Press, Austin, 1958).

——*The United States Navy in the Pacific, 1909–1922* (University of Texas Press, Austin, 1971).

Brodie, Bernard, *A Guide to Naval Strategy* (Princeton University Press, Princeton, N.J., 1944).

Burgoyne, Alan H., *The War Inevitable* (Griffiths, London, 1908). A prophetic novel by Bywater's mentor.

Butow, Robert J. C., *Tojo and the Coming of the War* (Stanford University Press, Stanford, Calif., 1961).

Byas, Hugh, *Government by Assassination* (Knopf, New York, 1942).

Bywater, Hector C., *Cruisers in Battle: Naval "Light Cavalry" Under Fire 1914–1918* (Constable, London, 1939).

———(unacknowledged coauthor), and Hurd, Archibald, *The Fleets at War* (Hodder & Stoughton, London, 1914).

———and Hurd, Archibald, *From Heligoland to Keeling Island* (Hodder & Stoughton, London, 1914).

———, *The Great Pacific War: A History of the American-Japanese Campaign of 1931–33* (Constable, London, 1925; also, Houghton Mifflin, Boston and New York, 1925; also, Houghton Mifflin, Boston and New York, 1932).

———, *The Great Pacific War: A Historic Prophecy Now Being Fulfilled*, with an introduction by Hanson W. Baldwin (Houghton Mifflin, Boston, 1942).

———, *Taiheiyo no Soha-sen, 1931–1933*, translated by Kyoji Kitagami (Hakuho-sha, Tokyo, 1925). A Japanese translation of Bywater's *The Great Pacific War*.

———, *Taiheiyo Senso to Sono Hihan (Pacific War and Comment)*, translated with commentary by Tota Ishimaru (Bunmei Kyokai Foundation Office, Tokyo, 1926). A Japanese translation of Bywater's *The Great Pacific War*.

———, *The Great Pacific War*, translated by Kojiro Sato (Japanese title and publisher unknown, 1925?). A Japanese translation of Bywater's *The Great Pacific War*.

———, *La Gran Guerra del Pacifico: Historia de la Campana Americana-Japonesa, 1931–1932, traducida por el Capitan de Fragata Manuel Ferrer Anton* (Editorial Naval, Madrid, 1931). A Spanish translation of *The Great Pacific War* published by the Spanish Ministry of Marine.

———, introduction to *Last Days of the German Fleet*, by Ludwig Freiwald, translated by Martin Moore (pseudonym?) (Constable, London, 1932).

———, *Navies and Nations: A Review of Naval Developments Since the Great War* (Constable, London, 1927; also, Houghton Mifflin, New York, 1927).

———, *Les marines de guerre et la politique navale des nations depuis la guerre. Editon francaise par J.-B. Gautreau. Preface du vice amiral Durand-Viel.* French translation of *Navies and Nations* by J.-B. Gautreau. Preface by Vice Admiral Durand-Viel. (Payot, Paris, 1930).

———, introduction to *On the Bottom*, by Edward Ellsberg (Constable, London, 1929).

———, *Sea-Power in the Pacific: A Study of the American-Japanese Naval*

Problem (Constable, London, 1921; also, Houghton Mifflin, Boston and New York, 1921).

———, *Taiheiyo kaiken ron* (Suiko-sha, Tokyo, July 1921). A Japanese translation of Bywater's *Sea Power in the Pacific*, authorized by the Office of the Imperial Navy General Staff. Available at the Library of Congress, Washington, D.C.

———, *Sea-Power in the Pacific: A Study of the American-Japanese Naval Problem*, new edition with new preface (Constable, London, 1934; also, Houghton Mifflin, Boston and New York, 1934).

———, *Sea-Power in the Pacific: A Study of the American-Japanese Naval Problem*, reproduced with the cooperation of the Hoover Institution of War, Revolution and Peace, Stanford University, Stanford, California (Arno Press and *The New York Times*, New York, 1970). Published in the series *American Imperialism—Viewpoints of United States Foreign Policy, 1898–1941*, selected by Charles Gregg of the Gregg Press.

———, *A Searchlight on the Navy* (Constable, London, 1934).

———, *A Searchlight on the Navy*, new edition with a foreword by Sir Roger J. B. Keyes Bt. GCB (Constable, London, 1935).

———, trans. *Spies Break Through: Memoirs of a German Secret Service Officer*, by Lieut. Alexander Bauermeister (Constable, London, 1934).

———, and Ferraby, H. C., *Strange Intelligence: Memoirs of Naval Secret Service* (Constable, London, 1931; also, Richard R. Smith, New York, 1931).

———, and Ferraby, H. C., *Strange Intelligence: Memoirs of Naval Secret Service*, second edition with preface by Admiral Sir Reginald Hall (Constable, London, 1934).

———, and Ferraby, H. C., *Englishe Marine-Spionage ins Deutsche Übertragen Ravi Ravendro*. A German translation of *Strange Intelligence* by Ravi Ravendro (Wilhelm Goldmann, Leipzig, 1933).

———, and Ferraby, H. C., *Intelligence service; souvenirs du service secret de l'Amiraute britannique; traduit de l'anglais par le capitaine de corvette Andre Guieu*. A French translation of *Strange Intelligence* by Captain Andre Guieu (Payot, Paris, 1932).

———, *Their Secret Purposes: Drama and Mysteries of the Naval War* (Constable, London, 1932).

———, trans., *The Two White Nations* (*Die Zwei Weissen Volker*), by Korvettenkapitan Georg von Hase, Intelligence Division, 1220 (Admiralty, Naval Staff, Intelligence Division, London, May, 1920). Bywater's translation of the book originally published in German by Kochler, Leipzig, in 1920.

Churchill, Randolph S., ed., *Winston S. Churchill, Companion Volume II, Part 2, 1907–1911* (Houghton Mifflin, Boston, 1969). Fisher letters to Churchill declare Bywater a "splendid spy."

Clarke, Ignatius Frederick, *Voices Prophesying War, 1763–1984* (Oxford University Press, Oxford, England, 1966).

Clarke, Joseph I. C., *My Life and Memoirs* (Dodd, Mead, New York, 1925). Clarke worked for the *New York Herald* as night city editor, 1870–83, and Sunday editor, 1903–06, when Bywater was on the staff.

Clowes, Sir William Laird, and Robinson, Commander Charles N., RN, *The Great Naval War of 1887*. A fifty-eight-page broadside available in the Naval History Library, Empress State Building, Earl's Court, London, England. Clowes, a prolific writer on naval subjects at the turn of the century, was the only Englishman other than Bywater to win the gold medal of the U.S. Naval Institute.

Colomb, Rear Admiral Philip, et al., *The Great War of 189—, A Forecast* (London, 1893).

Compilation Committee on the History of the Japanese Naval Air Force—see Government Documents, Japanese.

Cook, Nathalie Jarrold Kelley, *J. D. Jarrold Kelley, Commander, U.S. Navy* (New York, 1942, 1953). He was naval news editor of the *New York Herald* during the period when Bywater wrote for the newspaper.

Costello, John, *The Pacific War* (Rawson, Wade, New York, 1981).

Craigie, Sir Robert, *Behind the Japanese Mask* (Hutchinson, London, 1945).

The William Cramp & Sons Ship and Engine Building Company, *Cramp's Shipyard Founded by William Cramp, 1830* (William Cramp & Sons, Philadelphia, 1902). Details about *Variag*.

Dallek, Robert, *Franklin D. Roosevelt and American Foreign Policy, 1932–1945* (Oxford University Press, New York, 1979).

Daniels, Jonathan, *The End of Innocence* (Lippincott, Philadelphia, 1954). Recollections about his father, Josephus Daniels, including a story about Bennett and Franklin Roosevelt in 1913.

Davis, Burke, *Get Yamamoto* (Random House, New York, 1969).

Denlinger, Sutherland, and Gary, Charles B., *War in the Pacific: A Study of Navies, Peoples and Battle Problems* (McBride, New York, 1936). An imitation of Bywater's *The Great Pacific War*.

Dingman, Roger, *Power in the Pacific: The Origins of Naval Arms Limitation* (University of Chicago Press, Chicago, 1976). Outstanding bilingual study.

Dulin, Robert O., Jr., and Garzke, William H., Jr., *Battleships: United States Battleships in World War II* (U.S. Naval Institute Press, Annapolis, Md., 1976).

———, *Battleships: Allied Battleships in World War II* (U.S. Naval Institute Press, Annapolis, Md., 1980).

———, *Battleships: Axis and Neutral Battleships in World War II* (U.S. Naval Institute Press, Annapolis, Md., 1985).

Dull, Paul S., *A Battle History of the Imperial Japanese Navy (1941–1945)* (U.S. Naval Institute Press, Annapolis, Md., 1978).

Ellinger, Werner B., and Rosinski, Herbert, *Sea Power in the Pacific, 1936–1941, a Bibliography* (Princeton University Press, Princeton, N.J., 1942).

Ellsberg, Edward, *On the Bottom*, with an introduction by Hector Bywater (Constable, London, 1929).

Elting, Colonel John R., *The Super-Strategists: Great Captains, Theorists, and Fighting Men Who Have Shaped the History of Warfare* (Scribner's, New York, 1985).

Evans, David C., ed. and trans., *The Japanese Navy in World War II* (U.S. Naval Institute Press, Annapolis, Md., 1986).

Falk, Edwin A., *Togo and the Rise of Japanese Sea Power* (Longmans, Green, New York, 1936).

Farago, Ladislas, *Burn after Reading* (Pinacle Books, Los Angeles, 1961).

————, *The Broken Seal: The Story of Operation Magic and the Pearl Harbor Disaster* (Random House, New York, 1967).

Feis, Herbert, *The Road to Pearl Harbor: The Coming of the War Between the United States and Japan* (Princeton University Press, Princeton, N.J., 1950).

Fitzpatrick, Earnest Hugh, *The Coming Conflict of Nations, or the Japanese-American War* (H. W. Bokker, Springfield, Ill., 1909).

Fleisher, Wilfrid, *Volcanic Isle* (Doubleday, New York, 1941).

Freidel, Frank, *Franklin D. Roosevelt: The Apprenticeship*, vol. 1, and *Franklin D. Roosevelt: The Ordeal*, vol. 2 (Little, Brown, Boston, 1952, 1954).

Freiwald, Ludwig, *Last Days of the German Fleet*, translated by Martin Moore (pseudonym?) with an introduction by Hector C. Bywater (Constable, London, 1932).

Friedman, Norman, *Battleship Design and Development*, 1905–1945 (Conway, Greenwich, England, 1978).

Fuchida, Mitsuo, and Okumiya, Masatake, *Midway, the Battle That Doomed Japan* (U.S. Naval Institute Press, Annapolis, Md., 1955).

Gardner, Martin, ed., *The Wreck of the Titanic Foretold* (Prometheus, Buffalo, 1986).

Garrison, Oswald, *Some Newspapers and Newspaper-men*, new and revised edition (original 1923) (Books for Libraries Press, Freeport, N.Y., 1971).

Gelb, Arthur and Barbara, *O'Neill* (Harper, New York, 1962).

Gilbert, Martin, *Winston S. Churchill*, vols. 1–5 (Houghton Mifflin, Boston, 1977).

Grautoff, Ferdinand H., *Bansai!* (Weicher, Leipzig, 1908).

Gretton, Admiral Sir Peter, *Former Naval Person* (Cassell, London, 1968). Churchill and the Royal Navy.

Grew, Joseph C., *Ten Years in Japan: A Contemporary Record Drawn from the Diaries and Private and Official Papers of Joseph C. Grew, United States Ambassador to Japan, 1932–1942* (Simon & Schuster, New York, 1944).

Guderian, General Heinz, *Panzer Leader* (Michael Joseph, London, 1952). The German tank commander acknowledges his debt to Liddell Hart.

Hague, Paul, *Sea Battles in Miniature: A Guide to Naval Wargaming* (Stephens, Cambridge, England, 1980).

Hattori, Takushiro, *Daitoa Senso Zenshi* (*The Complete History of the Greater East Asia War*, 4 vols. (Masu Shobo, Tokyo, 1945).

Hodges, Peter, *The Big Gun: Battleship Main Armament, 1860–1945* (U.S. Naval Institute Press, Annapolis, Md., 1981).

Hough, Richard, *The Death of the Battleship* (Macmillan, New York, 1963).

———, *The Great War at Sea, 1914–1918* (Oxford University Press, Oxford, England, 1983).

Hovgaard, William, *Modern History of Warships, Comprising a Discussion of Present Standpoint and Recent War Experiences* (Conway Maritime Press, London, 1978). A reprint of the original 1920 edition.

Howarth, Stephen, *The Fighting Ships of the Rising Sun: The Drama of the Imperial Japanese Navy, 1895–1945* (Atheneum, New York, 1983).

Hoyt, Edwin P., *Blue Skies and Blood: The Battle of the Coral Sea* (Pinnacle, Los Angeles, 1976).

———, *The Life and Death of H.M.S. Hood* (Weindenfeld, London, 1977).

———, *The Lonely Ships: The Life and Death of the U.S. Asiatic Fleet* (Pinnacle, Los Angeles, 1977).

———, *Yamamoto: The Man Who Planned Pearl Harbor* (McGraw-Hill, New York, 1990).

Hughes, Richard, *Foreign Devil* (Deutsch, London, 1972). Includes chapter on Melville Cox.

Hunt, Frazier, *The Untold Story of Douglas MacArthur* (Devin-Adair, New York, 1954).

Hurd, Archibald Spicer, and Castle, Henry (pseudonym), *German Sea-Power, Its Rise, Progress and Economic Basis* (Scribner's, New York, 1913).

———, *The Fleets at War* (Hodder & Stoughton, London, 1914). Hector Bywater was unacknowledged coauthor.

———, and Bywater, H. C., *From Heligoland to Keeling Island* (Hodder & Stoughton, London, 1914).

———, *The Merchant Navy*, 3 vols. (Murray, London, 1921, 1929, 1930).

———, *Who Goes There?* (Hutchinson, London, 1942). Autobiography.

Ienaga, Saburo, *The Pacific War: World War II and the Japanese, 1931–1945* (Pantheon, New York, 1978). A translation of *Taiheiyo Senso* (Iwanami Shoten, Tokyo, 1968).

Ike, Nobutaka, ed. and trans., *Japan's Decision for War: Records of the 1941 Policy Conferences* (Stanford University Press, Stanford, Calif., 1967).

Inoguchi, Captain Rikihei, and Nakajima, Commander Tadashi, et al., *The Divine Wind: Japan's Kamikaze Force in World War II* (U.S. Naval Institute Press, Annapolis, Md., 1958).

Isely, Jeter A., and Crowl, Philip A., *The U.S. Marines and Amphibious War* (Princeton University Press, Princeton, N.J., 1951).

Ishimaru, Tota, *Japan Must Fight Britain*, translated by Captain G. V. Rayment, CBE, RN (Ret.) (Hurst and Blackett, London, 1936). Bywater reviewed the book for the *Daily Telegraph*.

————, *The Next World War* (Hurst and Blackett, London, 1937).

————, trans., see Japanese translations of Bywater's *The Great Pacific War*.

Ito, Masanori, with Pineau, Roger, *The End of the Japanese Imperial Navy*, translated by Y. Kuroda (Norton, New York, 1962).

James, Admiral Sir William, *The Code Breakers of Room 40* (St. Martin's Press, New York, 1956). Details on Admiral Sir Reginald Hall and British Secret Service.

Jane, Frederick T., *How to Play the Naval War Game* (Sampson, Low, Marston, London, 1912).

————, *The Imperial Japanese Navy* (Thacker, London, 1904).

————, *The Imperial Russian Navy* (Thacker, London, 1904).

————, *The Torpedo Book: A Series of Sketches with Torpedo Craft in Fair Weather and Foul* (Beeman, London, 1897).

Jentschura, Hansgeorge, et al., *Warships of the Imperial Japanese Navy, 1869–1945* (Arms and Armor Press, London, 1977).

Johnson, Chalmers, *An Instance of Treason: Ozaki Hotsumi and the Sorge Spy Ring* (Stanford University Press, Stanford, Calif., 1964).

Johnson, Gerald W., Kent, Frank R., Mencken, H. L., and Owens, Hamilton, *The Sunpapers of Baltimore* (Knopf, New York, 1937).

Jordan, Gerald, ed., *Naval Warfare in the Twentieth Century, 1900–1945: Essays in Honor of Arthur Marder* (Croom Helm, London, 1977). See chapter titled "Japanese Admirals and the Politics of Naval Limitation: Kato Tomosaburo Vs. Kato Kanji," by Sadao Asada.

Kennedy, Captain Malcolm D., *The Changing Fabric of Japan* (Constable, London, 1930).

————, *The Estrangement of Great Britain and Japan, 1917–35* (University of California Press, Berkeley and Los Angeles, 1969).

————, *The Military Side of Japanese Life* (Houghton Mifflin, Boston, 1923).

————, *Some Aspects of Japan and Her Defense Forces* (Kegan Paul, London, 1928).

Kenworthy, J. M. (Strabogli), *Peace or War?* (Boni & Liveright, New York, 1927).

Kimitada, Miwa, "Japanese Images of War with the United States," in *Mutual Images: Essays in American-Japanese Relations*, edited by Iriye Akira (Harvard University Press, Cambridge, Mass., 1975).

Kinkodo-Shoseki-Kabushiki-Kaisha, *The Russo-Japanese War* (Kindodo Publishing Company, Tokyo, 1904).

Kipling, Rudyard, *A Fleet in Being: Notes of Two Trips with the Channel Squadron* (Macmillan, New York, 1898).

Kitagami, Kyoji, trans.—see Japanese translations of Bywater's *The Great Pacific War*.

Klado, Nicolas, *The Battle of the Sea of Japan* (Hodder & Stoughton, London, 1905?).

Konoye, Fumimaro, *Ushinawareshi Seiji* (Lost Politics) (Asahi Shinbun-sha, Tokyo, 1946).

Kuzuoka, T., *The Life of Fleet Admiral Yamamoto-Isoroku* (Tokyo, 1943?).
Pamphlet available in the Library of Congress, Washington, D.C.

Landau, Captain Henry, *All's Fair, The Story of the British Secret Service* (Putnam's, New York, 1934).

Layton, Rear Admiral Edwin T., with Pineau, Captain Roger, and Costello,
John, *And I Was There: Pearl Harbor and Midway—Breaking the Secrets*
(Morrow, New York, 1985).

Lea, Homer, *The Valor of Ignorance*, with an introduction by Lieutenant-
General A. R. Chaffee (Harper, New York, 1909).

———, *The Valor of Ignorance: Introduction by Clare Boothe* (Harper, New
York, 1942).

Leahy, Fleet Admiral William D., *I Was There: The Personal Story of the Chief
of Staff to Presidents Roosevelt and Truman, Based on His Notes and
Diaries Made at the Time* (McGraw-Hill, New York, 1950).

Le Queux, William, *The Invasion of 1910*, with naval chapters by H. W. Wilson
(Eveleigh Nash, London, 1906).

Liddell Hart, Basil H., *The German Generals Talk* (Morrow, New York, 1948).

———, *The Memoirs of Captain Liddell Hart*, I (Cassell, London, 1965).

Link, Arthur, and Catton, William B., *American Epoch: A History of the U.S.
Since the 1890s* (Knopf, New York, 1963).

Livingston, Jon, et al., *Imperial Japan, 1800–1945*, edited, annotated, and with
introductions by Jon Livingston, Joe Moore, and Felicia Oldfather (Random
House, New York, 1973).

Lord, Walter, *Day of Infamy* (Holt, New York, 1957).

Lundstrom, John B., *The First South Pacific Campaign: Pacific Fleet Strategy
December 1941–June 1942* (U.S. Naval Institute Press, Annapolis, Md.,
1976).

Mackenzie, Compton, *Gallipoli Memories* (Cassell, London, 1929). First of the
author's war memoirs.

———, *First Athenian Memories* (Cassell, London, 1931). Second of the author's war memoirs.

———, *Greek Memories* (Cassell, London, 1932). Third of the author's war
memoirs. The original edition, presently available at the New York Public
Library, was suppressed in 1932 when the author was convicted of a violation of the Official Secrets Act. When *Greek Memories* was reissued in
1939 by Chatto & Windus, London, the author had changed all references
to Lieutenant Colonel Eric Holt-Wilson (who served as chief of staff of MI-
5 for twenty-three years) to "Major Dash," and most of his remarks were
deleted, including the fact that it was Holt-Wilson who revealed to Mackenzie the identity of C, the chief of the British Secret Service.

———, *Aegean Memories* (Chatto & Windus, London, 1940). Fourth and last
of the author's war memoirs.

Mahan, Alfred Thayer, *The Influence of Sea Power upon History, 1660–1783* (Little, Brown, Boston, 1890, 1918).

———, *Lessons of the War with Spain, and Other Articles* (Books for Libraries Press, Freeport, N.Y., 1970).

———, *Naval Strategy Compared and Contrasted with the Principles and Practice of Military Operations on Land; Lectures Delivered at the U.S. Naval War College, Newport, R.I., Between the Years 1887 and 1911* (Little, Brown, Boston, 1911).

Manchester, William, *American Caesar: Douglas MacArthur, 1880–1964* (Dell, New York, 1979).

Marder, Arthur J., *From the Dreadnought to Scapa Flow: The Royal Navy in the Fisher Era, 1904–1914*, vols. 1–5 (Oxford University Press, London, 1961–70).

———, *Old Friends, New Enemies: The Royal Navy and the Imperial Japanese Navy—Strategic Illusions, 1936–1941* (Clarendon Press, Oxford, 1981).

Matsuo, Kinoaki, *How Japan Plans to Win* (Little, Brown, Boston, 1942). A translation by Kilsoo K. Haan of the Japanese book *The Three-Power Alliance and a United States–Japanese War*, originally published in 1940.

Matsushima, Keizo, *Taiheiyo no Kyoshu Yamamoto Isoroku (Isoroku Yamamoto, Eagle of the Pacific)* (Kyoda Shuppan-sha, Tokyo, 1953).

Millett, Allan R., *Semper Fidelis: The History of the United States Marine Corps* (Macmillan, New York, 1980).

Mitchell, Donald W., *History of the American Navy* (Knopf, New York, 1946).

Mitchell, William, *Winged Victory* (Putnam, New York, 1924).

Mizuno, Hironori, *Tsugi no Issen (The Next Decisive Battle)* under pseudonym "A Naval Officer" (Tokyo, 1914).

Morison, Samuel Eliot, *The Rising Sun in the Pacific, 1931–April, 1942: History of United States Naval Operations in World War II*, vol. 3 (Little, Brown, Boston, 1948).

Morton, Louis, *The Fall of the Philippines: The War in the Pacific: United States Army in World War II* (Office of the Chief of Military History, Dept. of the Army, Washington, D.C., 1953).

———, *Strategy and Command: The First Two Years, United States Army in World War II, The War in the Pacific* (Center of Military History, United States Army, Washington, D.C., 1962, 1989).

Mott, Frank Luther, *American Journalism* (Macmillan, New York, 1942). Details on the *New York Herald*.

Mumby, Frank Arthur, *Publishing and Bookselling* (Cape, London, 1930). Details on Constable & Co.

Murdoch, James, *A History of Japan*, revised and edited by Joseph H. Longford (Frederick Ungar, New York, 1964).

Nachod, Oskar, *Bibliography of the Japanese Empire, 1906–26*, and subsequent vols. (Hiersemann, Leipzig, 1928, etc.).

O'Connor, Richard, *The Scandalous Mr. Bennett* (Doubleday, New York, 1962).

——, *Pacific Destiny: An Informal History of the U.S. in the Far East, 1776–1968* (Little, Brown, Boston, 1969).

Parkes, Oscar, *British Battleships: Warrior to Vanguard, A History of Design, Construction and Armament,* new and revised edition with a foreword by Admiral of the Fleet, the Earl Mountbatten of Burma (Seeley, London, 1973).

Peattie, Mark R., *Forecasting a Pacific War: Japanese Perspectives, 1913–1933.* An unpublished monograph presented at the Colloquium Center for Japanese and Korean Studies at the University of California at Berkeley, October 15, 1975. Superb bilingual study.

——, *Ishiwara Kanji and Japan's Confrontation with the West* (Princeton University Press, Princeton, N.J., 1975).

Pelz, Stephen E., *Race to Pearl Harbor* (Harvard University Press, Cambridge, Mass., 1974). Outstanding bilingual study.

Pineau, Roger—see Inoguchi, Captain Rikihei; Ito, Masanori; and Layton, Rear Admiral Edwin T.

Pitkin, Walter B., *Must We Fight Japan?* (Century, New York, 1921).

Potter, E. B., and Nimitz, Chester W., eds., *The Great Sea War* (Prentice-Hall, Englewood Cliffs, N.J., 1980).

——, *Nimitz* (U.S. Naval Institute Press, Annapolis, Md., 1976).

Potter, John Deane, *Yamamoto: The Man Who Menaced America* (Viking, New York, 1965).

Prange, Gordon W., et al., *At Dawn We Slept: The Untold Story of Pearl Harbor* (McGraw-Hill, New York, 1981).

——, *Miracle at Midway* (McGraw-Hill, New York, 1982).

Price, Alfred, *Battle of Britain: The Hardest Day, 18 August, 1940* (Scribner's, New York, 1979).

Puleston, Captain William Dilworth, *The Armed Forces of the Pacific* (Yale University Press, New Haven, Conn., 1941).

Reilly, John C., Jr., and Scheina, Robert L., *American Battleships, 1886–1923: Predreadnought Design and Construction* (U.S. Naval Institute Press, Annapolis, Md., 1980).

Reischauer, Edwin O., *The United States and Japan* (Harvard University Press, Cambridge, Mass., 1957).

Robinson, Rear Admiral Samuel S., and Robinson, Mary L., *A History of Naval Tactics from 1530 to 1930: The Evolution of Tactical Maxims* (U.S. Naval Institute, Annapolis, Md., 1942).

Rodger, N. A. M., *The Admiralty* (Terence Dalton, Lavenham, Suffolk, England, 1979).

Rosinski, Herbert, *The Development of Naval Thought* (Naval War College Press, Newport, R.I., 1977). See also Ellinger, Werner B.

Roskill, Stephen W., *Naval Policy Between the Wars,* vol 1: *The Period of*

Anglo-American Antagonism, 1919–1929; vol. 2: *The Period of Reluctant Rearmament, 1930–1939* (Collins, London, 1968 and 1976).

Saeki, Shoichi, "Images of the United States as a Hypothetical Enemy," in *Mutual Images: Essays in American-Japanese Relations*, edited by Iriye Akira (Harvard University Press, Cambridge, Mass., 1975).

Sato, Kojiro, *Nichi-Bei Moshi Tatakawaba (If Japan and America Fight)* (Tokyo, 1921).

———, *If Japan and America Fight*, English edition (Meguro Bunten, Tokyo, 1921).

———, *Nichi-Bei Senso Yume Monogatari (Japanese-American War Fantasy)* (Tokyo, Nippon Hyoron-sha, 1921).

———, see Japanese translations of Bywater's *The Great Pacific War*.

Schofield, B. B., *British Sea Power: Naval Policy in the Twentieth Century* (Batsford, London, 1967).

Scott, J. W. Robertson, *The Life and Death of a Newspaper* (London, 1952). Details on Garvin and Fleet Street.

Seitz, Don. Carlos, *The James Gordon Bennetts, Father and Son, Proprietors of the New York Herald* (Bobbs-Merrill, Indianapolis, 1928).

Smith, S. E., ed., *The United States Navy in World War II* (Morrow, New York, 1966).

Sorimachi, Eiichi, *Ningen Yamamoto Isoroku (The Biography of Isoroku Yamamoto)*, 2 vols. (Kohwa-do, Tokyo, 1956–57). A sympathetic biography written by a lifelong friend.

Spector, Ronald H., *Eagle Against the Sun: The American War With Japan* (Free Press, New York, 1985).

Sprout, Harold and Margaret, *Toward a New Order of Sea Power: American Naval Policy and the World Scene, 1918–1922* (Princeton University Press, Princeton, N.J., 1946).

———, *The Rise of American Naval Power, 1776–1918* (Princeton University Press, Princeton, N.J., 1966).

Stephan, John J., *Hawaii Under the Rising Sun: Japan's Plans for Conquest After Pearl Harbor* (University of Hawaii Press, Honolulu, 1984).

Stevens, Rowan, et al., *The Battle for the Pacific, and Other Adventures at Sea* (Harper, New York, 1908). An early example of *les guerres imaginaires*.

Stillwell, Paul, ed., *Air Raid: Pearl Harbor! Recollections of a Day of Infamy* (U.S. Naval Institute Press, Annapolis, Md., 1981).

Sweetman, Jack, *The U.S. Naval Academy: An Illustrated History* (U.S. Naval Institute Press, Annapolis, Md., 1979). Interesting details on Japanese officers who attended.

Takagi, Sokichi, *Shikan Taiheiyo Senso (A Personal View of the Pacific War)* (Bungei Shunju-sha, Tokyo, 1969).

Tanin, O., and Yohan, E., *When Japan Goes to War* (International Publishers, New York, 1936).

Tate, Merze, *The United States and the Hawaiian Kingdom, A Political History* (Yale University Press, New Haven and New York, 1965).

Toland, John, *The Rising Sun: The Decline and Fall of the Japanese Empire, 1936–1945* (Random House, New York, 1970).

———, *Infamy: Pearl Harbor and Its Aftermath* (Doubleday, Garden City, N.Y., 1982).

Tolischus, Otto D., *Tokyo Record* (Reynal & Hitchcock, New York, 1943).

Tuchman, Barbara, *The Proud Tower* (Macmillan, New York, 1966).

Tute, Warren, *The True Glory: The Story of the Royal Navy over a Thousand Years* (Harper & Row, New York, 1983).

Ubique (pseudonym), *Modern Warfare*. Mentioned by Maurice Prendergast in his review of *The Great Pacific War* in *Navy*, 9/10/1925.

Uyehara, Cecil H., compiler, *Checklist of Archives in the Japanese Ministry of Foreign Affairs, 1868–1945* (Library of Congress, Washington, D.C.).

Von Hase, Korvettenkapitan Georg—see Bywater, Hector C., trans.

Walder, David, *The Short Victorious War: The Russo-Japanese Conflict, 1904–5* (Hutchinson, London, 1973).

Warner, Denis and Peggy, *The Tide at Sunrise: A History of the Russo-Japanese War, 1904–1905* (Charterhouse, New York, 1974).

Watanabe, Ikujiro, *Shiden Yamamoto Gensui* (*A Biography of Admiral Yamamoto*) (Chikura Shobo, Tokyo, 1942).

Wells, H. G., *Little Wars: A Game for Boys from 12 Years of Age to One Hundred and Fifty and for That More Intelligent Sort of Girls Who Like Boys' Games* (Small, Maynard, Boston, 1913).

West, James H., *A Short History of the New York Navy Yard* (New York Navy Yard, New York, 1941).

Wheeler, Gerald E., *Prelude to Pearl Harbor: The U.S. Navy and the Far East, 1921–1931* (University of Missouri Press, Columbia, 1963).

Williams, Wythe, *Dusk of Empire* (Scribner's, New York, 1937). He knew staff members of the London bureau of the *New York Herald* before the First World War.

Willmott, H. P., *Empires in the Balance: Japanese and Allied Pacific Strategies to April 1942* (U.S. Naval Institute Press, Annapolis, Md., 1982).

———, *The Barrier and the Javelin: Japanese and Allied Strategies February to June 1942* (U.S. Naval Institute Press, Annapolis, Md., 1983).

Willoughby, Major General Charles A., and John Chamberlain, *MacArthur, 1941–1951* (McGraw-Hill, New York, 1954).

Wilson, H. W., *Ironclads in Action: A Sketch of Naval Warfare From 1855 to 1895* (Sampson Low, Marston, London, 1896). See Le Queux, William.

Wohlsetter, Roberta, *Pearl Harbor: Warning and Decision* (Stanford University Press, Stanford, Calif., 1962).

Yamamoto, Yoshimasa, *Chichi, Yamamoto Isoroku* (*My Father Isoroku Yamamoto*) (Kobun-sha, Tokyo, 1969).

Yamaoka, Sohachi, *Gensui, Yamamoto Isoroku* (*Admiral Isoroku Yamamoto*) (Dai Nihon Yuben-kai Kodan-sha, Tokyo, 1945).

Yano, Tohru, *Nanshinno Keifu* (*The Pedigree of Southern-Advance Thought*) (Chuo Koron-sha, Tokyo, 1975). An important history of the political movement that led to Japan's decision to expand her empire to the South Sea islands.

PERIODICALS

Bailey, Thomas, "Japan's Protest Against the American Annexation of Hawaii," *Journal of Modern History*, vol. 3 (1931), 46–61.

Ballendorf, Dirk Anthony, "Earl Hancock Ellis: The Man and His Mission," *USNIP*, 11/1983, 53–60.

Beard, Charles A., "Our Confusion over National Defense," *Harper's*, 2/1932.

Beigel, Harvey M., "The Battle Fleet's Home Port: 1919–1940," *USNIP*, Supplement, 1985.

Benjamin, Park, "Some Lessons of the Japanese Torpedo Attack," *Independent*, 2/18/1904.

Blackman, Raymond V. B., "A Century of Warship Development," Brassey's *Naval Annual*, 1968.

Naval and Shipping Annual (Brassey's, London, 1886–1943). Editors included Earl Brassey and Archibald Hurd.

Brown, D. K., "The Design and Construction of the Battleship *Dreadnought*," *Warship*, 1/1980.

Bywater, Hector C., "American Naval Policy," *Nineteenth Century*, London, 3/1928.

———, "Atlantic and Pacific Navies in 1937," *Navy*, London, 3/1937.

———, "The Battleship and Its Uses," *USNIP*, 3/1926, 407–26.

———, "Lord Brassey: A Tribute," *Nautical Magazine*, London, 4/1918.

———, "The British Navy To-Day," *Nineteenth Century*, London, 11/1928.

———, "The Coming Struggle for Sea Power," *Current History*, New York, 10/1934.

———, "Coming Struggle for Sea Power," *Far Eastern Review*, London, 11/1934.

———, "Coronel and the Falklands: Some Reflections," *Navy*, London, 1/1915, 9–10.

———, "The Great Pacific War," *Life*, 12/22/1941. A condensation of Bywater's book published posthumously as "the most current book of the week," yet without appreciation of the fact that the book might have influenced naval planners in Japan and the United States.

———, "The Imperial Japanese Navy," *Shipping Wonders of the World*, London, 1937, 1531–35.

———, "Japan: A Sequel to the Washington Conference," *Atlantic Monthly*, 2/1923. Reprinted by *USNIP*.

———, "Japanese and American Naval Power," *Atlantic Monthly*, 11/1921.

———, "Japanese and American Naval Power in the Pacific," *Pacific Affairs*, Institute of Pacific Relations, Honolulu, Hawaii, 6/1935. Reprinted in *Japan Times*, 9/6/1935, 12–17.

———, "Japanese Naval Policy," *Nineteenth Century*, London, 11/1925.

———, "The Japanese Navy," *Navy*, London, 12/1937.

———, "The Limitation of Naval Armaments," *Atlantic Monthly*, 2/1922.

———, "Limitation of Navies," *Fortnightly*, London, 12/1934.

———, "Mastodons of the Deep," *Navy*, London, 2/1924.

———, "Naval Warfare of To-morrow," *Navy*, London, 8/1936, 207–09.

———, "Our New Battleships," *Navy*, London, 5/21/1921, 133.

———, "Possible Features of a North Sea Campaign," *Navy League Annual*, 1911–12 edition, Navy League, London, edited by Alan H. Burgoyne, 1909–15.

———, "The Spirit of the Treaty: Recent Naval Developments in Japan," *Navy*, London, 5/1924.

———, "The War at Sea," *Foreign Affairs*, New York, 4/1940.

Clarke, I. F., "The Battle of Dorking, 1871–1914," *Victorian Studies*, vol. 8, no. 4, 6/1965, 309–28.

Costello, John E., "Remember Pearl Harbor," *USNIP*, 9/1983.

Davies, Robert B., "Hector C. Bywater and American Naval Journalism During the 1920s," in *New Aspects of Naval History, Selected Papers from the 5th Naval History Symposium (1981)*, edited by Department of History, U.S. Naval Academy (The Nautical and Aviation Publishing Co. of America, Baltimore, Md., 1985).

Dillingham, Walter F., "Pearl Harbor," *USNIP*, 5/1930.

Doyle, Michael K., "The U.S. Navy and War Plan Orange, 1933–1940," *Naval War College Review*, 5–6/1980, Newport, R.I.

Hiley, Nicholas P., "The Failure of British Espionage Against Germany, 1907–1914," *Historical Journal* (Great Britain), vol. 26, no. 4 (1983), 867–89. Interesting portrait of Mansfield Cumming, but the author regards Bywater as merely a journalist and is unaware of his personal involvement in British espionage.

Honan, William H., "Japan Strikes: 1941," *American Heritage*, 12/1970. The author's first article about Bywater's possible influence upon Yamamoto.

———, "Return of the Battleship," *New York Times Magazine*, 4/4 and 4/11/1982.

———, "Russian and American Pilots Play 'Chicken,'" *New York Times Magazine*, 11/22/1970.

Jane's Fighting Ships (Low, Marston, London, 1898–1943). Title varies: *All the World's Fighting Ships* (1898–1904); *Fighting Ships* (1905–15). Editors included Frederick T. Jane, Maurice Prendergast, Francis E. McMurtrie, and Raymond Blackman.

Knox, Dudley W., "The Navy and Public Indoctrination," *USNIP*, 6/1929.

Literary Digest, "War Cries From Japan" (unsigned), 7/17/1926. A report on Japanese-American war scenarios published in Japan by Seijiro Kawashima and Teisuke Akiyama.

Morton, Louis, "War Plan Orange: Evolution of a Strategy," *World Politics*, 1/1959, Center of International Studies, Princeton, N.J.

Niblack, Vice Admiral A. P., "The Maintenance of the Fleet," *Transactions*, vol. 23, 1915, 107–15. Society of Naval Architects and Marine Engineers, New York.

———, "Naval Stations and Naval Bases," *Transactions*, vol. 24, 1916, 139–48. Society of Naval Architects and Marine Engineers, New York.

Peattie, Mark R.,"Akiyama Saneyuki and the Emergence of Modern Japanese Naval Doctrine," *USNIP*, 1/1977.

———, and Evans, David C., "Sato Tetsutaro and Japanese Strategy," *Naval History*, Fall 1990.

Prendergast, Maurice, Review of SPP, *Navy*, London, 9/1925.

———, "The War of Wits," *Navy*, London, 12/1931.

Reber, Lieutenant Colonel John J., "Pete Ellis: Amphibious War Prophet," *USNIP*, 11/1977.

Redding, Leo, "James Gordon Bennett," *Everybody's Magazine*, New York, 6/1914, 846–58.

Robinson, Walton, "Mast and Funnel Design," *Navy*, London, 7/1935.

Roosevelt, Franklin D., "Shall We Trust Japan?" *Asia*, New York, 7/1923.

Storry, Richard, Roskill, Captain S. W., and McDonald, J. Kenneth, "The Second World War in the Pacific: Plans and Reality," papers read at a symposium at the National Maritime Museum, London, jointly with the Royal Naval College, Greenwich, on 5/6/1972. *Maritime Monographs and Reports*, National Maritime Museum, no. 9, 1974.

Tsunoda, Jun, and Uchida, Kazutomi, "The Pearl Harbor Attack: Admiral Yamamoto's Fundamental Concept," *Naval War College Review*, Fall 1978, 83–88.

Vaux, Patrick, "The Navy Men of Japan," *Navy*, London, 4/1933.

GOVERNMENT DOCUMENTS
British and American:

Admiralty Correspondence Index, the Admiralty Secretariat, 1924 and 1927, Bywater, H. C., Naval Journalist (ADM 12/1689) N.I.D. (Naval Intelligence Department) 034927, Public Record Office, Kew, London.

"Application for Appointment" to U.S. Department of State by Hector C. Bywater, 6/12/1913, Diplomatic Branch, Civil Archives Division, National Archives, Washington, D.C.

Combined Fleet Top Secret Operation Order Number 1, Exhibit 8 in Joint Congressional Investigation of the Attack on Pearl Harbor in Part 13 of Hearings Before the Joint Committee on the Investigation of the Pearl Harbor Attack, 431, 11/15/1945 to 7/15/1946.

Records of the Joint Army and Navy Board, 1903–1947; Microfilm M-1421, rolls 9 and 10, Military Reference Branch, National Archives, Washington, D.C.

"The Russo-Japanese War," Admiralty, Intelligence Department, Naval Library, Ministry of Defense, Empress State Building, London.

U.S. Strategic Bombing Survey (Pacific), Historical Records Branch, U.S. Army Center for Military History, Washington, D.C.

U.S. Congress, 75th, 4th Session, House Committee on Naval Affairs, "Hearings on H. R. 9218 to establish the composition of the U.S. Navy. . . ." 1/31– 2/28/1938. Washington, D.C. U.S. Government Printing Office, 1938. Admiral Leahy's testimony.

U.S. Navy Directory, GPO Publications, Washington, D.C.

Japanese:

Combined Fleet Top Secret Operation Order Number 1. See Government Documents, British and American.

Compilation Committee on the History of the Japanese Naval Air Force, *Nihon Kaigun Kokushi* (*History of the Japanese Naval Air Force*) (Jiji Tsusin-sha, Tokyo, 1970).

"The Debate Concerning a U.S.-Japanese War," Imperial Army General Staff (*Sanbo Honbu*), 6/20/1926, Collection of Miscellaneous Documents Concerning Japan and Other Countries (Japan and America), 1923–1926, vol. 5, *Gaiko Shiryokan* (Diplomatic Record Office), Tokyo.

"The Debate Concerning a U.S.-Japanese War and Observations About Japan Which Appeared Recently in the American Press," Imperial Army General Staff (*Sanbo Honbu*), 9/16/1926, Collection of Miscellaneous Documents Concerning Japan and Other Countries (Japan and America), 1923–1926, vol. 5, *Gaiko Shiryokan* (Diplomatic Record Office), Tokyo.

Reports from overseas diplomatic offices concerning Hector C. Bywater—Collection of Miscellaneous Documents Concerning Japan and Other Countries (Japan and America), 1923–1926, vol. 5. Also, Collection of Miscellaneous Documents Concerning Japan and Other Countries (Japan and Britain), 1902–23, classmark 1/1/4/1–7. Also Miscellaneous Documents of Japan-British Diplomatic Relations, 1940s. *Gaiko Shiryokan* (Diplomatic Record Office), Tokyo.

Senshi Sosho (War History Series), 102 vols., *Boeicho Boei Kenshujo Senshibu Shiryoko* (Archives of the Military History Department of the National Defense College, National Defense Agency), Tokyo. (Asagumo Shinbunsha, Tokyo, 1979).

PAPERS

Bywater, Hector C.—Bywater left no collection of papers. His son, Reverend Hector W. R. Bywater, has a few folders of clippings, hand-corrected typescripts, and a few pages of the manuscript of *Strange Intelligence* in a notebook. Bywater's daughter, Sylvia Newland, possesses a copy of her father's translation of *The Two White Nations* (see Bibliography). About three dozen letters from Bywater are to be found in the papers of Rudyard Kipling, Compton Mackenzie, Sir Roger Keyes, Constable & Co., Ferris Greenslet, and other collections listed in this section of the Bibliography.

There is also a small file of papers under Bywater's name in the Diplomatic Branch of the Civil Archives Division of the National Archives in Washington, D.C., including his job application to the U.S. State Department in 1913. Although Bywater falsified his nationality and age on this document, the other statements on the application are evidently correct and provide a valuable outline of his early life.

Bywater, Ulysses John Victor—His official papers as deputy consul general in Dresden are in the Diplomatic Branch, Civil Archives Division, National Archives, Washington, D.C. Access to certain documents requires the permission of his son, John Bywater.

Chevins, Hugh—The papers of the former news editor and industrial and labor correspondent of the London *Daily Telegraph*, who worked at the newspaper during many of the years when Bywater was on the staff, afford a good picture of conditions at the *Telegraph*, and on Fleet Street in general, in the 1930s (British Library of Political and Economic Science, 10 Portugal St., London). Chevins's daughter, Miss Barbara Chevins, possesses his well-written, unpublished autobiography, *It Ain't Easy, Brother*.

Constable & Company—The files of Bywater's British publisher include fourteen letters from Bywater written between 9/14/1921 and 11/5/1921, concerning his book *Sea Power in the Pacific* (Special Collections Department, Samuel Paley Library, Temple University, Philadelphia, Pa.). Also, Constable & Co., 10–12 Orange St., London, has a folder of Bywater's letters, contracts, and so forth.

Fisher, Sir John—Much material on Fisher's close relationship with the press (Archives Centre, Churchill College, Cambridge, England).

Gaffney, Thomas St. John—His official papers in the Diplomatic Branch of the Civil Archives Division of the National Archives in Washington, D.C., shed light on the activities of both Hector and Ulysses Bywater during their residence in Germany prior to World War I.

Gardiner, William Howard—The American naval expert and publicist was an early admirer of Bywater's *Sea Power in the Pacific*, and served, in a roundabout way, to bring Bywater's thesis to the attention of Franklin D. Roosevelt. He may also have tipped Bywater about War Plan Orange. See *52M-295, Item 32, Box 3, "Political & Military Miscellany," manila folder labeled Bywater, Hector C. (Houghton Library, Harvard University, Cambridge, Mass.).

Garvin, J. L.—Bywater's letters to Garvin, while the latter was editor of the London *Observer*, concern Bywater's efforts to publish his book about the rise of the German Navy. The letters are dated 11/10, 11/24, 12/15, and 12/29/1910; and 3/4/1911 (Humanities Research Center, University of Texas, Austin).

Godfrey, Admiral John H.—The unpublished memoirs of the director of British naval intelligence from 1938 to 1942 offer a wealth of information on how the Admiralty dealt with the press (Archives Centre, Churchill College, Cambridge, England).

Greenslet, Ferris—The editor and later editor-in-chief of Houghton Mifflin was the principal editor with whom Bywater discussed his idea for writing *The Great Pacific War*. Their correspondence, consisting of twenty-three letters and cables between 5/5/1924 and 10/31/1925, provide a rare window into the minds of the two men as they wrestled with such matters as the possibly provocative nature of the book (Houghton Library, Harvard University, Cambridge, Mass.).

Grew, Joseph C.—The man who was to become U.S. ambassador to Japan during the decade leading up to the Pearl Harbor attack befriended both Hector and Ulysses Bywater before World War I in Germany. Grew's letters home from Germany present an interesting view of life in the American and English colonies during that period (Houghton Library, Harvard University, Cambridge, Mass.).

Kipling, Rudyard—Bywater's correspondence with the poet reveal his admiration for Kipling, and despairing state of mind in 1933 (Manuscripts Section, University of Sussex Library, Brighton, England).

Keyes, Admiral of the Fleet, Sir Roger—An interesting letter from Bywater dated 4/7/1937 reveals how Bywater occasionally joined forces with influential naval officers in such common causes as the effort to improve *Dido*-class cruisers (Manuscript Division, British National Library, London, England).

Hurd, Archibald Spicer—The papers of Bywater's one-time mentor and predecessor as naval and shipping correspondent of the London *Daily Telegraph* contain interesting material on how Bywater came to succeed Hurd at the *Telegraph* (Archives Centre, Churchill College, Cambridge, England).

Liddell Hart, Basil H.—Two letters from Bywater dated 1/9/1928 and 1/20/1930 indicate Liddell Hart's respect for Bywater and their friendship (Liddell Hart Centre for Military Archives, King's College, Strand, London).

Mackenzie, Compton—The novelist and critic served in the British Secret Service under Sir Mansfield Cumming during the First World War, and corresponded on the subject with Bywater in 1932 (Humanities Research Center, University of Texas, Austin).

The New York Times Archives—Bywater's letters in 1931 to the *Times*' London correspondent, Charles A. Selden, led to his serving as European naval correspondent of the newspaper for nearly a decade (*The New York Times*, 229 West 43rd St., New York, N.Y.).

Newland, John—A memoir about his father-in-law, Hector C. Bywater, written in 1967 (author's collection).

Patterson, Donald H.—The files of Mr. Patterson, the late publisher of the Baltimore *Sun*, contain the correspondence and diaries of his father, Paul Patterson, who recorded his meetings with Bywater in London in 1921, which established Bywater's ten-year relationship with that newspaper.

Pratt, William V.—His papers include a reference to Bywater in "Thoughts and Notes Anent a Future Conference for Limitation of Naval Armament" (Box 2, Series 1, p. 27, Operational Archives, Naval History Division, Washington, D.C.).

Roosevelt, Franklin D.—Correspondence concerning his "debate" with Bywater, 1921–23, is in Papers Pertaining to Family, Business and Personal Affairs, 1882–1945, Group 14, FDR as author, Correspondence re *Asia* article, 1922–23, Box 106 (Franklin D. Roosevelt Library, Hyde Park, New York).

INDEX

ABOUT THE AUTHOR

WILLIAM H. HONAN'S *Visions of Infamy* is the result of an almost lifelong obsession with the Pacific war that took hold the year Admiral Isoroku Yamamoto attacked Pearl Harbor. Unable to explain why a diminutive nation like Japan would attack an industrial power like the United States, Honan, in the years following the war, amassed a considerable knowledge and library about the Pacific war. In 1967, in a small used bookstore in Greenwich Village, he found a copy of a book called *The Great Pacific War* by Hector C. Bywater. Honan was surprised to discover that the book, written sixteen years prior to the attack on Pearl Harbor, predicted with stunning accuracy and intricate detail the features and strategies used by Japan in the war in the Pacific.

Following the publication of an article on Bywater that he wrote for *American Heritage* magazine in 1970, Honan, while on assignment, wandered into the Library of Congress. Looking up Bywater's name in the card catalogue, he was surprised to discover that several of the titles under his name were in Japanese. Honan learned that the titles were books of Bywater's that had been translated into Japanese—one of which had been prepared by the Japanese Imperial Navy General Staff for the use of top naval officers. Suspecting that Bywater's books had influenced the Japanese who planned the attack against the United States, Honan began to actively research this possibility, traveling to Japan, Britain, and back and forth across the United States, corresponding with Bywater's children, historians, and Japanese war veterans. Honan was finally able to complete this revelatory biography after serving an eight-year stint as Cultural Editor of *The New York Times*, where he continues to write as Chief Cultural Correspondent.

THE 'HIGHWAY' TO JAPAN

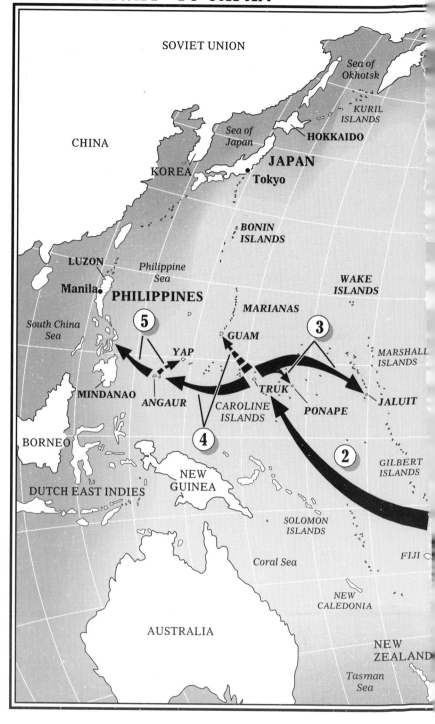